Handbook of
Construction Tolerances

Handbook of Construction Tolerances

David Kent Ballast

McGraw-Hill, Inc.

New York   San Francisco   Washington, D.C.   Auckland   Bogotá
Caracas   Lisbon   London   Madrid   Mexico City   Milan
Montreal   New Delhi   San Juan   Singapore
Sydney   Tokyo   Toronto

Library of Congress Cataloging-in-Publication Data

Ballast, David Kent.
    Handbook of construction tolerances / David Kent Ballast.
        p.   cm.
    Includes index.
    ISBN 0-07-003553-9
    1. Structural engineering.   2. Tolerance (Engineering) I. Title.
TH851.B35   1994
690—dc20   94-2368
                                                CIP

1 2 3 4 5 6 7 8 9 0   KGP/KGP   9 0 9 8 7 6 5 4

ISBN 0-07-003553-9

The sponsoring editor for this book was Joel Stein, the editing supervisor was Frank Kotowski, Jr., and the production supervisor was Donald F. Schmidt. It was set in Garamond Light by McGraw-Hill's Professional Book Group composition unit.

Printed and bound by Arcata Graphics/Kingsport.

Contents

List of Tables   *xi*
Acknowledgments   *xiii*
Introduction   *xv*

Part 1. Construction Tolerances

Chapter 1. Building Layout and Sitework   *3*

1-1. Horizontal Building Layout 3
1-2. Vertical Building Layout 5
1-3. Concrete Paving 7
1-4. Asphalt Paving..9
1-5. Pedestrian Paving..11
1-6. Rough and Finish Grading..13

Chapter 2. Concrete   *15*

2-1.   Reinforcement Placement for Flexural Members 15
2-2.   Reinforcement Placement in Walls and Columns 17
2-3.   Reinforcement Placement of Prestressing Steel..19
2-4.   Concrete Slabs-On-Grade 21
2-5.   Footings 23
2-6.   Piers 25
2-7.   Cast-in-Place Plumb Tolerances 27
2-8.   Cast-in-Place Sectional Tolerances 29
2-9.   Cast-in-Place Concrete Elements in Plan 31
2-10. Cast-in-Place Stairs 33
2-11. Glass Fiber Reinforced Concrete Panels 35
2-12. Architectural Precast Concrete Panels..37
2-13. Precast Ribbed Wall Panels 39
2-14. Precast Insulated Wall Panels 41
2-15. Hollow-Core Slabs..43
2-16. Precast Stairs 45
2-17. Precast Pilings...47
2-18. Prestressed Concrete Beams...49
2-19. Prestressed Single Tees 51
2-20. Prestressed Double Tees...53
2-21. Precast Columns..55
2-22. Prestressed Tee Joists or Keystone Joists...57
2-23. Precast Column Erection...59
2-24. Precast Beam and Spandrel Erection 61
2-25. Precast Floor and Roof Member Erection...63
2-26. Precast Structural Wall Panel Erection 65
2-27. Precast Architectural Wall Panel Erection..67
2-28. Glass Fiber Reinforced Concrete Panel Erection..69

Chapter 3. Steel   *71*

3-1.   Mill Tolerances for W and HP Shapes 71
3-2.   Mill Tolerances for Length of W and HP Shapes 75
3-3.   Mill Tolerances for S and M Shapes and Channels..........................77
3-4.   Mill Tolerances for Structural Angles and Tees................................79
3-5.   Mill Tolerances for Pipe and Tubing 81
3-6.   Steel Column Erection Tolerances 83
3-7.   Location of Exterior Steel Columns in Plan 85
3-8.   Beam/Column Connections..87
3-9.   Architecturally Exposed Structural Steel 89
3-10. Elevator Shaft Tolerances..91

Chapter 4. Unit Masonry   *93*

4-1.   Concrete Unit Masonry Manufacturing 93
4-2.   Concrete Unit Masonry Reinforcement Placement 95
4-3.   Concrete Unit Masonry Construction 97
4-4.   Prefabricated Masonry Panels...99
4-5.   Brick Manufacturing 101
4-6.   Brick Wall Construction 105
4-7.   Glazed Structural Clay Facing Tile 107
4-8.   Facing, Load-Bearing, and Non-Load-Bearing Clay Tile..............111
4-9.   Terra Cotta Manufacturing and Erection 113
4-10. Glass Block Manufacturing and Erection 115

Chapter 5. Stone   *117*

5-1.   Granite Fabrication..117
5-2.   Marble Fabrication 119
5-3.   Limestone Fabrication 121
5-4.   Granite and Marble Installation 123
5-5.   Limestone Installation 125
5-6.   Fabrication and Installation Tolerances for Slate 127
5-7.   Cast Stone Fabrication and Installation..129

Chapter 6. Structural Lumber   *131*

6-1.   Glued Laminated Timber Fabrication 131
6-2.   Manufacturing Tolerances for Structural Lumber 133
6-3.   Plywood Manufacturing..135
6-4.   Particleboard Manufacturing...137
6-5.   Fiberboard Manufacturing 139
6-6.   Rough Lumber Framing 141
6-7.   Wood Floor Framing and Subflooring 143
6-8.   Metal Plate Connected Wood Truss Fabrication 145
6-9.   Metal Plate Connected Wood Truss Erection 147
6-10. Prefabricated Structural Wood..149

Chapter 7. Finish Carpentry and Architectural Woodwork   *151*

7-1.   Manufacturing Tolerances for Board Lumber...................................151
7-2.   Site-Built Cabinets and Countertops..153
7-3.   Site-Built Stairs and Trim 155

7-4.   Standing and Running Trim...157
7-5.   Architectural Cabinets 161
7-6.   Modular Cabinets 163
7-7.   Countertops 165
7-8.   Flush Paneling 167
7-9.   Stile and Rail Paneling 171
7-10. Stairwork..175
7-11. Frames, Jambs, and Windows 177
7-12. Screens..179
7-13. Blinds and Shutters 181
7-14. Architectural Flush Doors 185
7-15. Stile and Rail Doors—Size and Flatness 187
7-16. Stile and Rail Doors—Joint Tightness and Flushness....................189
7-17. Architectural Woodwork Installation 193

Chapter 8. Curtain Walls   *197*

8-1.   Aluminum Curtain Wall Fabrication...197
8-2.   Aluminum Curtain Wall Installation 199
8-3.   Storefront and Entrance Manufacturing 201
8-4.   Storefront Installation..203

Chapter 9. Finishes   *205*

9-1.   Lightgage Framing for Gypsum Wallboard.....................................205
9-2.   Wallboard Partitions, Ceilings, and Trim 207
9-3.   Glass Reinforced Gypsum Products 209
9-4.   Installation of Lath and Plaster 211
9-5.   Floor and Wall Tile 213
9-6.   Terrazzo Flooring...217
9-7.   Wood Flooring 219
9-8.   Stone Flooring 221
9-9.   Acoustical Ceiling Installation..223
9-10. Linear Metal Ceiling Installation 225
9-11. Stainless Steel Ornamental Metal Products 227
9-12. Copper Alloy Ornamental Metal Products......................................229
9-13. Extruded Aluminum Tubes...231
9-14. Aluminum Rods, Bars, and Shapes 233

Chapter 10. Glazing   *235*

10-1. Manufacturing Tolerances for Flat Glass..235
10-2. Manufacturing Tolerances for Patterned and Wired Glass 237
10-3. Tempered, Heat-Strengthened, and Spandrel Glass........................239
10-4. Sealed Insulated Glass Units..243
10-5. All-Glass Entrances..245

Chapter 11. Doors and Windows   *247*

11-1. Standard Steel Doors and Frames 247
11-2. Insulated Steel Door Systems 249
11-3. Detention Security Hollow Metal Doors and Frames......................251
11-4. Standard Flush Wood Doors..253
11-5. Standard Stile and Rail Doors...255

11-6. Wood Swinging Patio Doors 257
11-7. Installation of Wood Doors 259
11-8. Wood Windows..261
11-9. Aluminum Windows and Sliding Doors 263
11-10. Steel Windows...265
11-11. Lockstrip Gasket Glazing..267

Part 2. Accommodating Construction Tolerances

Accommodating Construction Tolerances 269
Joint Design..271
Accumulated Tolerances..273

Chapter 12. Cast-in-Place Concrete Systems   *275*

12-1. Combined Concrete Frame Tolerances......................................275
12-2. Joint Tolerances..277
12-3. Detailing for Cast-in-Place and Precast Systems.......................279
12-4. Detailing Brick on Cast-in-Place Concrete 281
12-5. Detailing for Stone on Concrete 283
12-6. Detailing for Curtain Walls on Concrete Frames........................285
12-7. Detailing Doors in Cast-in-Place Concrete................................287
12-8. Detailing Windows in Cast-in-Place Concrete 289

Chapter 13. Precast Concrete Systems   *291*

13-1. Combined Precast Concrete Frame Tolerances............................291
13-2. Joint Tolerances..293
13-3. Detailing for Precast Systems..295
13-4. Detailing for Precast and Steel Systems 297
13-5. Detailing Masonry and Precast Systems...................................299
13-6. Detailing Doors in Precast Concrete 301
13-7. Detailing Windows in Precast Concrete....................................303

Chapter 14. Steel Frame Systems   *305*

14-1. Accumulated Column Tolerances..305
14-2. Accumulated Steel Frame Tolerances 307
14-3. Detailing for Steel Structural System Tolerances 309
14-4. Detailing for Precast on Steel 311
14-5. Detailing for Brick on Steel 313
14-6. Detailing for Stone on Steel Systems.......................................315
14-7. Detailing for Curtain Walls on Steel Frames 317

Chapter 15. Masonry Systems   *319*

15-1. Masonry Joint Tolerance 319
15-2. Detailing Brick and Masonry Systems......................................321
15-3. Detailing for Stone on Masonry Backup....................................323
15-4. Detailing Interior Stone on Masonry 325
15-5. Detailing Doors in Masonry...327
15-6. Detailing Windows in Masonry 329

Chapter 16. Timber and Carpentry Construction   *331*

16-1. Detailing Wood Joints..331
16-2. Detailing for Timber Columns...333
16-3. Detailing for Timber Beams..335
16-4. Detailing for Prefabricated Structural Wood................................337
16-5. Detailing for Paneling and Site-Built Substrates 339
16-6. Detailing for Cabinetry and Site-Built Substrates.........................341

List of Sources   *343*
Index   *353*

List of Tables

Table 2-1   Clear Distance Tolerance to Side Forms and Soffits   *15*
Table 2-2   Horizontal Dimension Tolerance for Footings Cast against Soil   *23*
Table 2-3   Sweep Tolerances for Prestressed Concrete Beams   *49*
Table 2-4   Tolerances for Top Elevation of Structural Wall Panels   *65*
Table 2-5   Tolerances for Top Elevation of Architectural Wall Panels   *67*

Table 3-1   Permissible Variation in Camber and Sweep for W and HP Shapes   *72*
Table 3-2   Permissible Variation in Length *L*   *75*
Table 3-3   Permissible Variation for Length and Squareness for Milled Shapes   *75*
Table 3-4   Permissible Variation in Cross-Sectional Shapes for S, M, C, and MC Shapes   *77*
Table 3-5   Permissible Variation in Length for S, M, and Channel Shapes   *77*
Table 3-6   Permissible Variation in Sizes for Angles and Tees   *79*
Table 3-7   Permissible Variation in Length for Angles and Tees   *79*
Table 3-8   Length Tolerances for Pipe and Tubing   *81*
Table 3-9   Twist Tolerances for Square and Rectangular Tubing   *81*

Table 4-1   UBC Reinforcement Placement Tolerances   *95*
Table 4-2   Top-of-Wall Alignment Envelope   *97*
Table 4-3   Dimensional Tolerances of Prefabricated Masonry Panels   *99*
Table 4-4   Brick Manufacturing Dimension Tolerances   *101*
Table 4-5   Brick Distortion Tolerances   *102*
Table 4-6   Face Dimension Tolerances for Glazed Clay Facing Tile   *107*
Table 4-7   Bed Depth (Thickness) Tolerances for Glazed Clay Facing Tile   *108*
Table 4-8   Distortion Tolerances for Glazed Clay Facing Tile   *109*
Table 4-9   Clay Facing Tile Manufacturing Dimension Tolerances   *111*
Table 4-10   Clay Facing Tile Distortion Tolerances   *111*

Table 5-1   Thickness Tolerances for Granite Veneer   *117*
Table 5-2   Size Tolerances for Marble   *119*
Table 5-3   Limestone Fabrication Tolerances   *121*

Table 6-1   Minimum Sizes of Dressed, Dry Dimensional Lumber   *133*
Table 6-2   Plywood Thickness Tolerances   *135*
Table 6-3   Tolerances for Particleboard   *137*
Table 6-4   Tolerances for Particleboard Flooring Products   *137*
Table 6-5   Manufacturing Tolerances for Wood Trusses   *145*

Table 7-1   Minimum Sizes of Dressed, Dry Finish, or Board Lumber   *151*
Table 7-2   Tightness and Flushness of Plant Assembled Joints   *158*
Table 7-3   Flushness and Flatness of Cabinet Joints and Panels   *161*
Table 7-4   Joint Tolerances for Factory Assembled Components   *165*
Table 7-5   Joint Tolerance for Separation between Factory Assembled Backsplash and Top   *165*
Table 7-6   Joint Tolerance for Factory Assembled Components for Wood Veneer Paneling   *168*

Table 7-7   Joint Tolerances for Factory Assembled Components for Stile and Rail Paneling   *172*
Table 7-8   Joint Tolerances for Factory Assembled Joints   *175*
Table 7-9   Joint Tolerances for Custom Windows   *177*
Table 7-10   Joint Tolerances for Screens   *179*
Table 7-11   Joint Tolerances for Blinds and Shutters   *182*
Table 7-12   Tightness of Plant Assembled Joints   *190*
Table 7-13   Flushness of Plant Assembled Joints   *191*
Table 7-14   Wood-to-Wood Field Joints up to 118 in (3 m) above Finished Floor   *193*
Table 7-15   Wood-to-Nonwood Field Joints up to 118 in (3 m) above Finished Floor   *193*
Table 7-16   Nonwood-to-Nonwood Field Joints up to 118 in (3 m) above Finished Floor   *194*

Table 9-1   Tile Manufacturing Tolerances   *213*
Table 9-2   Required Tolerance for Plane of Substrate for Tile Installation   *214*
Table 9-3   Recommended Concrete Slab Tolerances for Wood Flooring   *219*
Table 9-4   Twist Tolerances for Stainless Steel Tube Sections   *227*
Table 9-5   Size and Squareness Tolerances for Stainless Steel Tee Sections   *227*
Table 9-6   Straightness Tolerances for Round Tubing   *229*
Table 9-7   Straightness Tolerances for Bars Made from Square-Sheared Metal   *229*
Table 9-8   Selected Tolerances for Extruded Aluminum Tube Sections   *231*
Table 9-9   Selected Tolerances for Aluminum Rods, Bars, and Shapes   *233*

Table 10-1   Allowable Tolerances for Clear, Flat Glass   *235*
Table 10-2   Tolerances for Patterned Glass   *237*
Table 10-3   Tolerances for Wired Glass   *237*
Table 10-4   Dimensional Tolerances for Tempered, Heat-Strengthened, and Spandrel Glass   *239*
Table 10-5   Bow Tolerances for Tempered, Heat-Strengthened, and Spandrel Glass   *240*
Table 10-6   Dimensional Tolerances for Insulating Glass Units   *243*

Table 11-1   Standard Insulated Steel Door Opening Sizes   *249*
Table 11-2   AWI Joint Tolerances for Factory Assembled Windows   *261*

Acknowledgments

I thank the many people who provided vital information to make this book complete. Credit goes to Ken Lerch and Harold Rovins, Structural Slate Company; Jim Owens, Indiana Limestone Institute; Michael Baklarz, Facing Tile Institute; Phil Pederson, Gladding, McBean; and Bruce Pooley, American Institute of Timber Construction.

Thanks is also due to Greg Martensen, Timberweld Company; David Kretschmann, Forest Products Laboratory; Charlie Goehring, Truss Plate Institute; Paul Nicholas, Trus-Joist Macmillan; Cynthia Mitlo, American Society of Landscape Architects; Jeff Lowinski, American Architectural Manufacturers Association; Bill Lingnell, Lingnell Consulting Services; Bob Ford, Laser Alignment, Inc.; and Derrick Hardy, National Terrazzo and Mosaic Association.

Introduction

In the construction industry, all materials are assumed to have specific dimensions, and the locations of construction elements are dimensioned on the drawings to a theoretically exact position relative to one or more datum points. Of course, in reality all dimensions and positions of installed materials vary somewhat. The acceptable amount of this variation is the tolerance of the material or installed position of the material. For some materials, such as shop-fabricated windows, the variation may be so slight as to be insignificant. For other materials, such as cast-in-place concrete, the allowable tolerance may be in an order of magnitude of several inches and may adversely affect the installation of other components. While some materials can be custom cut and fit at the job site, others come from the factory in a fixed size and must be attached to a previously constructed frame. All of the materials must be fit together to satisfy the functional requirements of the building while being reasonably economic to build.

The construction industry is unique in that tolerances range from thousandths of an inch for many manufactured items to several inches for many field installed components. Each range of tolerances is important in its own right and the architect and contractor must know what tolerances apply for any given situation. Then the tolerances must be accommodated with adequate clearances between adjacent elements and with adjustable connections or appropriately sized joints.

Acceptable construction tolerances have become established over a long time. Some are simply considered standard practice based on years of field experience about what is practical and readily achievable. Many are based on standards that specific industries have published and reflect what each industry agrees is reasonable as a balance between ease of construction, quality, and cost. Because of this evolution there are innumerable tolerances that architects, engineers, suppliers, fabricators, and contractors must know about and accommodate to build well.

For the first time, the *Handbook of Construction Tolerances* assembles the thousands of industry standard and standard practice tolerances for the manufacture, fabrication, and installation of hundreds of construction assemblies from structural steel to ceramic tile and shows how dimensional variations must be accommodated in today's buildings. Whether you are an architect, interior designer, contractor, or specification writer, you will find this book invaluable for designing and detailing, establishing what normal practice is, settling disputes in the field, and writing more accurate specifications.

Because current construction techniques require using a combination of factory-built and site-built components assembled in complex ways, it is more important than ever that you understand what normal tolerances are, how they can accumulate during construction, and how you can plan for them before they cause trouble. Too often, when the reality of tolerances is ignored, the results can include costly field modifications, delays, design compromises, or even failure of a building component. This book arms you with the knowledge you need to help avoid these kinds of problems on your projects.

Part 1 of this book includes all types of material and assembly tolerances, from structural concrete and masonry to finish components like architectural woodwork and ceilings. Each material, fabrication, installation, or erection tolerance is shown graphically, making it easy to quickly pull out exactly what you need. In addition, you will find guidance on how one material tolerance relates to another and how dimensional variations should be accounted for in design and construction. Among the many tolerance data you will find, this handbook:

- shows what variation to expect when architectural precast concrete comes from the plant.
- lays out guidelines for concrete, asphalt, and pedestrian paving.

- gives the standards for cast-in-place concrete construction.
- explains how to anticipate dimensional differences for structural steel construction and how to provide for attachment of other construction materials to the steel frame.
- blocks out the basic requirements for unit masonry including concrete block, brick, and even terra cotta.
- presents the tolerances for exterior stone cladding and illustrates how to detail it to structural framing.
- demonstrates the fine points of accommodating interior material tolerances of finishes such as stone, paneling, ceilings, and more.
- organizes what you need to know for detailing fine cabinetry and other woodwork.
- identifies the variances involved with aluminum curtain wall construction.
- sets forth the generally accepted limits for gypsum wallboard construction including glass reinforced gypsum.
- illustrates the tolerances for ceramic and quarry tile so you know what kinds of finish installations to expect.
- provides the basic data for flooring materials such as terrazzo, stone, and wood.
- discusses the degree of perfection you can expect with various types of glazing materials.
- gives guidelines for how to get the most from decorative and ornamental metals for high-quality interior detailing.
- illustrates the variations common with wood and metal door and frame construction and installation.
- shows the common dimensional variations of windows and their installation, including wood, steel, and aluminum products.
- illustrates how to accommodate combinations of tolerances commonly found in building construction such as masonry veneer on a steel or concrete frame and precast concrete on a steel frame.
- provides suggested details for particularly troublesome material and assembly tolerances that are often overlooked.

The information about each tolerance follows an identical format to help speed your research. First, a drawing shows the material or installed assembly with the pertinent dimensional variation allowed by an industry standard or by common practice. Next, on the facing page, there is a brief written description about the essential facts concerning the component shown and the tolerances involved. The applicable industry standard organization and relevant standard number are listed in case you want to do more research. After this, there is a brief discussion of the tolerances and how they can be accommodated with proper detailing and construction methods. Finally, cross-references to related sections in the book are included so you can coordinate the assembly of several materials, if necessary.

Part 2 of this book addresses the all-important subject of accumulated dimensional variations. These occur when seemingly minor tolerances build on one another or when several materials are combined in such a way that normally acceptable, small, variations add up to a large difference. Knowing how this can occur and how you can plan for it will minimize many field problems. Dozens of detail drawings show how typical assemblies are put together to accommodate common tolerances.

Because tolerances can vary so much, always discuss them with the supplier, fabricator, contractor, and installer to determine acceptable amounts for a specific application. Then include the tolerances in the specifications. In the field contractors often do not build to the theoretical tolerances given in industry standards (or even know them) so they should be listed in each section of the specifications, especially when they are critical or serve as the basis for subsequent finish work. In some cases, the required tolerances may be more stringent than industry standards, so unless they are clearly spelled out in the specifications the contractor may build to the less exacting dimension.

Throughout this book both English and SI units are used. In most cases the English measurement or unit is given first with the equivalent SI unit in parentheses. The equivalent SI unit may not be consistent in all parts of the book. For example, ¼ in may be considered 6.4 mm in some places while it may be 6 mm in others. This is because in some cases the equivalent SI unit is a mathematical conversion using standard conversion factors and rounded off while in other cases the SI equivalent is the standard adopted by a particular trade association or testing agency and published to a specific degree of accuracy. These published SI tolerances have been reproduced without adjusting them for consistency with non-standardized SI units. As the United States slowly converts to the metric system, more and more tolerances will be published in both systems.

Whether you are involved with the design, construction, or evaluation of buildings, you will find this book a valuable addition to your reference collection. It will give you an easy-to-use guide to the thousands of construction tolerances currently in use and help you avoid countless detailing problems.

David Kent Ballast

Handbook of
Construction Tolerances

Part 1

Construction Tolerances

Figure 1-1

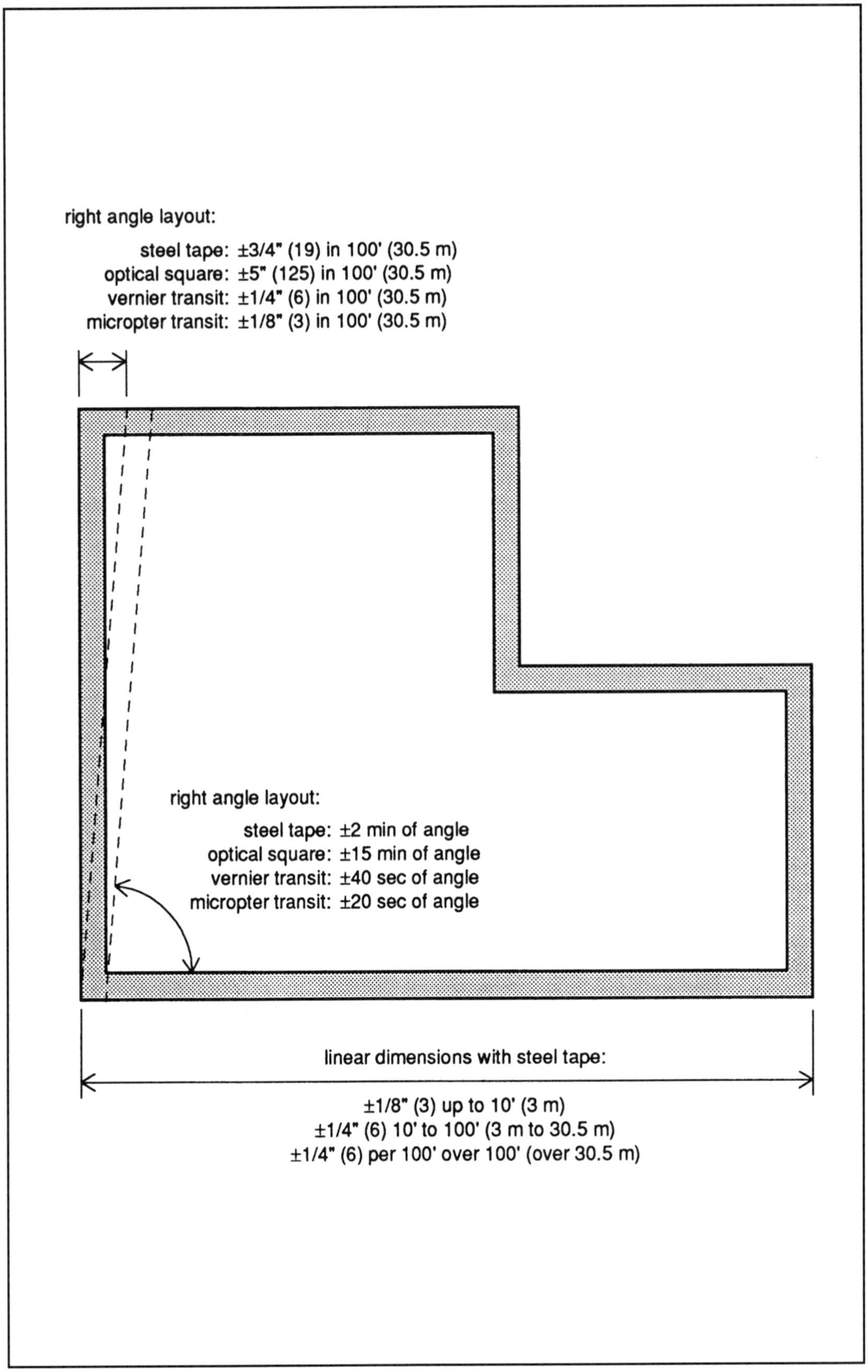

right angle layout:

> steel tape: ±3/4" (19) in 100' (30.5 m)
> optical square: ±5" (125) in 100' (30.5 m)
> vernier transit: ±1/4" (6) in 100' (30.5 m)
> micropter transit: ±1/8" (3) in 100' (30.5 m)

right angle layout:

> steel tape: ±2 min of angle
> optical square: ±15 min of angle
> vernier transit: ±40 sec of angle
> micropter transit: ±20 sec of angle

linear dimensions with steel tape:

±1/8" (3) up to 10' (3 m)
±1/4" (6) 10' to 100' (3 m to 30.5 m)
±1/4" (6) per 100' over 100' (over 30.5 m)

Chapter 1

Building Layout and Sitework

1-1. Horizontal Building Layout

Description

One of the first sources of inaccuracies in building construction is the establishment of horizontal and vertical referencing systems for the layout of a building and subsequent marking of lines and benchmarks for horizontal and vertical dimensions as construction proceeds. Layout is dependent on the accuracy of the instruments used as well as the skill of the people doing the layout. This section includes some of the horizontal layout accuracies possible with various instruments assuming a normal degree of skill on the part of the worker.

Recommendation

J. K. Latta, "Inaccuracies in Construction," Canadian Building Digest 171, April 1975, in *Canadian Building Digests,* 151–200, Institute for Research in Construction, National Research Council of Canada, Ottawa, March 1989.

Allowable Tolerances

For horizontal layout there are two primary concerns: the accuracy of linear dimensions compared with those shown on the drawings and the accuracy of establishing angles to form foundations and other structural elements.

The dimensional accuracy for a 100-ft (30.5-m) steel tape depends on the amount of sag, temperature, tension, and angle of use. However, for typical situations and when sag is minimized, the tolerances shown in Fig. 1-1 can be expected. If higher accuracy is required, a laser should be used or steel tapes with correction factors included for temperature and other variables.

Right angles for many buildings, such as houses and small commercial structures, can be laid out with a steel tape measuring a 3:4:5 triangle. When greater accuracy is required, a transit or theodolite should be used. Transits have the added advantage of being useful to lay out angles other than right angles.

Related Section

1-2. Vertical Building Layout

Figure 1-2

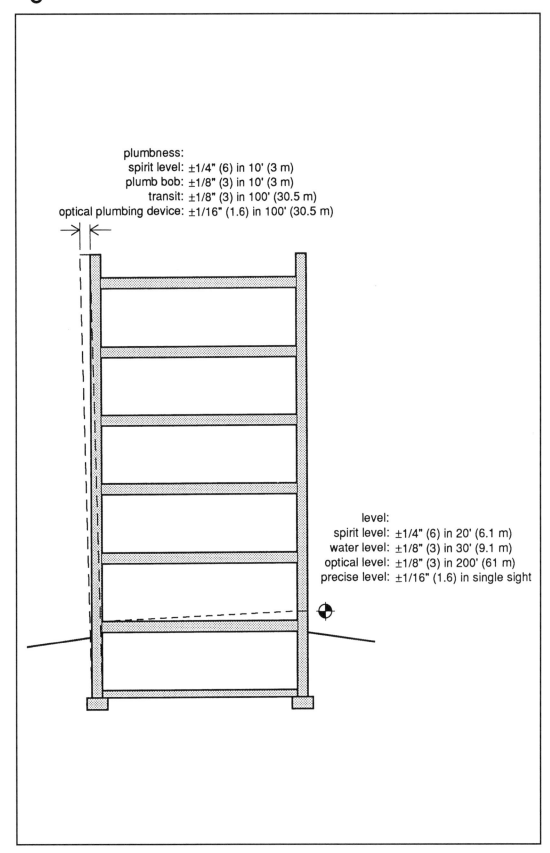

plumbness:
spirit level: ±1/4" (6) in 10' (3 m)
plumb bob: ±1/8" (3) in 10' (3 m)
transit: ±1/8" (3) in 100' (30.5 m)
optical plumbing device: ±1/16" (1.6) in 100' (30.5 m)

level:
spirit level: ±1/4" (6) in 20' (6.1 m)
water level: ±1/8" (3) in 30' (9.1 m)
optical level: ±1/8" (3) in 200' (61 m)
precise level: ±1/16" (1.6) in single sight

1-2. Vertical Building Layout

Description

After the horizontal form and dimensions of a building are established, the next source of inaccuracy is plumbing vertical elements and maintaining levels. These are dependent on the accuracy of the instruments used as well as the skill of the people doing the layout. This section includes some of the layout accuracies possible in establishing plumbness and level with various instruments assuming a normal degree of skill on the part of the worker.

Recommendation

J. K. Latta, "Inaccuracies in Construction," Canadian Building Digest 171, April 1975, in *Canadian Building Digests,* 151–200, Institute for Research in Construction, National Research Council of Canada, Ottawa, March 1989.

Allowable Tolerances

Spirit levels and plumb bobs are often used for residential and small commercial buildings. The typical accuracies for these instruments are shown in Fig. 1-2. For greater accuracies over longer distances, transits, optical devices, or lasers can be used.

The tolerances shown in other sections of this book for plumbness and level for individual construction materials and assemblies are often larger or smaller than those shown in this section. Refer to individual sections for more specific information on industry standards for specific materials.

Related Section

1-1. Horizontal Building Layout

Figure 1-3

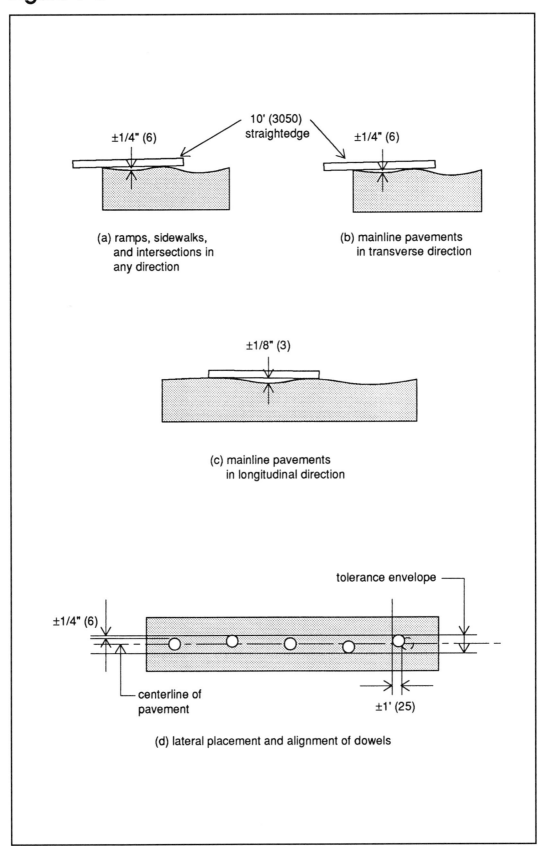

10' (3050) straightedge

±1/4" (6)

±1/4" (6)

(a) ramps, sidewalks, and intersections in any direction

(b) mainline pavements in transverse direction

±1/8" (3)

(c) mainline pavements in longitudinal direction

tolerance envelope

±1/4" (6)

centerline of pavement

±1' (25)

(d) lateral placement and alignment of dowels

1-3. Concrete Paving

Description

Concrete paving includes drives, parking surfaces, sidewalks, and other site paving. In many cases tight tolerances for exterior paving are not critical. However, when existing building and site elevations require minimum slopes for drainage (usually $\frac{1}{4}$ in per ft or 6 mm per 300 mm) the tolerances shown in this section should be specified. When ponding of water might create hazards in any situation, these tolerances should also be specified.

Industry Standard

ACI 117-90, *Standard Tolerances for Concrete Construction and Materials and Commentary*, American Concrete Institute, Detroit, 1990.

Allowable Tolerances

Allowable tolerances based on American Concrete Institute (ACI) standards are shown in Fig. 1-3. These tolerances are probably the best that will be achieved in most concrete paving projects when tolerances are important. For less critical applications such as residential sidewalks, for steeply sloped paving, or when tolerances are not explicitly specified, expect greater variations from true plane.

Related Sections

1-4. Asphalt Paving

1-5. Pedestrian Paving

Figure 1-4

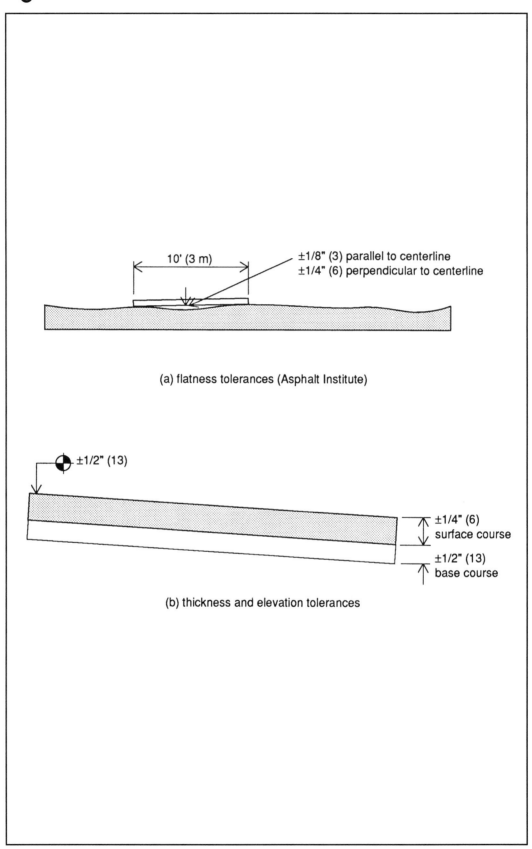

(a) flatness tolerances (Asphalt Institute)

(b) thickness and elevation tolerances

1-4. Asphalt Paving

Description

Asphalt paving includes drives and parking surfaces. As with concrete paving, asphalt paving tolerances are not always critical if sufficient slope is built into the paving for drainage. However, when a minimum drainage slope of $\frac{1}{4}$ in per ft (6 mm per 300 mm) is required, the tolerances shown in this section should be specified.

Industry Standards

SITESPEC Section 02510, "Asphalt Concrete Paving," p. 1, *SITESPEC Handbook, Version II,* James Burkart, Upper Arlington, OH, 1991.

Spectext Section 02510, *Asphaltic Concrete Paving,* p. 8, Construction Sciences Research Foundation, Baltimore, July 1989.

SS-1, *Model Construction Specifications for Asphalt Concrete and Other Plant-Mix Types,* Asphalt Institute, Lexington, KY, November 1984.

Allowable Tolerances

The Asphalt Institute's model specifications for flatness are shown in Fig. 1-4a. The term *centerline* refers to the centerline of the compaction roller. In most cases, it is preferable to specify a tolerance of $\pm\frac{1}{4}$ in (6 mm) in both directions. The SITESPEC master specifications suggest a surface course smoothness of $\pm\frac{1}{4}$ in (6 mm) in any direction.

The variation of actual elevation from spot elevations shown on the drawings should be within $\pm\frac{1}{2}$ in (13 mm). This is consistent with the Spectext model specifications and the Asphalt Institute's recommendations.

According to the Asphalt Institute's model specifications, the thickness T should not have an average value less than that shown on the plans. The SITESPEC master specifications suggest a base course thickness tolerance of $\pm\frac{1}{2}$ in (13 mm) and a surface course thickness tolerance of $\pm\frac{1}{4}$ in (6 mm).

Related Sections

1-3. Concrete Paving

1-5. Pedestrian Paving

Figure 1-5

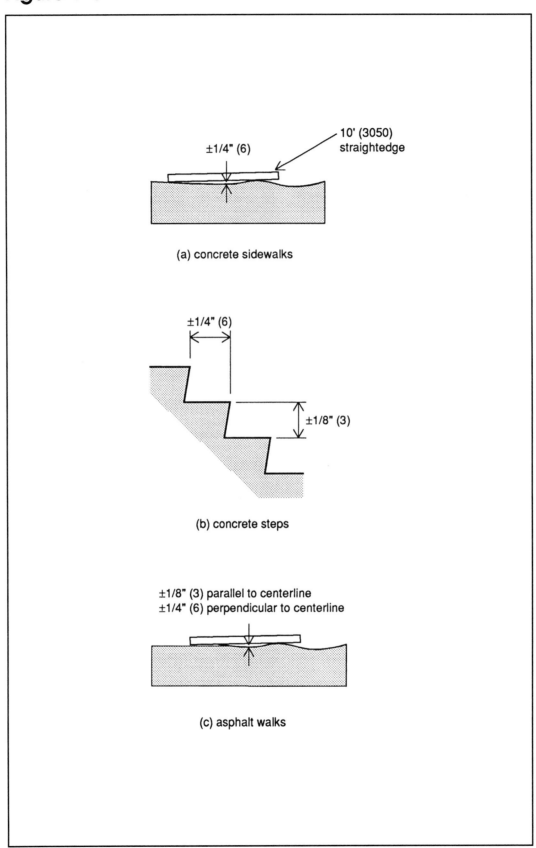

(a) concrete sidewalks

(b) concrete steps

(c) asphalt walks

1-5. Pedestrian Paving

Description

This section includes paving of concrete, asphalt, and concrete steps. For safety reasons, pedestrian paving should be constructed to close tolerances to avoid ponding and freezing of water, to prevent water buildup which could damage the paving, and to drain water away from the building and other important site structures. This is especially important because pedestrian paving is normally shown at low slopes, from $\frac{1}{4}$ in per ft (6 mm per 300 mm) to $\frac{1}{2}$ in per ft (13 mm per 300 mm).

Industry Standards

ACI 117-90, *Standard Tolerances for Concrete Construction and Materials and Commentary,* American Concrete Institute, Detroit, 1990.

SS-1, *Model Construction Specifications for Asphalt Concrete and Other Plant-Mix Types,* Asphalt Institute, Lexington, KY, November 1984.

Allowable Tolerances

Tolerances for pedestrian paving are shown in Fig. 1-5. Concrete tolerances for sidewalks and concrete steps are based on American Concrete Institute (ACI) standards. Asphalt walks are based on the Asphalt Institute's model specifications. There are no standard tolerances for brick or stone paving so if these are critical they should be specified based on the requirements of the project.

Related Sections

1-3. Concrete Paving

1-4. Asphalt Paving

Figure 1-6

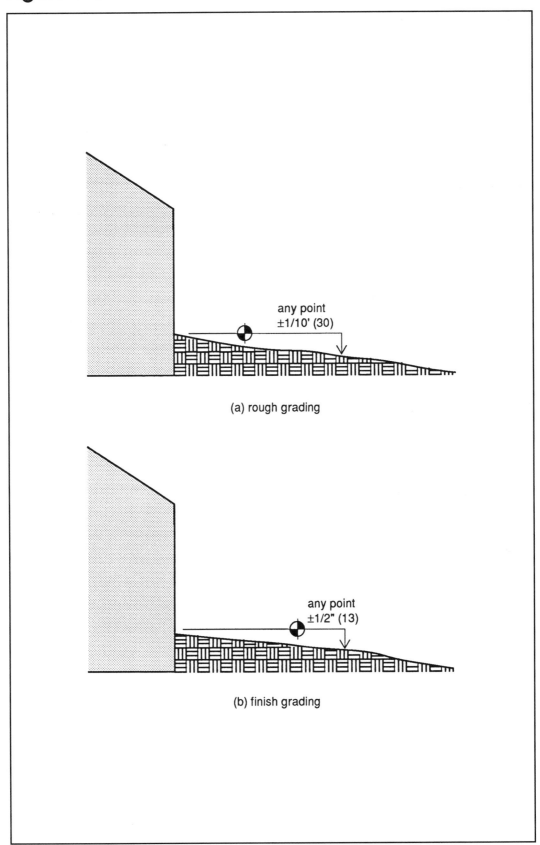

any point
±1/10' (30)

(a) rough grading

any point
±1/2" (13)

(b) finish grading

1-6. Rough and Finish Grading

Description

Although grading tolerances are not always critical, they can affect drainage away from a building, the appearance of ground cover material at the building line, and the final appearance of finish landscaping. Because of its nature, soil grading cannot be very accurate and is subject to the skills of the people grading as well as natural forces such as rain, snow, and freeze-thaw cycles. This section includes some of the various recommended tolerances for grading.

Industry Recommendations

Landscape Specification Guidelines, 3d ed., Associated Landscape Contractors of America, Falls Church, VA, 1986.

SITESPEC Section 02200, *Earthwork,* p. 1, *SITESPEC Handbook, Version II,* James Burkart, Upper Arlington, OH, 1991.

Spectext Section 02211, *Rough grading,* p. 6, Construction Sciences Research Foundation, Baltimore, July 1989.

Spectext Section 02923, *Landscape Grading,* p. 3, Construction Sciences Research Foundation, Baltimore, July 1989.

Allowable Tolerances

There are several recommended tolerances for rough and finish grading. The Associated Landscape Contractors of America suggest the landscape contractor not proceed with final work until the topsoil has been uniformly graded to within 0.2 in (about $\frac{3}{16}$ in or 5 mm). The Spectext master specifications suggest the topsoil be within $\frac{1}{2}$ in (13 mm) of specified elevations.

For rough grading, Spectext master specifications suggest a tolerance of ± 0.1 ft or $1\frac{3}{16}$ in (30 mm) as shown in Fig. 1-6a. The SITESPEC master specifications also recommend a rough grading elevation tolerance of ± 0.1 ft (30 mm). For granular base, the SITESPEC master specifications recommend a subgrade tolerance of $\pm\frac{1}{2}$ in in 10 ft (13 mm in 3050 mm).

Related Section

1-5. Pedestrian Paving

Figure 2-1

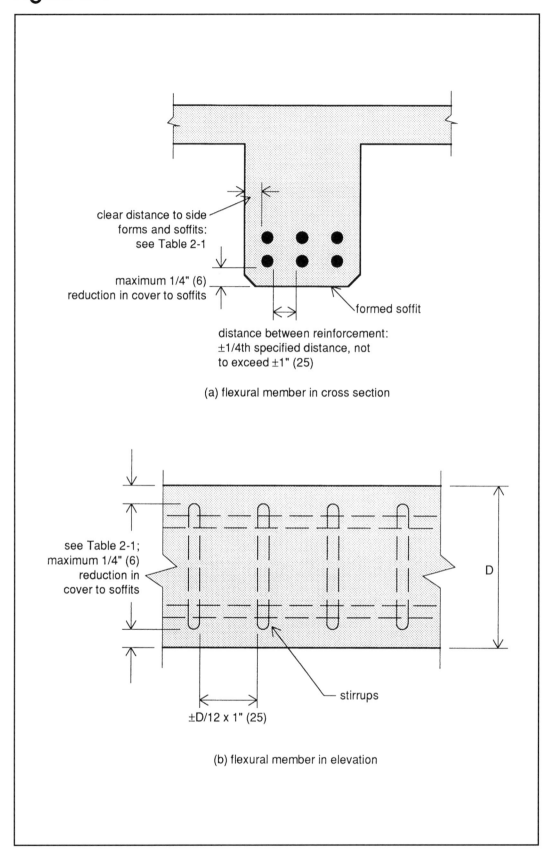

clear distance to side
forms and soffits:
see Table 2-1

maximum 1/4" (6)
reduction in cover to soffits

formed soffit

distance between reinforcement:
±1/4th specified distance, not
to exceed ±1" (25)

(a) flexural member in cross section

see Table 2-1;
maximum 1/4" (6)
reduction in
cover to soffits

D

stirrups

±D/12 x 1" (25)

(b) flexural member in elevation

Chapter 2

Concrete

2-1. Reinforcement Placement for Flexural Members

Description

This section includes some of the typical tolerances for rebar placement for cast-in-place beams and other flexural members. Refer to ACI 117 for a complete listing of all placement tolerances and for fabrication of individual pieces of reinforcing steel.

Industry Standard

ACI 117-90, *Standard Tolerances for Concrete Construction and Materials,* American Concrete Institute, Detroit, 1990.

Allowable Tolerances

In reinforcement placement a tolerance envelope is created by two limitations: the maximum reduction on concrete cover or clear distance between the rebar and forms, and the reduction in distance between reinforcement. The clear distance between side forms or formed soffits is shown in Fig. 2-1a and given in Table 2-1. However, the specified concrete cover cannot be reduced more than $\frac{3}{8}$ in (10 mm) for members 12 in (305 mm) or less in dimension or more than $\frac{1}{2}$ in (13 mm) for members over 12 in. In any case, the reduction in cover cannot exceed one-third of the specified concrete cover. For soffits, the reduction in cover cannot exceed $\frac{1}{4}$ in (6 mm). The distance between reinforcement is shown in Fig. 2-1b, but the distance cannot be less than the greater of the bar diameter or 1 in (25 mm) for unbundled bars.

Table 2-1
Clear Distance Tolerance to Side Forms and Soffits

Member size, in (mm)	Tolerance, in (mm)
4 (102) or less	$+\frac{1}{4}, -\frac{3}{8}$ (+6 , 210)
Over 4 (102), but not over 12 (305)	$\pm\frac{3}{8}$ (10)
Over 12 (305) but not over 2 ft (610)	$\pm\frac{1}{2}$ (13)
Over 2 ft (610)	± 1 (25)

SOURCE: ACI 117-90; reproduced with permission, American Concrete Institute.

Related Section

2-2. Reinforcement Placement in Walls and Columns

Figure 2-2

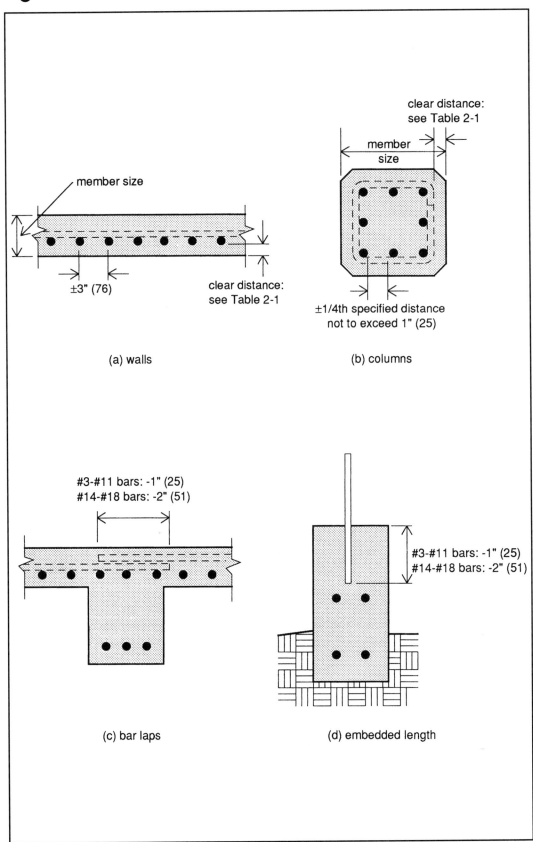

(a) walls

(b) columns

(c) bar laps

(d) embedded length

2-2. Reinforcement Placement in Walls and Columns

Description

Reinforcement placement for cast-in-place walls and columns follows many of the same requirements as for flexural members. Refer to ACI 117 for a complete listing of all placement tolerances and for fabrication of individual pieces of reinforcing steel.

Industry Standard

ACI 117-90, *Standard Tolerances for Concrete Construction and Materials,* American Concrete Institute, Detroit, 1990.

Allowable Tolerances

As with flexural members, placement tolerances for walls and columns depend on the specified clear cover and the spacing between individual members. The clear distance tolerances given in Table 2-1 apply to walls and columns. As with flexural members, the specified cover cannot be reduced more than $\frac{3}{8}$ in (10 mm) for members 12 in (305 mm) or less in dimension or more than $\frac{1}{2}$ in (13 mm) for members over 12 in. In any case, the reduction in cover cannot exceed one-third of the specified concrete cover. The spacing of reinforcement in walls (other than ties) shown in Fig. 2-2a cannot exceed ±3 in (76 mm) except that the total number of bars cannot be less than that specified. For columns, the distance between reinforcement is shown in Fig. 2-2b, but the distance cannot be less than the greater of the bar diameter or 1 in (25 mm) for unbundled bars.

For bar laps and embedded length there is no positive tolerance; that is, bars may overlap or be embedded more than specified by any amount but not less than shown in Figs. 2-2c and 2-2d.

Related Section

2-1. Reinforcement Placement for Flexural Members

Figure 2-3

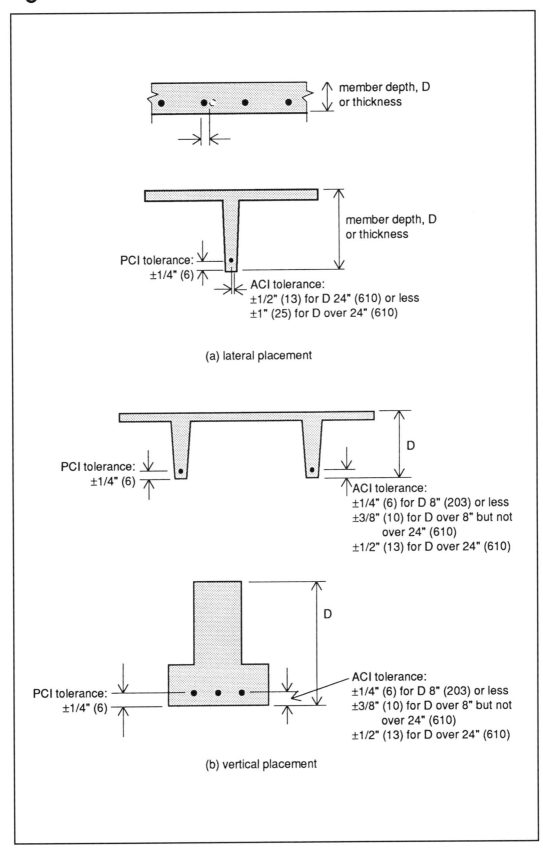

member depth, D or thickness

member depth, D or thickness

PCI tolerance: ±1/4" (6)

ACI tolerance:
±1/2" (13) for D 24" (610) or less
±1" (25) for D over 24" (610)

(a) lateral placement

D

PCI tolerance: ±1/4" (6)

ACI tolerance:
±1/4" (6) for D 8" (203) or less
±3/8" (10) for D over 8" but not
over 24" (610)
±1/2" (13) for D over 24" (610)

D

PCI tolerance: ±1/4" (6)

ACI tolerance:
±1/4" (6) for D 8" (203) or less
±3/8" (10) for D over 8" but not
over 24" (610)
±1/2" (13) for D over 24" (610)

(b) vertical placement

Concrete

2-3. Reinforcement Placement of Prestressing Steel

Description

Prestressing steel includes tendons used for reinforcement of precast, prestressed concrete sections. Simple precast reinforcing steel placement tolerances are governed by ACI 117.

Industry Standards

ACI 117-90, *Standard Tolerances for Concrete Construction and Materials,* American Concrete Institute, Detroit, 1990.

Tolerances for Precast and Prestressed Concrete, Precast/Prestressed Concrete Institute, reprinted from *Journal of the Prestressed Concrete Institute,* vol. 30, no. 1, January–February 1985.

Allowable Tolerances

Lateral and vertical placement tolerances for prestressing steel and prestressing steel ducts are shown in Fig. 2-3. ACI 117 sets tolerances based on member depth while the Precast/Prestressed Concrete Institute sets tolerances based on member type.

The Precast/Prestressed Concrete Institute recommends that the position of tendons be $\pm\frac{1}{4}$ in (6 mm) for individual tendons and $\pm\frac{1}{2}$ in (13 mm) for bundled tendons for prestressed sections such as single tees, double tees, beams, spandrels, columns, ribbed wall panels, insulated wall panels, and tee joists.

Related Sections

2-1. Reinforcement Placement for Flexural Members

2-2. Reinforcement Placement in Walls and Columns

Figure 2-4

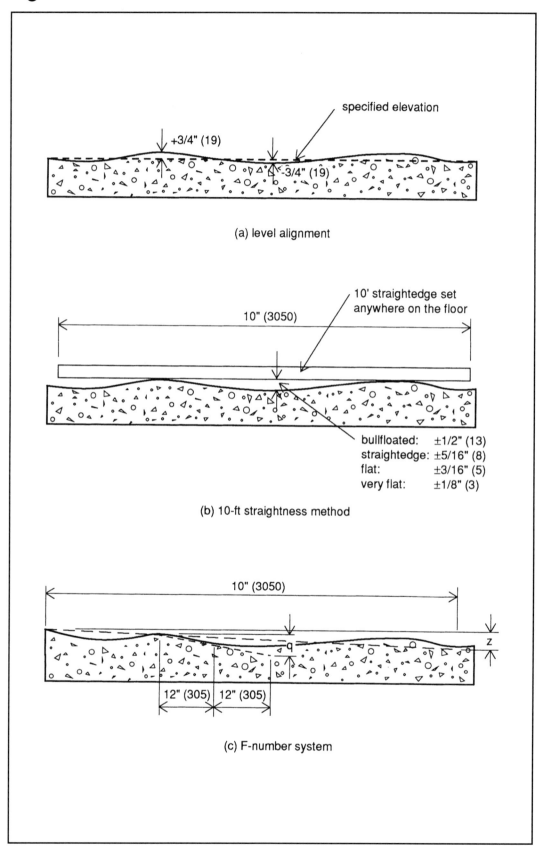

(a) level alignment

(b) 10-ft straightness method

(c) F-number system

2-4. Concrete Slabs-on-Grade

Description

Both slabs-on-grade and elevated slabs are subject to two tolerances. One is the overall tolerance above and below the specified elevation and the other is the flatness and levelness of the floor finish. *Flatness* is the degree to which the surface approximates a plane. *Levelness* is the degree to which the surface parallels horizontal. For a complete discussion of the new F-numbering system refer to ACI 302.1R-89, *Guide for Concrete Floor and Slab Construction* and ACI Compilation no. 9, *Concrete Floor Flatness and Levelness*.

Industry Standards

ACI 117-90, *Standard Tolerances for Concrete Construction and Materials,* American Concrete Institute, Detroit, 1990.

ASTM E1155-87, *Standard Test Method for Determining Floor Flatness and Levelness Using the F-Number System,* American Society for Testing and Materials, Philadelphia, 1987.

Allowable Tolerances

Level alignment tolerance is shown in Fig. 2-4*a*. This means that over the entire surface of a concrete slab all points must fall within an envelope $\frac{3}{4}$ in (19 mm) above or below the theoretical elevation plane.

Floor finish tolerances may be specified either by the traditional 10-ft straightedge method, as shown in Fig. 2-4*b*, or by the newer F-number system. The F-number system is a statistical method to measure and specify both the local flatness of a floor within adjacent, 12-in intervals (the F_F number) and the local levelness of a floor (the F_L number) over a 10-ft (3050 mm) distance. The higher the F_F or F_L number, the flatter or more level the floor. To determine if a floor falls within the tolerances of a particular F_F and F_L number, measurements must be taken according to the procedure set forth in ASTM E1155-87. Although there is no direct correlation, an F_{F50} roughly corresponds to a $\frac{1}{8}$-in (3.2-mm) gap under a 10-ft straightedge.

For slabs-on-grade the F-numbering system works well. However, to determine the F numbers, measurements must be taken within 72 h of floor installation and before shoring and forms are removed. Therefore, for elevated slabs specified levelness of a floor may be compromised when the floor deflects when the shoring is removed and loads applied.

Related Sections

1-3. Concrete Paving

2-8. Cast-in-Place Sectional Tolerances

Figure 2-5

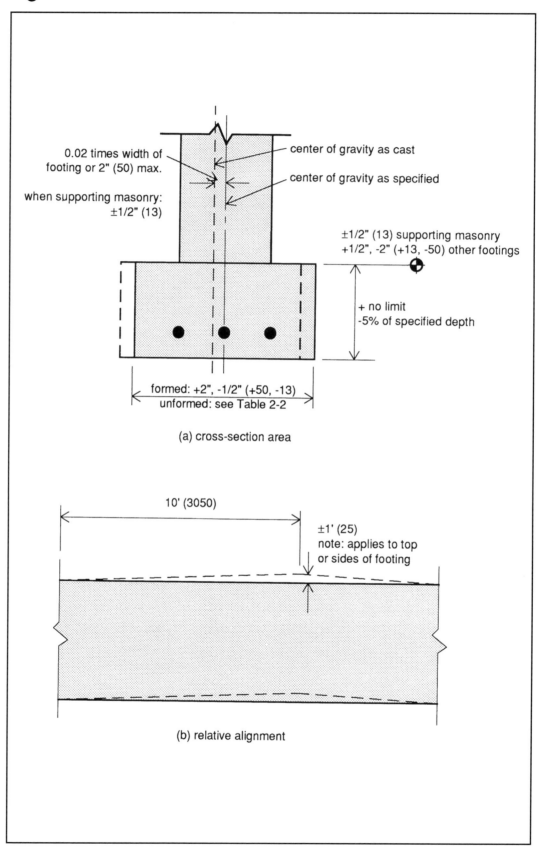

0.02 times width of footing or 2" (50) max.

when supporting masonry: ±1/2" (13)

center of gravity as cast

center of gravity as specified

±1/2" (13) supporting masonry
+1/2", -2" (+13, -50) other footings

+ no limit
-5% of specified depth

formed: +2", -1/2" (+50, -13)
unformed: see Table 2-2

(a) cross-section area

10' (3050)

±1' (25)
note: applies to top or sides of footing

(b) relative alignment

2-5. Footings

Description

Footings include continuous spread footings and pad footings. They include foundations poured in forms or directly against the soil.

Industry Standard

ACI 117-90, *Standard Tolerances for Concrete Construction and Materials,* American Concrete Institute, Detroit, 1990.

Allowable Tolerances

Tolerances for footings include lateral and level alignment as well as cross-sectional dimensions and relative alignment of the length along the sides and tops. As shown in Fig. 2-5 lateral alignment depends on the width of the footing in the least dimension based on the center of gravity of the footing as specified and as cast. For unformed footings the horizontal cross-sectional dimension depends on the specified width of the footing and is given in Table 2-2.

Table 2-2
Horizontal Dimension Tolerance
for Footings Cast against Soil

Specified width of footing, ft (mm)	Tolerance, in (mm)
2 (610) or less	$+3, -\frac{1}{2}$ (+76, −13)
Greater than 2 (610) but less than 6 (1830)	$+6, -\frac{1}{2}$ (+152, −13)
Over 6 (1830)	$+12, -\frac{1}{2}$ (+305, −13)

SOURCE: ACI 117-90; reproduced with permission, American Concrete Institute.

The sides and top of footings may slope at a rate not to exceed 1 in in 10 ft (25 mm in 3050 mm) as shown in Fig. 2-5*b*. Note that thickness tolerance and the top elevation tolerance cannot be combined to give a tolerance greater than formed top surface tolerance.

Related Sections

2-6. Piers

2-17. Precast Pilings

Figure 2-6

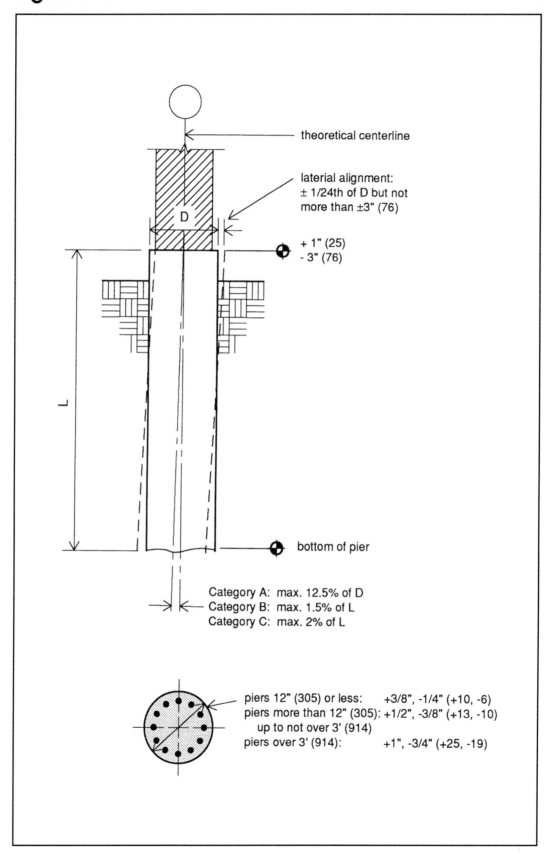

theoretical centerline

laterial alignment:
± 1/24th of D but not
more than ±3" (76)

+ 1" (25)
- 3" (76)

bottom of pier

Category A: max. 12.5% of D
Category B: max. 1.5% of L
Category C: max. 2% of L

piers 12" (305) or less: +3/8", -1/4" (+10, -6)
piers more than 12" (305):   +1/2", -3/8" (+13, -10)
     up to not over 3' (914)
piers over 3' (914):   +1", -3/4" (+25, -19)

2-6. Piers

Description

This section includes drilled piers of three categories. Category A includes unreinforced shafts extending through materials offering no or minimal lateral restraint, such as water, normally consolidated organic soils, or soils that might liquefy during an earthquake. Category B includes unreinforced shafts extending through materials offering lateral restraint which are soils other than those in Category A. Category C is for reinforced shafts.

Industry Standard

ACI 117-90, *Standard Tolerances for Concrete Construction and Materials,* American Concrete Institute, Detroit, 1990.

Allowable Tolerances

Tolerances for drilled piers are shown in Fig. 2-6. Note that vertical alignment tolerances depend on either the diameter of the pier or its length, depending on the category.

Related Sections

2-5. Footings

2-17. Precast Pilings

Figure 2-7

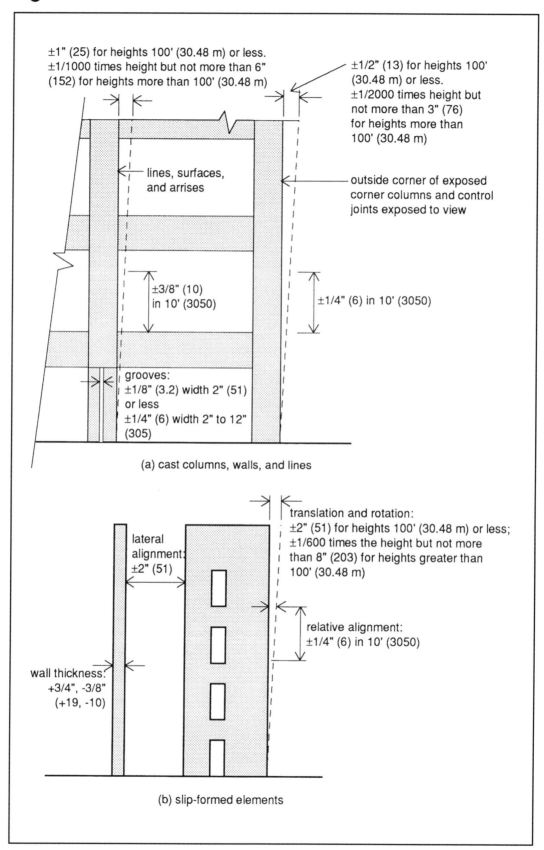

±1" (25) for heights 100' (30.48 m) or less.
±1/1000 times height but not more than 6"
(152) for heights more than 100' (30.48 m)

±1/2" (13) for heights 100'
(30.48 m) or less.
±1/2000 times height but
not more than 3" (76)
for heights more than
100' (30.48 m)

lines, surfaces,
and arrises

outside corner of exposed
corner columns and control
joints exposed to view

±3/8" (10)
in 10' (3050)

±1/4" (6) in 10' (3050)

grooves:
±1/8" (3.2) width 2" (51)
or less
±1/4" (6) width 2" to 12"
(305)

(a) cast columns, walls, and lines

translation and rotation:
±2" (51) for heights 100' (30.48 m) or less;
±1/600 times the height but not more
than 8" (203) for heights greater than
100' (30.48 m)

lateral
alignment:
±2" (51)

relative alignment:
±1/4" (6) in 10' (3050)

wall thickness:
+3/4", -3/8"
(+19, -10)

(b) slip-formed elements

2-7. Cast-in-Place Plumb Tolerances

Description

This section includes tolerances for both cast-in-place and vertically slip-formed elements. It includes visible elements, such as exposed columns, grooves, and expansion joints, as well as plumb tolerances for concealed column edges, walls, and slab edges.

Industry Standard

ACI 117-90, *Standard Tolerances for Concrete Construction and Materials,* American Concrete Institute, Detroit, 1990.

Allowable Tolerances

Vertical alignment tolerances (plumb) depend on the height of the structure and the location of the line in question. These conditions are shown in Fig. 2-7a. Note that the vertical tolerance envelope for exterior corner columns and interior lines and the slope tolerances within any 10 ft (3050 mm) also apply to the edges of concealed suspended slabs to which other building elements may be attached.

For slip-formed structures such as those shown in Fig. 2-7b, *rotation* is the twisting of a structure based on a fixed point at the base while *translation* is the change in horizontal position perpendicular to the original position of the structure at the base. The lateral alignment tolerance of ±2 in (51 mm) is between adjacent elements.

Related Sections

2-8. Cast-in-Place Sectional Tolerances

2-9. Cast-in-Place Concrete Elements in Plan

Figure 2-8

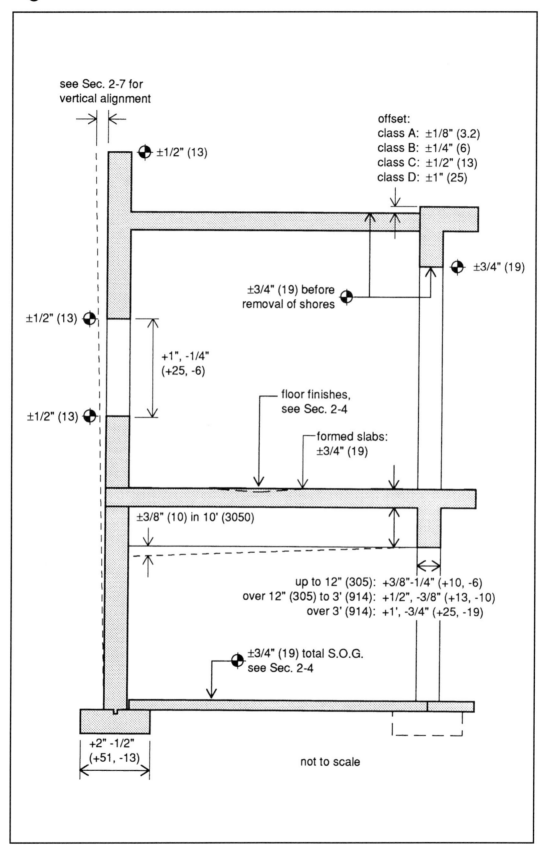

see Sec. 2-7 for
vertical alignment

⊕ ±1/2" (13)

offset:
class A: ±1/8" (3.2)
class B: ±1/4" (6)
class C: ±1/2" (13)
class D: ±1" (25)

⊕ ±3/4" (19)

±3/4" (19) before
removal of shores

±1/2" (13) ⊕

+1", -1/4"
(+25, -6)

floor finishes,
see Sec. 2-4

±1/2" (13) ⊕

formed slabs:
±3/4" (19)

±3/8" (10) in 10' (3050)

up to 12" (305): +3/8"-1/4" (+10, -6)
over 12" (305) to 3' (914): +1/2", -3/8" (+13, -10)
over 3' (914): +1', -3/4" (+25, -19)

±3/4" (19) total S.O.G.
see Sec. 2-4

+2" -1/2"
(+51, -13)

not to scale

2-8. Cast-in-Place Sectional Tolerances

Description

This section includes dimensional tolerances for cast-in-place concrete elements. It includes elevation tolerances as well as cross-sectional tolerances for elements such as columns, beams, walls, and slabs.

Industry Standard

ACI 117-90, *Standard Tolerances for Concrete Construction and Materials,* American Concrete Institute, Detroit, 1990.

Allowable Tolerances

The various sectional tolerances are shown diagrammatically in Fig. 2-8. The level alignment tolerance of $\pm\frac{1}{2}$ in (13 mm) for lintels, sills, and parapets also applies to horizontal grooves and other lines exposed to view. Offsets listed as Class A, B, C, and D are for adjacent pieces of formwork facing material. Note that the level alignment of the top surface of formed slabs and for other formed surfaces is measured *before* the removal of shoring.

Related Sections

2-4. Concrete Slabs-on-Grade

2-5. Footings

2-7. Cast-in-Place Plumb Tolerances

2-9. Cast-in-Place Concrete Elements in Plan

Figure 2-9

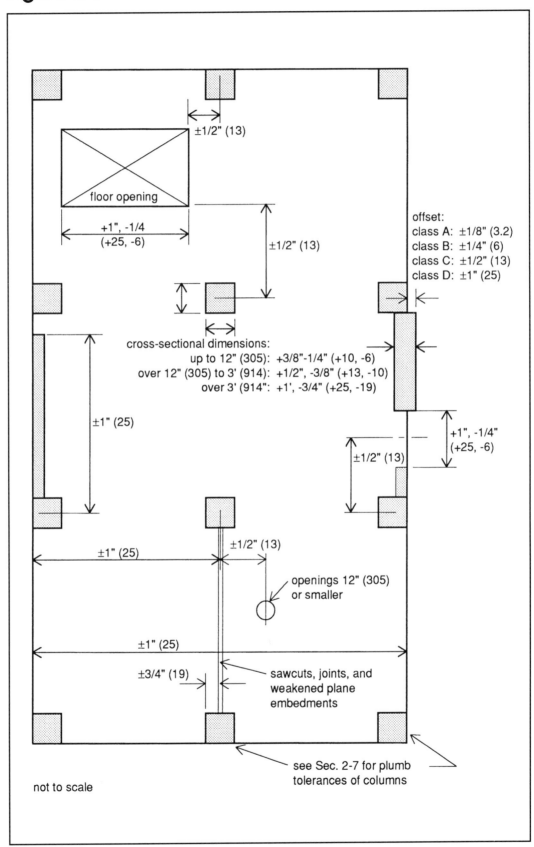

not to scale

     Concrete

2-9. Cast-in-Place Concrete Elements in Plan

Description

This section includes lateral dimensional tolerances for cast-in-place concrete construction. It includes location tolerances for elements such as columns and walls as well as opening tolerances.

Industry Standard

ACI 117-90, *Standard Tolerances for Concrete Construction and Materials,* American Concrete Institute, Detroit, 1990.

Allowable Tolerances

Tolerances for lateral alignment of cast-in-place building elements are shown in Fig. 2-9. The cross-section dimensions apply to columns, beams, piers, and walls.

Related Sections

2-7. Cast-in-Place Plumb Tolerances
2-8. Cast-in-Place Sectional Tolerances

Figure 2-10

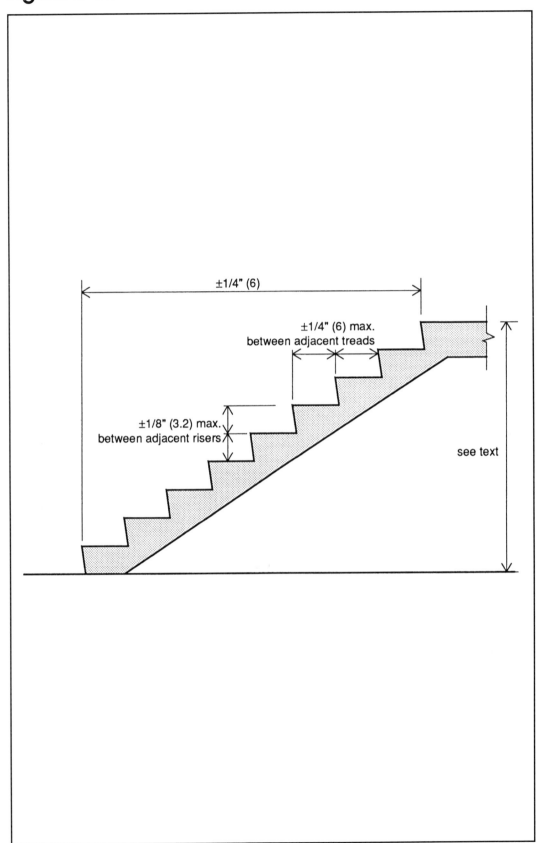

±1/4" (6)

±1/4" (6) max.
between adjacent treads

±1/8" (3.2) max.
between adjacent risers

see text

2-10. Cast-in-Place Stairs

Description

The American Concrete Institute's tolerances for cast-in-place concrete only require adjacent risers and treads to be within a listed tolerance. However, the *Uniform Building Code* and other codes require that the largest tread run (or riser height) within any flight not exceed the smallest tread (or riser) by more than $\frac{3}{8}$ in (10 mm).

Industry Standards

ACI 117-90, *Standard Tolerances for Concrete Construction and Materials,* American Concrete Institute, Detroit, 1990.

Section 3306(c), *Uniform Building Code,* International Conference of Building Officials, Whittier, CA, 1991.

Allowable Tolerances

Current ACI tolerances only give allowable variations in height and width between adjacent risers and treads, respectively, as shown in Fig. 2-10. Previous versions of ACI 117 also limited the total rise in a flight of stairs to $\pm\frac{1}{8}$ in (3.2 mm) and the total run to $\pm\frac{1}{4}$ in (6 mm), but these tolerances are no longer included as part of ACI 117. If the elevation of the top surfaces of formed slabs is $\pm\frac{3}{4}$ in (19 mm) as stated in Sec. 2-8, there could be a maximum difference of $1\frac{1}{2}$ in (38 mm) beyond what is shown on the drawings. This could require riser heights to be adjusted to match actual floor-to-floor heights.

Related Sections

2-8. Cast-in-Place Sectional Tolerances

2-9. Cast-in-Place Concrete Elements in Plan

2-16. Precast Stairs

Figure 2-11

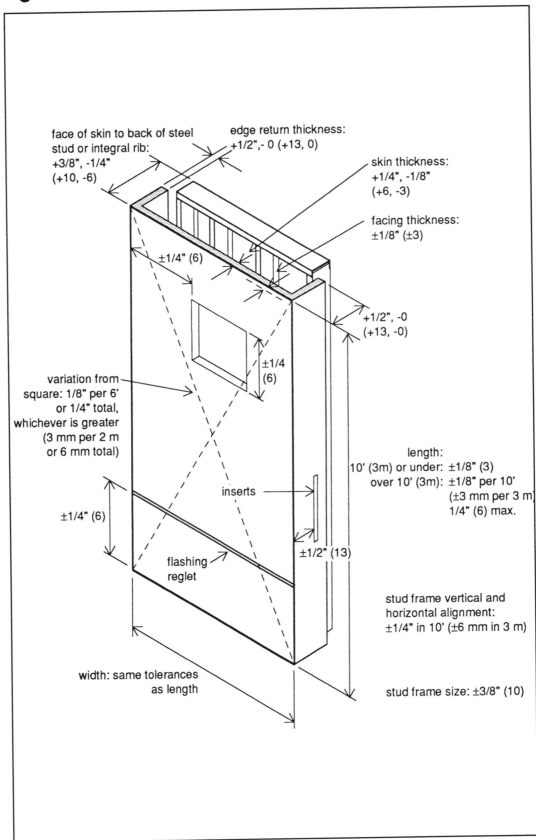

face of skin to back of steel stud or integral rib: +3/8", -1/4" (+10, -6)

edge return thickness: +1/2",- 0 (+13, 0)

skin thickness: +1/4", -1/8" (+6, -3)

facing thickness: ±1/8" (±3)

±1/4" (6)

+1/2", -0 (+13, -0)

±1/4 (6)

variation from square: 1/8" per 6' or 1/4" total, whichever is greater (3 mm per 2 m or 6 mm total)

length:
10' (3m) or under: ±1/8" (3)
over 10' (3m): ±1/8" per 10'
(±3 mm per 3 m)
1/4" (6) max.

±1/4" (6)

inserts

±1/2" (13)

flashing reglet

stud frame vertical and horizontal alignment: ±1/4" in 10' (±6 mm in 3 m)

width: same tolerances as length

stud frame size: ±3/8" (10)

Concrete

2-11. Glass Fiber Reinforced Concrete Panels

Description

The term *glass fiber reinforced concrete* (GFRC) applies to products manufactured with a cement/aggregate slurry reinforced with alkali resistant glass fibers. GFRC panels are typically used for exterior cladding, column covers, and interior finish panels. They can be manufactured with or without a face mix of conventional concrete with decorative aggregates. When a face mix is used, GFRC panels have the same appearance as standard precast concrete panels. Panels are normally $\frac{3}{8}$ to $\frac{1}{2}$ in (10 to 13 mm) thick not including any exposed aggregate or veneer finish, if used.

Industry Standard

Recommended Practice for Glass Fiber Reinforced Concrete Panels, Precast/Prestressed Concrete Institute, Chicago, 1993.

Allowable Tolerances

Most of the tolerances for GFRC panel manufacturing are shown in Fig. 2-11. Where tolerances for thickness are shown, increased tolerances should be allowed at a change in plane, a radius section, stiffening ribs, and similar construction elements. Generally, manufacturing tolerances can be compensated for during erection by making adjustments in the clearance space, modifying joint width slightly, and by forcing out minor variations in bow and warpage during attachment of the panel to the supporting framework. See the *Recommended Practice for Glass Fiber Reinforced Concrete Panels* for a complete listing and discussion of GFRC panel tolerances.

Related Section

2-28. Glass Fiber Reinforced Concrete Panel Erection

Figure 2-12

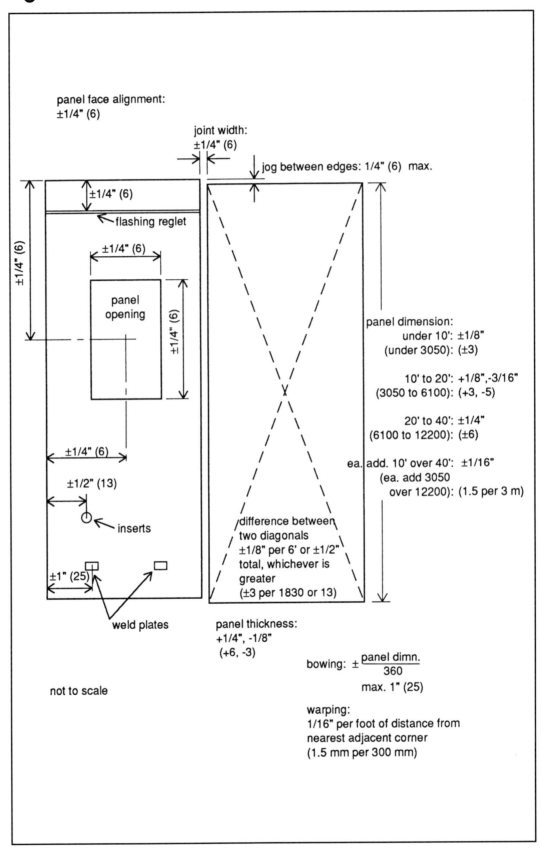

panel face alignment:
±1/4" (6)

joint width:
±1/4" (6)

jog between edges: 1/4" (6) max.

±1/4" (6)

← flashing reglet

±1/4" (6)

±1/4" (6)

panel
opening

±1/4" (6)

panel dimension:
    under 10': ±1/8"
(under 3050): (±3)

10' to 20': +1/8",-3/16"
(3050 to 6100): (+3, -5)

20' to 40': ±1/4"
(6100 to 12200): (±6)

ea. add. 10' over 40': ±1/16"
(ea. add 3050
    over 12200): (1.5 per 3 m)

±1/4" (6)

±1/2" (13)

← inserts

difference between
two diagonals
±1/8" per 6' or ±1/2"
total, whichever is
greater
(±3 per 1830 or 13)

±1" (25)

weld plates

panel thickness:
+1/4", -1/8"
(+6, -3)

bowing: ± $\dfrac{\text{panel dimn.}}{360}$

max. 1" (25)

warping:
1/16" per foot of distance from
nearest adjacent corner
(1.5 mm per 300 mm)

not to scale

2-12. Architectural Precast Concrete Panels

Description

This section includes tolerances for plant-cast and site-cast precast and precast prestressed concrete panels commonly used as exterior cladding. The tolerances shown are some of the most common with which architects are concerned. Manufacturing tolerances (sometimes referred to as "product tolerances") must be coordinated with erection tolerances and tolerances for other building systems for a successful project. During construction one surface is usually designated as the primary control surface, the location of which is controlled during erection. The product tolerances given in this section are *not* additive to the erection tolerances of the primary control surfaces. However, product tolerances are additive to secondary control surface erection tolerances.

Industry Standards

ACI 117-90, *Standard Tolerances for Concrete Construction and Materials,* American Concrete Institute, Detroit, 1990.

Tolerances for Precast and Prestressed Concrete, Precast/Prestressed Concrete Institute, reprinted from *Journal of the Prestressed Concrete Institute,* vol. 30, no. 1, January–February 1985.

Allowable Tolerances

Some of the primary casting tolerances for flat panels are shown in Fig. 2-12. Other tolerances exist for items such as haunch dimensions and positions, hidden blockouts, and other inserts. Refer to *Tolerances for Precast and Prestressed Concrete* for a complete listing. The *bowing* tolerances refer to the overall out-of-planeness which can occur in one direction along a length of panel or in two directions. *Warping,* on the other hand, refers to the variation of one corner from adjacent corners. The difference between diagonals applies to major openings as well as the panel itself.

Related Sections

2-13. Precast Ribbed Wall Panels

2-14. Precast Insulated Wall Panels

2-26. Precast Structural Wall Panel Erection

2-27. Precast Architectural Wall Panel Erection

Chapter 13. Precast Concrete Systems

Figure 2-13

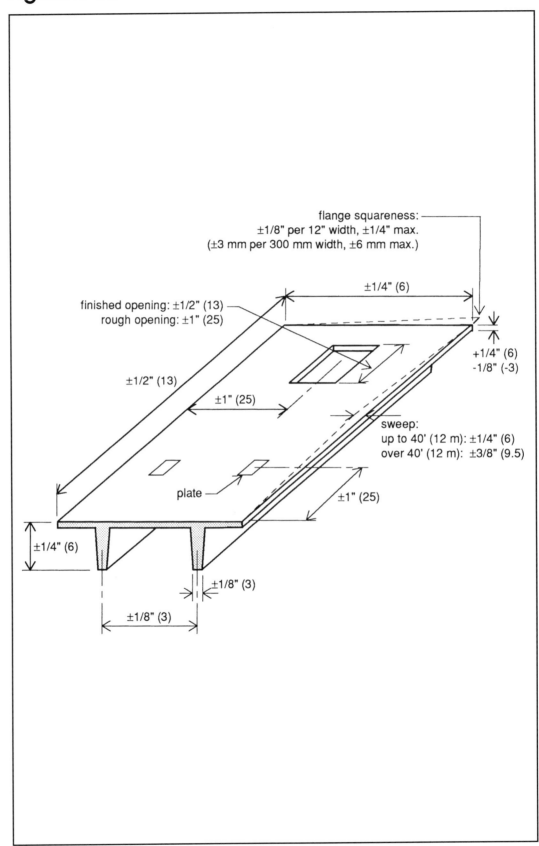

flange squareness:
±1/8" per 12" width, ±1/4" max.
(±3 mm per 300 mm width, ±6 mm max.)

±1/4" (6)

finished opening: ±1/2" (13)
rough opening: ±1" (25)

+1/4" (6)
-1/8" (-3)

±1/2" (13)

±1" (25)

sweep:
up to 40' (12 m): ±1/4" (6)
over 40' (12 m): ±3/8" (9.5)

plate

±1" (25)

±1/4" (6)

±1/8" (3)

±1/8" (3)

Concrete

2-13. Precast Ribbed Wall Panels

Description

This section includes tolerances for plant-cast and site-cast precast and precast prestressed concrete ribbed wall panels. These are similar to double tees but have a slightly different configuration.

Manufacturing tolerances (sometimes referred to as "product tolerances") must be coordinated with erection tolerances and tolerances for other building systems for a successful project. During construction one surface is usually designated as the primary control surface, the location of which is controlled during erection. The product tolerances given in this section are *not* additive to the erection tolerances of the primary control surfaces. However, product tolerances are additive to secondary control surface erection tolerances.

Industry Standard

Tolerances for Precast and Prestressed Concrete, Precast/Prestressed Concrete Institute, reprinted from *Journal of the Prestressed Concrete Institute,* vol. 30, no. 1, January–February 1985.

Allowable Tolerances

Many of the tolerances for ribbed wall panels are shown in Fig. 2-13. Refer to *Tolerances for Precast and Prestressed Concrete* for a complete listing.

The variation from end squareness is $\pm\frac{1}{8}$ in per 12 in (±3 mm per 300 mm). Bowing is limited to the length of the member divided by 360. Differential bowing between adjacent panels of the same design is limited to $\pm\frac{1}{2}$ in (13 mm). Warping cannot exceed $\frac{1}{16}$ in per ft (1.5 mm per 300 mm) of the distance from the nearest adjacent corner. The local smoothness of any surface is $\pm\frac{1}{4}$ in per 10 ft (6 mm per 3 m).

The tolerance for the tipping and flushness of plates as well as tendon location is $\pm\frac{1}{4}$ in (6 mm). Inserts for structural connections are located within $\pm\frac{1}{2}$ in (13 mm).

Related Sections

2-1. Architectural Precast Concrete Panels

2-20. Prestressed Double Tees

2-26. Precast Structural Wall Panel Erection

Chapter 13. Precast Concrete Systems

Figure 2-14

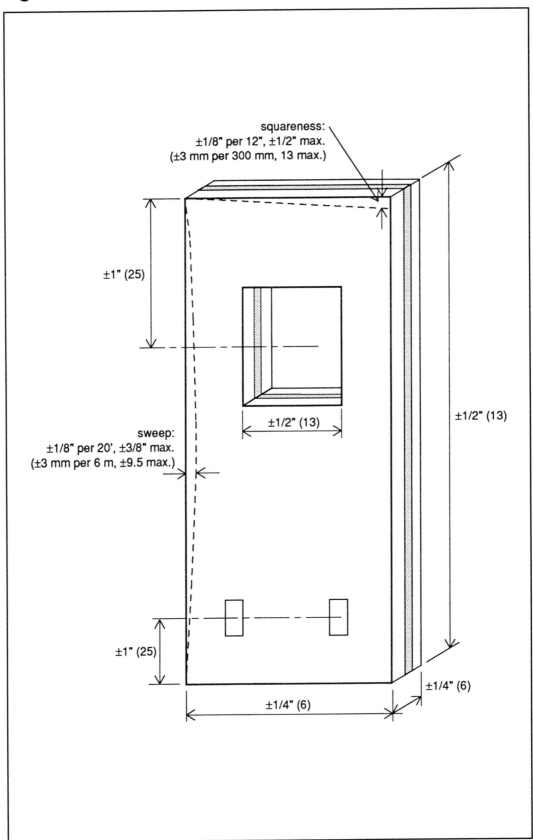

squareness:
±1/8" per 12", ±1/2" max.
(±3 mm per 300 mm, 13 max.)

±1" (25)

±1/2" (13)

sweep:
±1/8" per 20', ±3/8" max.
(±3 mm per 6 m, ±9.5 max.)

±1/2" (13)

±1" (25)

±1/4" (6)

±1/4" (6)

2-14. Precast Insulated Wall Panels

Description

This section includes tolerances for multiwythe wall panels used in single-story structures. The manufacturing tolerances (sometimes referred to as "product tolerances") shown here must be coordinated with erection tolerances and tolerances for other building systems for a successful project. During construction one surface is usually designated as the primary control surface, the location of which is controlled during erection. The product tolerances given in this section are *not* additive to the erection tolerances of the primary control surfaces. However, product tolerances are additive to secondary control surface erection tolerances.

Industry Standard

Tolerances for Precast and Prestressed Concrete, Precast/Prestressed Concrete Institute, reprinted from *Journal of the Prestressed Concrete Institute,* vol. 30, no. 1, January–February 1985.

Allowable Tolerances

Many of the tolerances for insulated wall panels are shown in Fig. 2-14. Refer to *Tolerances for Precast and Prestressed Concrete* for a complete listing.

The variation from end squareness is $\pm\frac{1}{8}$ in per 12 in (±3 mm per 300 mm). Bowing is limited to the length of the member divided by 360. Differential bowing between adjacent panels of the same design is limited to $\pm\frac{1}{2}$ in (13 mm). Warping cannot exceed $\frac{1}{16}$ in per ft (1.5 mm per 300 mm) of the distance from the nearest adjacent corner. The local smoothness of any surface is $\pm\frac{1}{4}$ in per 10 ft (6 mm per 3 m).

The tolerance for the tipping and flushness of plates as well as tendon location is $\pm\frac{1}{4}$ in (6 mm). Inserts for structural connections are located within $\pm\frac{1}{2}$ in (13 mm).

Related Sections

2-12.   Architectural Precast Concrete Panels

2-26.   Precast Structural Wall Panel Erection

Chapter 13. Precast Concrete Systems

Figure 2-15

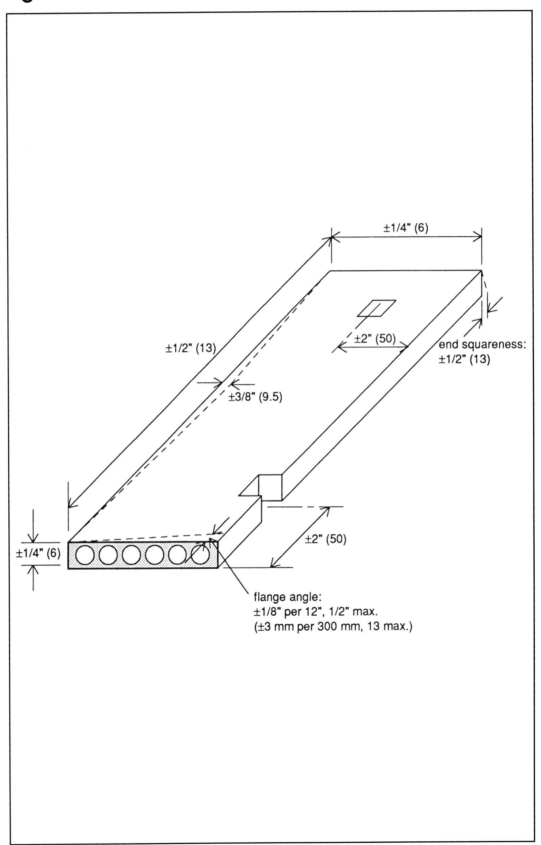

±1/4" (6)

±1/2" (13)

±2" (50)

end squareness:
±1/2" (13)

±3/8" (9.5)

±2" (50)

±1/4" (6)

flange angle:
±1/8" per 12", 1/2" max.
(±3 mm per 300 mm, 13 max.)

Concrete

2-15. Hollow-Core Slabs

Description

This section includes tolerances for cored slabs used for floor and roof construction.

Manufacturing tolerances (sometimes referred to as "product tolerances") must be coordinated with erection tolerances and tolerances for other building systems for a successful project. During construction one surface is usually designated as the primary control surface, the location of which is controlled during erection. The product tolerances given in this section are *not* additive to the erection tolerances of the primary control surfaces. However, product tolerances are additive to secondary control surface erection tolerances.

Industry Standard

Tolerances for Precast and Prestressed Concrete, Precast/Prestressed Concrete Institute, reprinted from *Journal of the Prestressed Concrete Institute,* vol. 30, no. 1, January–February 1985.

Allowable Tolerances

Many of the tolerances for hollow-core slabs are shown in Fig. 2-15. Refer to *Tolerances for Precast and Prestressed Concrete* for a complete listing.

The variation from end squareness is $\pm\frac{1}{2}$ in (13 mm). When differential camber between adjacent members of the same design is critical, the amount of tolerance should be verified with the producer. The local smoothness of any surface is $\pm\frac{1}{4}$ in in 10 ft (6 mm in 3 m). However, this does not apply to the top deck surface that is to receive a topping or other visually concealed surface. The tolerance for the tipping and flushness of plates is $\pm\frac{1}{4}$ in (6 mm).

Related Sections

2-18. Prestressed Concrete Beams

2-25. Precast Floor and Roof Member Erection

Chapter 13. Precast Concrete Systems

Figure 2-16

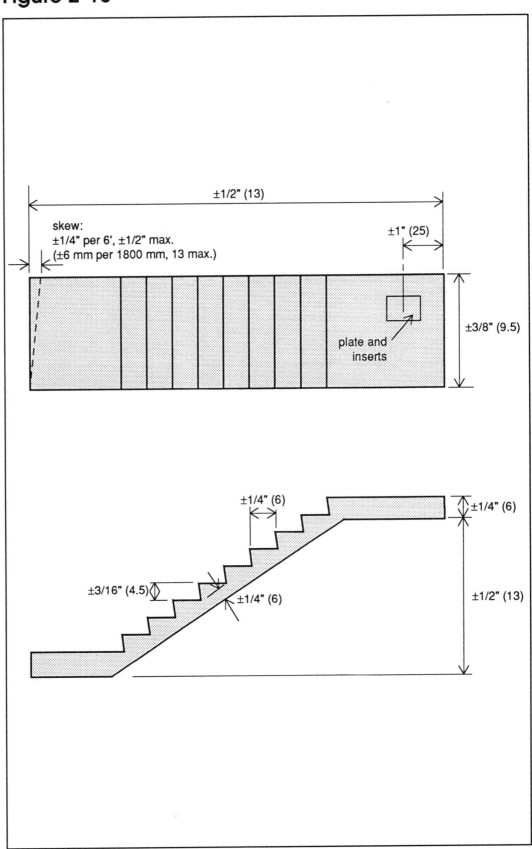

2-16. Precast Stairs

Description

Precast stairs may be part of a larger precast building or be incorporated into a cast-in-place concrete structure or a composite structure of steel and concrete. The applicable fabrication and erection tolerances of the base structure must be coordinated with the tolerances in this section to assure that code maximums for variance of riser heights are not exceeded.

Industry Standard

Tolerances for Precast and Prestressed Concrete, Precast/Prestressed Concrete Institute, reprinted from *Journal of the Prestressed Concrete Institute,* vol. 30, no. 1, January–February 1985.

Allowable Tolerances

Overall tolerances and individual step tolerances are shown in Fig. 2-16. In addition, the maximum difference between two risers is $\pm\frac{1}{4}$ in (6 mm). These step tolerances are within the *Uniform Building Code*'s requirement that the largest tread run (or riser height) within any flight not exceed the smallest tread (or riser) by more than $\frac{3}{8}$ in (10 mm).

The square tolerance for the entire assembly (the difference in length of the two diagonals) is $\pm\frac{1}{4}$ in per 6 ft with a $\frac{1}{2}$-in maximum (±6 mm per 1.8 m, with a 13-mm maximum variance). The position of inserts for structural connections must fall within $\frac{3}{8}$ in (9.5 mm) of the specified location.

Related Sections

2-10. Cast-in-Place Stairs

2-25. Precast Floor and Roof Member Erection

Chapter 13. Precast Concrete Systems

Figure 2-17

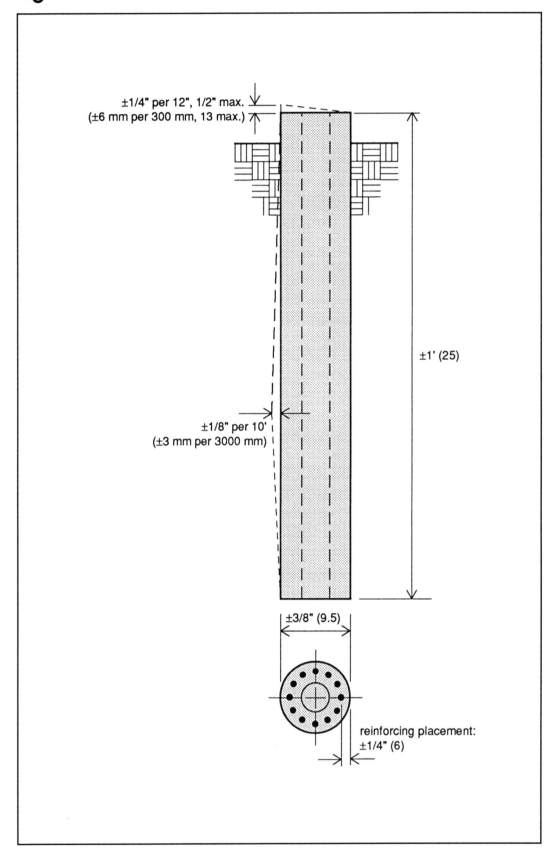

±1/4" per 12", 1/2" max.
(±6 mm per 300 mm, 13 max.)

±1' (25)

±1/8" per 10'
(±3 mm per 3000 mm)

±3/8" (9.5)

reinforcing placement:
±1/4" (6)

2-17. Precast Pilings

Description

This section includes tolerances for both solid and hollow pilings. The dimensions illustrated are for round-, square-, and octagonal-shaped pilings.

Industry Standard

Tolerances for Precast and Prestressed Concrete, Precast/Prestressed Concrete Institute, reprinted from *Journal of the Prestressed Concrete Institute,* vol. 30, no. 1, January–February 1985.

Allowable Tolerances

The primary tolerances are shown in Fig. 2-17. Note that the length tolerance of ± 1 in (25 mm) is smaller than is often necessary. In many instances a tolerance of $+6$ in (150 mm) and -2 in (50 mm) is acceptable.

For hollow pilings, the wall thickness has a tolerance of $+\frac{1}{2}$ in and $-\frac{1}{4}$ in ($+13$ mm, -6 mm). Smoothness tolerance is $\pm\frac{1}{4}$ in in 10 ft (6 mm in 3 m).

Related Sections

2-5. Footings

2-6. Piers

Figure 2-18

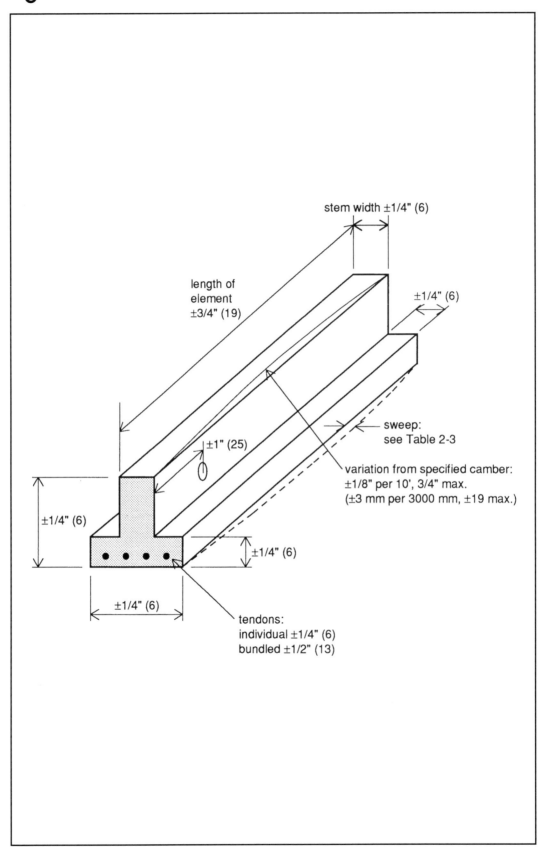

stem width ±1/4" (6)

length of
element
±3/4" (19)

±1/4" (6)

±1" (25)

sweep:
see Table 2-3

variation from specified camber:
±1/8" per 10', 3/4" max.
(±3 mm per 3000 mm, ±19 max.)

±1/4" (6)

±1/4" (6)

±1/4" (6)

tendons:
individual ±1/4" (6)
bundled ±1/2" (13)

2-18. Prestressed Concrete Beams

Description

This section includes tolerances for rectangular, T-shaped, and L-shaped beams.

Manufacturing tolerances (sometimes referred to as "product tolerances") must be coordinated with erection tolerances and tolerances for other building systems for a successful project. During construction one surface is usually designated as the primary control surface, the location of which is controlled during erection. The product tolerances given in this section are *not* additive to the erection tolerances of the primary control surfaces. However, product tolerances are additive to secondary control surface erection tolerances.

Industry Standard

Tolerances for Precast and Prestressed Concrete, Precast/Prestressed Concrete Institute, reprinted from *Journal of the Prestressed Concrete Institute,* vol. 30, no. 1, January–February 1985.

Allowable Tolerances

Many of the tolerances for precast beams are shown in Fig. 2-18. Refer to *Tolerances for Precast and Prestressed Concrete* for a complete listing. The sweep tolerances shown in Fig. 2-18 are given in Table 2-3.

Table 2-3
Sweep Tolerances for Prestressed Concrete Beams

Member length, ft (m)	Sweep tolerance, in (mm)
Up to 40 (12)	$\pm\frac{1}{4}$ (±6)
40 to 60 (12 to 18)	$\pm\frac{1}{2}$ (±13)
Over 60 (18)	$\pm\frac{5}{8}$ (±16)

SOURCE: Precast/Prestressed Concrete Institute.

The variation from end squareness is $\pm\frac{1}{8}$ in per 12 in of depth, with a $\frac{1}{2}$-in maximum (±3 mm per 300 mm of depth, 13-mm maximum). Camber variation from the design camber is $\pm\frac{1}{8}$ in per 10 ft, with a $\frac{3}{4}$-in maximum (±3 mm per 3 m, with a 19-mm maximum). However, for members with a span-to-depth ratio approaching or exceeding 30, this camber tolerance may not apply. If camber tolerances must be controlled with such span-to-depth ratios, premium production measures may be required. Specific job requirements should be verified with the producer.

Plate position tolerance is ±1 in (25 mm) for miscellaneous plates and $\frac{1}{2}$ in (13 mm) for bearing plates. The tolerance for the tipping and flushness of miscellaneous plates is $\pm\frac{1}{4}$ in (6 mm) and for bearing plates it is $\pm\frac{1}{8}$ in (3 mm). Inserts for structural connections are located within $\pm\frac{1}{2}$ in (13 mm).

Smoothness of any surface must be within $\frac{1}{4}$ in in 10 ft (6 mm in 3 m), except that surface requirements do not apply to top surfaces left rough to receive a topping.

Related Sections

2-19. Prestressed Single Tees

2-20. Prestressed Double Tees

2-21. Precast Columns

2-24. Precast Beam and Spandrel Erection

Chapter 13. Precast Concrete Systems

Figure 2-19

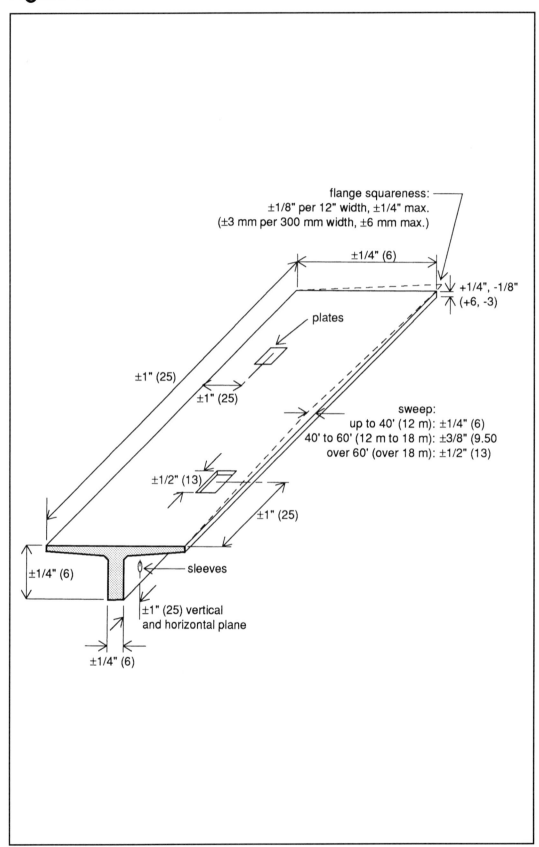

flange squareness:
±1/8" per 12" width, ±1/4" max.
(±3 mm per 300 mm width, ±6 mm max.)

±1/4" (6)

+1/4", -1/8"
(+6, -3)

plates

±1" (25)

±1" (25)

sweep:
up to 40' (12 m): ±1/4" (6)
40' to 60' (12 m to 18 m): ±3/8" (9.50
over 60' (over 18 m): ±1/2" (13)

±1/2" (13)

±1" (25)

±1/4" (6)

sleeves

±1" (25) vertical
and horizontal plane

±1/4" (6)

2-19. Prestressed Single Tees

Description

This section includes tolerances for single tees as commonly used for floor and roof structure. The manufacturing tolerances (sometimes referred to as "product tolerances") shown here must be coordinated with erection tolerances and tolerances for other building systems for a successful project. During construction one surface is usually designated as the primary control surface, the location of which is controlled during erection. The product tolerances given in this section are *not* additive to the erection tolerances of the primary control surfaces. However, product tolerances are additive to secondary control surface erection tolerances.

Industry Standard

Tolerances for Precast and Prestressed Concrete, Precast/Prestressed Concrete Institute, reprinted from *Journal of the Prestressed Concrete Institute,* vol. 30, no. 1, January–February 1985.

Allowable Tolerances

Many of the tolerances for single tees are shown in Fig. 2-19. Refer to *Tolerances for Precast and Prestressed Concrete* for a complete listing.

The variation from end squareness is $\pm 1/8$ in per 12 in of depth, with a $\frac{1}{2}$-in maximum (± 3 mm per 300 mm of depth, 13-mm maximum) for depths greater than 24 in (600 mm). For depths 24 in (600 mm) or less the end squareness tolerance is $\pm \frac{1}{4}$ in (± 6 mm). Camber variation from the design camber is $\pm \frac{1}{4}$ in per 10 ft, with a $\frac{3}{4}$-in maximum (± 6 mm per 3 m, with a 19-mm maximum). However, for members with a span-to-depth ratio approaching or exceeding 30, this camber tolerance may not apply. If camber tolerances must be controlled with such span-to-depth ratios, premium production measures may be required. Specific job requirements should be verified with the producer. Differential camber between adjacent members of the same design is $\pm \frac{1}{4}$ in per 10 ft, with a $\frac{3}{4}$-in maximum (6 mm per 3 m, 19-mm maximum).

Plate position tolerance is ± 1 in (25 mm) for miscellaneous plates and $\frac{1}{2}$ in (13 mm) for bearing plates. The tolerance for the tipping and flushness of miscellaneous plates is $\pm \frac{1}{4}$ in (6 mm) and for bearing plates it is $\pm \frac{1}{8}$ in (3 mm). Inserts for structural connections are located within $\pm \frac{1}{2}$ in (13 mm).

Smoothness of any surface must be within $\frac{1}{4}$ in in 10 ft (6 mm in 3 m), except that surface requirements do not apply to top surfaces left rough to receive a topping.

Related Sections

2-18. Prestressed Concrete Beams

2-20. Prestressed Double Tees

2-25. Precast Floor and Roof Member Erection

Chapter 13. Precast Concrete Systems

Figure 2-20

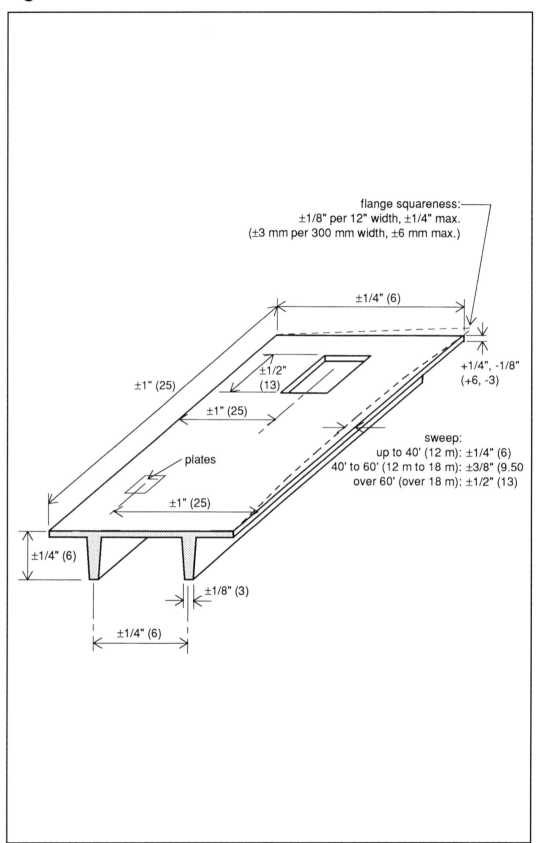

flange squareness:
±1/8" per 12" width, ±1/4" max.
(±3 mm per 300 mm width, ±6 mm max.)

±1/4" (6)

+1/4", -1/8"
(+6, -3)

±1/2"
(13)

±1" (25)

±1" (25)

plates

±1" (25)

sweep:
up to 40' (12 m): ±1/4" (6)
40' to 60' (12 m to 18 m): ±3/8" (9.50
over 60' (over 18 m): ±1/2" (13)

±1/4" (6)

±1/8" (3)

±1/4" (6)

2-20. Prestressed Double Tees

Description

This section includes tolerances for double tees as commonly used for floor and roof structure. The manufacturing tolerances (sometimes referred to as "product tolerances") shown here must be coordinated with erection tolerances and tolerances for other building systems for a successful project. During construction one surface is usually designated as the primary control surface, the location of which is controlled during erection. The product tolerances given in this section are *not* additive to the erection tolerances of the primary control surfaces. However, product tolerances are additive to secondary control surface erection tolerances.

Industry Standard

Tolerances for Precast and Prestressed Concrete, Precast/Prestressed Concrete Institute, reprinted from *Journal of the Prestressed Concrete Institute,* vol. 30, no. 1, January–February 1985.

Allowable Tolerances

Many of the tolerances for double tees are shown in Fig. 2-20. Refer to *Tolerances for Precast and Prestressed Concrete* for a complete listing.

The variation from end squareness is $\pm\frac{1}{8}$ in per 12 in of depth, with a $\frac{1}{2}$-in maximum (±3 mm per 300 mm of depth, 13-mm maximum) for depths greater than 24 in (600 mm). For depths 24 in (600 mm) or less the end squareness tolerance is $\pm\frac{1}{4}$ in (±6 mm). Camber variation from the design camber is $\pm\frac{1}{4}$ in per 10 ft, with a $\frac{3}{4}$-in maximum (±6 mm per 3 m, with a 19-mm maximum). However, for members with a span-to-depth ratio approaching or exceeding 30, this camber tolerance may not apply. If camber tolerances must be controlled with such span-to-depth ratios, premium production measures may be required. Specific job requirements should be verified with the producer. Differential camber between adjacent members of the same design is $\pm\frac{1}{4}$ in per 10 ft, with a $\frac{3}{4}$-in maximum (6 mm per 3 m, 19-mm maximum).

Plate position tolerance is ±1 in (25 mm) for miscellaneous plates and $\frac{1}{2}$ in (13 mm) for bearing plates. The tolerance for the tipping and flushness of miscellaneous plates is $\pm\frac{1}{4}$ in (6 mm) and for bearing plates it is $\pm1/8$ in (3 mm). Inserts for structural connections are located within $\pm\frac{1}{2}$ in (13 mm).

Smoothness of any surface must be within $\frac{1}{4}$ in in 10 ft (6 mm in 3 m), except that surface requirements do not apply to top surfaces left rough to receive a topping.

Related Sections

2-18. Prestressed Concrete Beams

2-19. Prestressed Single Tees

2-25. Precast Floor and Roof Member Erection

Chapter 13. Precast Concrete Systems

Figure 2-21

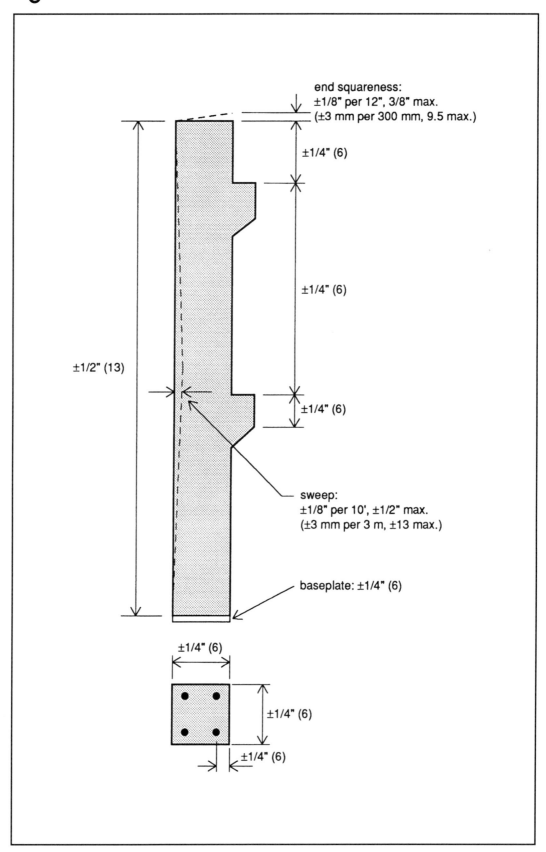

end squareness:
±1/8" per 12", 3/8" max.
(±3 mm per 300 mm, 9.5 max.)

±1/4" (6)

±1/4" (6)

±1/2" (13)

±1/4" (6)

sweep:
±1/8" per 10', ±1/2" max.
(±3 mm per 3 m, ±13 max.)

baseplate: ±1/4" (6)

±1/4" (6)

±1/4" (6)

±1/4" (6)

2-21. Precast Columns

Description

This section includes tolerances for precast concrete columns commonly used to support precast beams or other structural members. The manufacturing tolerances shown here must be coordinated with erection tolerances and tolerances for other building systems for a successful project. During construction one surface is usually designated as the primary control surface, the location of which is controlled during erection. The product tolerances given in this section are *not* additive to the erection tolerances of the primary control surfaces. However, product tolerances are additive to secondary control surface erection tolerances.

Industry Standard

Tolerances for Precast and Prestressed Concrete, Precast/Prestressed Concrete Institute, reprinted from *Journal of the Prestressed Concrete Institute,* vol. 30, no. 1, January–February 1985.

Allowable Tolerances

Many of the tolerances for precast columns are shown in Fig. 2-21. Refer to *Tolerances for Precast and Prestressed Concrete* for a complete listing. Note that the tolerances for the size and position of haunches are not cumulative. Plate position tolerance is ± 1 in (25 mm). The tolerance for the tipping and flushness of plates is $\pm \frac{1}{4}$ in (6 mm). Inserts for structural connections are located within $\pm \frac{1}{2}$ in (13 mm). Smoothness of any surface must be within $\frac{1}{4}$ in in 10 ft (6 mm in 3 m), except that surface requirements do not apply to visually concealed surfaces.

Related Sections

2-23. Precast Column Erection

Chapter 13. Precast Concrete Systems

Figure 2-22

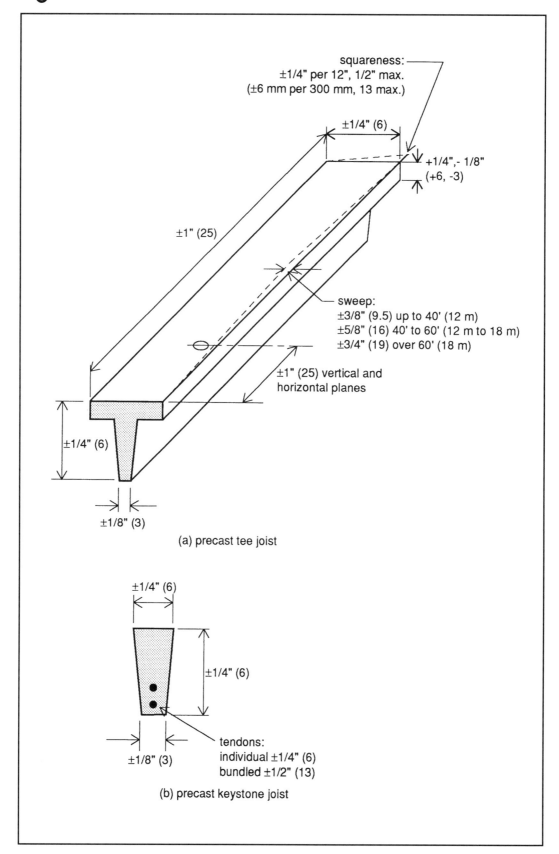

squareness:
±1/4" per 12", 1/2" max.
(±6 mm per 300 mm, 13 max.)

±1/4" (6)

+1/4",- 1/8"
(+6, -3)

±1" (25)

sweep:
±3/8" (9.5) up to 40' (12 m)
±5/8" (16) 40' to 60' (12 m to 18 m)
±3/4" (19) over 60' (18 m)

±1" (25) vertical and
horizontal planes

±1/4" (6)

±1/8" (3)

(a) precast tee joist

±1/4" (6)

±1/4" (6)

±1/8" (3)

tendons:
individual ±1/4" (6)
bundled ±1/2" (13)

(b) precast keystone joist

2-22. Precast Tee Joists or Keystone Joists

Description

This section includes tolerances for tee joists and keystone joists. The manufacturing tolerances (sometimes referred to as "product tolerances") shown here must be coordinated with erection tolerances and tolerances for other building systems for a successful project. During construction one surface is usually designated as the primary control surface, the location of which is controlled during erection. The product tolerances given in this section are *not* additive to the erection tolerances of the primary control surfaces. However, product tolerances are additive to secondary control surface erection tolerances.

Industry Standard

Tolerances for Precast and Prestressed Concrete, Precast/Prestressed Concrete Institute, reprinted from *Journal of the Prestressed Concrete Institute,* vol. 30, no. 1, January–February 1985.

Allowable Tolerances

Many of the tolerances for tee and keystone joists are shown in Fig. 2-22. Refer to *Tolerances for Precast and Prestressed Concrete* for a complete listing.

The variation from end squareness is $\pm\frac{1}{4}$ in per 12 in, with a $\frac{1}{2}$-in maximum (±6 mm per 300 mm of depth, 13-mm maximum). Camber variation from the design camber is $\pm\frac{1}{4}$ in per 10 ft, with a $\frac{3}{4}$-in maximum (±6 mm per 3 m, with a 19-mm maximum). However, for members with a span-to-depth ratio approaching or exceeding 30, this camber tolerance may not apply. If camber tolerances must be controlled with such span-to-depth ratios, premium production measures may be required. Specific job requirements should be verified with the producer. For some types of combined precast and cast-in-place construction these tolerances may not be required.

Plate position tolerance is ±1 in (25 mm) for miscellaneous plates and $\frac{1}{2}$ in (13 mm) for bearing plates. The tolerance for the tipping and flushness of miscellaneous plates is $\pm\frac{1}{4}$ in (6 mm) and for bearing plates it is $\pm\frac{1}{8}$ in (3 mm). Inserts for structural connections are located within $\pm\frac{1}{2}$ in (13 mm).

Smoothness of any surface must be within $\frac{1}{4}$ in in 10 ft (6 mm in 3 m), except that surface requirements do not apply to top surfaces left rough to receive a topping.

Related Sections

2-18. Prestressed Concrete Beams

2-19. Prestressed Single Tees

2-20. Prestressed Double Tees

2-24. Precast Beam and Spandrel Erection

Chapter 13. Precast Concrete Systems

Figure 2-23

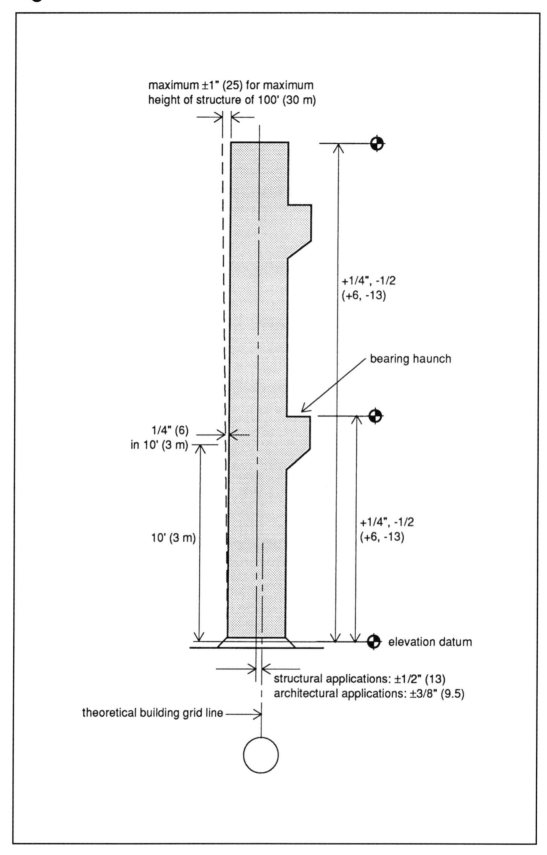

maximum ±1" (25) for maximum
height of structure of 100' (30 m)

+1/4", -1/2
(+6, -13)

bearing haunch

1/4" (6)
in 10' (3 m)

+1/4", -1/2
(+6, -13)

10' (3 m)

elevation datum

structural applications: ±1/2" (13)
architectural applications: ±3/8" (9.5)

theoretical building grid line

Concrete

2-23. Precast Column Erection

Description

The tolerances given in this section are recommended tolerances rather than strict standards. They are reasonable variations that can be expected in most situations. However, because precast erection is subject to many variables and some situations are visually more critical than others, tolerances should be reviewed with the precast supplier prior to finalizing specifications. To minimize costs the tolerances in this section can be increased where the members will be covered with other finish material or in structures where visual appearance is not critical.

The erection tolerances shown in this section must be coordinated with manufacturing tolerances and tolerances for other building systems to which the precast system is connected. The erection tolerances are based on the primary control surfaces, which are the surfaces that are controlled during erection. The erection tolerances are *not* additive to the product tolerances given in previous sections. However, erection tolerances are additive to the product tolerances for secondary control surfaces.

The erection tolerances shown in this section are primarily for precast element to precast element.

Industry Standard

Tolerances for Precast and Prestressed Concrete, Precast/Prestressed Concrete Institute, reprinted from *Journal of the Prestressed Concrete Institute,* vol. 30, no. 1, January–February 1985.

Allowable Tolerances

Tolerances for precast column erection are shown in Fig. 2-23. Note that the tolerance in placement from the theoretical building grid line is for the plan location, so it applies to two directions. In addition, the maximum jog in the alignment of matching edges is $\pm\frac{1}{4}$ in (6 mm) for architectural exposed edges and $\pm\frac{1}{2}$ in (13 mm) for visually noncritical edges.

Related Sections

2-21. Precast Columns

2-24. Precast Beam and Spandrel Erection

Chapter 13. Precast Concrete Systems

Figure 2-25

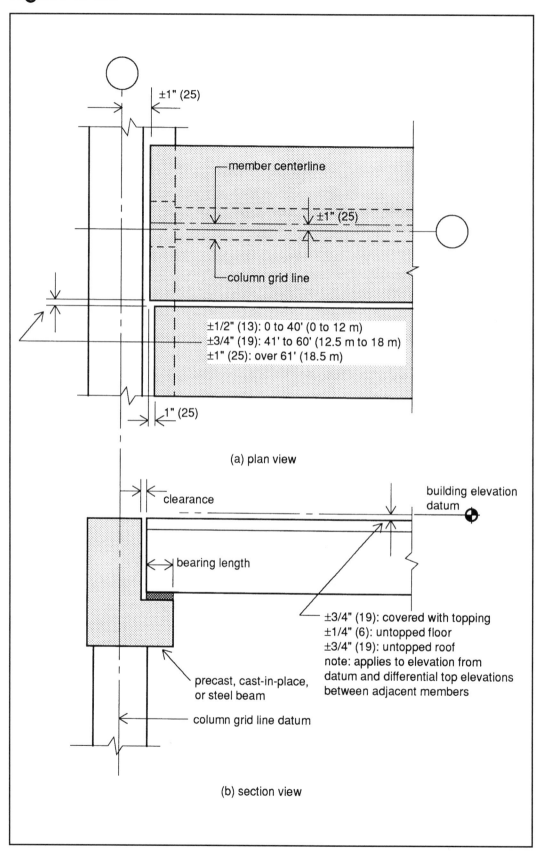

±1" (25)

member centerline

±1" (25)

column grid line

±1/2" (13): 0 to 40' (0 to 12 m)
±3/4" (19): 41' to 60' (12.5 m to 18 m)
±1" (25): over 61' (18.5 m)

1" (25)

(a) plan view

clearance

building elevation datum

bearing length

±3/4" (19): covered with topping
±1/4" (6): untopped floor
±3/4" (19): untopped roof
note: applies to elevation from datum and differential top elevations between adjacent members

precast, cast-in-place, or steel beam

column grid line datum

(b) section view

2-25. Precast Floor and Roof Member Erection

Description

The tolerances given in this section are recommended tolerances rather than strict standards for floor and roof members. They are reasonable variations that can be expected in most situations. However, because precast erection is subject to many variables and some situations are visually more critical than others, tolerances should be reviewed with the precast supplier prior to finalizing specifications. To minimize costs the tolerances in this section can be increased where the members will be covered with other finish material or in structures where visual appearance is not critical.

The erection tolerances shown in this section must be coordinated with manufacturing tolerances and tolerances for other building systems to which the precast system is connected. The erection tolerances are based on the primary control surfaces, which are the surfaces that are controlled during erection. The erection tolerances are *not* additive to the product tolerances given in previous sections. However, erection tolerances are additive to the product tolerances for secondary control surfaces.

The erection tolerances shown in this section apply to precast elements attached to other precast elements, to cast-in-place concrete or masonry, and to steel members.

Industry Standard

Tolerances for Precast and Prestressed Concrete, Precast/Prestressed Concrete Institute, reprinted from *Journal of the Prestressed Concrete Institute,* vol. 30, no. 1, January–February 1985.

Allowable Tolerances

Tolerances for floor and roof members are shown in Fig. 2-25. When a precast floor or roof member is placed on a steel beam, the 1-in (25-mm) tolerance from end of member to building grid still applies but it is measured from the centerline of the steel support structure. When hollow-core slabs are used, the differential bottom elevation of exposed slabs is $\pm\frac{1}{4}$ in (6 mm). In addition, the bearing length (in the direction of the floor or roof member span) is $\pm\frac{3}{4}$ in (19 mm) and the bearing width is $\pm\frac{1}{2}$ in (13 mm).

Related Sections

2-15. Hollow-Core Slabs

2-19. Prestressed Single Tees

2-20. Prestressed Double Tees

2-24. Precast Beam and Spandrel Erection

Chapter 13. Precast Concrete Systems

Figure 2-26

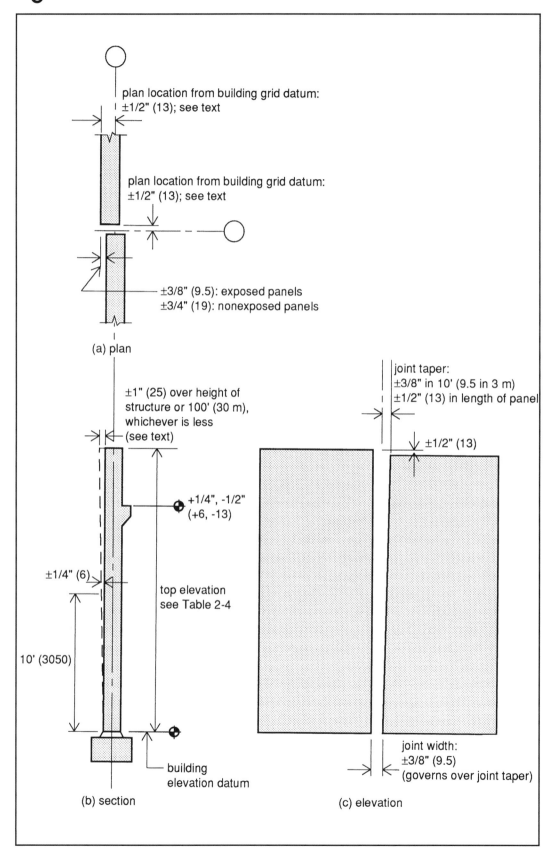

plan location from building grid datum:
±1/2" (13); see text

plan location from building grid datum:
±1/2" (13); see text

±3/8" (9.5): exposed panels
±3/4" (19): nonexposed panels

(a) plan

±1" (25) over height of
structure or 100' (30 m),
whichever is less
(see text)

+1/4", -1/2"
(+6, -13)

±1/4" (6)

top elevation
see Table 2-4

10' (3050)

building
elevation datum

(b) section

joint taper:
±3/8" in 10' (9.5 in 3 m)
±1/2" (13) in length of panel

±1/2" (13)

joint width:
±3/8" (9.5)
(governs over joint taper)

(c) elevation

2-26. Precast Structural Wall Panel Erection

Description

The tolerances given in this section are recommended tolerances rather than strict standards. They are reasonable variations that can be expected in most situations. However, because precast erection is subject to many variables and some situations are visually more critical than others, tolerances should be reviewed with the precast supplier prior to finalizing specifications. To minimize costs the tolerances in this section can be increased where the members will be covered with other finish material or in structures where visual appearance is not critical.

The erection tolerances shown in this section must be coordinated with manufacturing tolerances and tolerances for other building systems to which the precast system is connected. The erection tolerances are based on the primary control surfaces, which are the surfaces that are controlled during erection. The erection tolerances are *not* additive to the product tolerances given in previous sections. However, erection tolerances are additive to the product tolerances for secondary control surfaces.

The erection tolerances shown in this section apply to precast elements attached to other precast elements, to cast-in-place concrete or masonry, and to steel members.

Industry Standard

Tolerances for Precast and Prestressed Concrete, Precast/Prestressed Concrete Institute, reprinted from *Journal of the Prestressed Concrete Institute,* vol. 30, no. 1, January–February 1985.

Allowable Tolerances

Tolerances for the erection of precast structural wall panels are shown in Fig. 2-26. When a precast panel is placed on a steel beam, the $\frac{1}{2}$-in (13-mm) tolerance still applies but it is measured from the centerline of the steel support structure. Tolerances for the distance from the building elevation datum to the top of the panel are listed in Table 2-4. Note that the toler-

Table 2-4
Tolerances for Top Elevation of Structural Wall Panels

Type of panel	Tolerance, top elevation from nominal top elevation, in (mm)
Exposed individual panel	$\pm\frac{1}{2}$ (13)
Nonexposed individual panel	$\pm\frac{3}{4}$ (19)
Exposed panel relative to adjacent panel	$\pm\frac{1}{2}$ (13)
Nonexposed panel relative to adjacent panel	$\pm\frac{3}{4}$ (19)

SOURCE: Precast/Prestressed Concrete Institute.

ances for the plan location and maximum plumb can increase $\frac{1}{8}$ in (3 mm) per story for buildings over 100 ft (30 m) high, up to a maximum out-of-plumb of 2 in (50 mm). Differential bowing between adjacent members of the same design is limited to $\pm\frac{1}{2}$ in (13 mm).

Related Sections

2-5. Footings

2-12. Architectural Precast Concrete Panels

2-13. Precast Ribbed Wall Panels

2-14. Precast Insulated Wall Panels

2-18. Prestressed Concrete Beams

Chapter 13. Precast Concrete Systems

Figure 2-27

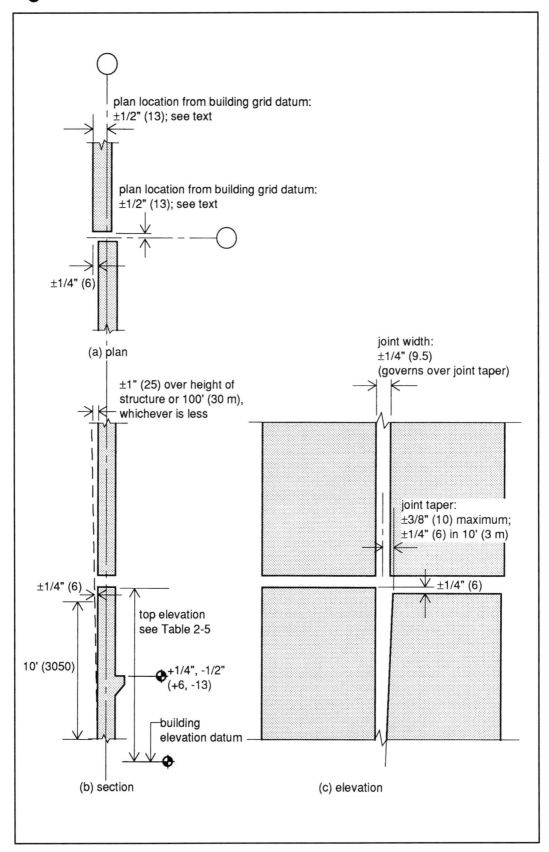

plan location from building grid datum: ±1/2" (13); see text

plan location from building grid datum: ±1/2" (13); see text

±1/4" (6)

(a) plan

joint width: ±1/4" (9.5) (governs over joint taper)

±1" (25) over height of structure or 100' (30 m), whichever is less

joint taper: ±3/8" (10) maximum; ±1/4" (6) in 10' (3 m)

±1/4" (6)

±1/4" (6)

top elevation see Table 2-5

10' (3050)

+1/4", -1/2" (+6, -13)

building elevation datum

(b) section

(c) elevation

2-27. Precast Architectural Wall Panel Erection

Description

The tolerances given in this section are for precast panels where appearance is a primary concern. They are recommended tolerances rather than strict standards and include reasonable variations that can be expected in most situations. However, because precast erection is subject to many variables and some situations are visually more critical than others, tolerances should be reviewed with the precast supplier prior to finalizing specifications. To minimize costs the tolerances in this section can be increased where the members will be covered with other finish material or in structures where visual appearance is not critical.

The erection tolerances shown in this section must be coordinated with manufacturing tolerances and tolerances for other building systems to which the precast system is connected. The erection tolerances are based on the primary control surfaces, which are the surfaces that are controlled during erection. The erection tolerances are *not* additive to the product tolerances given in previous sections. However, erection tolerances are additive to the product tolerances for secondary control surfaces.

The erection tolerances shown in this section apply to precast elements attached to other precast elements, to cast-in-place concrete or masonry, and to steel members.

Industry Standard

Tolerances for Precast and Prestressed Concrete, Precast/Prestressed Concrete Institute, reprinted from *Journal of the Prestressed Concrete Institute,* vol. 30, no. 1, January–February 1985.

Allowable Tolerances

Tolerances for the erection of precast architectural wall panels are shown in Fig. 2-27. When a precast panel is placed on a steel beam, the $\frac{1}{2}$-in (13-mm) tolerance still applies but it is measured from the centerline of the steel support structure. Tolerances for the distance from the building elevation datum to the top of the panel are listed in Table 2-5. Note that the toler-

Table 2-5
Tolerances for Top Elevation of Architectural Wall Panels

Type of panel	Tolerance, top elevation from nominal top elevation, in (mm)
Exposed individual panel	$\pm\frac{1}{4}$ (6)
Nonexposed individual panel	$\pm\frac{1}{2}$ (13)
Exposed panel relative to adjacent panel	$\pm\frac{1}{4}$ (6)
Nonexposed panel relative to adjacent panel	$\pm\frac{1}{2}$ (13)

SOURCE: Precast/Prestressed Concrete Institute.

ances for the plan location and maximum plumb can increase $\frac{1}{8}$ in (3 mm) per story for buildings over 100 ft (30 m) high, up to a maximum out-of-plumb of 2 in (50 mm). Differential bowing or camber between adjacent members of the same design is limited to $\pm\frac{1}{4}$ in (6 mm).

Related Sections

2-5. Footings

2-12. Architectural Precast Concrete Panels

2-18. Prestressed Concrete Beams

Chapter 13. Precast Concrete Systems

Figure 2-28

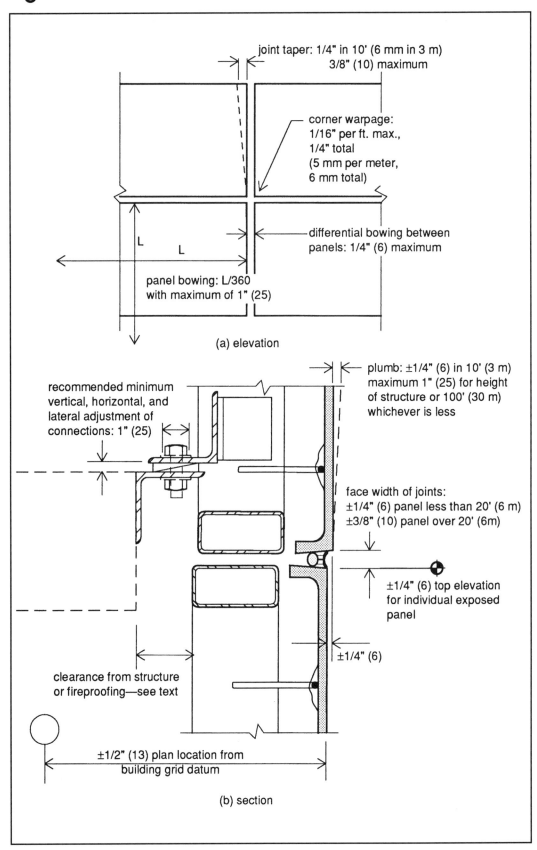

joint taper: 1/4" in 10' (6 mm in 3 m)
3/8" (10) maximum

corner warpage:
1/16" per ft. max.,
1/4" total
(5 mm per meter,
6 mm total)

differential bowing between
panels: 1/4" (6) maximum

L

L

panel bowing: L/360
with maximum of 1" (25)

(a) elevation

recommended minimum
vertical, horizontal, and
lateral adjustment of
connections: 1" (25)

plumb: ±1/4" (6) in 10' (3 m)
maximum 1" (25) for height
of structure or 100' (30 m)
whichever is less

face width of joints:
±1/4" (6) panel less than 20' (6 m)
±3/8" (10) panel over 20' (6m)

±1/4" (6) top elevation
for individual exposed
panel

±1/4" (6)

clearance from structure
or fireproofing—see text

±1/2" (13) plan location from
building grid datum

(b) section

2-28. Glass Fiber Reinforced Concrete Panel Erection

Description

Glass fiber reinforced concrete (GFRC) panels, described in Sec. 2-11, are normally attached to a stiffening assembly of metal studs. The stiffeners are then attached to the building structure. As long as sufficient clearance and adequate adjustable fasteners are provided, GFRC panels can be installed to fairly tight tolerances.

Industry Standard

Recommended Practice for Glass Fiber Reinforced Concrete Panels, Precast/Prestressed Concrete Institute, Chicago, 1993.

Allowable Tolerances

Guideline tolerances for GFRC panels are shown in Fig. 2-28. Because GFRC panels have some flexibility, some of the bowing and warpage can be compensated for during installation. It is important that tolerances for the structural frame be stated in the specifications and held during construction in order to achieve the GFRC tolerances shown here.

Clearances between the GFRC panels and the supporting structure are important and should be maintained. At least 1 in (25 mm) should be maintained between a GFRC panel and steel fireproofing, but $1\frac{1}{2}$ in (38 mm) is preferred. If no fireproofing is used, $1\frac{1}{2}$ to 2 in (38 to 51 mm) clearance should be detailed in tall, irregular structures. For precast concrete $1\frac{1}{2}$ in (38 mm) clearance is preferred with 1 in (25 mm) as the minimum. A clearance of 2 in (51 mm) between GFRC panels and cast-in-place concrete is preferred, with $1\frac{1}{2}$ in (38 mm) as the minimum. Clearance between columns and GFRC covers should be at least 2 in (51 mm), with 3 in (76 mm) preferred.

Related Section

2-11.Glass Fiber Reinforced Concrete Panels

Figure 3-1

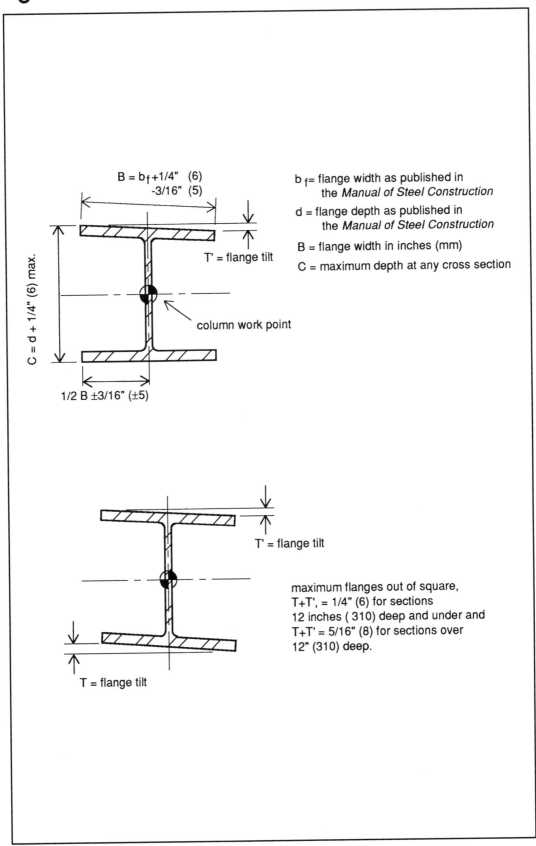

$B = b_f + 1/4"$ (6)
      $-3/16"$ (5)

T' = flange tilt

$C = d + 1/4"$ (6) max.

column work point

$1/2\ B \pm 3/16"$ (± 5)

b_f = flange width as published in
      the *Manual of Steel Construction*

d = flange depth as published in
      the *Manual of Steel Construction*

B = flange width in inches (mm)

C = maximum depth at any cross section

T' = flange tilt

maximum flanges out of square,
$T+T'$, = 1/4" (6) for sections
12 inches (310) deep and under and
$T+T'$ = 5/16" (8) for sections over
12" (310) deep.

T = flange tilt

Chapter 3

3-1. Mill Tolerances for W and HP Shapes

Description

Figure 3-1 illustrates some of the allowable variations in cross-sectional size and straightness of standard rolled W and HP shapes, commonly used for columns. A W shape is a doubly symmetric, wide-flange shape used as a beam or column whose inside flange surfaces are substantially parallel. An HP shape is a wide-flange shape generally used as a bearing pile whose flanges and webs are of the same nominal thickness and whose depth and width are essentially the same. The tolerances shown are those that most affect architectural detailing and coordination with other materials. Tolerances for web thickness and web depth are not included.

Industry Standard

ASTM A6/A6M, *General Requirements for Rolled Steel Plates, Shapes, Sheet Piling, and Bars for Structural Use,* American Society for Testing and Materials, Philadelphia, 1991.

Allowable Tolerances

In addition to the tolerances shown in Fig. 3-1, Table 3-1 gives the allowable variations in camber, sweep, and length. Camber is the deviation in straightness parallel to the web. Sweep is the deviation in straightness parallel to the flanges.

Related Sections

3-2. Mill Tolerances for Length of W and HP Shapes

3-3. Mill Tolerances for S and M Shapes and Channels

3-6. Steel Column Erection Tolerances

3-7. Location of Exterior Steel Columns in Plan

14-1. Accumulated Column Tolerances

Table 3-1
Permissible Variation in Camber and Sweep for W and HP Shapes

Size	Permissible variation, in (mm)		
	Length	Camber	Sweep
Flange width less than 6 in (150 mm)	Any	$\frac{1}{8}$ in $\times \dfrac{L,\text{ft}}{10}$ (1 mm $\times$ L, m)	$\frac{1}{8}$ in $\times \dfrac{L,\text{ft}}{5}$ (2 mm $\times$ L, m)
Flange width equal to or greater than 6 in (150 mm)	Any	$\frac{1}{8}$ in $\times \dfrac{L,\text{ft}}{10}$ (1 mm $\times$ L, m)	
Certain sections used as columns*	45 ft (14 m) and under	$\frac{1}{8}$ in $\times \dfrac{L,\text{ft}}{10}$ with $\frac{3}{8}$ in max. (1 mm $\times$ L, m, with 10 mm max.)	
	Over 45 ft (14 m)	$\frac{3}{8}$ in $+ (\frac{1}{8}$ in $\times \dfrac{L,\text{ft} - 45}{10})$ (10 mm $+ [1$ mm $\times (L,$ m, $- 14$ m)])	

*Sections include W 8 × 31 and heavier, W 10 × 49 and heavier, W 12 × 65 and heavier, W 14 × 90 and heavier (200 mm deep, 46.1 kg/m and heavier; 250 mm deep, 73 kg/m and heavier; 310 mm deep, 97 kg/m and heavier; 360 mm deep, 116 kg/m and heavier).

SOURCE: ASTM A6/A6M; copyright ASTM; reprinted with permission.

Figure 3-2

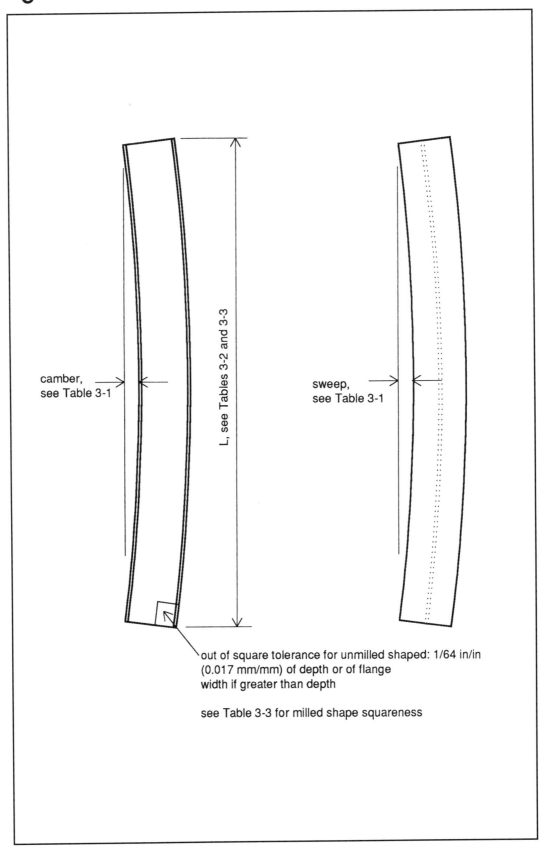

camber,
see Table 3-1

L, see Tables 3-2 and 3-3

sweep,
see Table 3-1

out of square tolerance for unmilled shaped: 1/64 in/in
(0.017 mm/mm) of depth or of flange
width if greater than depth

see Table 3-3 for milled shape squareness

3-2. Mill Tolerances for Length of W and HP Shapes

Description

These tolerances are a continuation of those given in Sec. 3-1 and include allowable variations in length and end squareness for both unmilled and milled sections.

Industry Standard

ASTM A6/A6M, *General Requirements for Rolled Steel Plates, Shapes, Sheet Piling, and Bars for Structural Use,* American Society for Testing and Materials, Philadelphia, 1991.

Allowable Tolerances

Allowable tolerances are shown in Tables 3-2 and 3-3, as illustrated in Fig. 3-2.

Related Sections

3-1. Mill Tolerances for W and HP Shapes

3-6. Steel Column Erection Tolerances

3-7. Location of Exterior Steel Columns in Plan

14-1. Accumulated Column Tolerances

14-2. Accumulated Steel Frame Tolerances

Table 3-2
Permissible Variation in Length *L*

W shapes	30 ft (9 m) and under		Over 30 ft (9 m)	
	Over	Under	Over	Under
Beams 24 in (610 mm) and under	$\frac{3}{8}$ (10)	$\frac{3}{8}$ (10)	$\frac{3}{8}$ (10) plus $\frac{1}{16}$ (1) for each additional 5 ft (1 m) or fraction thereof	$\frac{3}{8}$ (10)
Beams over 24 in (610 mm) and all columns	$\frac{1}{2}$ (13)	$\frac{1}{2}$ (13)	$\frac{1}{2}$ (13) plus $\frac{1}{16}$ (1) for each additional 5 ft (1 m) or fraction thereof	$\frac{1}{2}$ (13)

Heading spanning: "Permissible variation from specified length, in (mm)"

SOURCE: ASTM A6/A6M; copyright ASTM; reprinted with permission.

Table 3-3
Permissible Variation for Length and Squareness for Milled Shapes*

	Milled both ends			Milled one end		
	Length, in (mm)		End out of square, max., in (mm)	Length, in (mm)		End out of square, max., in (mm)
	Over	Under		Over	Under	
Depth: 6 to 36 in (150 to 920 mm) Length: 6 to 70 ft (2 to 21 m)	$\frac{1}{32}$ (1)	$\frac{1}{32}$ (1)	$\frac{1}{32}$ (1)	$\frac{1}{4}$ (6)	$\frac{1}{4}$ (6)	$\frac{1}{32}$ (1)

*Length variation and out-of-square variation are additive. Length is measured along centerline of web.
SOURCE: ASTM A6/A6M; copyright ASTM; reprinted with permission.

Figure 3-3

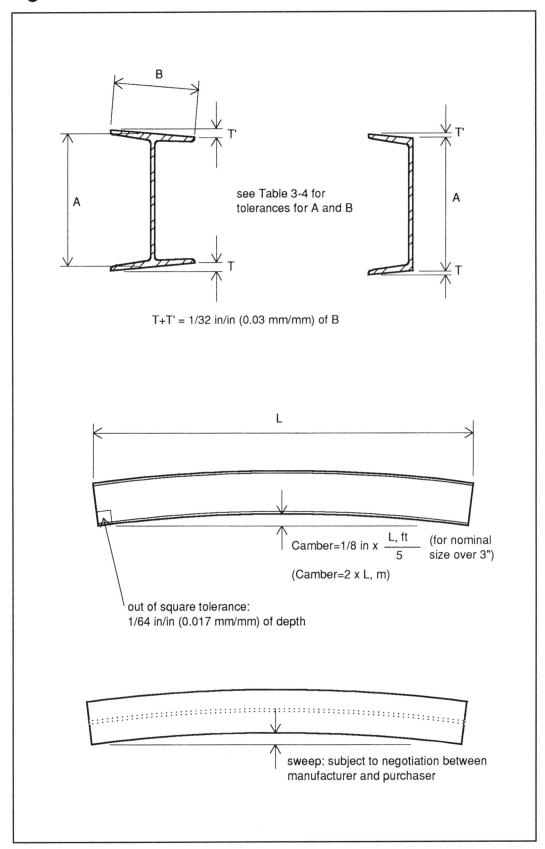

see Table 3-4 for
tolerances for A and B

T+T' = 1/32 in/in (0.03 mm/mm) of B

Camber=1/8 in x $\dfrac{L, ft}{5}$ (for nominal size over 3")

(Camber=2 x L, m)

out of square tolerance:
1/64 in/in (0.017 mm/mm) of depth

sweep: subject to negotiation between
manufacturer and purchaser

3-3. Mill Tolerances for S and M Shapes and Channels

Description

Figure 3-3 illustrates some of the allowable variations in cross-sectional size and straightness of standard rolled S, M, and channel shapes. The tolerances shown are those that most affect architectural detailing and coordination with other materials. Tolerances for web thickness and web depth are not included.

Industry Standard

ASTM A6/A6M, *General Requirements for Rolled Steel Plates, Shapes, Sheet Piling, and Bars for Structural Use,* American Society for Testing and Materials, Philadelphia, 1991.

Allowable Tolerances

In addition to the tolerances shown in Fig. 3-3, Tables 3-4 and 3-5 give the allowable variations in cross-sectional sizes and length.

Table 3-4
Permissible Variation in Cross-Sectional Shapes for S, M, C, and MC Shapes

Nominal size, in (mm)	A, depth, in (mm)		B, flange width, in (mm)	
	Over	Under	Over	Under
S and M shapes				
3 to 7, inclusive (75 to 180)	$\frac{3}{32}$ (2)	$\frac{1}{16}$ (2)	$\frac{1}{8}$ (3)	$\frac{1}{32}$ (1)
Over 7 to 14, inclusive (180 to 360)	$\frac{1}{8}$ (3)	$\frac{3}{32}$ (2)	$\frac{5}{32}$ (4)	$\frac{5}{32}$ (4)
Over 14 to 24, inclusive (360 to 610)	$\frac{3}{16}$ (5)	$\frac{1}{8}$ (3)	$\frac{3}{16}$ (5)	$\frac{3}{16}$ (5)
C and MC shapes				
Over $1\frac{1}{2}$ to 3, exclusive (40 to 75)	$\frac{1}{16}$ (2)	$\frac{1}{16}$ (2)	$\frac{1}{16}$ (2)	$\frac{1}{32}$ (1)
3 to 7, inclusive (75 to 180)	$\frac{3}{32}$ (3)	$\frac{1}{16}$ (2)	$\frac{1}{8}$ (3)	$\frac{1}{8}$ (3)
Over 7 to 14, inclusive (180 to 360)	$\frac{1}{8}$ (3)	$\frac{3}{32}$ (3)	$\frac{1}{8}$ (3)	$\frac{5}{32}$ (4)
Over 14 (360)	$\frac{3}{16}$ (5)	$\frac{1}{8}$ (3)	$\frac{3}{16}$ (3)	$\frac{3}{16}$ (5)

SOURCE: ASTM A6/A6M; copyright ASTM; reprinted with permission.

Table 3-5
Permissible Variation in Length for S, M, and Channel Shapes*

	Allowable variation from specified length, in (mm)									
	To 30 ft (9 m), inclusive		Over 30 to 40 ft (9 to 12 m), inclusive		Over 40 to 50 ft (12 to 15 m), inclusive		Over 50 to 65 ft (15 to 20 m), inclusive		Over 65 ft (20 m)	
	Over	Under	Over	Under	Over	Under	Over	Under	Over	Under
S, M, and channels	$\frac{1}{2}$ (13)	$\frac{1}{4}$ (6)	$\frac{3}{4}$ (19)	$\frac{1}{4}$ (6)	1 (25)	$\frac{1}{4}$ (6)	$1\frac{1}{8}$ (29)	$\frac{1}{4}$ (6)	$1\frac{1}{4}$ (32)	$\frac{1}{4}$ (6)

*Tolerances apply to sections with greatest cross-sectional dimension 3 in (75 mm) and over.
SOURCE: ASTM A6/A6M; copyright ASTM; reprinted with permission.

Related Sections

3-7. Location of Exterior Steel Columns in Plan
14-2. Accumulated Steel Frame Tolerances

Figure 3-4

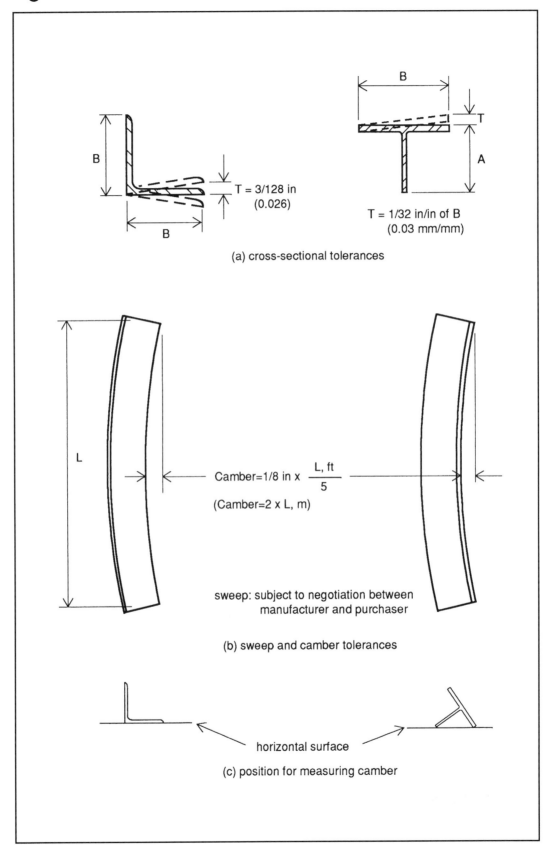

T = 3/128 in
(0.026)

T = 1/32 in/in of B
(0.03 mm/mm)

(a) cross-sectional tolerances

$$Camber = 1/8 \text{ in} \times \frac{L, \text{ft}}{5}$$

(Camber = 2 × L, m)

sweep: subject to negotiation between
manufacturer and purchaser

(b) sweep and camber tolerances

horizontal surface

(c) position for measuring camber

3-4. Mill Tolerances for Structural Angles and Tees

Description

This section includes information for rolled tees and structural-size angles. There are additional tolerances for bar-size angles which include those with legs less than 3 in (75 mm). Refer to ASTM A6 for information on these smaller angles and for zee sections.

Industry Standard

ASTM A6/A6M, *General Requirements for Rolled Steel Plates, Shapes, Sheet Piling, and Bars for Structural Use,* American Society for Testing and Materials, Philadelphia, 1991.

Allowable Tolerances

Allowable variations in angle and tee sizes are shown in Table 3-6, as illustrated in Fig. 3-4. Length tolerances for sizes up to 40 ft (12.2 m) are shown in Table 3-7. Ends out-of-square tolerance is $\frac{3}{128}$ in per in (0.026 mm per 25 mm) of leg length ($1\frac{1}{2}°$).

Table 3-6
Permissible Variation in Sizes for Angles and Tees

Nominal size,* in (mm)	Variation in depth of tee *A*, in (mm)		Variation in length of angle leg, or width of tee *B*, in (mm)	
	Over, *A*	Under, *A*	Over, *B*	Under, *B*
Angles				
3 to 4, inclusive (75 to 100)	——	——	$\frac{1}{8}$ (3)	$\frac{3}{32}$ (2)
Over 4 to 6, inclusive (over 100 to 150)	——	——	$\frac{1}{8}$ (3)	$\frac{1}{8}$ (3)
Over 6 (over 150)	——	——	$\frac{3}{16}$ (5)	$\frac{1}{8}$ (3)
Tees				
$1\frac{1}{4}$ (30) and under	$\frac{3}{64}$ (1)	$\frac{3}{64}$ (1)	$\frac{3}{64}$ (1)	$\frac{3}{64}$ (1)
Over $1\frac{1}{4}$ to 2, inclusive (30 to 50)	$\frac{1}{16}$ (2)	$\frac{1}{16}$ (2)	$\frac{1}{16}$ (2)	$\frac{1}{16}$ (2)
Over 2 to 3, exclusive (50 to 75)	$\frac{3}{32}$ (2)	$\frac{3}{32}$ (2)	$\frac{3}{32}$ (2)	$\frac{3}{32}$ (2)
3 to 5, inclusive (75 to 125)	$\frac{3}{32}$ (2)	$\frac{1}{16}$ (2)	$\frac{1}{8}$ (3)	$\frac{1}{8}$ (3)
Over 5 to 7, inclusive (125 to 180)	$\frac{3}{32}$ (2)	$\frac{1}{16}$ (2)	$\frac{1}{8}$ (3)	$\frac{1}{8}$ (3)

*For angles with unequal legs the longer leg determines the classification.
SOURCE: ASTM A6/A6M; copyright ASTM; reprinted with permission.

Table 3-7
Permissible Variation in Length for Angles and Tees

Nominal size, in (mm)	Variation from specified length, in (mm)							
	5 to 10 ft (1.5 to 3 m), excl.		10 to 20 ft (3 to 6 m), excl.		20 to 30 ft (6 to 9 m), incl.		Over 30 to 40 ft (9 to 12 m), incl.	
	Over	Under	Over	Under	Over	Under	Over	Under
Under 3 (75)	$\frac{5}{8}$ (16)	0	1 (25)	0	$1\frac{1}{2}$ (38)	0	2 (51)	0
3 (75) and over	$\frac{1}{2}$ (13)	$\frac{1}{4}$ (6)	$\frac{1}{2}$ (13)	$\frac{1}{4}$ (6)	$\frac{1}{2}$ (13)	$\frac{1}{4}$ (6)	$\frac{3}{4}$ (19)	$\frac{1}{4}$ (6)

SOURCE: ASTM A6/A6M; copyright ASTM; reprinted with permission.

Figure 3-5

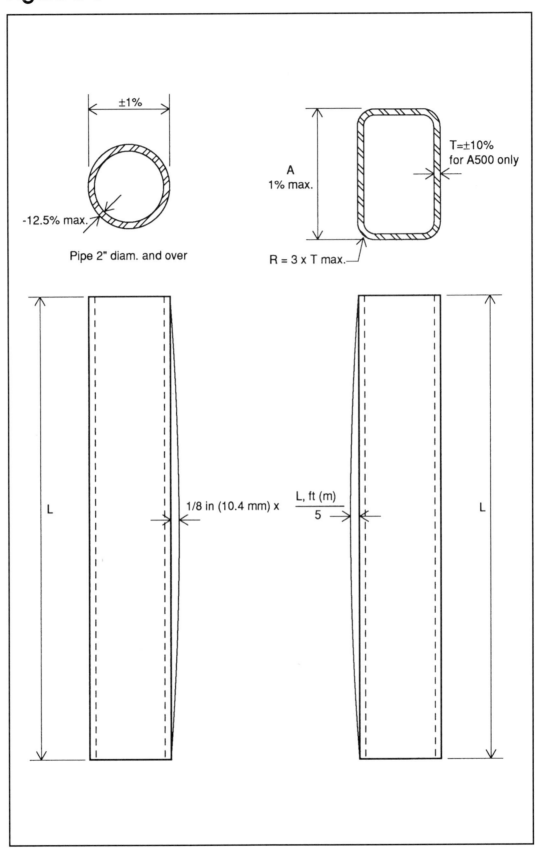

±1%

-12.5% max.

Pipe 2" diam. and over

A
1% max.

T=±10%
for A500 only

R = 3 x T max.

L

1/8 in (10.4 mm) x

L, ft (m)
―――――
5

L

3-5. Mill Tolerances for Pipe and Tubing

Description

This section includes information for structural pipe and tubing that are commonly used for columns in residential and light commercial construction. In most cases, the allowable mill tolerances are small enough that problems with architectural detailing are not encountered. The relatively large mill tolerances for length are adjusted at the fabricating plant to more precise measurements if necessary.

Industry Standards

ASTM A500, *Standard Specification for Cold-Formed Welded and Seamless Carbon Steel Structural Tubing in Rounds and Shapes,* American Society for Testing and Materials, Philadelphia, 1990.

ASTM A618, *Standard Specification for Hot-Formed Welded and Seamless High-Strength Low-Alloy Structural Tubing,* American Society for Testing and Materials, Philadelphia, 1990.

Allowable Tolerances

In addition to the tolerances shown in Fig. 3-5, allowable tolerances in length for both round and rectangular tubing are shown in Table 3-8.

Table 3-8
Length Tolerances for Pipe and Tubing

	22 ft (6.7 m) and under		Over 22 to 44 ft (6.7 to 13.4 m), incl.	
	Over	Under	Over	Under
Length tolerance for specified lengths, in (mm)	$\frac{1}{2}$ (12.7)	$\frac{1}{4}$ (6.4)	$\frac{3}{4}$ (19.0)	$\frac{1}{4}$ (6.4)

SOURCE: ASTM A500. Copyright ASTM. Reprinted with permission.

The dimensional tolerances A for square and rectangular tubing vary with the largest outside dimension, but never exceed 1 percent for sections over $5\frac{1}{2}$ in (139.7 mm). Because this is only about $\frac{1}{16}$ in (1.6 mm) for a 6-in section, it seldom presents a problem for detailing. Twist tolerances for square and rectangular tubing are measured by placing one end of the section on a flat surface and measuring the height that either corner, at the opposite end of the section, extends above the surface. These tolerances are summarized in Table 3-9.

Table 3-9
Twist Tolerances for Square and Rectangular Tubing

Specified dimension of the longest side, in (mm)	Maximum twist in the first 3 ft (1 m) and in each additional 3 ft, in (mm)
$1\frac{1}{2}$ (38.1) and under	0.050 (1.39)
Over $1\frac{1}{2}$ (38.1) to $2\frac{1}{2}$ (63.5), inclusive	0.062 (1.72)
Over $2\frac{1}{2}$ (63.5) to 4 (101.6), inclusive	0.075 (2.09)
Over 4 (101.6) to 6 (152.4), inclusive	0.087 (2.42)
Over 6 (152.4) to 8 (203.2), inclusive	0.100 (2.78)
Over 8 (203.2)	0.112 (3.11)

SOURCE: ASTM A500; copyright ASTM; reprinted with permission.

Figure 3-6

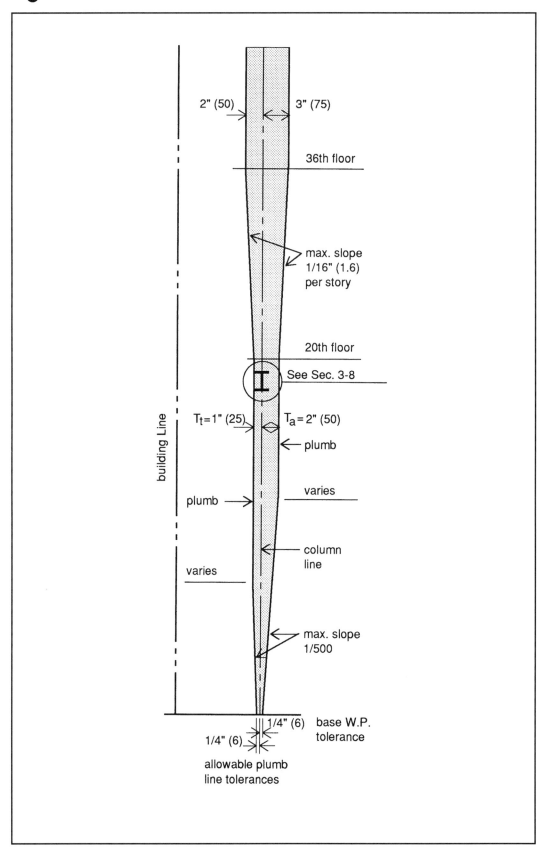

3-6. Steel Column Erection Tolerances

Description

Figure 3-6 illustrates some of the erection tolerances permitted by the American Institute of Steel Construction (AISC) for the plumbness of columns and attached spandrel beams. Along with the mill tolerances and plan tolerances shown in Secs. 3-1, 3-2, 3-7, and 3-8, this diagram permits realistic detailing of the attachment of other materials, such as exterior cladding, to a steel frame. Some of the methods by which accumulated tolerances can be accommodated are shown in Chap. 14.

The diagram in Fig. 3-6 shows the permissible envelope within which the working points of columns can fall. When misalignment of beams is caused by an acceptable variation in column alignment the beams are considered acceptable as well. The *working point of a column* is the actual center of the column at each end of the column as shipped. The *working point of a beam* is the actual centerline of the top flange at each end.

Industry Standard

Code of Standard Practice for Steel Buildings and Bridges, American Institute of Steel
  Construction, Chicago, 1992.

Allowable Tolerances

A column is considered plumb if the deviation of the working line of the column from true plumb does not exceed 1:500. However, AISC standard practices limit the total variation to 1 in (25 mm) toward the building line and 2 in (50 mm) away from the building line up to the twentieth floor and a maximum deviation of $\frac{1}{16}$ in (1.6 mm) per floor above the twentieth up to a maximum of 2 in (50 mm) toward and 3 in (75 mm) away from the building line. For exterior columns, the deviation parallel to the building line is limited to a maximum of 1 in (25 mm) up to the twentieth floor and 2 in (50 mm) beyond that.

Although tolerances for anchor bolt placement are not the responsibility of the fabricator or the erector, the AISC code requires that the center-to-center dimension between adjacent anchor bolt groups and from the established column line not vary by more than $\frac{1}{4}$ in (6 mm). The center-to-center distance between any two bolts within an anchor bolt group cannot vary by more than $\frac{1}{8}$ in (3 mm).

For members with both ends finished for contact bearing, a variation of $\frac{1}{32}$ in (0.8 mm) in the overall length of columns is permitted.

Related Sections

3-1.   Mill Tolerances for W and HP Shapes

3-2.   Mill Tolerances for Length of W and HP Shapes

3-7.   Location of Exterior Steel Columns in Plan

3-8.   Beam/Column Connections

3-10. Elevator Shaft Tolerances

Chapter 14. Steel Frame Systems

Figure 3-7

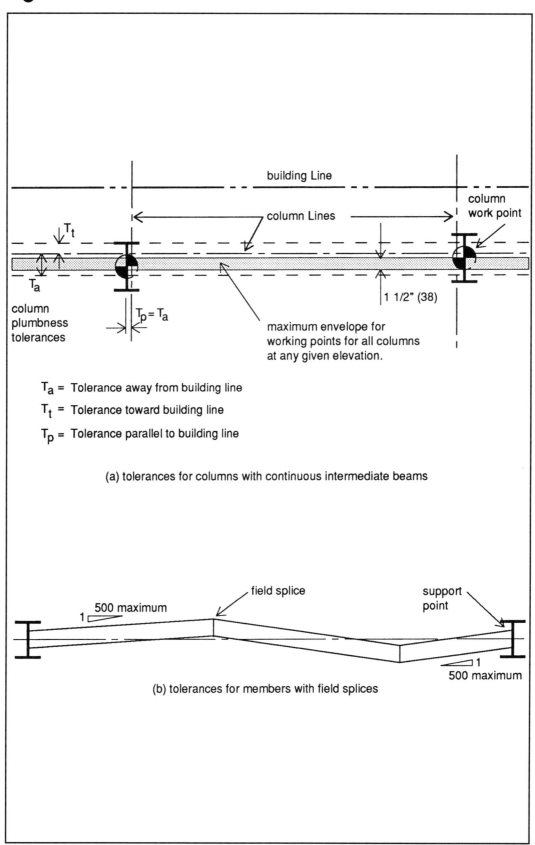

building Line

column Lines

column work point

T_t

T_a

1 1/2" (38)

column plumbness tolerances

$T_p = T_a$

maximum envelope for working points for all columns at any given elevation.

T_a = Tolerance away from building line

T_t = Tolerance toward building line

T_p = Tolerance parallel to building line

(a) tolerances for columns with continuous intermediate beams

field splice

support point

1
500 maximum

1
500 maximum

(b) tolerances for members with field splices

3-7. Location of Exterior Steel Columns in Plan

Description

In addition to individual column tolerances for plumb, a row of columns must fall within specified limits. This determines the alignment of the total length of a building and the alignment of individual beams between columns. Figure 3-7 shows the tolerances for this alignment as well as permissible alignment for members with field splices.

Industry Standard

Code of Standard Practice for Steel Buildings and Bridges, American Institute of Steel Construction, Chicago, 1992.

Allowable Tolerances

The working points at the tops of exterior columns in a single-tier building or the working points of exterior columns at any splice level for multitier buildings must fall within a horizontal envelope parallel to the building line. This is shown diagrammatically in Fig. 3-7a. For each column, the working points must also fall within the envelope shown in Fig. 3-6. This horizontal envelope is $1\frac{1}{2}$ in (38 mm) wide for buildings up to 300 ft (91 m) long and is increased $\frac{1}{2}$ in (13 mm) for each 100 ft (30 m) but cannot exceed 3 in (75 mm).

The horizontal location of this $1\frac{1}{2}$-in (38-mm) envelope does not necessarily have to fall directly above or below the adjacent envelope but must be within the allowable 1:500 tolerance in plumbness for columns as shown in Fig. 3-6.

If the alignment of the columns is within acceptable limits, then any single-piece beam connected to them is considered in acceptable alignment. However, if the horizontal member consists of two or more splices, the field-fabricated member is considered acceptable if the misalignment does not exceed 1:500 between adjacent members. This is shown diagrammatically in Figure 3-7b for a beam between two columns. The same 1:500 misalignment tolerance applies to field-spliced vertical members.

For cantilevered members alignment is checked by extending a straight line from the working point at the member's supported end and comparing it with the working line of the cantilevered member. If the misalignment does not exceed an angle of 1:500 then the member is considered aligned, level, or plumb, depending on the direction of the cantilever.

Related Sections

3-1. Mill Tolerances for W and HP Shapes

3-2. Mill Tolerances for Length of W and HP Shapes

3-6. Steel Column Erection Tolerances

3-8. Beam/Column Connections

Chapter 14. Steel Frame Systems

Figure 3-8

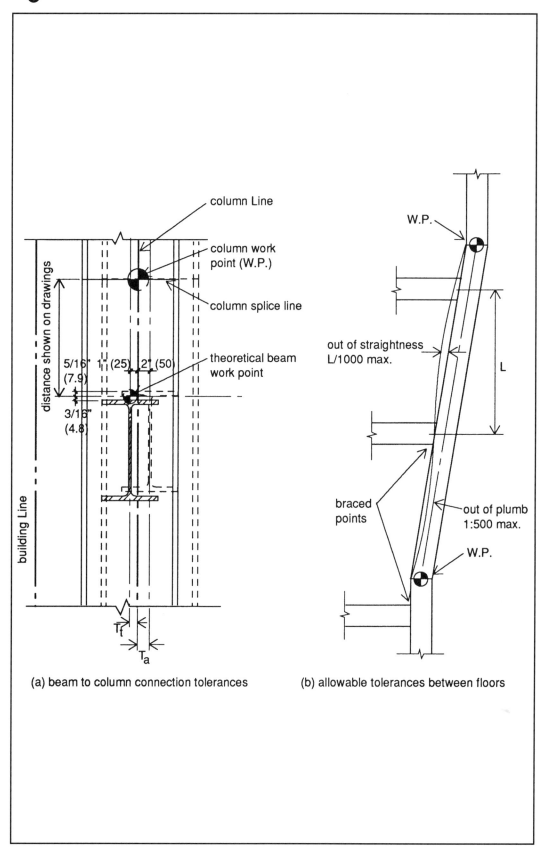

(a) beam to column connection tolerances

(b) allowable tolerances between floors

3-8. Beam/Column Connections

Description

As stated in Sec. 3-7, horizontal alignment of beams is considered acceptable when the ends are connected to columns that fall within acceptable tolerances. This section describes acceptable variations in both horizontal and vertical placement of beams and tolerances of individual columns between floors.

Industry Standard

Code of Standard Practice for Steel Buildings and Bridges, American Institute of Steel Construction, Chicago, 1992.

Allowable Tolerances

Figure 3-8*a* illustrates how the horizontal position of an individual beam work point must fall within the allowable column tolerances shown in Fig. 3-6. In addition, the allowable vertical tolerance is determined by measuring from the upper column splice line to the theoretical beam work point. This distance cannot be greater than $\frac{3}{16}$ in (5 mm) or less than $\frac{5}{16}$ in (8 mm).

Related Sections

3-1.   Mill Tolerances for W and HP Shapes

3-3.   Mill Tolerances for S and M Shapes and Channels

3-6.   Steel Column Erection Tolerances

3-7.   Location of Exterior Steel Columns in Plan

3-10.   Elevator Shaft Tolerances

Chapter 14.   Steel Frame Systems

Figure 3-9

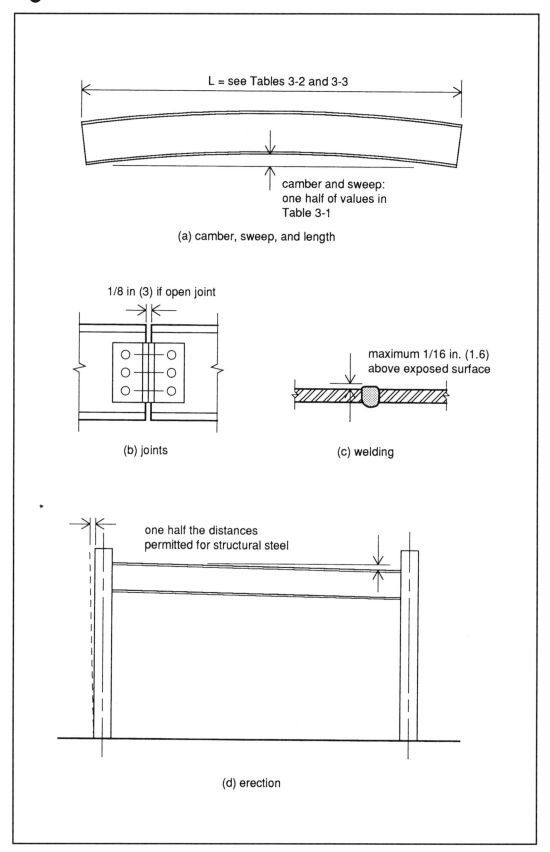

L = see Tables 3-2 and 3-3

camber and sweep:
one half of values in
Table 3-1

(a) camber, sweep, and length

1/8 in (3) if open joint

(b) joints

maximum 1/16 in. (1.6)
above exposed surface

(c) welding

one half the distances
permitted for structural steel

(d) erection

3-9. Architecturally Exposed Structural Steel

Description

Architecturally exposed structural steel (AESS) is steel subject to normal view by pedestrians or occupants of a building. It includes, but is not limited to, weathering steel. Because it is clearly visible, AESS is subject to closer tolerances than standard structural steel that is hidden from view.

The individual members that must conform to AESS tolerances must be clearly identified on the drawings so the fabricator knows which pieces must meet the more stringent requirements.

Industry Standards

Code of Standard Practice for Steel Buildings and Bridges, American Institute of Steel Construction, Chicago, 1992.

ASTM A6/A6M, *General Requirements for Rolled Steel Plates, Shapes, Sheet Piling, and Bars for Structural Use,* American Society for Testing and Materials, Philadelphia, 1991.

Allowable Tolerances

Mill tolerances for out-of-square, out-of-parallel, depth, width, and symmetry are the same as those for other structural steel shapes. Length tolerances are given in Tables 3-2 and 3-3. Camber and sweep tolerances are one-half those given in Table 3-1. See Fig. 3-9a.

As indicated in Fig. 3-9b, all miters, copes, and butt cuts in exposed surfaces are made with uniform gaps of $\frac{1}{8}$ in (3 mm) if the designer wants open joints or in reasonable contact if designed without gaps. Butt and plug welds cannot project more than $\frac{1}{16}$ in (1.6 mm) above any exposed surface. If grinding or finishing is required, it must be specifically included in the contract documents.

Erection tolerances are one-half those for structural steel as described in Secs. 3-6, 3-7, and 3-8. However, the designer is responsible for providing adjustable connections between AESS and any other structural steel or masonry or concrete supports.

Related Sections

3-1. Mill Tolerances for W and HP Shapes

3-2. Mill Tolerances for Length of W and HP Shapes

3-3. Mill Tolerances for S and M Shapes and Channels

3-4. Mill Tolerances for Structural Angles and Tees

3-6. Steel Column Erection Tolerances

3-7. Location of Exterior Steel Columns in Plan

3-8. Beam/Column Connections

Chapter 14. Steel Frame Systems

Figure 3-10

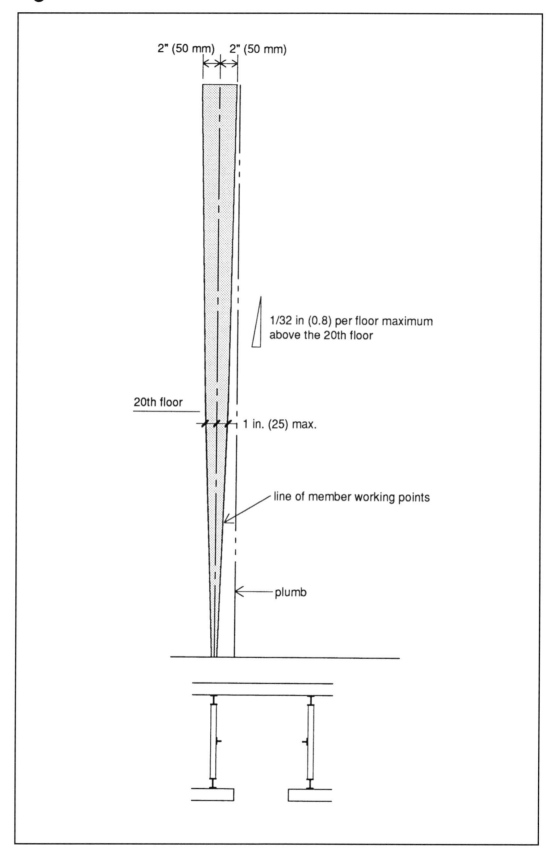

2" (50 mm)   2" (50 mm)

1/32 in (0.8) per floor maximum
above the 20th floor

20th floor

1 in. (25) max.

line of member working points

plumb

3-10. Elevator Shaft Tolerances

Description

Because guide rails of elevators must be adjusted to extremely close tolerances, the structural framing to which they are attached must be built to a tolerance closer than other construction. Because tolerances required by the National Elevator Industry are more stringent, you may want to include the closer tolerances in the specifications if recommended by the elevator supplier rather than rely on American Institute of Steel Construction (AISC) standard tolerances.

Industry Standards

Code of Standard Practice for Steel Buildings and Bridges, American Institute of Steel Construction, Chicago, 1992.

Vertical Transportation Standards, National Elevator Industry, Inc., Fort Lee, NJ, 1990.

Allowable Tolerances

The AISC *Code of Standard Practice* requires the member working points of columns adjacent to elevator shafts to be displaced no more than 1 in (25 mm) from the established column line in the first 20 stories as shown in Fig. 3-10. Above the twentieth floor, the displacement can be increased $\frac{1}{32}$ in (0.8 mm) for each additional story up to a maximum of 2 in (50 mm).

However, hoistway tolerances set by the National Elevator Industry are slightly more stringent. They require a clear hoistway plumb from top to bottom with variations not to exceed 1 in (25 mm) at any point in the first 100 ft (30 m). Above that, the tolerance may increase $\frac{1}{32}$ in (0.8 mm) for each additional 10 ft (3 m) up to a maximum displacement of 2 in (50 mm).

When entrance walls are constructed of reinforced concrete, the National Elevator Industry requires that the depth of the hoistway door space be increased by 1 in (25 mm). Further, concrete rough openings should be 12 in (300 mm) wider than the clear opening width and 6 in (150 mm) higher than the clear opening height.

Related Sections

3-1. Mill Tolerances for W and HP Shapes

3-2. Mill Tolerances for Length of W and HP Shapes

3-7. Location of Exterior Steel Columns in Plan

3-8. Beam/Column Connections

Chapter 14. Steel Frame Systems

Figure 4-1

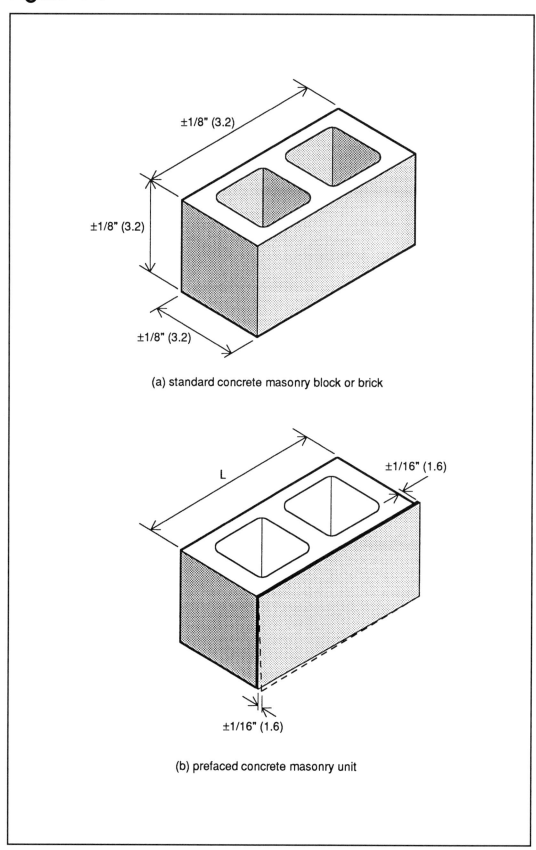

±1/8" (3.2)

±1/8" (3.2)

±1/8" (3.2)

(a) standard concrete masonry block or brick

L

±1/16" (1.6)

±1/16" (1.6)

(b) prefaced concrete masonry unit

Chapter 4

Unit Masonry

4-1. Concrete Unit Masonry Manufacturing

Description

The information in this section includes dimensional tolerances for concrete building brick and similar solid units, standard hollow load-bearing and non-load-bearing concrete block, and prefaced concrete block. The tolerances shown in Fig. 4-1 are measured from the standard, or actual, size of the concrete block units, whether modular or nonmodular, rather than from the nominal sizes of the blocks. The actual sizes of concrete bricks are the manufacturers' designated dimensions. The actual size of modular concrete bricks is usually $\frac{3}{8}$ in (9.5 mm) less than the nominal dimension (the width of one mortar joint). The actual size of nonmodular building brick is usually $\frac{1}{8}$ to $\frac{1}{4}$ in (3.2 to 6.4 mm) less than the nominal dimension. Standard concrete blocks are $\frac{3}{8}$ in (9.5 mm) less than the nominal dimension.

Industry Standards

ASTM C 55, *Standard Specification for Concrete Building Brick,* American Society for Testing and Materials, Philadelphia, 1985.

ASTM C 90, *Standard Specification for Hollow Load-Bearing Concrete Masonry Units,* American Society for Testing and Materials, Philadelphia, 1992.

ASTM C 129, *Standard Specification for Non-Load-Bearing Concrete Masonry Units,* American Society for Testing and Materials, Philadelphia, 1992.

ASTM C 744, *Standard Specification for Prefaced Concrete and Calcium Silicate Masonry Units,* American Society for Testing and Materials, Philadelphia, 1985.

Allowable Tolerances

Allowable dimensional tolerance for standard non-load-bearing and load-bearing concrete masonry units based on ASTM standards is $\pm\frac{1}{8}$ in (3.2 mm) from the standard (actual) dimension. This includes width, height, and length. However, in practice, units are usually manufactured to a $\frac{1}{16}$-in (1.6-mm) tolerance. For non-load-bearing concrete masonry units, the shell dimension cannot be less than $\frac{1}{2}$ in (13 mm).

For concrete building brick the tolerance is also $\pm\frac{1}{8}$ in (3.2 mm) in width, height, and length from the standard (actual) dimension.

Concrete masonry units used for prefaced block must meet the tolerances described above. In addition, the total variation in finished face dimensions of prefaced units cannot exceed $\pm\frac{1}{16}$ in (1.6 mm) between the largest and smallest unit in any lot of each size. The distortion of the plane and edges of the face of prefaced units from the corresponding plane and edges of the concrete masonry unit cannot exceed $\frac{1}{16}$ in (1.6 mm).

Related Sections

4-2. Concrete Unit Masonry Reinforcement Placement
4-3. Concrete Unit Masonry Construction

Figure 4-2

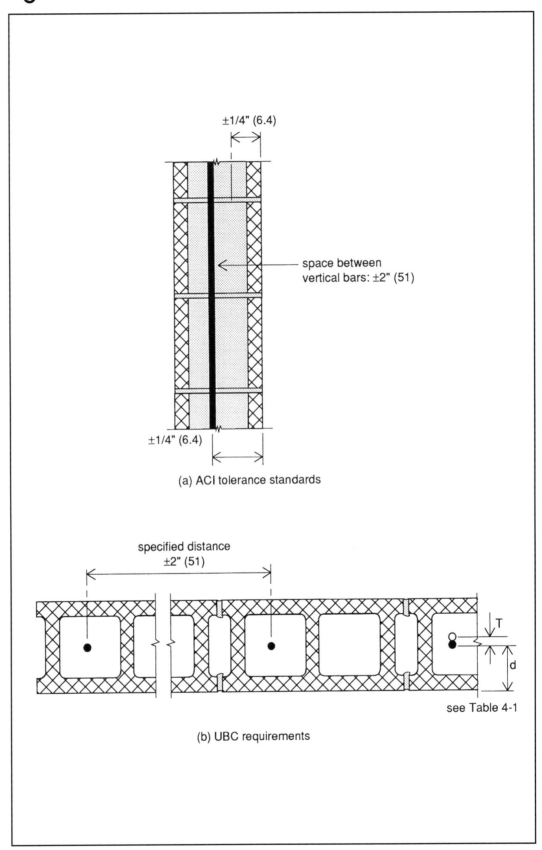

±1/4" (6.4)

space between
vertical bars: ±2" (51)

±1/4" (6.4)

(a) ACI tolerance standards

specified distance
±2" (51)

T

d

see Table 4-1

(b) UBC requirements

4-2. Concrete Unit Masonry Reinforcement Placement

Description

Reinforced concrete unit masonry is often used for walls, columns and pilasters, lintels, and beams. The placement of the reinforcing is critical to the strength and performance of these construction elements and can affect the placement of other embedded items, such as electrical boxes, plumbing, and structural fasteners. Both the American Concrete Institute (ACI) and the model codes prescribe allowable variations in reinforcement placement.

Industry Standards

ACI 117-90, *Standard Tolerances for Concrete Construction and Materials,* American Concrete Institute, Detroit, 1990.

ACI 531.1-76 (Rev. 1983), *Specification for Concrete Masonry Construction,* American Concrete Institute, Detroit, 1983.

Section 2404(e), *Uniform Building Code,* Placement of Reinforcing Steel in Concrete Masonry Units, International Conference of Building Officials, Whittier, CA, 1991.

Allowable Tolerances

ACI standards for reinforcement placement in masonry are shown in Fig. 4-2a. Both vertical and horizontal bars must be placed within $\frac{1}{4}$ in (6.4 mm) of the face of the masonry. Longitudinal spacing must be within 2 in (51 mm).

Uniform Building Code (*UBC*) tolerances for the placement of steel in walls and flexural elements are not at tight as ACI standards. *UBC* tolerances depend on d, the distance from the compression face of a flexural member to the centroid of the longitudinal tensile reinforcement. For d equal to 8 in (203 mm) or less the tolerance is $\pm\frac{1}{2}$ in (13 mm). For d greater than 8 in (203 mm) but equal to or less than 24 in (610 mm) the tolerance is ± 1 in (25 mm). For d greater than 24 in (610 mm) the tolerance is $1\frac{1}{4}$ in (32 mm). See Fig. 4-2b and Table 4-1.

Table 4-1
UBC Reinforcement Placement Tolerances

d, in (mm)	Placement tolerance T, in (mm)
$d \leq 8$ (203)	$\pm\frac{1}{2}$ (13)
8 (203) $\leq d \leq$ 24 (610)	± 1 (25)
d > 24 (610)	$\pm 1\frac{1}{4}$ (32)

Related Sections

4.1. Concrete Unit Masonry Manufacturing

4.3. Concrete Unit Masonry Construction

4.4. Prefabricated Masonry Panels

Figure 4-3

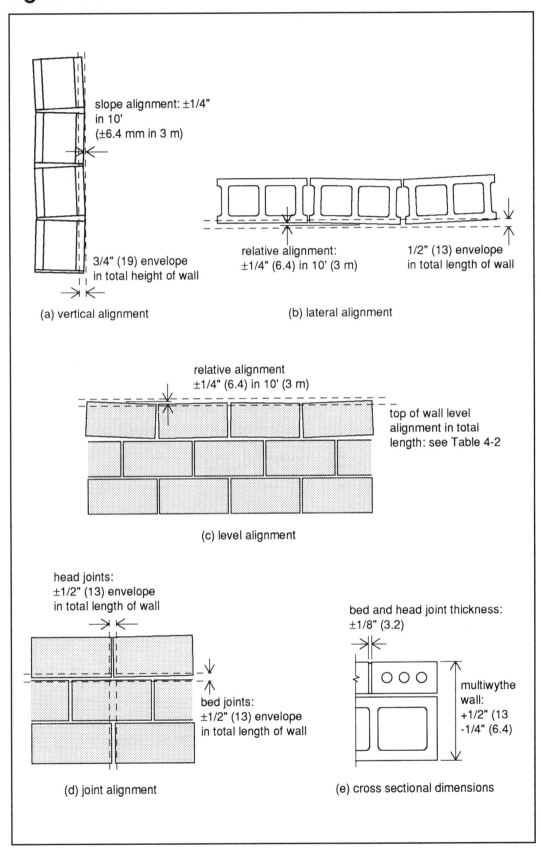

slope alignment: ±1/4"
in 10'
(±6.4 mm in 3 m)

3/4" (19) envelope
in total height of wall

(a) vertical alignment

relative alignment:
±1/4" (6.4) in 10' (3 m)

1/2" (13) envelope
in total length of wall

(b) lateral alignment

relative alignment
±1/4" (6.4) in 10' (3 m)

top of wall level
alignment in total
length: see Table 4-2

(c) level alignment

head joints:
±1/2" (13) envelope
in total length of wall

bed joints:
±1/2" (13) envelope
in total length of wall

(d) joint alignment

bed and head joint thickness:
±1/8" (3.2)

multiwythe
wall:
+1/2" (13
-1/4" (6.4)

(e) cross sectional dimensions

4-3. Concrete Unit Masonry Construction

Description

This section describes tolerances for laying up standard concrete unit masonry walls, either single wythe or multiple wythe.

Industry Standard

ACI 117-90, *Standard Tolerances for Concrete Construction and Materials,* Section 6—
    "Masonry," American Concrete Institute, Detroit, 1990.

Allowable Tolerances

American Concrete Institute (ACI) standards define both a total tolerance envelope within which the plane and edges of a wall must fall and relative alignment tolerances for adjacent elements and construction within a 10-ft (3-m) distance. (See Fig. 4-3.) For top-of-wall alignment, the tolerance depends on whether the wall is exposed and whether it is a bearing surface. These are summarized in Table 4-2 below. All of the ACI tolerances apply to concrete masonry walls as well as brick and other types of masonry.

Table 4-2
Top-of-Wall Alignment Envelope

Condition	Tolerance
Exposed	$\pm\frac{1}{2}$ (13)
Not exposed	± 1 (25)
Bearing surface	$\pm\frac{1}{2}$ (13)
Top of wall, other than bearing surface	$\pm\frac{3}{4}$ (19)

SOURCE: ACI 117-90; reproduced with permission, American Concrete Institute.

Related Sections

4.1. Concrete Unit Masonry Manufacturing

4.2. Concrete Unit Masonry Reinforcement Placement

4.4. Prefabricated Masonry Panels

Chapter 15. Masonry Systems

Figure 4-4

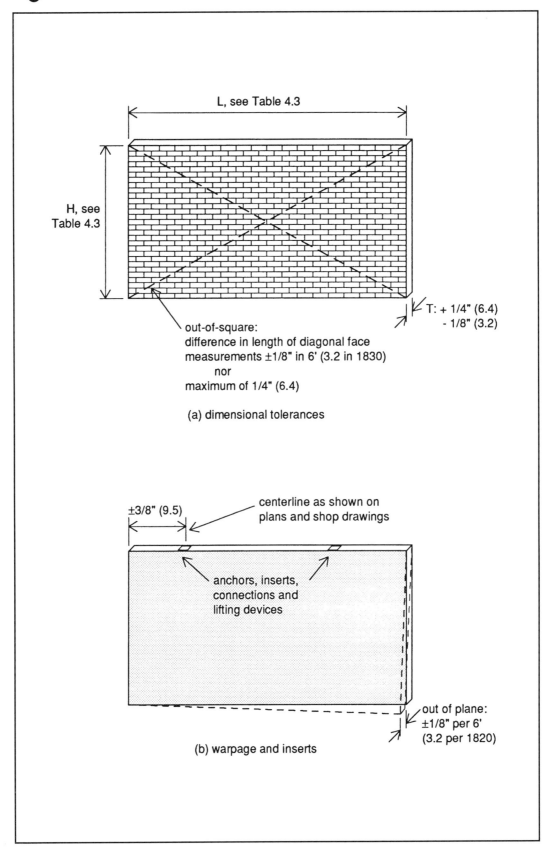

L, see Table 4.3

H, see
Table 4.3

T: + 1/4" (6.4)
    - 1/8" (3.2)

out-of-square:
difference in length of diagonal face
measurements ±1/8" in 6' (3.2 in 1830)
nor
maximum of 1/4" (6.4)

(a) dimensional tolerances

±3/8" (9.5)

centerline as shown on
plans and shop drawings

anchors, inserts,
connections and
lifting devices

out of plane:
±1/8" per 6'
(3.2 per 1820)

(b) warpage and inserts

4-4. Prefabricated Masonry Panels

Description

Prefabricated masonry panels include shop-fabricated assemblies made from concrete units, concrete block, brick, or structural clay tile.

Industry Standard

ASTM C 901, *Standard Specification for Prefabricated Masonry Panels,* American Society for Testing and Materials, Philadelphia, 1990.

Allowable Tolerances

ASTM tolerance specifications only relate to the fabrication of load-bearing and non-load-bearing panels. These are shown in Fig. 4-4. Erection tolerances are generally required to conform to American Concrete Institute (ACI) standards as described in Sec. 4-3. Dimensional tolerances depend on the size of the panel and are listed in Table 4-3.

Table 4-3
Dimensional Tolerances of Prefabricated Masonry Panels

Size of panel, L or H, ft (mm)*	Tolerance, in (mm)
10 or under (3050 or under)	$\pm\frac{1}{8}$ (3.2)
10 to 20 (3050 to 6100)	$+\frac{1}{8}, -\frac{3}{16}$ (+3.2, −4.8)
20 to 30 (6096 to 9144)	$+\frac{1}{8}, -\frac{1}{4}$ (+3.2, −6.4)

*For each additional 10 ft (3050 mm): $\pm\frac{1}{16}$ (1.6 mm).
source: ASTM C901; copyright ASTM; reprinted with permission.

Related Sections

4.1. Concrete Unit Masonry Manufacturing

4.2. Concrete Unit Masonry Reinforcement Placement

4-5. Brick Manufacturing

4-7. Glazed Structural Clay Facing Tile

Chapter 15. Masonry Systems

Figure 4-5

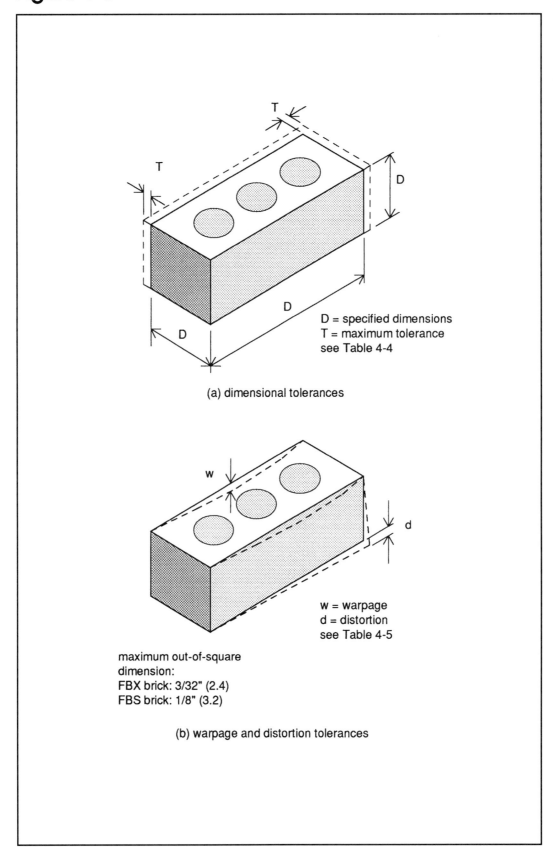

D = specified dimensions
T = maximum tolerance
see Table 4-4

(a) dimensional tolerances

w = warpage
d = distortion
see Table 4-5

maximum out-of-square
dimension:
FBX brick: 3/32" (2.4)
FBS brick: 1/8" (3.2)

(b) warpage and distortion tolerances

4-5. Brick Manufacturing

Description

This section covers four categories of brick. The first category is *facing brick,* which is available in three types, FBS, FBX, and FBA. Only types FBS and FBX have manufacturing tolerances established by ASTM specifications. The other three categories are building brick, hollow brick, and thin veneer brick units. *Building brick* is a solid clay masonry unit used where external appearance is not a concern. *Hollow brick* is clay masonry whose net cross-sectional solid area is less than 75 percent of its gross cross-sectional area. *Thin brick veneer* is a clay masonry unit with a maximum thickness of $1\frac{3}{4}$ in (44 mm).

Industry Standards

ASTM C 62, *Standard Specification for Building Brick,* American Society for Testing and Materials, Philadelphia, 1991.

ASTM C 216, *Standard Specification for Facing Brick,* American Society for Testing and Materials, Philadelphia, 1991.

ASTM C 652, *Standard Specification for Hollow Brick,* American Society for Testing and Materials, Philadelphia, 1991.

ASTM C 1088, *Standard Specification for Thin Veneer Brick Units Made from Clay or Shale,* American Society for Testing and Materials, Philadelphia, 1991.

Allowable Tolerances

ASTM manufacturing tolerances apply to each of the four categories of brick mentioned above. There are several types of brick in each of the four categories but only two types in each category (except building brick) have established manufacturing tolerances. These are listed in Table 4-4 and shown diagrammatically in Fig. 4-5*a*. The tolerances for each of the

Table 4-4
Brick Manufacturing Dimension Tolerances

Specified dimension, in (mm)	Maximum variation from specified dimension, in (mm)	
	Facing brick, type FBX Hollow brick, type HBX Thin veneer brick, type TBX	Facing brick, type FBS, & building brick Hollow brick, types HBS and HBB Thin veneer brick, type TBS
3 and under (76 and under)	$\frac{1}{16}$ (1.6)	$\frac{3}{32}$ (2.4)
Over 3 up to and including 4 (76 to 102 inclusive)	$\frac{3}{32}$ (2.4)	$\frac{1}{8}$ (3.2)
Over 4 up to and including 6 (102 to 152 inclusive)	$\frac{1}{8}$ (3.2)	$\frac{3}{16}$ (4.7)
Over 6 up to and including 8 (152 to 203 inclusive)	$\frac{5}{32}$ (4.0)	$\frac{1}{4}$ (6.4)
Over 8 up to and including 12 (203 to 305 inclusive)	$\frac{7}{32}$ (5.6)	$\frac{5}{16}$ (7.9)
Over 12 up to and including 16 (305 to 406 inclusive)	$\frac{9}{32}$ (7.1)	$\frac{3}{8}$ (9.5)

SOURCE: ASTM C 62, C 216, C 652, and C 1088; copyright ASTM; reprinted with permission.

four categories are the same. Distortion tolerances are shown in Table 4-5. Tolerances for other types of brick in each category must be specified by the purchaser.

**Table 4-5
Brick Distortion Tolerances**

Maximum dimension, in (mm)	Maximum permissible distortion, in (mm)	
	Facing brick, type FBX Hollow brick, type HBX Thin veneer brick, type TBX	Facing brick, type FBS Hollow brick, type HBS Thin veneer brick, type TBS
8 and under (203 and under)	$\frac{1}{16}$ (1.6)	$\frac{3}{32}$ (2.4)
Over 8 up to and including 12 (203 to 305 inclusive)	$\frac{3}{32}$ (2.4)	$\frac{1}{8}$ (3.2)
Over 12 up to and including 16 (305 to 406 inclusive)	$\frac{1}{8}$ (3.2)	$\frac{5}{32}$ (4.0)

SOURCE: ASTM C 216, C 652, and C 1088; copyright ASTM; reprinted with permission.

Related Sections

4-5. Brick Wall Construction

4-7. Glazed Structural Clay Facing Tile

Figure 4-6

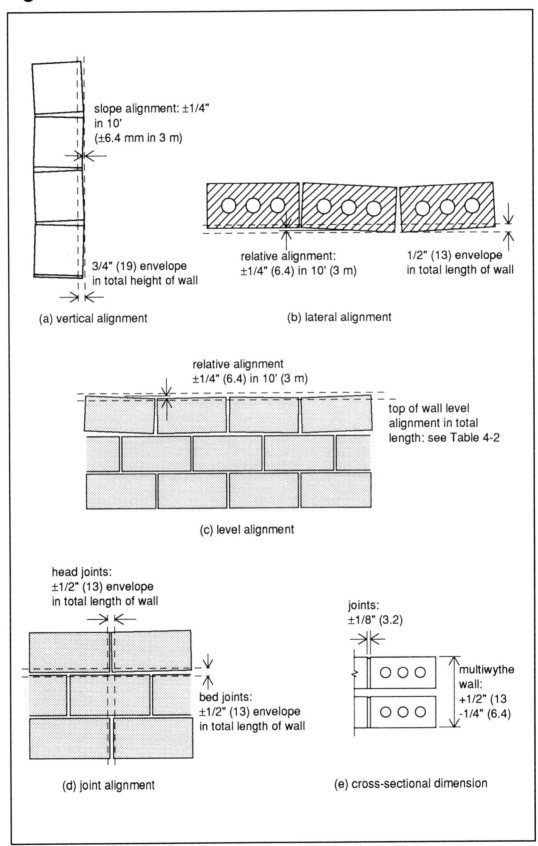

slope alignment: ±1/4" in 10' (±6.4 mm in 3 m)

3/4" (19) envelope in total height of wall

(a) vertical alignment

relative alignment: ±1/4" (6.4) in 10' (3 m)

1/2" (13) envelope in total length of wall

(b) lateral alignment

relative alignment ±1/4" (6.4) in 10' (3 m)

top of wall level alignment in total length: see Table 4-2

(c) level alignment

head joints: ±1/2" (13) envelope in total length of wall

bed joints: ±1/2" (13) envelope in total length of wall

(d) joint alignment

joints: ±1/8" (3.2)

multiwythe wall: +1/2" (13 -1/4" (6.4)

(e) cross-sectional dimension

4-6. Brick Wall Construction

Description

This section describes tolerances for laying up standard brick walls, either single wythe or multiple wythe. The same standards apply to brick walls as apply to concrete masonry walls.

Industry Standard

ACI 117-90, *Standard Tolerances for Concrete Construction and Materials,* Section 6— "Masonry," American Concrete Institute, 1990.

Allowable Tolerances

American Concrete Institute (ACI) standards define both a total tolerance envelope within which the plane and edges of a wall must fall and relative alignment tolerances for adjacent elements and construction within a 10-ft (3-m) distance. See Fig. 4-6. For top-of-wall alignment, the tolerance depends on whether the wall is exposed and whether it is a bearing surface. These are summarized in Table 4-2. All of the ACI tolerances apply to brick walls as well as concrete masonry walls and other types of masonry construction.

Related Sections

4-4. Prefabricated Masonry Panels

4-5. Brick Manufacturing

14-5. Detailing for Brick on Steel

15-2. Detailing Brick and Masonry Systems

Figure 4-7

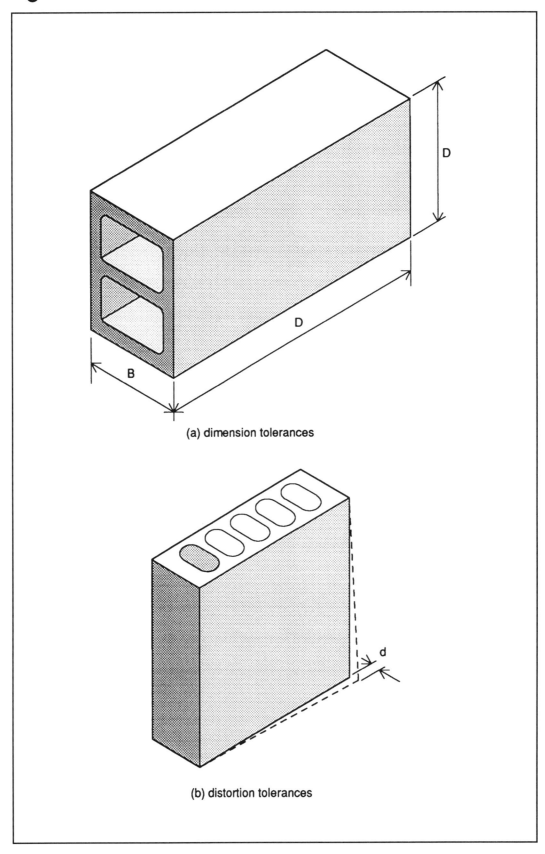

(a) dimension tolerances

(b) distortion tolerances

4-7. Glazed Structural Clay Facing Tile

Description

Structural clay facing tile is load-bearing clay tile having a finish consisting of ceramic glaze fused to the body at above 1500°F (665°C). Tolerance standards established by ASTM C 126 also apply to facing brick and other solid masonry units that have a ceramic glazed finish.

There are two grades: S grade (select) is for use with relatively narrow mortar joints and SS grade (select sized or ground edge) is for use where the variation of face dimensions must be very small. There are various types and core configurations, but tolerances depend on which of the two grades is specified.

Industry Standard

ASTM C 126, *Standard Specification for Ceramic Glazed Structural Clay Facing Tile, Facing Brick, and Solid Masonry Units,* American Society for Testing and Materials, Philadelphia, 1991.

Allowable Tolerances

Tolerances are established for face dimensions *D*, bed-depth dimension (thickness) *B*, and distortion tolerances *d*, as shown in Fig. 4-7. Tables 4-6 through 4-8 give the tolerances based on the size of the unit used.

Table 4-6
Face Dimension Tolerances for Glazed Clay Facing Tile

Specified face dimension *D*, in (mm)	Maximum difference between any unit and the specified dimension, in (mm)*		Maximum difference between largest and smallest unit in one lot, in (mm)
Grade S units			
$2\frac{3}{8}$ (60.3)	$+\frac{1}{16}$ (+1.6)	$-\frac{3}{32}$ (−2.4)	$\frac{3}{32}$ (2.4)
$3\frac{3}{4}$ (95.3)	$+\frac{1}{16}$ (+1.6)	$-\frac{3}{32}$ (−2.4)	$\frac{3}{32}$ (2.4)
$5\frac{1}{16}$ (128.6)	$+\frac{1}{16}$ (+1.6)	$-\frac{3}{32}$ (−2.4)	$\frac{3}{32}$ (2.4)
$5\frac{3}{4}$ (146.1)	$+\frac{1}{16}$ (+1.6)	$-\frac{3}{32}$ (−2.4)	$\frac{3}{32}$ (2.4)
$7\frac{3}{4}$ (196.9)	$+\frac{1}{16}$ (+1.6)	$-\frac{1}{8}$ (−3.2)	$\frac{5}{32}$ (4.0)
$11\frac{3}{4}$ (198.5)	$+\frac{1}{16}$ (+1.6)	$-\frac{5}{32}$ (−4.0)	$\frac{3}{16}$ (4.8)
Grade SS units			
$7\frac{3}{4}$ (196.9)	$+\frac{1}{16}$ (+1.6)	$-\frac{1}{16}$ (−1.6)	$\frac{3}{32}$ (2.4)
$15\frac{3}{4}$ (400.1)	$+\frac{1}{16}$ (+1.6)	$-\frac{1}{16}$ (−1.6)	$\frac{3}{32}$ (2.4)

*When a unit has a dimension more than $\frac{1}{4}$ in (6.4 mm) greater than shown, its tolerance is the same as for the next larger dimension.

SOURCE: ASTM C 126; copyright ASTM; reprinted with permission.

Table 4-7
Bed Depth (Thickness) Tolerances for Glazed Clay Facing Tile

Specified bed depth (thickness) B, in (mm)	Maximum difference between any unit and the specified dimension, in (mm)*		Maximum difference between largest and smallest unit in one lot, in (mm)†
Type I, single-faced units			
$1\frac{3}{4}$ (44.5)	$+\frac{1}{8}$ (+3.2)	$-\frac{1}{8}$ (−3.2)	$\frac{1}{8}$ (3.2)
$3\frac{3}{4}$ (95.3)	$+\frac{1}{8}$ (+3.2)	$-\frac{3}{16}$ (−4.8)	$\frac{3}{16}$ (4.8)
$5\frac{3}{4}$ (146.1)	$+\frac{1}{8}$ (+3.2)	$-\frac{1}{4}$ (−6.4)	$\frac{1}{4}$ (6.4)
$7\frac{3}{4}$ (196.9)	$+\frac{1}{8}$ (+3.2)	$-\frac{5}{16}$ (−7.9)	$\frac{5}{16}$ (7.9)
Type II, two-faced units			
$3\frac{3}{4}$ (95.3)	$+\frac{1}{8}$ (+3.2)	$-\frac{1}{8}$ (−3.2)	$\frac{1}{8}$ (3.2)
$5\frac{3}{4}$ (146.1)	$+\frac{1}{8}$ (+3.2)	$-\frac{1}{8}$ (−3.2)	$\frac{1}{8}$ (3.2)

*When a unit has a dimension more than $\frac{1}{4}$ in (6.4 mm) greater than shown, its tolerance is the same as for the next larger dimension.

†Lot size is determined by agreement between purchaser and the seller.

SOURCE: ASTM C 126; copyright ASTM; reprinted with permission.

Table 4-8
Distortion Tolerances for Glazed Clay Facing Tile

Specified face dimensions D, (height × length) in (mm)*	Grade	Maximum distortion d, in (mm)
$2\frac{3}{8} \times 7\frac{3}{4}$ (60.3 × 196.9)	S	$\frac{1}{16}$ (1.6)
$5\frac{1}{16} \times 7\frac{3}{4}$ (128.6 × 196.9)	S	$\frac{1}{16}$ (1.6)
$5\frac{1}{16} \times 11\frac{3}{4}$ (128.6 × 298.5)	S	$\frac{1}{16}$ (1.6)
$3\frac{3}{4} \times 11\frac{3}{4}$ (95.3 × 298.5)	S	$\frac{1}{16}$ (1.6)
$5\frac{3}{4} \times 11\frac{3}{4}$ (146.1 × 298.5)	S	$\frac{1}{16}$ (1.6)
$7\frac{3}{4} \times 11\frac{3}{4}$ (196.9 × 298.5)	S	$\frac{5}{32}$ (4.0)
$7\frac{3}{4} \times 15\frac{3}{4}$ (196.9 × 400.1)	SS	$\frac{3}{32}$ (2.4)

SOURCE: ASTM C 126; copyright ASTM; reprinted with permission.

Related Section

4-8. Facing, Load-Bearing, and Non-Load-Bearing Clay Tile

Figure 4-8

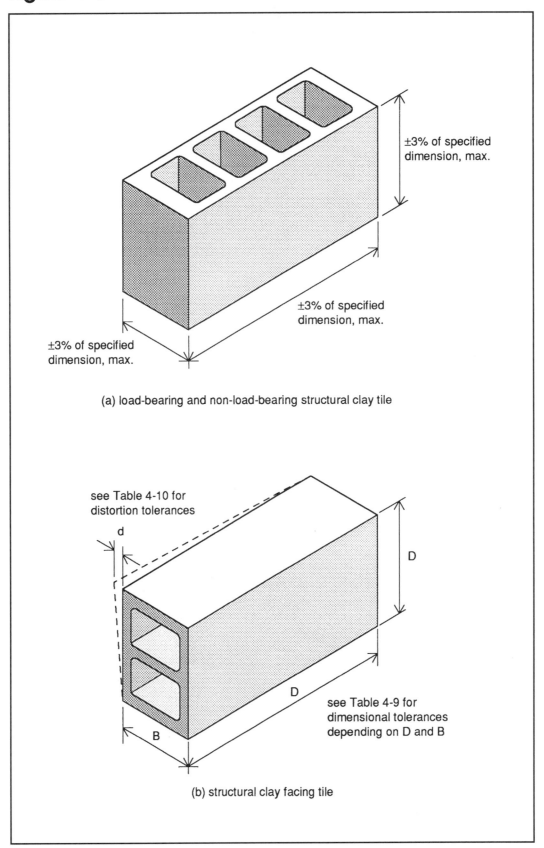

±3% of specified dimension, max.

±3% of specified dimension, max.

±3% of specified dimension, max.

(a) load-bearing and non-load-bearing structural clay tile

see Table 4-10 for distortion tolerances

d

D

D

B

see Table 4-9 for dimensional tolerances depending on D and B

(b) structural clay facing tile

4-8. Facing, Load-Bearing, and Non-Load-Bearing Clay Tile

Description

Tile conforming to ASTM C 34 and C 56 is used for concealed walls and partitions, furring, backup tile, and fireproofing. Load-bearing facing tile conforming to ASTM C 212 is used for exposed exterior and interior walls and partitions where low absorption and high stain resistance are required.

Industry Standards

ASTM C34, *Standard Specification for Structural Clay Load-Bearing Wall Tile,* American Society for Testing and Materials, Philadelphia, 1991.

ASTM C 56, *Standard Specification for Structural Clay Non-Load-Bearing Tile,* American Society for Testing and Materials, Philadelphia, 1991.

ASTM C 212, *Standard Specification for Structural Clay Facing Tile,* American Society for Testing and Materials, Philadelphia, 1991.

Allowable Tolerances

As shown in Fig. 4-8a the tolerance for tile conforming to ASTM C 34 and C 56 is only ±3 percent of the specified dimension.

Tolerances for structural clay facing tile depend on the type and are illustrated in Fig. 4-8b and detailed in Tables 4-9 and 4-10.

Table 4-9
Clay Facing Tile Manufacturing Dimension Tolerances

Specified dimension, in (mm)	Maximum variation from specified dimension, in (mm)	
	Type FTX	Type FTS
3 and under (76.2 and under)	$\frac{1}{16}$ (1.6)	$\frac{3}{32}$ (2.4)
Over 3 up to and including 4 (76.2 to 101.6 inclusive)	$\frac{3}{32}$ (2.4)	$\frac{1}{8}$ (3.2)
Over 4 up to and including 6 (101.6 to 152.4 inclusive)	1/8 (3.2)	$\frac{3}{16}$ (4.7)
Over 6 up to and including 8 (152.4 to 203.2 inclusive)	$\frac{5}{32}$ (4.0)	$\frac{1}{4}$ (6.4)
Over 8 up to and including 12 (203.2 to 304.8 inclusive)	$\frac{7}{32}$ (5.6)	$\frac{5}{16}$ (7.9)
Over 12 up to and including 16 (304.8 to 406.4 inclusive)	$\frac{9}{32}$ (7.1)	$\frac{3}{8}$ (9.5)

SOURCE: ASTM C212; copyright ASTM; reprinted with permission.

Table 4-10
Clay Facing Tile Distortion Tolerances

Maximum dimension, in (mm)	Maximum permissible distortion, in (mm)	
	Type FTX	Type FTS
8 and under (203.2 and under)	$\frac{3}{32}$ (2.4)	$\frac{1}{8}$ (3.2)
Over 8 up to and including 12 (203.2 to 304.8 inclusive)	$\frac{1}{8}$ (3.2)	$\frac{3}{16}$ (4.8)
Over 12 up to and including 16 (304.8 to 406.4 inclusive)	$\frac{3}{16}$ (4.8)	$\frac{1}{4}$ (6.4)

SOURCE: ASTM C212; copyright ASTM; reprinted with permission.

Related Section

4-7. Glazed Structural Clay Facing Tile

Figure 4-9

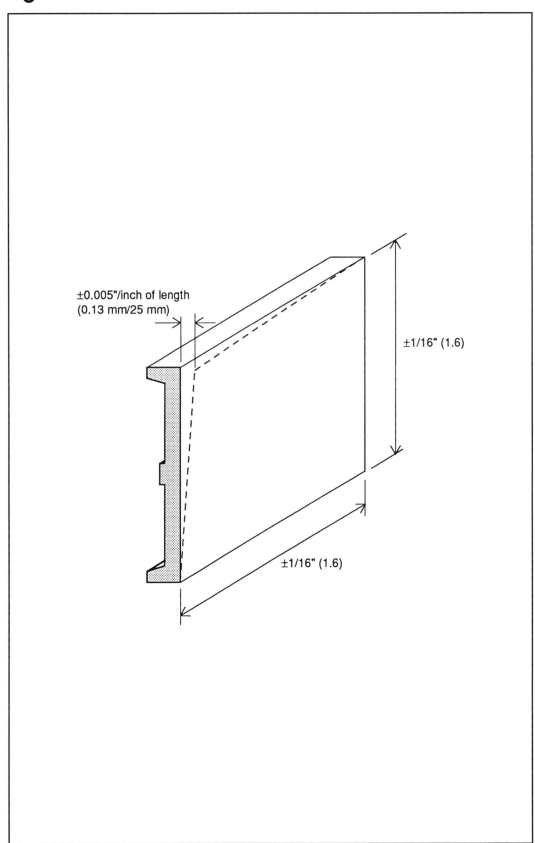

±0.005"/inch of length
(0.13 mm/25 mm)

±1/16" (1.6)

±1/16" (1.6)

4-9. Terra Cotta Manufacturing and Erection

Description

Terra cotta is made by machine extrusion, pressing into molds, or by hand carving for ornate work. Machine extruded terra cotta is often called "ceramic veneer." Because terra cotta is not used much there are very few manufacturers and each may have its own tolerances for manufacturing and erection.

Industry Standards

Public Works Specifications, Ceramic Veneer, Architectural Terra Cotta Institute (now defunct), October 1961 (AIA File no. 9).

ASTM C 126, *Standard Specification for Ceramic Glazed Structural Clay Facing Tile, Facing Brick, and Solid Masonry Units,* American Society for Testing and Materials, Philadelphia, 1991.

Allowable Tolerances

Tolerances for machine extruded terra cotta generally follow the requirements of ASTM C 126 for type SS units. In addition, specifications developed by the Architectural Terra Cotta Institute (which are still used by one manufacturer) correspond with the ASTM requirements for finished face dimension tolerances.

However, there is a slight variance between the two specifications concerning flatness tolerances. For sizes up to about 18 in (457 mm) this tolerance is $\pm\frac{1}{16}$ in (1.6 mm). For larger sizes the tolerance only increases to about $\frac{3}{32}$ in (2.4 mm). The 1961 specifications call for a flatness tolerance of 0.005 inch per inch of length (0.13 mm per 25 mm) as shown in Fig. 4-9. Tolerances for erection and for pressed or hand carved work should be verified with the manufacturer.

Related Section

4-7. Glazed Structural Clay Facing Tile

Figure 4-10

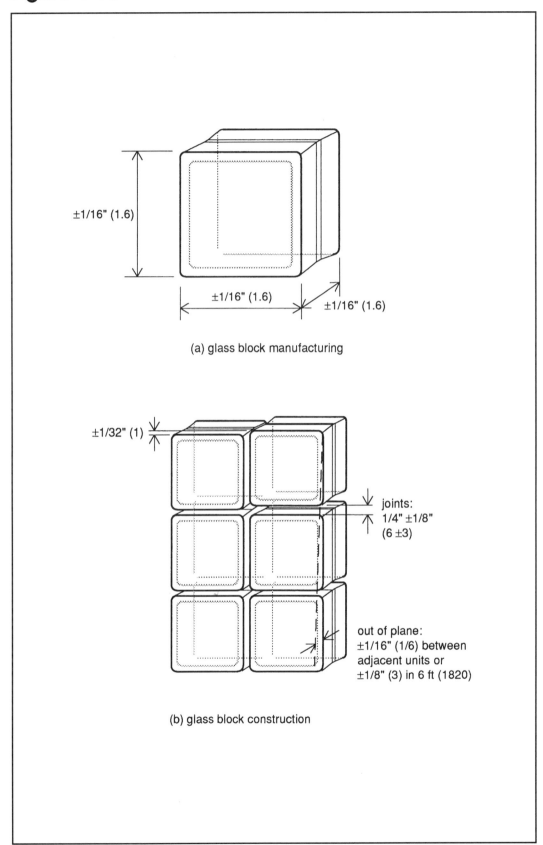

±1/16" (1.6)

±1/16" (1.6)   ±1/16" (1.6)

(a) glass block manufacturing

±1/32" (1)

joints:
1/4" ±1/8"
(6 ±3)

out of plane:
±1/16" (1/6) between
adjacent units or
±1/8" (3) in 6 ft (1820)

(b) glass block construction

4-10. Glass Block Manufacturing and Erection

Description

Glass block consists of individual masonry units made from partially evacuated hollow glass units or solid glass units. Because glass block cannot be cut, openings must be precisely formed based on the modular unit size plus allowances for expansion joints, reinforcing, and framing.

Industry Standards

There are currently no industry standards for either glass block manufacturing or erection. Specific tolerances must be verified with each manufacturer and erection tolerances stated in the specifications.

Allowable Tolerances

In spite of the lack of industry standards, most glass block is manufactured to within $\pm\frac{1}{16}$ in (1.6 mm) of the actual specified size of the unit, as shown in Fig. 4-10a. In most cases the mortar joints can accommodate these minor variations without visible misalignment.

Variations in vertical and horizontal alignment between adjacent units should be specified, but can be as small as $\pm\frac{1}{32}$ in (1 mm), as shown in Fig. 4-10b. Variations out of plane can be as little as $\pm\frac{1}{16}$ in (1.6 mm) between adjacent units.

No standards exist for out-of-plane tolerances for an entire wall section between framing, but it should be possible to build to the same tolerances as a brick wall or no more than $\pm\frac{1}{8}$ in in 6 ft (3.2 mm in 1820 mm). Masonry construction tolerances given in ACI 117 could also apply (see Sec. 4-3). For walls a single story high, out-of-plumb tolerances may be specified as a total of $\pm\frac{1}{8}$ in (3 mm). Joints should be laid $\frac{1}{4}$ in (6 mm) thick with a tolerance of $\pm\frac{1}{8}$ in (3 mm).

Related Section

4-3. Concrete Unit Masonry Construction

Figure 5-1

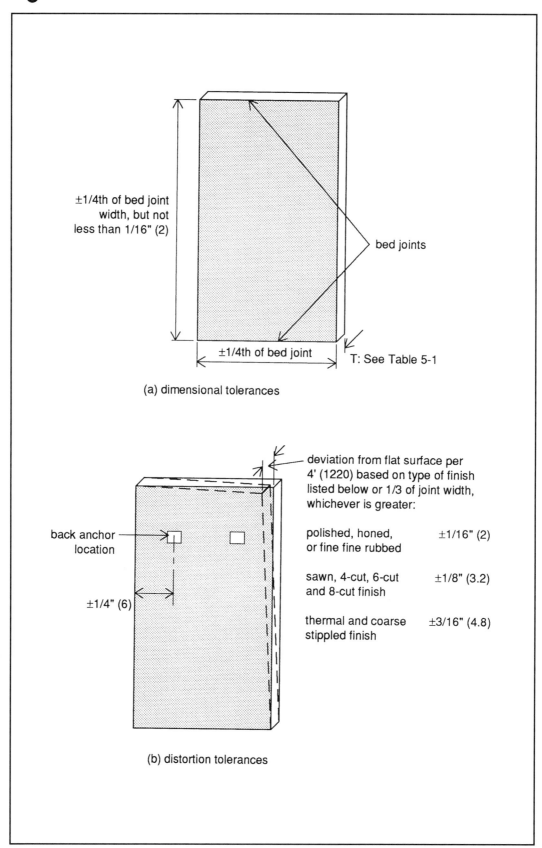

±1/4th of bed joint width, but not less than 1/16" (2)

bed joints

±1/4th of bed joint

T: See Table 5-1

(a) dimensional tolerances

back anchor location

±1/4" (6)

deviation from flat surface per 4' (1220) based on type of finish listed below or 1/3 of joint width, whichever is greater:

polished, honed, or fine fine rubbed   ±1/16" (2)

sawn, 4-cut, 6-cut and 8-cut finish   ±1/8" (3.2)

thermal and coarse stippled finish   ±3/16" (4.8)

(b) distortion tolerances

Chapter 5

Stone

5-1. Granite Fabrication

Description

This section includes tolerances for thick-veneer granite and dimensional stone. It also includes the newer, reinforced, thin granite panels.

Industry Standard

Dimension Stone Design Manual IV, Marble Institute of America, Inc., Farmington, 1991.

Allowable Tolerances

Maximum length tolerances, as shown in Fig. 5-1*a,* are one-fourth of the specified bed joint width, but no less than $\frac{1}{16}$ in (2 mm). Thickness tolerances depend on the nominal thickness and are listed in Table 5-1.

Flatness tolerances depend on the finish of the stone. For polished, honed, and fine rubbed finishes, flatness tolerances cannot exceed those shown in Fig. 5-1*b* or one-third of the specified joint width, whichever is greater. On surfaces with other finishes the tolerance is that shown in Fig. 5-1*b* or one-half the specified joint width, whichever is greater. Flatness tolerances are determined by a 4-ft (1220-mm) dimension in any direction on the surface.

Anchors must be as shown in Fig. 5-1*b* with sinkages within $\pm\frac{1}{16}$ in (2 mm). The width and location of slots or kerfs cut into the edge of granite must be within $\pm\frac{1}{16}$ in (2 mm). The depth of kerfs and anchor holes must be within $-\frac{1}{8}$ in (3 mm) or $+\frac{3}{8}$ in (10 mm).

Related Section

5-4. Granite and Marble Installation

Table 5-1
Tolerances for Granite Veneer

Thickness (all material)*	Finished one face, in (mm)		Face dimensions (all material), in (mm)		
			Thin stock	$+\frac{1}{16}, -\frac{1}{32}$	$(+2, -1)$
Thin stock: 3⁄4 in to 2 in (2 cm to 5 cm)	$\pm\frac{1}{8}$	(±3)	Cubic stock	$\pm\frac{1}{8}$	(±3)
			Stone tile	$\pm\frac{1}{32}$	(±1)
Cubic stock: 2 in+ (5 cm+)	$\pm\frac{1}{2}$ in	(±13)	Squareness (all material), in (mm)		
			Thin stock	$\pm\frac{1}{32}$	(±1)
Stone tile: 3⁄4 in or less (15 mm)	$\pm\frac{1}{64}$ in	(±0.5)	Cubic stock	$\pm\frac{1}{16}$	(±2)
			Stone tile	$\pm\frac{1}{32}$	(±1)

*Thickness variations are *not* gauged.
    SOURCE: "Product description—Granite," *Dimension Stone Design Manual IV,* Marble Institute of America, Inc.

Figure 5-2

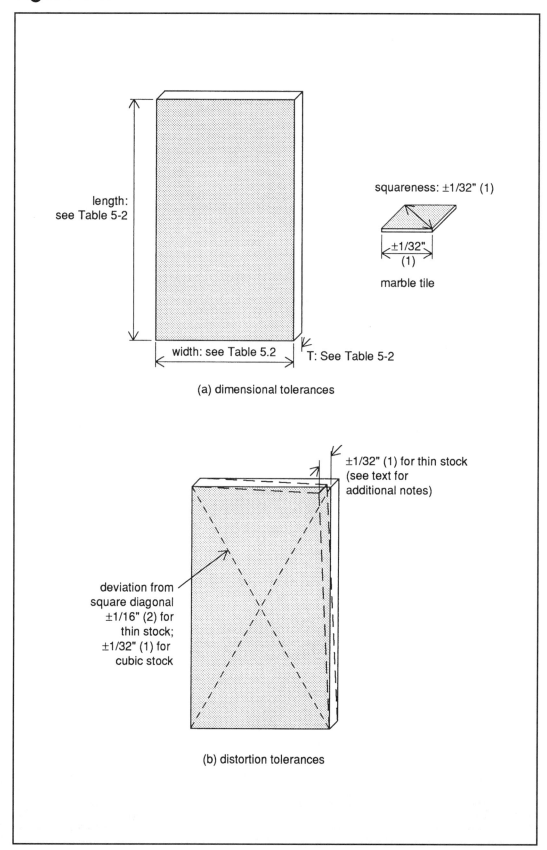

length:
see Table 5-2

width: see Table 5.2

T: See Table 5-2

squareness: ±1/32" (1)

±1/32"
(1)

marble tile

(a) dimensional tolerances

±1/32" (1) for thin stock
(see text for
additional notes)

deviation from
square diagonal
±1/16" (2) for
thin stock;
±1/32" (1) for
cubic stock

(b) distortion tolerances

5-2. Marble Fabrication

Description

Marble tolerances include those for thin veneer slabs, cubic stock, and marble tile. This section does not include tolerances for the newer reinforced thin marble panels.

Industry Standards

Dimension Stone Design Manual IV, Marble Institute of America, Inc., Farmington, MI, 1991.

Allowable Tolerances

Dimensional tolerances, as shown in Fig. 5-2a, for thin and cubic stock are $\pm\frac{1}{16}$ (2 mm). Thickness tolerances depend on the type of stone and whether it is finished on one or both sides as listed in Table 5-2.

Table 5-2
Size Tolerances for Marble

Thickness (all material)*	Finished both faces, in (mm)		Finished one face, in (mm)	
Thin stock: $\frac{3}{4}$ in to 2 in (2 cm to 5 cm)	$+0, -\frac{1}{32}$	$(+0, -1)$	$\pm\frac{1}{32}$	(±1)
Cubic stock: 2 in + (5 cm+)	$\pm\frac{1}{16}$	(±2)	$\pm\frac{1}{8}$	(±3)
Stone tile: $\frac{5}{8}$ in or less (15 mm)			$\pm\frac{1}{64}$	(±0.5)
Face dimensions (all material), in (mm)				
Thin stock	$+\frac{1}{16}, -\frac{1}{32}$	$(+2, -1)$	$+\frac{1}{16}, -\frac{1}{32}$	$(+2, -1)$
Cubic stock	$\pm\frac{1}{16}$	(±2)	$\pm\frac{1}{16}$	(±2)
Stone tile			$\pm\frac{1}{32}$	(±1)
Squareness (all material), in (mm)				
Thin stock	$\pm\frac{1}{32}$	(±1)	$\pm\frac{1}{32}$	(±1)
Cubic stock	$\pm\frac{1}{16}$	(±2)	$\pm\frac{1}{16}$	(±2)
Stone tile			$\pm\frac{1}{32}$	(±1)

*All thicknesses are subject to gauged fabrication tolerances.
SOURCE: "Product description—Marble," *Dimension Stone Design Manual IV,* Marble Institute of America, Inc.

The tolerance of $\pm\frac{1}{32}$ in (1 mm) shown in Fig. 5-2b is for variation from a flat surface on the exposed face. The maximum variation on the bed and joint arris (the visible edges along the horizontal and vertical joints) from true line as measured by a 4-ft (1200-mm) straightedge is $\frac{3}{64}$ in (1.2 mm) or one-sixth of the specified joint width, whichever is greater. This tolerance is for polished, honed, and fine rubbed finishes. For other finishes the tolerance is plus or minus one-fourth of the joint width.

Related Section

5-4. Granite and Marble Installation

Figure 5-3

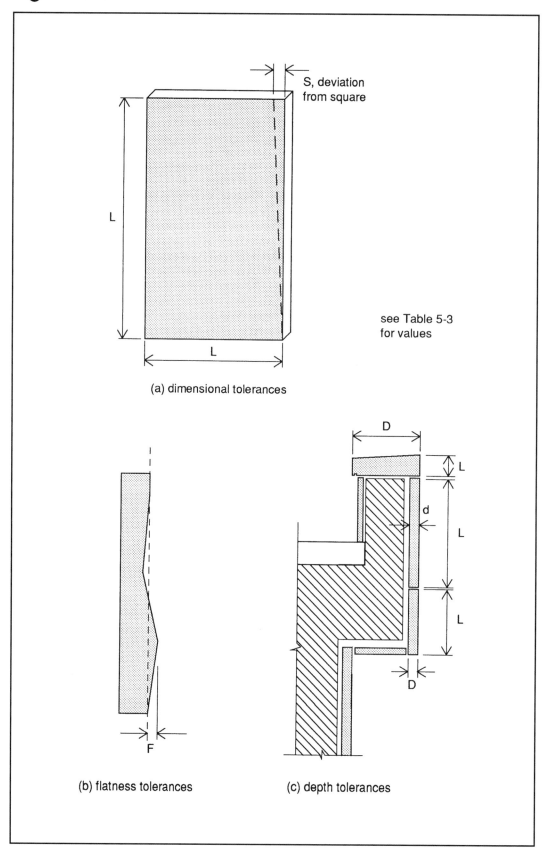

(a) dimensional tolerances

see Table 5-3
for values

S, deviation
from square

(b) flatness tolerances

(c) depth tolerances

5-3. Limestone Fabrication

Description

This section includes standard limestone construction using both single panels and shop-fabricated assemblies. Tolerances for ornately carved work should be verified with the supplier.

Industry Standard

Indiana Limestone Handbook, 19th ed., Indiana Limestone Institute of America, Inc., Bedford, IN, 1992.

Allowable Tolerances

Common tolerances are shown in Fig. 5-3 and listed in Table 5-3. Common finishes are indicated in Table 5-3, but special finishes are available which may affect the tolerance of various pieces. *Preassembled units* are stone assemblies consisting of two or more stones assembled at the plant using adhesives and metal accessories where required.

Table 5-3
Limestone Fabrication Tolerances

Finish type	Length L, in (mm)	Deviation from flat surface F, in (mm)	Critical depth D, in (mm)	Noncritical depth d, in (mm)	Deviation from square S, in (mm)
Smooth machine finish	$\pm\frac{1}{16}$ (2)	$\pm\frac{1}{16}$ (2)	$\pm\frac{1}{16}$ (2)	$\pm\frac{1}{2}$ (13)	$\pm\frac{1}{16}$ (2)
Diamond gang finish	$\pm\frac{1}{16}$ (2)	$\pm\frac{1}{4}$ (6)	$\pm\frac{1}{8}$ (3)	$\pm\frac{1}{2}$ (13)	$\pm\frac{1}{16}$ (2)
Chat sawed finish	$\pm\frac{1}{16}$ (2)	$\pm\frac{1}{4}$ (6)	$\pm\frac{1}{8}$ (3)	$\pm\frac{1}{2}$ (13)	$\pm\frac{1}{16}$ (2)
Shot sawed finish	$\pm\frac{1}{16}$ (2)	$\pm\frac{1}{2}$ (13)	$\pm\frac{1}{4}$ (6)	$\pm\frac{1}{2}$ (13)	$\pm\frac{1}{16}$ (2)
Preassembled units*	$\pm\frac{1}{8}$ (3)	$\pm\frac{1}{8}$ (3)	$\pm\frac{1}{8}$ (3)	$\pm\frac{1}{2}$ (13)	$\pm\frac{1}{8}$ (3)
Panels over 50 ft² (4.6 m²)	$\pm\frac{1}{8}$ (3)	$\pm\frac{1}{8}$ (3)	$\pm\frac{1}{8}$ (3)	$\pm\frac{1}{2}$ (13)	$\pm\frac{1}{8}$ (3)

*When multiple stone units increase beyond 50 ft² and as steel or other framing members become more complex to accomplish a single plane change, tolerances may be affected. Acceptable tolerances should be verified between the architect, contractor, supplier, and erector.

SOURCE: *Indiana Limestone Handbook,* 19th ed., Indiana Limestone Institute of America, Inc.; reproduced with permission.

Related Section

5-5. Limestone Installation

Figure 5-4

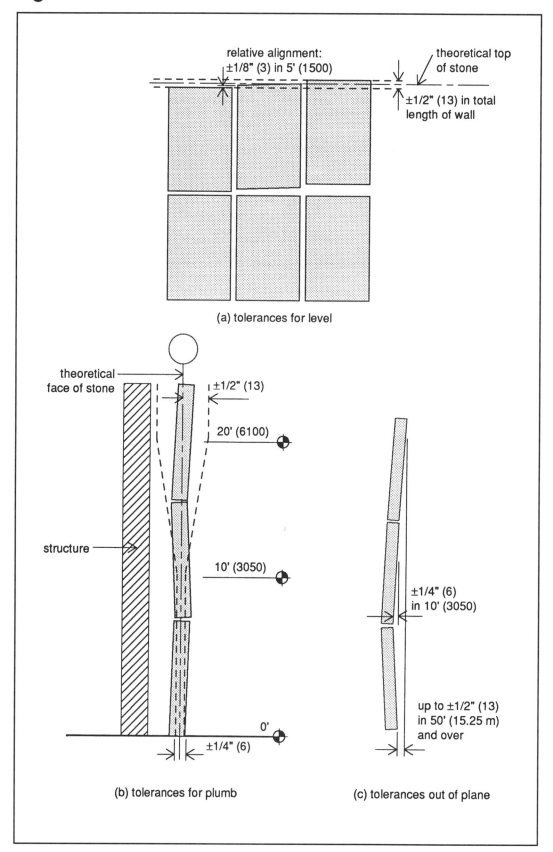

relative alignment:
±1/8" (3) in 5' (1500)

theoretical top of stone

±1/2" (13) in total length of wall

(a) tolerances for level

theoretical face of stone

±1/2" (13)

20' (6100)

structure

10' (3050)

0'

±1/4" (6)

(b) tolerances for plumb

±1/4" (6) in 10' (3050)

up to ±1/2" (13) in 50' (15.25 m) and over

(c) tolerances out of plane

5-4. Granite and Marble Installation

Description

Granite and marble can be installed on a variety of substrates including steel framing, concrete, and masonry. In addition, stone can be installed on a steel grid framework anchored to other structural backup systems. The accuracy with which stone can be installed depends on the tolerance of the structural framework and the clearances between materials as well as the amount of adjustment designed into the connections.

Industry Standard

Dimension Stone Design Manual IV, Marble Institute of America, Inc., Farmington, MI, 1991.

Allowable Tolerances

There are no industry standards for installation tolerances for exterior granite and marble. Specific tolerances should be developed in conjunction with the fabricator and installation contractor based on the expected tolerances of the building frame and the specific details of the stone cladding. The installation tolerances shown in Fig. 5-4 are those recommended in the Spectext master specifications.

The recommended maximum variation for interior stone wall veneer as published by the Marble Institute of America is $\pm\frac{1}{8}$ in (4 mm) cumulative over a 10-ft (3-m) linear measurement, with a maximum of $\frac{1}{32}$ in (1 mm) variation between adjacent tiles.

Related Sections

5-1. Granite Fabrication

5-2. Marble Fabrication

12-5. Detailing for Stone on Concrete

14-6. Detailing for Stone on Steel Systems

15-3. Detailing for Stone on Masonry Backup

Figure 5-5

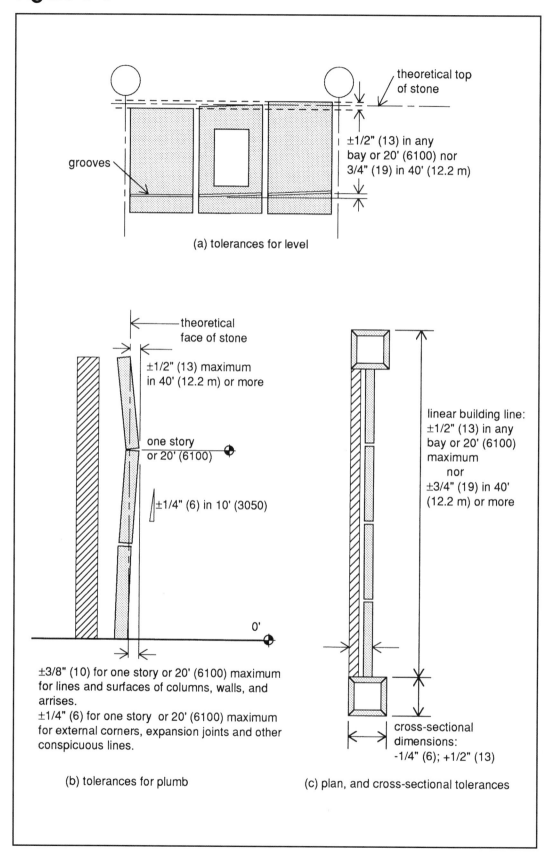

theoretical top of stone

grooves

±1/2" (13) in any bay or 20' (6100) nor 3/4" (19) in 40' (12.2 m)

(a) tolerances for level

theoretical face of stone

±1/2" (13) maximum in 40' (12.2 m) or more

one story or 20' (6100)

±1/4" (6) in 10' (3050)

0'

±3/8" (10) for one story or 20' (6100) maximum for lines and surfaces of columns, walls, and arrises.
±1/4" (6) for one story or 20' (6100) maximum for external corners, expansion joints and other conspicuous lines.

(b) tolerances for plumb

linear building line: ±1/2" (13) in any bay or 20' (6100) maximum nor ±3/4" (19) in 40' (12.2 m) or more

cross-sectional dimensions: -1/4" (6); +1/2" (13)

(c) plan, and cross-sectional tolerances

5-5. Limestone Installation

Description

This section describes the allowable setting tolerances for limestone regardless of the type of structural system being used. These tolerances assume that sufficient clearance and correct anchorage devices have been detailed and specified.

Industry Standards

The tolerances in this section are compiled from various industry standards.

Allowable Tolerances

Tolerances for level are shown in Fig. 5-5a and include exposed lintels, sills, parapets, horizontal grooves, and other conspicuous lines.

As shown in Fig. 5-5b, plumb tolerances require that deviations not exceed $\frac{1}{4}$ in (6 mm) in any 10-ft (3050-mm) length nor $\frac{3}{8}$ in (10 mm) for a single story or in any 20-ft (6100-mm) section. For external corners, expansion joints, and other conspicuous lines the tolerance is neither more than $\pm\frac{1}{4}$ in (6 mm) in 20 ft (6100 mm) nor $\frac{3}{4}$ in (19 mm) in 40 ft (12.2 m) or more.

For the position of limestone components shown in plan and related portions of columns, walls, and partitions, the tolerance is $\pm\frac{1}{2}$ in (13 mm) in any bay or 20 ft (6100 mm) maximum. Plan dimensions must not vary more than $\frac{3}{4}$ in (19 mm) total in 40 ft (12.2 m) or more. Thickness tolerances are $-\frac{1}{4}$ in (6 mm) and $+\frac{1}{2}$ in (13 mm).

Related Sections

5-3. Limestone Fabrication

12-5. Detailing for Stone on Concrete

14-6. Detailing for Stone on Steel Systems

15-3. Detailing for Stone on Masonry Backup

Figure 5-6

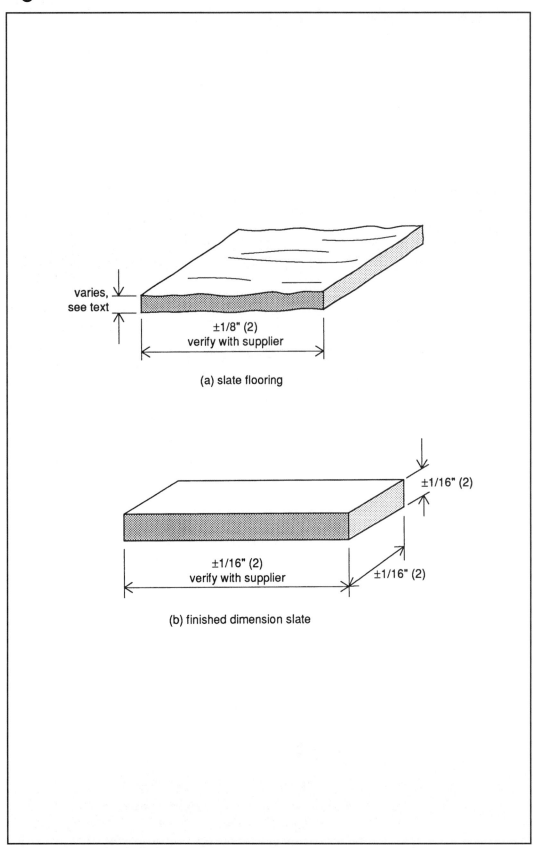

varies,
see text

±1/8" (2)
verify with supplier

(a) slate flooring

±1/16" (2)

±1/16" (2)
verify with supplier

±1/16" (2)

(b) finished dimension slate

5-6. Fabrication and Erection Tolerances for Slate

Description

Structural slate (slate used for uses other than roofing) is used for flooring, interior wall facing, stair treads and risers, window sills, and occasionally for exterior spandrels and facings. Because slate has natural cleavage planes and is often fabricated with a natural split face, tolerances for thickness can vary widely, depending on the fabricator, job conditions, size of panel, and other variables.

Industry Standards

There are no established industry standards for slate tolerances. However, for dimensional stone the standards of the Marble Institute of America, Inc., are often used.

Allowable Tolerances

As shown in Fig. 5-6, many manufacturers cut structural split-face and flooring slate to within $\pm\frac{1}{8}$ in (3 mm) in length and width. Dimensional stone is often finished by honing or sand rubbing to within $\pm\frac{1}{16}$ in (2 mm).

For natural cleft flooring, slabs are often specified by a thickness range: $\frac{3}{8}$ to $\frac{1}{2}$ in, $\frac{1}{2}$ to $\frac{5}{8}$ in, $\frac{5}{8}$ to $\frac{3}{4}$ in, and $\frac{3}{4}$ to 1 in. Construction details should account for this possible range of thickness, even if the bottom of the slab is gauged, or smoothed.

Larger tolerances for both size and thickness may exist for imported slate.

Related Section

5-2. Marble Fabrication

Figure 5-7

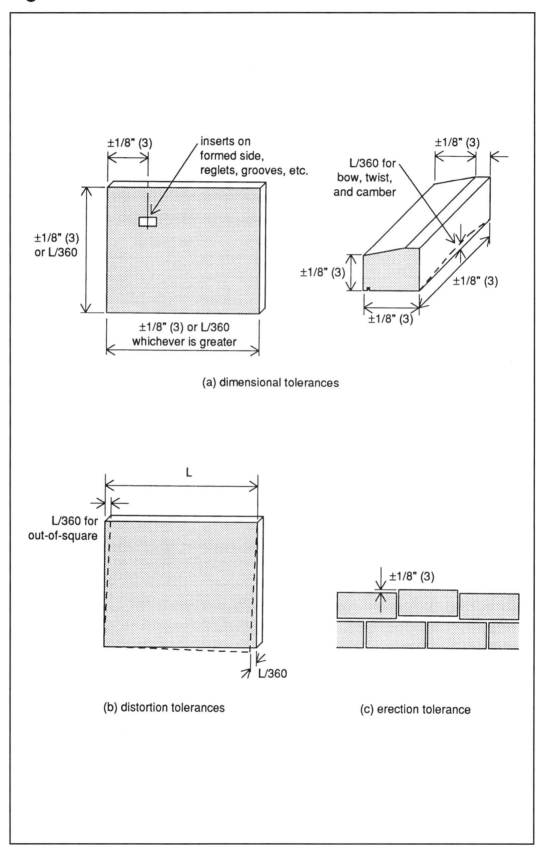

(a) dimensional tolerances

(b) distortion tolerances

(c) erection tolerance

5-7. Cast Stone Fabrication and Erection

Description

Cast stone is an architectural precast concrete building stone manufactured from Portland cement and coarse and fine aggregates to simulate natural stone. It is used for facing, trim, ornaments, columns, moldings, and copings, among other architectural elements.

Industry Standard

Technical Manual, Cast Stone Institute, Winter Park, FL, 1990.

Allowable Tolerances

Fabrication and erection tolerances established by the Cast Stone Institute are illustrated in Fig. 5-7. The tolerances of $\frac{1}{8}$ in (3 mm) or length divided by 360, whichever is greater, apply to all sectional dimensions, to length, and to distortions of twist, square, and camber.

For inserts and dowel holes on the back, or unformed side, the location tolerance is increased from $\frac{1}{8}$ in (3 mm) to $\frac{3}{8}$ in (10 mm).

Related Sections

12-5. Detailing for Stone on Concrete

14-6. Detailing for Stone on Steel Systems

Figure 6-1

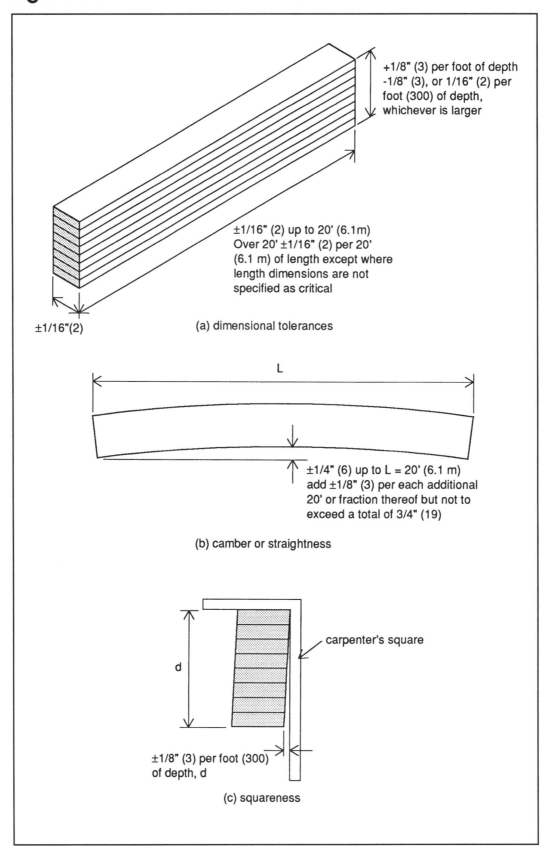

+1/8" (3) per foot of depth
-1/8" (3), or 1/16" (2) per foot (300) of depth, whichever is larger

±1/16" (2) up to 20' (6.1m)
Over 20' ±1/16" (2) per 20' (6.1 m) of length except where length dimensions are not specified as critical

±1/16"(2)

(a) dimensional tolerances

L

±1/4" (6) up to L = 20' (6.1 m) add ±1/8" (3) per each additional 20' or fraction thereof but not to exceed a total of 3/4" (19)

(b) camber or straightness

d

carpenter's square

±1/8" (3) per foot (300) of depth, d

(c) squareness

Chapter 6

Structural Lumber

6-1. Glued Laminated Timber Fabrication

Description

The tolerances shown here are for standard glued laminated timber for either interior or exterior use. The depth tolerances do not apply to special tapered or curved shapes.

Industry Standards

AITC 113-86, *Standard for Dimensions of Structural Glued Laminated Timber,* American Institute of Timber Construction, Englewood, CO, 1986.

ANSI/AITC 190.1, *American National Standard for Wood Products—Structural Glued Laminated Timber,* American Institute of Timber Construction, Englewood, CO, 1992.

Allowable Tolerances

The tolerances established by the American Institute of Timber Construction are shown in Fig. 6-1 and are based on dimensions at the time of manufacture. When length dimensions are not specified as critical the tolerances shown in the diagram do not apply. The camber or straightness tolerances are for the section at the time of manufacture without any tolerance for dead load deflection. Camber tolerances do not apply to curved members. Squareness tolerances are for standard rectangular sections and do not apply to specially shaped sections.

Related Section

6-6. Rough Lumber Framing

Figure 6-2

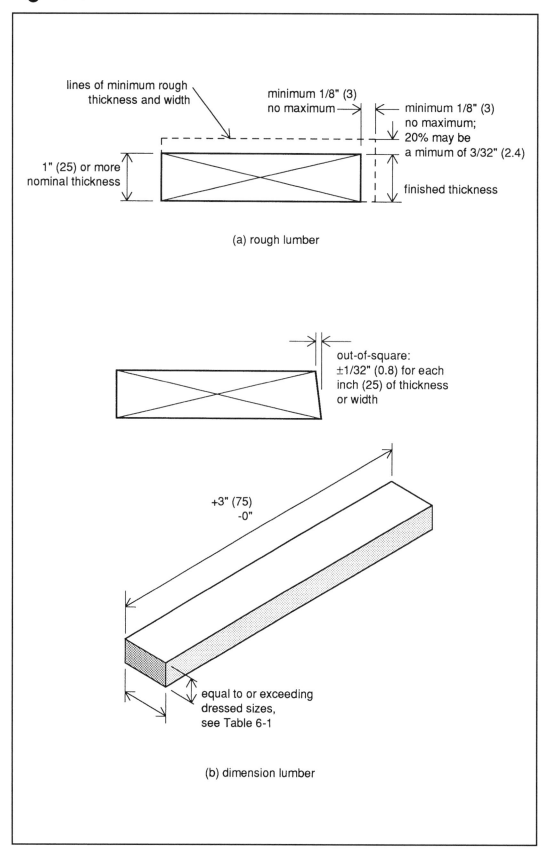

lines of minimum rough
thickness and width

minimum 1/8" (3)
no maximum

minimum 1/8" (3)
no maximum;
20% may be
a mimum of 3/32" (2.4)

1" (25) or more
nominal thickness

finished thickness

(a) rough lumber

out-of-square:
±1/32" (0.8) for each
inch (25) of thickness
or width

+3" (75)
-0"

equal to or exceeding
dressed sizes,
see Table 6-1

(b) dimension lumber

6-2. Manufacturing Tolerances for Structural Lumber

Description

This section includes dimensional lumber and timbers generally used for structural and rough framing. It does not include board lumber often used for site-built finish carpentry items.

The *American Softwood Lumber Standard* classifies dimensional lumber as lumber from 2 in (51 mm) in nominal thickness to, but not including, 5 in (127 mm) in nominal thickness, and 2 in or more in nominal width. Timber is lumber 5 in or more (127 mm or more) nominally in the least dimension.

Industry Standard

PS20-70, *Voluntary Product Standard PS20-70, American Softwood Lumber Standard,* National Institute of Standards and Technology, Gaithersberg, MD, 1986.

Allowable Tolerances

Dimensional lumber may be ordered either as dry or green lumber. *Dry lumber* is lumber which has been seasoned or dried to a moisture content of 19 percent or less, while *green lumber* has a moisture content greater than 19 percent. As shown in Fig. 6-2a, rough lumber size cannot be less than $\frac{1}{8}$ in (3.2 mm) thicker or wider than the corresponding minimum finished thickness or width, except that 20 percent of a shipment cannot be less than $\frac{3}{32}$ in (2.4 mm) thicker or wider.

Dressed sizes for dimensional lumber must be equal to or exceed those shown in Table 6-1. These sizes are for dry lumber. Shrinkage that may occur after dressing to dry sizes can be up to 1 percent for each 4 points of moisture content below the applicable maximum or 0.7 percent for each 4 points of moisture content reduction for redwood, western red cedar, and northern white cedar. Sizes for timbers are only applicable for green lumber and are $\frac{1}{2}$ in (13 mm) smaller than the nominal dimension.

Table 6-1
Minimum Sizes of Dressed, Dry Dimensional Lumber

Nominal thickness, in (mm)	Minimum actual thickness, in (mm)	Nominal width, in (mm)	Minimum actual width, in (mm)
2 (51)	$1\frac{1}{2}$ (38)	4 (100)	$3\frac{1}{2}$ (89)
$2\frac{1}{2}$ (64)	2 (51)	6 (150)	$5\frac{1}{2}$ (140)
3 (76)	$2\frac{1}{2}$ (64)	8 (200)	$7\frac{1}{4}$ (184)
$3\frac{1}{2}$ (89)	3 (76)	10 (250)	$9\frac{1}{4}$ (235)
4 (100)	$3\frac{1}{2}$ (89)	12 (300)	$11\frac{1}{4}$ (286)
$4\frac{1}{2}$ (114)	4 (102)	14 (357)	$13\frac{1}{4}$ (336)

SOURCE: *Voluntary Product Standard, PS20-70,* National Institute of Standards and Technology.

Related Sections

6-3. Plywood Manufacturing

6-4. Particleboard Manufacturing

7-1. Manufacturing Tolerances for Board Lumber

Figure 6-3

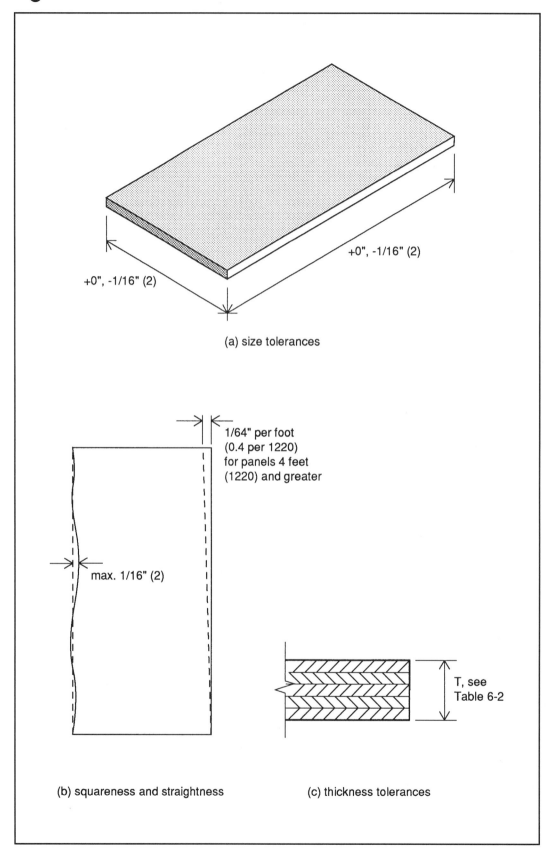

+0", -1/16" (2)

+0", -1/16" (2)

(a) size tolerances

1/64" per foot
(0.4 per 1220)
for panels 4 feet
(1220) and greater

max. 1/16" (2)

T, see
Table 6-2

(b) squareness and straightness

(c) thickness tolerances

6-3. Plywood Manufacturing

Description

This section includes tolerances for plywood intended for construction and industrial use and which conform to *U.S. Product Standard PS 1-83.*

Industry Standard

PS 1-83, *U.S. Product Standard PS 1-83 for Construction and Industrial Plywood,* National Institute of Standards and Technology, Gaithersberg, MD, 1983. Office of Product Standards Policy.

Allowable Tolerances

Tolerances are shown in Fig. 6-3. Squareness tolerances for panels 4 ft (1220 mm) and greater are shown in the diagram. For panels less than 4 ft wide the squareness tolerance is $\frac{1}{16}$ in (2 mm) measured along the short dimension.

Thickness tolerances for various thicknesses and types of plywood are shown in Table 6-2. Thickness tolerances are based on a moisture content of 9 percent oven dry weight and are measured with a micrometer using an anvil pressure of not less than 5 psi (34 kPa) or more than 10 psi (69 kPa).

Table 6-2
Plywood Thickness Tolerances

Panel type	Tolerance, in (mm)
Sanded panels $\frac{3}{4}$ in (19 mm) and less	$\pm\frac{1}{64}$ (0.4)
Sanded panels over $\frac{3}{4}$ in (19 mm)	$\pm3\%$ of specified thickness
Unsanded, touch sanded, and overlaid panels $\frac{13}{16}$ in (20 mm) and less	$\pm\frac{1}{32}$ (0.8)
Unsanded, touch sanded, and overlaid panels over $\frac{13}{16}$ in (20 mm)	$\pm5\%$ of specified thickness

SOURCE: *Voluntary Product Standard PS 1-83,* National Institute of Standards and Technology.

Related Sections

6-4. Particleboard Manufacturing

6-5. Fiberboard Manufacturing

Figure 6-4

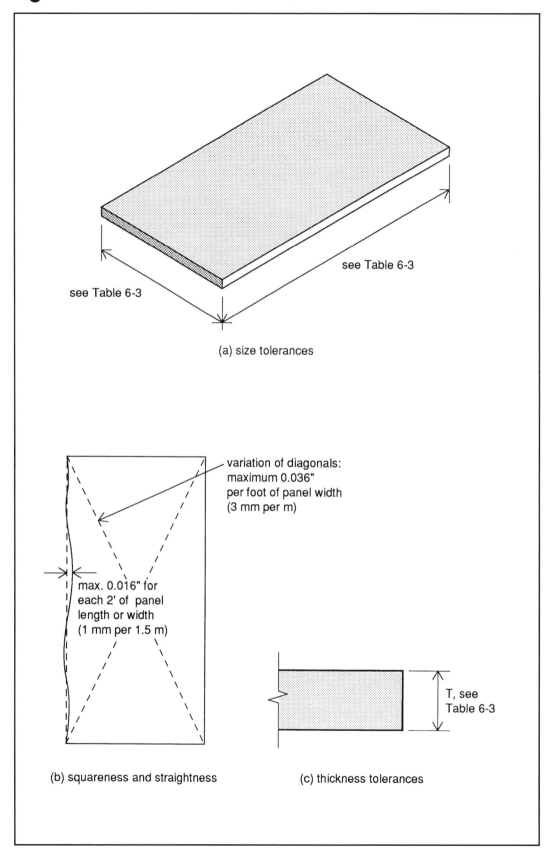

(a) size tolerances

variation of diagonals:
maximum 0.036"
per foot of panel width
(3 mm per m)

max. 0.016" for
each 2' of panel
length or width
(1 mm per 1.5 m)

T, see
Table 6-3

(b) squareness and straightness

(c) thickness tolerances

6-4. Particleboard Manufacturing

Description

Particleboard is a panel product made from particles of wood and wood fibers bonded together with synthetic resins or other suitable bonding systems. There are two basic categories, one for general construction and one for flooring products. Within each category are several grades developed for various uses. In the grade designations in Tables 6-3 and 6-4, H means high density, M means medium density, LD means low density, D means decking, and PBU means underlayment.

Industry Standards

ANSI/NPA A 208.1-1993, *American National Standard, Particleboard,* National Particleboard Association, Gaithersberg, MD, 1993.

Allowable Tolerances

Tolerances for squareness and straightness are illustrated in Fig. 6-4. Tolerances for squareness are measured when the length and width tolerances are satisfied. Tolerances for length, width, and thickness of particleboard depend on the type and grade. The tolerances for the two categories are listed in Tables 6-3 and 6-4. The average thickness is the average of eight measurements taken at each panel corner and at the midlength of each panel edge.

Table 6-3
Tolerances for Particleboard

Grade tolerances, in (mm)								
H-1	H-2	H-3	M-1	M-2	M-3	M-S	LD-1	LD-2
Length and width								
±0.080 (2.0)	±0.080 (2.0)	±0.080 (2.0)	±0.080 (2.0)	±0.080 (2.0)	±0.080 (2.0)	±0.080 (2.0)	±0.080 (2.0)	±0.080 (2.0)
Average panel thickness from nominal (sanded panels only)								
±0.008 (0.200)	±0.008 (0.200)	±0.008 (0.200)	±0.010 (0.250)	±0.008 (0.200)	±0.008 (0.200)	±0.010 (0.250)	+0.005 (+0.125) −0.015 (−0.375)	+0.005 (+0.125) −0.015 (−0.375)

SOURCE: ANSI/NPA A208.1-1993, National Particleboard Association.

Related Sections

6-3. Plywood Manufacturing

6-5. Fiberboard Manufacturing

Table 6-4
Tolerances for Particleboard Flooring Products

Grade tolerances, in (mm)		
PBU	D-2	D-3
Length and width		
+0, −0.160 (+0, −4.0)	±0.080 (2.0)	±0.080 (2.0)
Average panel thickness from nominal (sanded panels only)		
±0.015 (0.375)	±0.015 (0.375)	±0.015 (0.375)

SOURCE: ANSI/NPA A208.1-1993, National Particleboard Association.

Figure 6-5

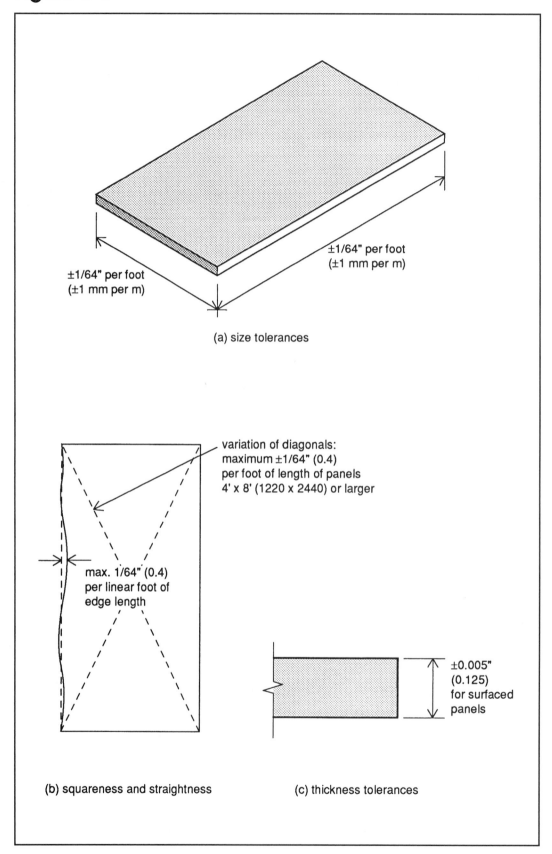

±1/64" per foot
(±1 mm per m)

±1/64" per foot
(±1 mm per m)

(a) size tolerances

variation of diagonals:
maximum ±1/64" (0.4)
per foot of length of panels
4' x 8' (1220 x 2440) or larger

max. 1/64" (0.4)
per linear foot of
edge length

±0.005"
(0.125)
for surfaced
panels

(b) squareness and straightness

(c) thickness tolerances

6-5. Fiberboard Manufacturing

Description

Medium-density fiberboard is a panel product made from lignocellulosic fibers bonded together with a synthetic resin or other suitable binders under heat and pressure.

Industry Standard

ANSI/NPA A 208.2-1994, *Medium Density Fiberboard for Interior Use,* National Particleboard Association, Gaithersberg, MD, 1994.

Allowable Tolerances

Tolerances for fiberboard are illustrated in Fig. 6-5. For panels smaller than 4 ft by 8 ft (1220 mm by 2440 mm) the length and width tolerance is $\pm\frac{1}{64}$ in (0.4 mm) per linear foot. The thickness tolerances shown are for surfaced panels only. Tolerances for unsurfaced panels must be agreed to by the buyer and seller.

Related Sections

6-3. Plywood Manufacturing

6-4. Particleboard Manufacturing

Figure 6-6

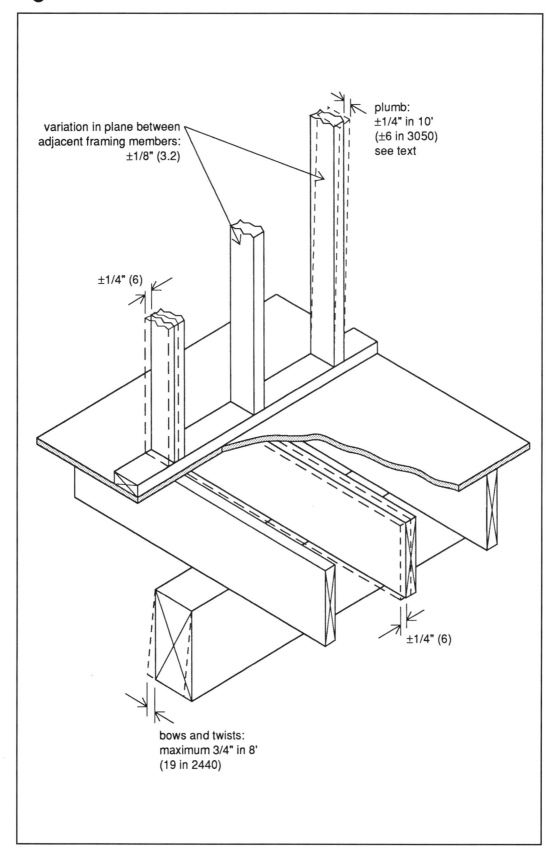

variation in plane between
adjacent framing members:
±1/8" (3.2)

plumb:
±1/4" in 10'
(±6 in 3050)
see text

±1/4" (6)

±1/4" (6)

bows and twists:
maximum 3/4" in 8'
(19 in 2440)

6-6. Rough Lumber Framing

Description

Rough lumber framing includes posts, beams, joists, rafters, studs, and other wood framing for residential or commercial construction. It also includes glued laminated timber and heavy timber construction.

Industry Standards

Quality Standards for the Professional Remodeler, 2nd ed., 1991, National Association of Home Builders Remodelors™ Council, Washington, DC, 1991.

Insurance/Warranty Documents, Home Owners Warranty Corporation, Arlington, VA, 1987.

Spectext Section 06112, *Framing and Sheathing,* Construction Sciences Research Foundation, Baltimore, 1989.

Allowable Tolerances

There is not a single, fixed standard for rough lumber framing tolerances. Various documents and industry practices refer to a variety of measurements, as shown in Fig. 6-6. In most cases, positional tolerances of framing members of dimensional lumber [less than 5 in (127 mm) in nominal dimension] are not critical for the application of finish materials. A tolerance of $\pm\frac{1}{4}$ in (6 mm) is frequently used and is acceptable. For heavy timber construction a tolerance of $\pm\frac{1}{2}$ in (13 mm) is often used.

However, plumbness tolerance is important because out-of-plumb walls and partitions can be noticeable and can affect the successful application of many finish materials. The *Quality Standards for the Professional Remodeler* and the *Insurance/Warranty Documents* require that walls be plumb to within $\frac{1}{4}$ in (6 mm) in any 32-in (813-mm) vertical measurement. However, a smaller tolerance of $\frac{1}{4}$ in in 10 ft (6 mm in 3050 mm) is often recommended for gypsum wallboard and plaster applications. For gypsum wallboard application, the maximum misalignment of adjacent framing members must not exceed $\frac{1}{8}$ in (3.2 mm).

A tolerance of $\frac{1}{4}$ in in 10 ft provides a reasonable tolerance for carpenters while allowing gypsum wallboard to be installed without excessive shimming when tighter tolerances of the wallboard surface are required. For example, if a $\frac{1}{8}$ in in 8 ft (3.2 mm in 2440 mm) plumbness is required for a thin-set mortar application of ceramic tile, the gypsum board can be shimmed from a $\frac{1}{4}$-in tolerance to the $\frac{1}{8}$-in tolerance. However, most wallboard contractors prefer not to shim, so the specifier may want to require that the smaller tolerance be built into the framing specifications.

Related Sections

6-2. Manufacturing Tolerances for Structural Lumber

6-7. Wood Floor Framing and Subflooring

6-9. Metal Plate Connected Wood Truss Erection

6-10. Prefabricated Structural Wood

9-1. Lightgage Framing for Gypsum Wallboard

9-5. Floor and Wall Tile

Figure 6-7

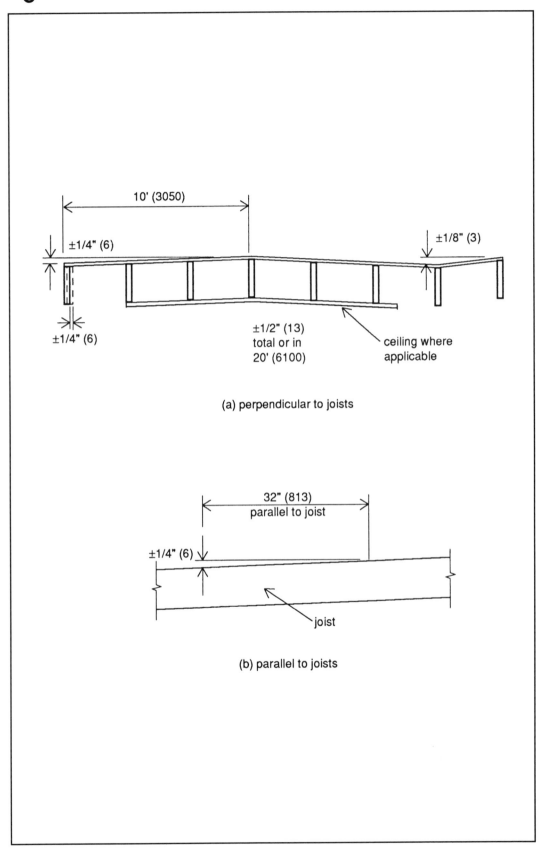

10' (3050)

±1/4" (6)

±1/8" (3)

±1/4" (6)

±1/2" (13)
total or in
20' (6100)

ceiling where
applicable

(a) perpendicular to joists

32" (813)
parallel to joist

±1/4" (6)

joist

(b) parallel to joists

6-7. Wood Floor Framing and Subflooring

Description

This section includes wood floors framed with standard wood joists and covered with sub-flooring of plywood, particleboard, or other sheet material as a base for underlayment and other finish flooring.

Industry Standards

Quality Standards for the Professional Remodeler, 2nd ed., National Association of Home Builders Remodelors™ Council, Washington, DC, 1991.

Insurance/Warranty Documents, Home Owners Warranty Corporation, Arlington, VA, 1987.

GA-216, *Standard Specification for the Application and Finishing of Gypsum Board,* The Gypsum Association, Washington, DC, 1993.

Spectext Section 06112, *Framing and Sheathing,* Construction Sciences Research Foundation, Baltimore, 1989.

Section 2307, "Deflection," *Uniform Building Code,* International Conference of Building Officials, Whittier, CA, 1991.

Allowable Tolerances

As with rough framing, there is no single accepted tolerance for flatness of wood subfloors. (See Fig. 6-7.) In most cases, the required level depends on the type of finish surface used and other considerations, such as whether factory built cabinets will be placed on an uneven floor, requiring shimming.

In general, a level tolerance of $\pm\frac{1}{4}$ in in 10 ft (6 mm in 3050 mm) for new construction is a reasonable expectation and is less than the maximum allowable deflection ($L/240$ for dead and live load) stated by the *Uniform Building Code.* It also allows for slight misalignments of supporting members. However, the *Quality Standards for the Professional Remodeler* and *Insurance/Warranty Documents* state a more generous maximum out-of-level tolerance of $\frac{1}{4}$ in in 32 in (6 mm in 813 mm) measured parallel to the joists.

For total variation in a floor surface of a room, the *Quality Standards for the Professional Remodeler* state a tolerance of $\pm\frac{1}{2}$ in in 20 ft (13 mm in 6100 mm) while the recommended specification of the Spectext master specifications is $\frac{1}{2}$ in in 30 ft (13 mm in 9144 mm).

If the floor framing is also supporting a gypsum wallboard ceiling below, The Gypsum Association requires that deflection not exceed $L/240$ of the span at full design load, where L is the span. In addition, the fastening surface of adjacent joists should not vary by more than $\frac{1}{8}$ in (3 mm).

As with other rough framing, if a smaller tolerance that those mentioned above is required for finish materials, such as ceramic tile or wood flooring, it should be specified.

Related Sections

6-2. Manufacturing Tolerances for Structural Lumber

6-6. Rough Lumber Framing

6-10. Prefabricated Structural Wood

9-5. Floor and Wall Tile

9-7. Wood Flooring

Figure 6-8

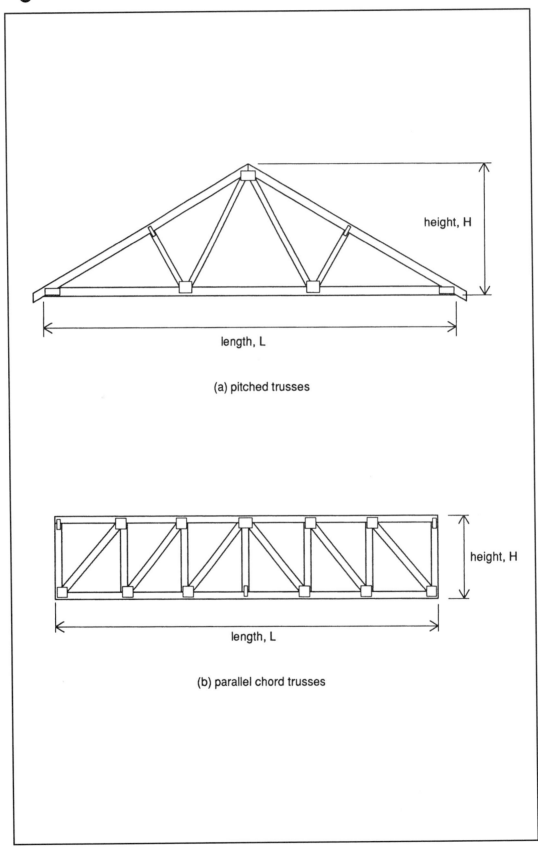

(a) pitched trusses

(b) parallel chord trusses

6-8. Metal Plate Connected Wood Truss Fabrication

Description

This section includes tolerances for wood trusses fabricated in accordance with the Truss Plate Institute's quality standards. Although the standards include many details of fabrication, the tolerances shown in this section include only those that are of most interest to architects and that can affect the final appearance of a structure.

Industry Standard

TPI-85, *TPI-85 Addendum, Appendix P, Quality Standard for Metal Plate Connected Wood Trusses,* Truss Plate Institute, Madison, WI, 1985.

Allowable Tolerances

Overall dimensional fabrication tolerances for wood trusses are shown in Fig. 6-8 and listed in Table 6-5. In addition, the Truss Plate Institute's *Quality Standard* includes tolerances for connector plate positioning, wood member joint tolerances, and other aspects of truss fabrication. Refer to TPI-85 for these details.

Table 6-5
Manufacturing Tolerances for Wood Trusses

Type of truss	Length		Height	
	Length L, ft (mm)	Variance from design dimension, in (mm)	Height H, ft (mm)	Variance from design dimension, in (mm)
Pitched*	Up to 30 (9144)	$\pm\frac{1}{4}$ (6)	Up to 5 (1524)	$\pm\frac{1}{8}$ (3)
	30 to 50 (9144 to 15,240)	$\pm\frac{3}{8}$ (10)	5 to 12 (1524 to 3660)	$\pm\frac{1}{4}$ (6)
	Over 50 (15,240)	$\pm\frac{1}{2}$ (13)	Over 12 (3660)	$\pm\frac{3}{8}$ (10)
Parallel chord†	Up to 30 (9144)	$\pm\frac{1}{4}$ (6)	Up to 2 (610)	$\pm\frac{1}{8}$ (3)
	Over 30 (9144)	$\pm\frac{3}{8}$ (10)	2 to 5 (610 to 1524)	$\pm\frac{1}{4}$ (6)
			Over 5 (1524)	$\pm\frac{3}{8}$ (10)

*Pitched trusses are defined as having slopes greater than 1:12.
†Parallel chord trusses are defined as having slopes equal to or less than 1:12.
SOURCE: Truss Plate Institute; reproduced with permission.

Related Section

6-9. Metal Plate Connected Wood Truss Erection

Figure 6-9

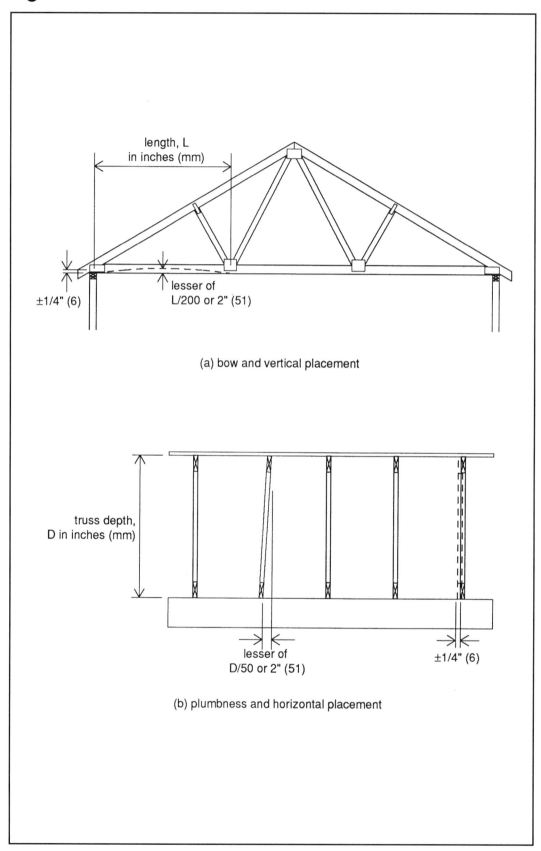

length, L
in inches (mm)

lesser of
L/200 or 2" (51)

±1/4" (6)

(a) bow and vertical placement

truss depth,
D in inches (mm)

lesser of
D/50 or 2" (51)

±1/4" (6)

(b) plumbness and horizontal placement

6-9. Metal Plate Connected Wood Truss Erection

Description

This section includes tolerances for wood trusses erected in accordance with the Truss Plate Institute's quality standards.

Industry Standard

HIB-91, *Handling, Installing & Bracing Metal Plate Connected Wood Trusses,* Truss Plate Institute, Madison, WI, 1991.

Allowable Tolerances

Placement tolerances are shown in Fig. 6-9. Bow tolerances include the overall bow or the bow in any chord or panel. Vertical and horizontal placement must be within $\pm \frac{1}{4}$ in (6 mm) of the placement points shown on the drawings. Special hangers or supports should be designed to accommodate this tolerance. In addition, top chord bearing parallel chord trusses will have a maximum gap of $\frac{1}{2}$ in (13 mm) between the inside of the bearing point and the first diagonal or vertical web at both ends of the truss.

Related Section

6-8. Metal Plate Connected Wood Truss Fabrication

Figure 6-10

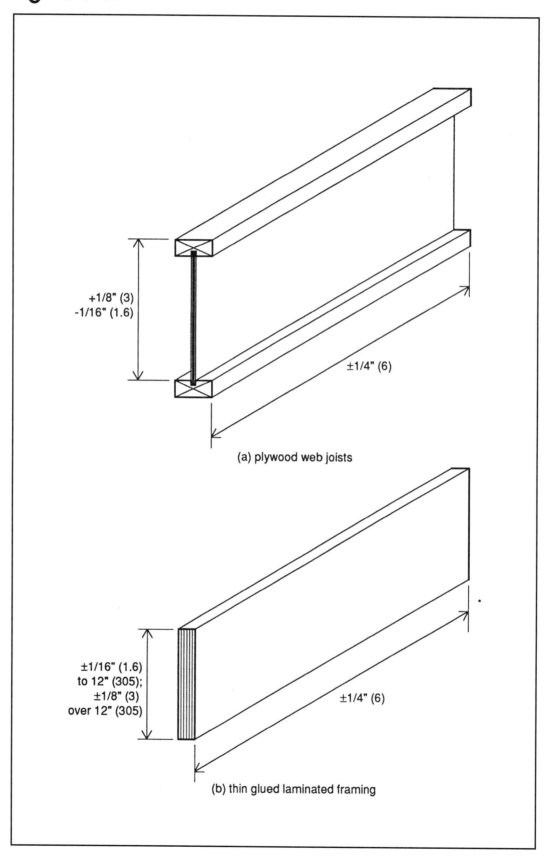

+1/8" (3)
-1/16" (1.6)

±1/4" (6)

(a) plywood web joists

±1/16" (1.6)
to 12" (305);
±1/8" (3)
over 12" (305)

±1/4" (6)

(b) thin glued laminated framing

6-10. Prefabricated Structural Wood

Description

Prefabricated structural wood includes products such as plywood web joists, thin glued laminated framing, wood chord metal joists, or any product fabricated in the factory and comprised entirely or mostly of wood products. Structural glued laminated timber is generally considered in a category by itself.

Industry Standards

Spectext Section 06151, *Wood Chord Metal Joists,* Construction Sciences Research Foundation, Baltimore, 1990.

Spectext Section 06196, *Plywood Web Joists,* Construction Sciences Research Foundation, Baltimore, 1990.

Allowable Tolerances

There are no industry standards for the fabrication or placement of prefabricated structural wood products. Each manufacturer has its own fabricating tolerances. In critical situations these tolerances should be verified with the manufacturer. However, the tolerances shown in Fig. 6-10 are representative of several proprietary products at the time of manufacturing.

Although master specifications may suggest a placement tolerance of $\pm\frac{1}{2}$ in (13 mm), prefabricated structural wood products can usually be placed within a $\frac{1}{4}$-in (6-mm) positional tolerance like rough carpentry.

Related Sections

6-1. Glued Laminated Timber Fabrication

6-6. Rough Lumber Framing

Figure 7-1

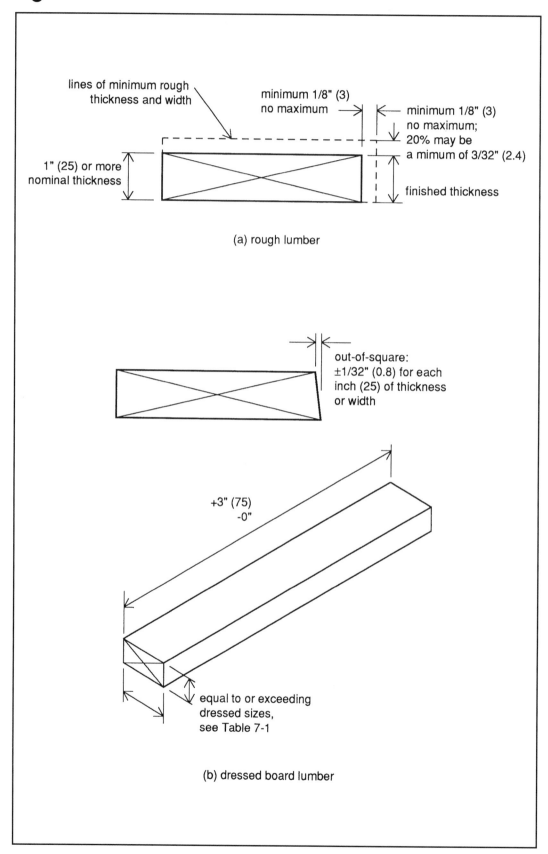

lines of minimum rough thickness and width

minimum 1/8" (3) no maximum

minimum 1/8" (3) no maximum; 20% may be a mimum of 3/32" (2.4)

1" (25) or more nominal thickness

finished thickness

(a) rough lumber

out-of-square: ±1/32" (0.8) for each inch (25) of thickness or width

+3" (75) -0"

equal to or exceeding dressed sizes, see Table 7-1

(b) dressed board lumber

Chapter 7

Finish Carpentry and Architectural Woodwork

7-1. Manufacturing Tolerances for Board Lumber

Description

This section includes board lumber generally used for site-fabricated finish carpentry and miscellaneous framing and blocking for other finish carpentry or architectural woodwork. It does not include standard wood molding shapes.

The *American Softwood Lumber Standard* classifies *board lumber* as lumber less than 2 in (51 mm) in nominal thickness and 2 in or more (51 mm or more) in nominal width. Boards less than 6 in (150 mm) in nominal width may be classified as *strips*. Southern pine board lumber is classified similarly except that boards are 1 in (25 mm) or more in width.

Industry Standard

PS20-70, *Voluntary Product Standard PS20-70, American Softwood Lumber Standard,* National Institute of Standards and Technology, Gaithersburg, MD, 1986.

Allowable Tolerances

Board lumber may be ordered either as rough lumber or dressed lumber, although dressed is the most common use. As shown in Fig. 7-1*a*, rough lumber size cannot be less than $\frac{1}{8}$ in (3.2 mm) thicker or wider than the corresponding minimum finished thickness or width, except that 20 percent of a shipment cannot be less than $\frac{3}{32}$ in (2.4 mm) thicker or wider.

Dressed sizes must be equal to or exceed those shown in Table 7-1. These sizes are for dry lumber at 19 percent moisture content or less. Shrinkage that may occur after dressing to dry sizes can be up to 1 percent for each 4 points of moisture content below the applicable maximum or 0.7 percent for each 4 points of moisture content reduction for redwood, western red cedar, and northern white cedar.

Table 7-1 Minimum Sizes of Dressed, Dry Finish, or Board Lumber

Nominal thickness, in (mm)	Minimum actual thickness, in (mm)	Nominal width, in (mm)	Minimum actual width, in (mm)
$\frac{1}{2}$ (13)	$\frac{7}{16}$ (11)	2 (50)	$1\frac{1}{2}$ (38)
$\frac{5}{8}$ (16)	$\frac{9}{16}$ (14)	3 (76)	$2\frac{1}{2}$ (64)
$\frac{3}{4}$ (19)	$\frac{5}{8}$ (16)	4 (100)	$3\frac{1}{2}$ (89)
1 (25)	$\frac{3}{4}$ (19)	5 (125)	$4\frac{1}{2}$ (114)
$1\frac{1}{4}$ (32)	1 (25)	6 (150)	$5\frac{1}{2}$ (140)
$1\frac{1}{2}$ (38)	$1\frac{1}{4}$ (32)	8 (200)	$7\frac{1}{4}$ (184)

SOURCE: Product Standard PS 20-70, National Institute of Standards and Technology.

Related Sections

6-2. Manufacturing Tolerances for Structural Lumber

6-3. Plywood Manufacturing

6-4. Particleboard Manufacturing

Figure 7-2

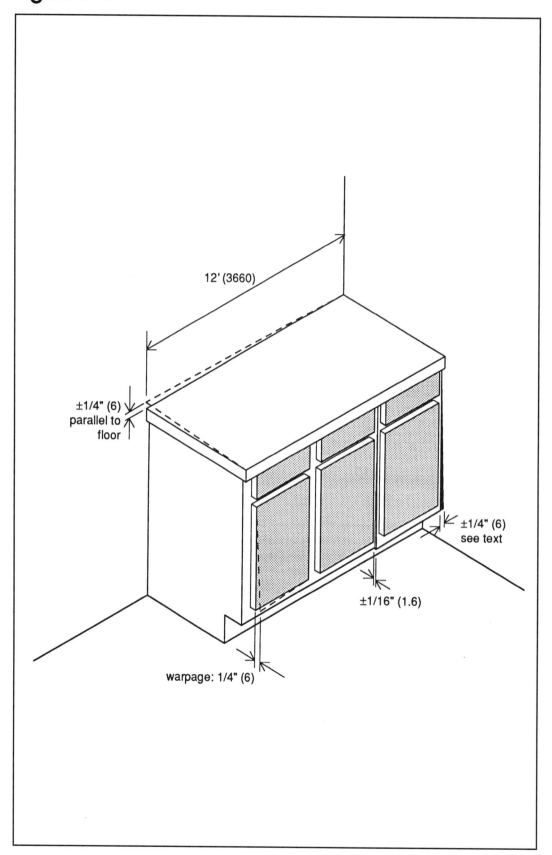

12' (3660)

±1/4" (6)
parallel to
floor

±1/4" (6)
see text

±1/16" (1.6)

warpage: 1/4" (6)

Finish Carpentry and Architectural Woodwork

7-2. Site-Built Cabinets and Countertops

Description

For some residential and small commercial projects, cabinets and countertops are built on site. In other cases, prebuilt cabinets are installed by finish carpenters. Such site-built and installed cabinets do not follow the tolerances of the Architectural Woodwork Institute described in later sections unless specifically stated in the specifications.

Few standards exist for finish carpentry work and tolerances for construction and installation often depend on the skill of the individual worker. Two standards that are often used for residential construction are included in this section. However, these should be considered maximum tolerances, as most competent finish carpenters work to tighter limits.

Industry Standards

Quality Standards for the Professional Remodeler, 2nd ed., National Association of Home Builders Remodelors™ Council, Washington, DC, 1991.

Insurance/Warranty Documents, Home Owners Warranty Corporation, Arlington, VA, 1987.

Spectext Section 06200, *Finish Carpentry,* Construction Sciences Research Foundation, Baltimore, 1990.

Allowable Tolerances

As shown in Fig. 7-2, the NAHB *Quality Standards* limit gaps between cabinets and the walls or ceiling to not more than $\frac{1}{4}$ in (6 mm). However, the Spectext master specifications recommend that finish carpentry be scribed when abutting other components with a maximum gap of $\frac{1}{32}$ in (0.8 mm). Adjacent cabinets should not be out of alignment by more than $\frac{1}{16}$ in (1.6 mm) nor should cabinet corners be out more than $\frac{1}{8}$ in (3.2 mm). Cabinet warpage should not exceed $\frac{1}{4}$ in (6.4 mm) as measured from the face frame to the point of furthermost warpage.

The NAHB *Quality Standards* state that countertops should be not more than $\frac{1}{4}$ in in 12 ft (6.4 mm in 3660 mm) out of parallel with the floor. However, NAHB quality standards for remodeling allow the countertop to be installed proportionately out of level if the floor is not level. In new construction, it is possible to shim below the base cabinets to bring a countertop level and conceal the shim space with the finish base.

Related Sections

7-5. Architectural Cabinets

7-6. Modular Cabinets

7-7. Countertops

Figure 7-3

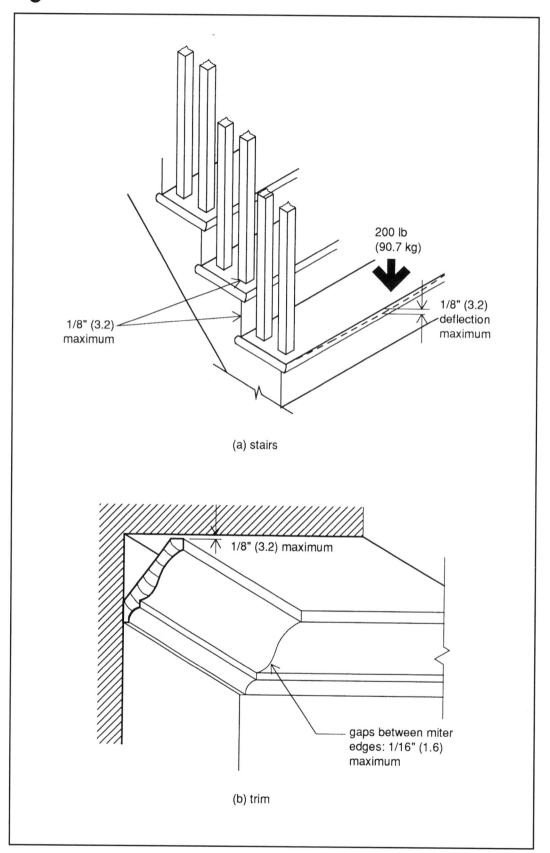

200 lb
(90.7 kg)

1/8" (3.2)
deflection
maximum

1/8" (3.2)
maximum

(a) stairs

1/8" (3.2) maximum

gaps between miter
edges: 1/16" (1.6)
maximum

(b) trim

7-3. Site-Built Stairs and Trim

Description

This section includes woodwork built at the job site by finish carpenters. Site-built stairs and trim are commonly used in residential and small commercial projects where factory built architectural woodwork is not required.

Industry Standard

Quality Standards for the Professional Remodeler, 2nd ed., National Association of Home Builders Remodelors™ Council, Washington, DC, 1991.

Allowable Tolerances

There are few standards for finish carpentry items such as stairs, shelving, and trim. Some of these are shown in Fig. 7-3. The NAHB *Quality Standards* recommend that the maximum vertical deflection of interior stair treads not exceed $\frac{1}{8}$ in (3.2 mm) under a load of 200 lb (90.7 kg). Cracks between adjoining parts that are designed to meet flush and cracks between interior stair railing parts should not exceed $\frac{1}{8}$ in (3.2 mm). As with site-built cabinets, most competent carpenters should be able to construct stairs and trim to tolerances closer to $\frac{1}{16}$ in (1.6 mm).

For trim and moldings, openings at joints between adjacent pieces of trim and at joints between moldings and adjacent surfaces should not exceed $\frac{1}{8}$ in (3.2 mm). Gaps at miter corners should not exceed $\frac{1}{16}$ in (1.6 mm).

Related Sections

7-4. Standing and Running Trim

7-10. Stairwork

Figure 7-4

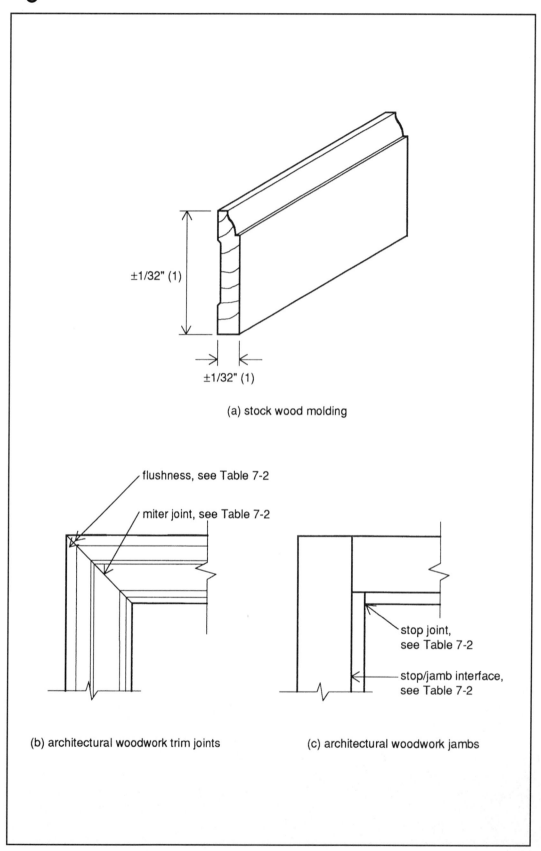

±1/32" (1)

±1/32" (1)

(a) stock wood molding

flushness, see Table 7-2

miter joint, see Table 7-2

stop joint,
see Table 7-2

stop/jamb interface,
see Table 7-2

(b) architectural woodwork trim joints

(c) architectural woodwork jambs

7-4. Standing and Running Trim

Description

Standing and running trim are shop-fabricated items such as door and window casings, base, cornice molding, and rails. *Standing trim* is an item of fixed length installed with a single length of wood. *Running trim* is a continuous item requiring more than one length, such as chair rails or baseboards.

Industry Standards

Architectural Woodwork Quality Standards, 6th ed., Architectural Woodwork Institute, Centreville, VA, 1993.

WM 4-85, *General Requirements for Wood Moulding,* Wood Moulding and Millwork Producers, Inc., Portland, OR, 1985.

Allowable Tolerances

For standard stock molding made to the Wood Moulding and Millwork Producers, Inc., standards, dimensional tolerances are $\pm\frac{1}{32}$ in (1 mm) as shown in Fig. 7-4a.

As with all tolerances for architectural woodwork built according to the AWI *Quality Standards,* tolerances depend on which of the three grades is specified. Premium is the highest grade. Test locations are shown in Fig. 7-4b and 7-4c. Joint tolerances for plant assembled joints are shown in Table 7-2. Methods of plant assembly of mitered joints are shown in Fig. 7-4.1.

Related Sections

7-3. Site-Built Stairs and Trim

7-17. Architectural Woodwork Installation

Table 7-2
Tightness and Flushness of Plant Assembled Joints

AWI grade tolerances, in (mm)

Location	Premium		Custom		Economy	
	Interior	Exterior	Interior	Exterior	Interior	Exterior
Miter joint	0.015 (0.38) wide by 20% of joint length	0.025 (0.6) wide by 30% of joint length	0.025 (0.6) wide by 20% of joint length	0.050 (1.3) wide by 30% of joint length	0.050 (1.3) wide by 20% of joint length	0.075 (1.9) wide by 30% of joint length
Stop/jamb interface	0.015 (0.38) × 3 (75), and no gap may occur within 48 (1200) of a similar gap	0.025 (0.6) × 6 (150), and no gap may occur within 24 (600) of a similar gap	0.025 (0.6) × 6 (150), and no gap may occur within 60 (1500) of a similar gap	0.050 (1.3) × 8 (200), and no gap may occur within 30 (760) of a similar gap	0.050 (1.3) × 8 (200), and no gap may occur within 72 (1830) of a similar gap	0.075 (1.9) × 10 (250), and no gap may occur within 36 (900) of a similar gap
Stop joint	0.015 (0.38)	0.025 (0.6)	0.025 (0.6)	0.050 (1.3)	0.050 (1.3)	0.075 (1.9)
Flushness	None	0.015 (0.38)	0.005 (0.13)	0.025 (0.6)	0.025 (0.6)	0.050 (1.3)

SOURCE: Reprinted with permission from *Architectural Woodwork Quality Standards*, 6th ed., Architectural Woodwork Institute.

Figure 7-4.1

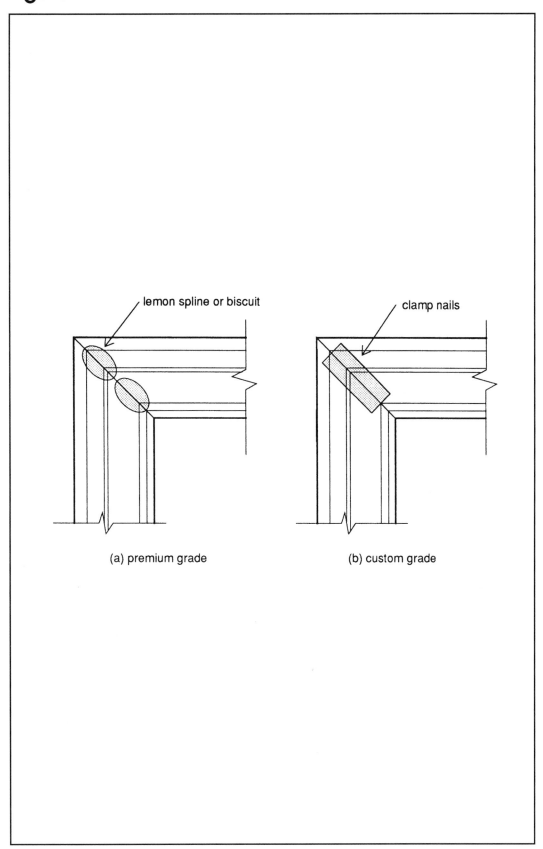

lemon spline or biscuit

clamp nails

(a) premium grade

(b) custom grade

Figure 7-5

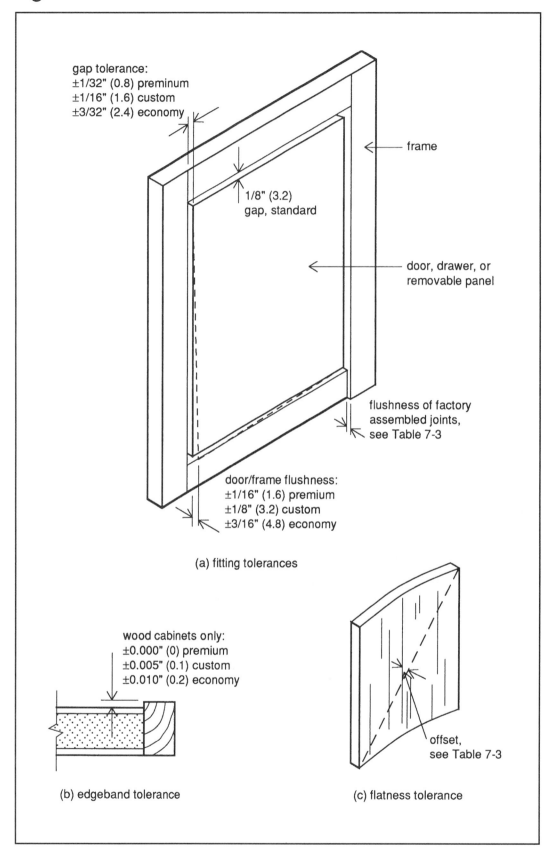

gap tolerance:
±1/32" (0.8) preminum
±1/16" (1.6) custom
±3/32" (2.4) economy

frame

1/8" (3.2)
gap, standard

door, drawer, or
removable panel

flushness of factory
assembled joints,
see Table 7-3

door/frame flushness:
±1/16" (1.6) premium
±1/8" (3.2) custom
±3/16" (4.8) economy

(a) fitting tolerances

wood cabinets only:
±0.000" (0) premium
±0.005" (0.1) custom
±0.010" (0.2) economy

offset,
see Table 7-3

(b) edgeband tolerance

(c) flatness tolerance

7-5. Architectural Cabinets

Description

This section includes custom-fabricated cabinets, teller lines, desks, display cases, and similar items designed for a particular project. Items included as architectural cabinets are completely manufactured and finished in the millshop with only minor assembly and finish touchup on the job site. The tolerances included here are for both wood veneer and high-pressure decorative laminate (HPDL) clad cabinets.

Industry Standard

Architectural Woodwork Quality Standards, 6th ed., Architectural Woodwork Institute, Centreville, VA, 1993.

Allowable Tolerances

Fabrication tolerances for the three standard Architectural Woodwork Institute (AWI) grades are shown in Fig. 7-5. These tolerances are the same for both wood veneer and laminate clad cabinets except where noted.

The gap tolerances are for the fitting of cabinet doors, drawers, and removable panels and are subject to the size of the component, allowable warp, hardware, and other installation variables. The gap tolerances listed are AWI recommended targeted deviations and are subject to such variables.

Flatness tolerances shown in Fig. 7-5*c* are measured diagonally after installation and the permitted values are listed in Table 7-3. These values are per linear foot or fraction thereof.

Table 7-3
Flushness and Flatness of Cabinet Joints and Panels

	Tolerance, in (mm)		
	Premium	Custom	Economy
Flushness, wood veneer	0.000 (0.0)	0.005 (0.1)	0.010 (0.2)
Flushness, laminate clad	0.010 (0.2)	0.020 (0.4)	0.030 (0.6)
Flatness (per linear foot)	0.027 (0.7)	0.036 (0.9)	0.050 (1.3)

SOURCE: Compiled from information in *Architectural Woodwork Quality Standards,* 6th ed., Architectural Woodwork Institute.

Related Sections

7-2. Site-Built Cabinets and Countertops

7-6. Modular Cabinets

7-7. Countertops

Figure 7-6

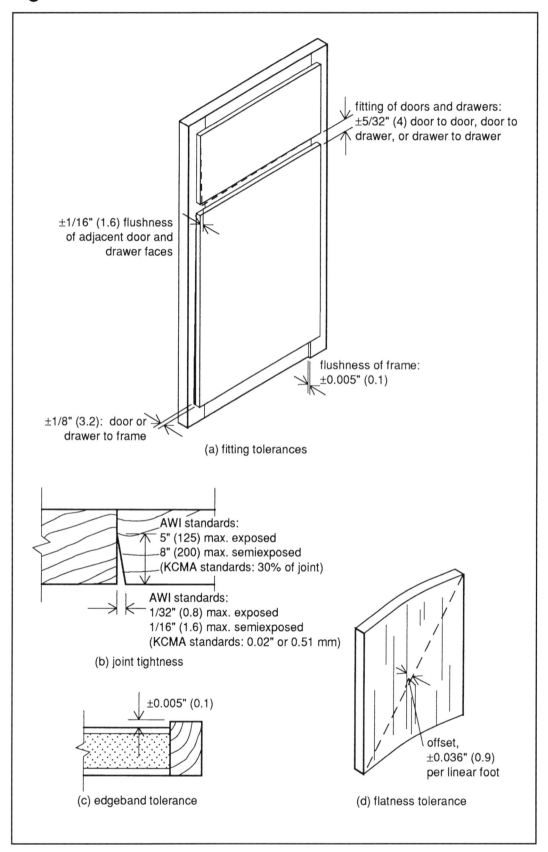

fitting of doors and drawers:
±5/32" (4) door to door, door to
drawer, or drawer to drawer

±1/16" (1.6) flushness
of adjacent door and
drawer faces

flushness of frame:
±0.005" (0.1)

±1/8" (3.2): door or
drawer to frame

(a) fitting tolerances

AWI standards:
5" (125) max. exposed
8" (200) max. semiexposed
(KCMA standards: 30% of joint)

AWI standards:
1/32" (0.8) max. exposed
1/16" (1.6) max. semiexposed
(KCMA standards: 0.02" or 0.51 mm)

(b) joint tightness

±0.005" (0.1)

(c) edgeband tolerance

offset,
±0.036" (0.9)
per linear foot

(d) flatness tolerance

7-6. Modular Cabinets

Description

Modular cabinets are mass-produced casework using a manufacturer's standard details and sizes. Modular cabinets are adapted for a particular job by using appropriate sizes and filler panels and finishing with custom countertops. The tolerances included here are for both wood veneer and high-pressure decorative laminate (HPDL) clad cabinets.

Industry Standards

Architectural Woodwork Quality Standards, 6th ed., Architectural Woodwork Institute, Centreville, VA, 1993.

ANSI/KCMA A161.1-1990, *Recommended Performance and Construction Standards for Kitchen and Vanity Cabinets,* Kitchen Cabinet Manufacturers Association, Reston, VA, 1990.

Allowable Tolerances

The various tolerances are shown in Fig. 7-6. The Architectural Woodwork Institute (AWI) standards do not have different tolerances for the three grades normally used; there is only one tolerance for each cabinet part.

In considering the tightness and flushness of plant assembled joints (Fig. 7-6*b*) a reasonable assessment should be made between the finished product and absolute compliance with the AWI standard. The Kitchen Cabinet Manufacturers Association standards are more stringent. For exposed exterior joints on the face of the cabinet a maximum gap of 0.02 in (0.51 mm) is allowed, with a maximum length of the gap of 30 percent of the total length of the joint. Refer to ANSI/KCMA A161.1-1990 for other gap limitations.

Related Sections

7-2. Site-Built Cabinets and Countertops

7-5. Architectural Cabinets

7-7. Countertops

Figure 7-7

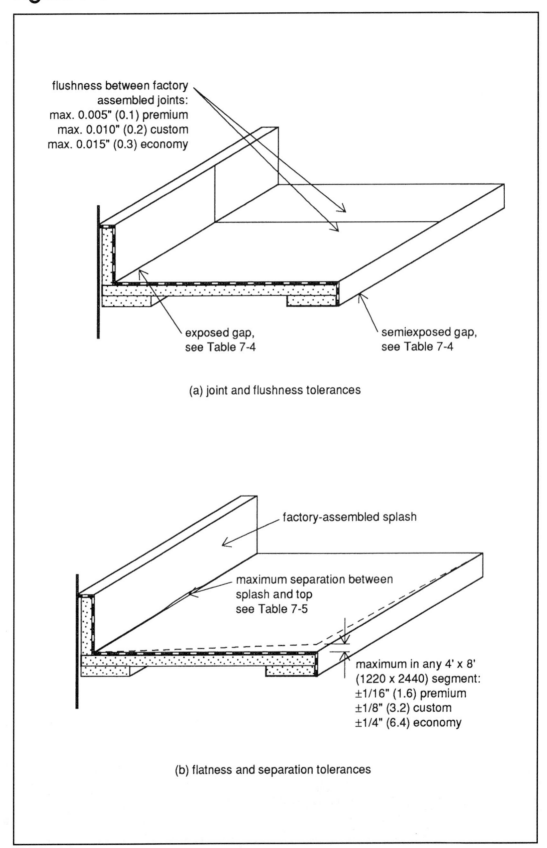

flushness between factory
assembled joints:
max. 0.005" (0.1) premium
max. 0.010" (0.2) custom
max. 0.015" (0.3) economy

exposed gap,
see Table 7-4

semiexposed gap,
see Table 7-4

(a) joint and flushness tolerances

factory-assembled splash

maximum separation between
splash and top
see Table 7-5

maximum in any 4' x 8'
(1220 x 2440) segment:
±1/16" (1.6) premium
±1/8" (3.2) custom
±1/4" (6.4) economy

(b) flatness and separation tolerances

7-7. Countertops

Description

The tolerances included in this section include Architectural Woodwork Institute (AWI) standards for countertops made with wood veneer, high-pressure decorative laminate (HPDL), post-formed HPDL, combination material tops, solid laminated tops (butcher block), and solid wood tops.

Industry Standard

Architectural Woodwork Quality Standards, 6th ed., Architectural Woodwork Institute, Centreville, VA, 1993.

Allowable Tolerances

Countertop tolerances are shown in Fig. 7-7. When the entire countertop is factory assembled the joint gap tolerances are as listed in Table 7-4 and shown in Fig. 7-7*a.*. When a factory assembled backsplash is jointed with a countertop in the field the tolerances are as listed in Table 7-5 and shown in Fig. 7-7*b.*

Table 7-4
Joint Tolerances for Factory Assembled Components*

	AWI grade tolerances, in (mm)		
	Premium	Custom	Economy
Maximum gap between exposed components	$\frac{1}{64}$ (0.4)	$\frac{1}{32}$ (0.8)	$\frac{1}{16}$ (1.6)
Maximum length of gap in exposed components	3 (76)	5 (127)	8 (204)
Maximum gap between semi-exposed components	$\frac{1}{32}$ (0.8)	$\frac{1}{64}$ (0.4)	$\frac{1}{8}$ (3.2)
Maximum length of gap in semi-exposed components	6 (152)	8 (204)	12 (305)

*No gap may occur within 48 in (1220 mm) of another gap (except adjustable shelf ends).
SOURCE: Compiled from information in *Architectural Woodwork Quality Standards,* 6th ed., Architectural Woodwork Institute.

Table 7-5
Joint Tolerance for Separation between Factory Assembled Backsplash and Top

	AWI grade tolerances, in (mm)		
	Premium	Custom	Economy
Maximum separation	$\frac{1}{64}$ (0.4) × 3 (76) and no more than 1 in per 4-ft (1220-mm) section of top	$\frac{1}{32}$ (0.8) × 5 (127) and no more than 1 in per 4-ft (1220-mm) section of top	$\frac{1}{16}$ (1.6) × 8 (203) and no more than 1 in per 4-ft (1220-mm) section of top

SOURCE: Compiled from information in *Architectural Woodwork Quality Standards,* 6th ed., Architectural Woodwork Institute.

Edges of laminate tops are eased and there can be a maximum visible overlap of 0.005 in (0.13 mm) for a length of not more than 1 in (25.4 mm) in any 24-in (610-mm) run.

Related Section

7-2. Site-Built Cabinets and Countertops

Figure 7-8

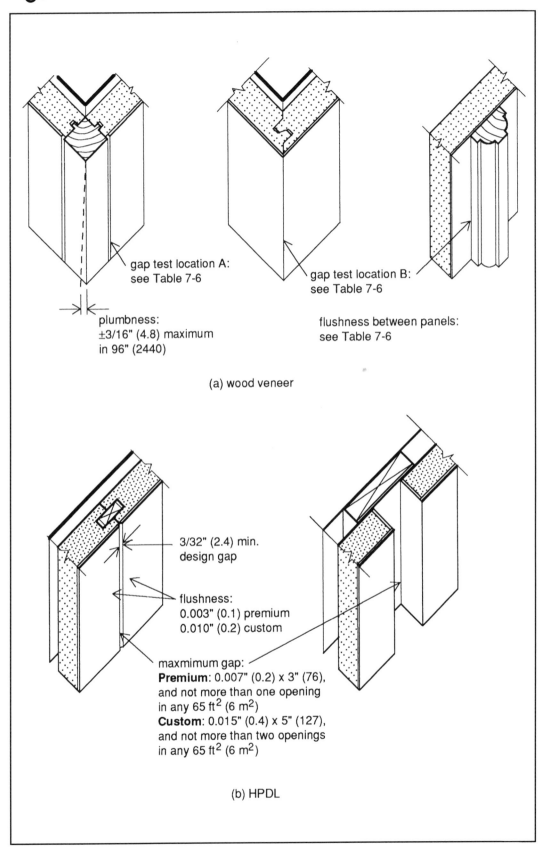

gap test location A:
see Table 7-6

plumbness:
±3/16" (4.8) maximum
in 96" (2440)

gap test location B:
see Table 7-6

flushness between panels:
see Table 7-6

(a) wood veneer

3/32" (2.4) min.
design gap

flushness:
0.003" (0.1) premium
0.010" (0.2) custom

maxmimum gap:
Premium: 0.007" (0.2) x 3" (76),
and not more than one opening
in any 65 ft^2 (6 m^2)
Custom: 0.015" (0.4) x 5" (127),
and not more than two openings
in any 65 ft^2 (6 m^2)

(b) HPDL

7-8. Flush Paneling

Description

This section includes tolerances for both flat wood veneer paneling and high-pressure decorative laminate (HPDL) paneling. Tolerances also include surface applied moldings. For stile and rail paneling refer to Sec. 7-9.

Industry Standard

Architectural Woodwork Quality Standards, 6th ed., Architectural Woodwork Institute, Centreville, VA, 1993.

Allowable Tolerances

Tolerances for wood veneer flush paneling are shown in Fig. 7-8*a* and 7-8.1 and listed in Table 7-6.

Tolerances for HPDL panels are shown in Fig. 7-8*b*. Note that there is no plant assembled economy grade. In considering the tightness and flushness of plant assembled joints for wood veneer paneling (Fig. 7-8*a*) a reasonable assessment should be made between the finished product and absolute compliance with the Architectural Woodwork Institute (AWI) standard.

Related Sections

7-4. Standing and Running Trim

7-9. Stile and Rail Paneling

Table 7-6
Joint Tolerances for Factory Assembled Components for Wood Veneer Paneling

AWI grade tolerances, in (mm)

	Premium		Custom		Economy	
	Interior	Exterior	Interior	Exterior	Interior	Exterior
Maximum gap: test location A	0.015 (0.38) wide by 20% of joint length	0.025 (0.6) wide by 30% of joint length	0.025 (0.6) wide by 20% of joint length	0.050 (1.3) wide by 30% of joint length	0.050 (1.3) wide by 20% of joint length	0.075 (1.9) wide by 30% of joint length
Maximum gap: test location B	0.015 (0.38) × 3 (75), and no gap may occur within 48 (1200) of a similar gap	0.025 (0.6) × 6 (150), and no gap may occur within 24 (600) of a similar gap	0.025 (0.6) × 6 (150), and no gap may occur within 60 (1500) of a similar gap	0.050 (1.3) × 8 (200), and no gap may occur within 30 (760) of a similar gap	0.050 (1.3) × 8 (200), and no gap may occur within 72 (1830) of a similar gap	0.075 (1.9) × 10 (250), and no gap may occur within 36 (900) of a similar gap
Flushness	None	0.015 (0.38)	0.005 (0.13)	0.025 (0.6)	0.025 (0.6)	0.050 (1.3)

SOURCE: Reprinted with permission from *Architectural Woodwork Quality Standards*, 6th ed., Architectural Woodwork Institute.

Figure 7-8.1

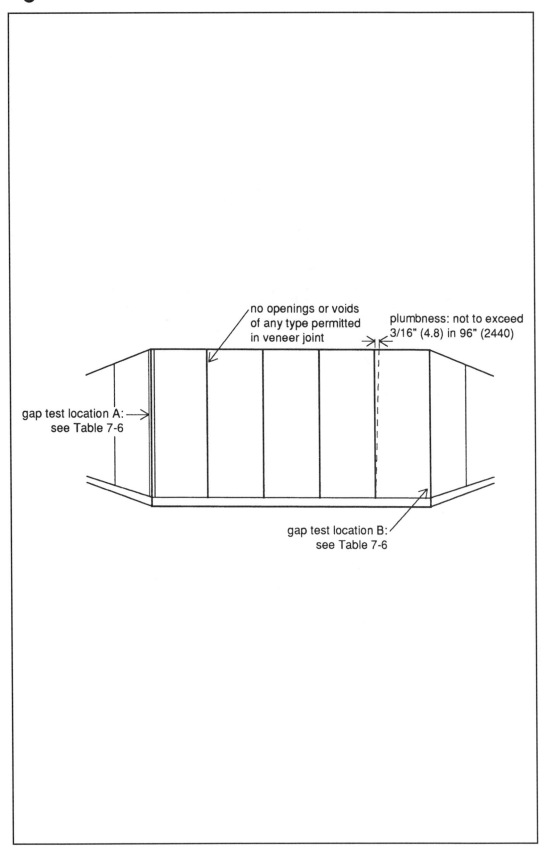

no openings or voids
of any type permitted
in veneer joint

plumbness: not to exceed
3/16" (4.8) in 96" (2440)

gap test location A:
see Table 7-6

gap test location B:
see Table 7-6

Figure 7-9

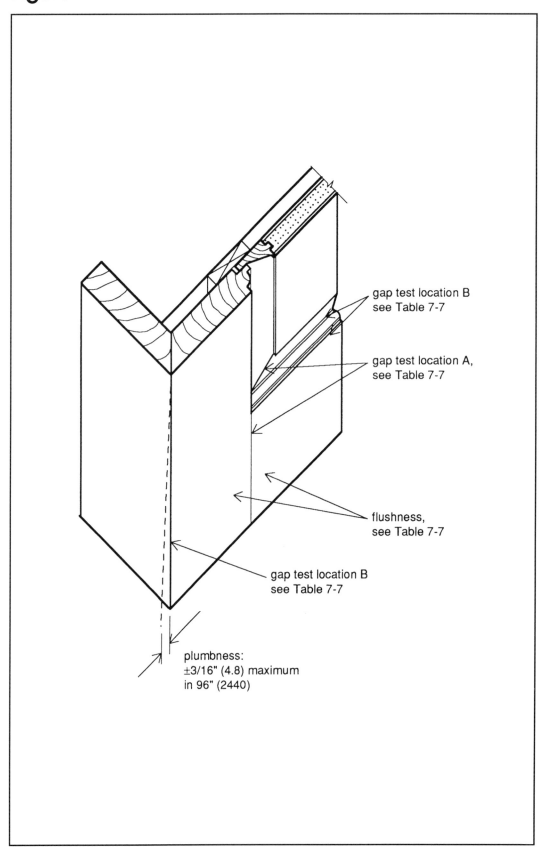

gap test location B
see Table 7-7

gap test location A,
see Table 7-7

flushness,
see Table 7-7

gap test location B
see Table 7-7

plumbness:
±3/16" (4.8) maximum
in 96" (2440)

7-9. Stile and Rail Paneling

Description

Stile and rail paneling consists either of flat or raised panels with wood veneer faces or of solid lumber, combined in a framework of stiles and rails. Surface applied molding may also be a part of the design.

Industry Standard

Architectural Woodwork Quality Standards, 6th ed., Architectural Woodwork Institute, Centreville, VA, 1993.

Allowable Tolerances

Tolerances for stile and rail paneling are shown in Fig. 7-9 and Fig. 7-9.1 and listed in Table 7-7.

In considering the tightness and flushness of plant assembled joints a reasonable assessment should be made between the finished product and absolute compliance with the Architectural Woodwork Institute (AWI) standard.

Related Sections

7-4. Standing and Running Trim

7-8. Flush Paneling

Table 7-7
Joint Tolerances for Factory Assembled Components for Stile and Rail Paneling

	AWI grade tolerances, in (mm)					
	Premium		Custom		Economy	
	Interior	Exterior	Interior	Exterior	Interior	Exterior
Maximum gap: test location A	0.015 (0.38) wide by 20% of joint length	0.025 (0.6) wide by 30% of joint length	0.025 (0.6) wide by 20% of joint length	0.050 (1.3) wide by 30% of joint length	0.050 (1.3) wide by 20% of joint length	0.075 (1.9) wide by 30% of joint length
Maximum gap: test location B	0.015 (0.38) × 3 (75), and no gap may occur within 48 (1200) of a similar gap	0.025 (0.6) × 6 (150), and no gap may occur within 24 (600) of a similar gap	0.025 (0.6) × 6 (150), and no gap may occur within 60 (1500) of a similar gap	0.050 (1.3) × 8 (200), and no gap may occur within 30 (760) of a similar gap	0.050 (1.3) × 8 (200), and no gap may occur within 72 (1830) of a similar gap	0.075 (1.9) × 10 (250), and no gap may occur within 36 (900) of a similar gap
Flushness	None	0.015 (0.38)	0.005 (0.13)	0.025 (0.6)	0.025 (0.6)	0.050 (1.3)

SOURCE: Reprinted with permission from *Architectural Woodwork Quality Standards*, 6th ed., Architectural Woodwork Institute.

Figure 7-9.1

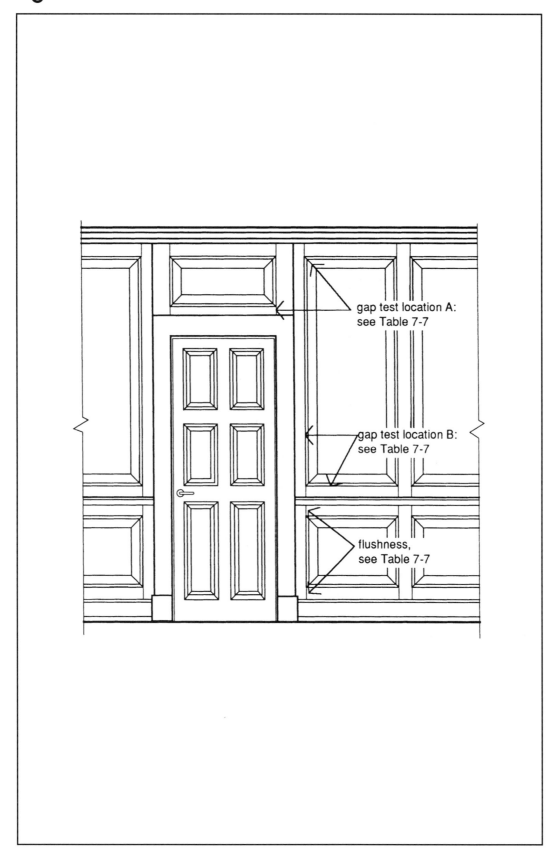

gap test location A:
see Table 7-7

gap test location B:
see Table 7-7

flushness,
see Table 7-7

Figure 7-10

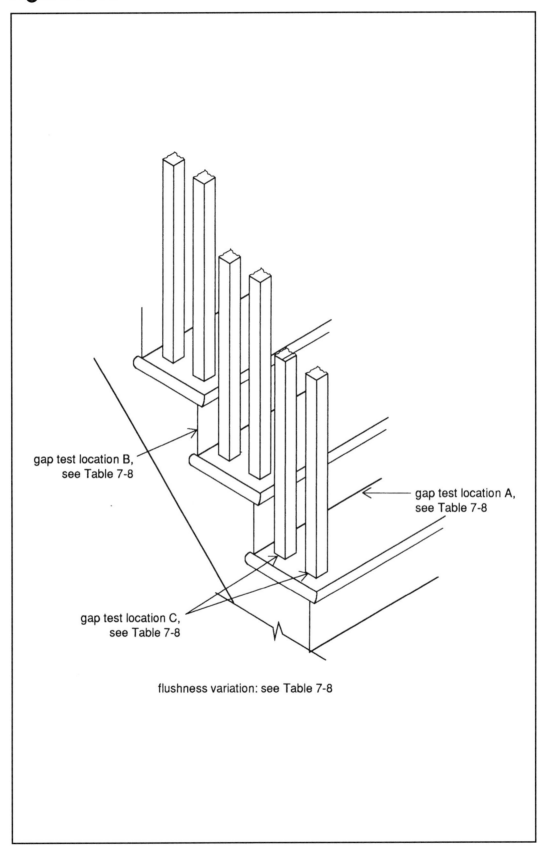

gap test location B,
see Table 7-8

gap test location A,
see Table 7-8

gap test location C,
see Table 7-8

flushness variation: see Table 7-8

7-10. Stairwork

Description

This section includes tolerances for fabrication of stairs in the millshop according to Architectural Woodwork Institute (AWI) quality standards.

Industry Standard

Architectural Woodwork Quality Standards, 6th ed., Architectural Woodwork Institute, Centreville, VA, 1993.

Allowable Tolerances

Tolerances for stairwork are listed in Table 7-8. The corresponding test locations for factory assembled joints are shown in Fig. 7-10. These tolerances apply to the stair components shown in the diagram as well as to handrail joints. Note that there are no joint tightness or flushness tolerances for economy grade stairs.

Table 7-8
Joint Tolerances for Factory Assembled Joints

	AWI grade tolerances, in (mm)			
	Premium		Custom	
	Interior	Exterior	Interior	Exterior
Maximum gap: test location A	0.015 (0.38) wide by 20% of joint length	0.025 (0.6) wide by 30% of joint length	0.025 (0.6) wide by 20% of joint length	0.025 (0.6) wide by 30% of joint length
Maximum gap: test location B	0.015 (0.38) × 3 (75), and no gap may occur within 48 (1200) of a similar gap	0.025 (0.6) × 6 (150), and no gap may occur within 24 (600) of a similar gap	0.025 (0.6) × 6 (150), and no gap may occur within 60 (1500) of a similar gap	0.050 (1.3) × 8 (200), and no gap may occur within 30 (760) of a similar gap
Maximum gap: test location C	0.015 (0.38)	0.025 (0.6)	0.025 (0.6)	0.050 (1.3)
Flushness	None	0.015 (0.38)	0.005 (0.13)	0.025 (0.6)

SOURCE: Reprinted with permission from *Architectural Woodwork Quality Standards,* 6th ed., Architectural Woodwork Institute.

In considering the tightness and flushness of plant assembled joints a reasonable assessment should be made between the finished product and absolute compliance with the AWI standard.

Related Section

7-3. Site-Built Stairs and Trim

Figure 7-11

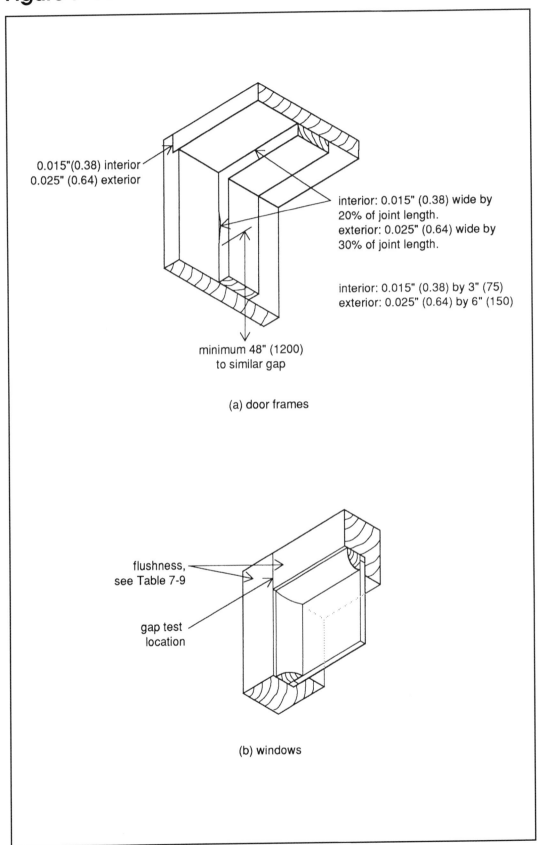

0.015"(0.38) interior
0.025" (0.64) exterior

interior: 0.015" (0.38) wide by
20% of joint length.
exterior: 0.025" (0.64) wide by
30% of joint length.

interior: 0.015" (0.38) by 3" (75)
exterior: 0.025" (0.64) by 6" (150)

minimum 48" (1200)
to similar gap

(a) door frames

flushness,
see Table 7-9

gap test
location

(b) windows

Finish Carpentry and Architectural Woodwork

7-11. Frames, Jambs, and Windows

Description

This section includes components manufactured under Architectural Woodwork Institute (AWI) quality standards and includes frames and jambs for interior and exterior doors, sidelights, transoms, and similar elements; also included are frames, sash, and exterior trim for custom-made wood windows.

Industry Standard

Architectural Woodwork Quality Standards, 6th ed., Architectural Woodwork Institute, Centreville, VA, 1993.

Allowable Tolerances

Tolerances for frames and jambs are shown in Fig. 7-11*a*. These only include tolerances for premium grade as there are no plant assembled frames and jambs in custom or economy grade. Tolerances for windows are shown in Fig. 7-11*b* and listed in Table 7-9.

Table 7-9
Joint Tolerances for Custom Windows

| | AWI grade tolerances, in (mm) | | | | | |
| | Premium | | Custom | | Economy | |
	Interior	Exterior	Interior	Exterior	Interior	Exterior
Maximum gap at test location	0.015 (0.38)	0.025 (0.6)	0.025 (0.6)	0.050 (1.3)	0.050 (1.3)	0.075 (1.9)
Flushness	None	0.015 (0.38)	0.005 (0.13)	0.025 (0.6)	0.025 (0.6)	0.050 (1.3)

SOURCE: Reprinted with permission from *Architectural Woodwork Quality Standards,* 6th ed., Architectural Woodwork Institute.

In considering the tightness and flushness of plant assembled joints a reasonable assessment should be made between the finished product and absolute compliance with the AWI standard.

Related Sections

7-4. Standing and Running Trim

7-14. Architectural Flush Doors

Figure 7-12

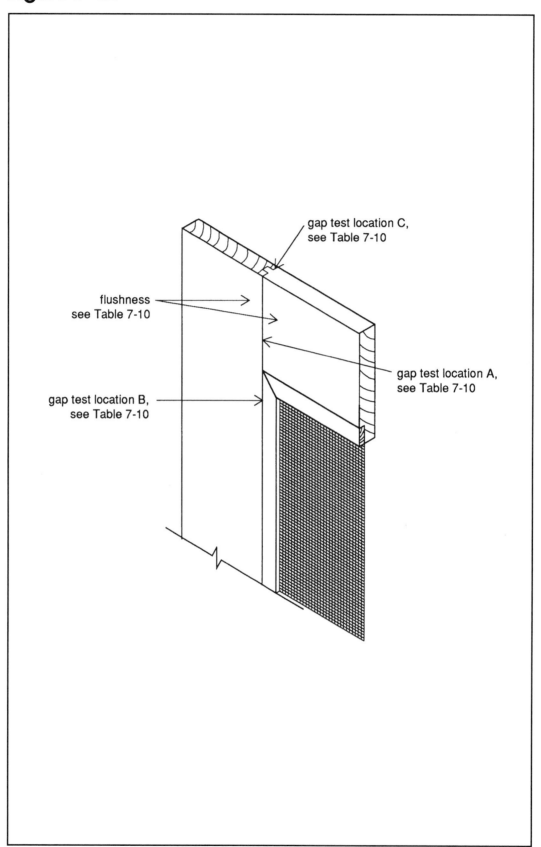

gap test location C,
see Table 7-10

flushness
see Table 7-10

gap test location A,
see Table 7-10

gap test location B,
see Table 7-10

7-12. Screens

Description

This section includes custom-made insect screens for windows and doors.

Industry Standard

Architectural Woodwork Quality Standards, 6th ed., Architectural Woodwork Institute, Centreville, VA, 1993.

Allowable Tolerances

Tolerances for screens are shown in Fig. 7-12 and listed in Table 7-10.

In considering the tightness and flushness of plant assembled joints a reasonable assessment should be made between the finished product and absolute compliance with the Architectural Woodwork Institute (AWI) standard.

Table 7-10
Joint Tolerances for Screens

	AWI grade tolerances, in (mm)		
	Premium, exterior	Custom, exterior	Economy, exterior
Maximum gap: test location A	0.025 (0.6) wide by 30% of joint length	0.050 (1.3) wide by 30% of joint length	.075 (1.9) wide by 30% of joint length
Maximum gap: test location B	0.025 (0.6) × 6 (150), and no gap may occur within 24 (600) of a similar gap	0.050 (1.3) × 8 (200), and no gap may occur within 30 (760) of a similar gap	0.075 (1.9) × 10 (250), and no gap may occur within 36 (900) of a similar gap
Maximum gap: test location C	0.025 (0.6)	0.050 (1.8)	0.075 (1.9)
Flushness	0.015 (0.38)	0.025 (0.6)	0.050 (1.3)

SOURCE: Reprinted with permission from *Architectural Woodwork Quality Standards,* 6th ed., Architectural Woodwork Institute.

Related Section

7-11. Frames, Jambs, and Windows

Figure 7-13

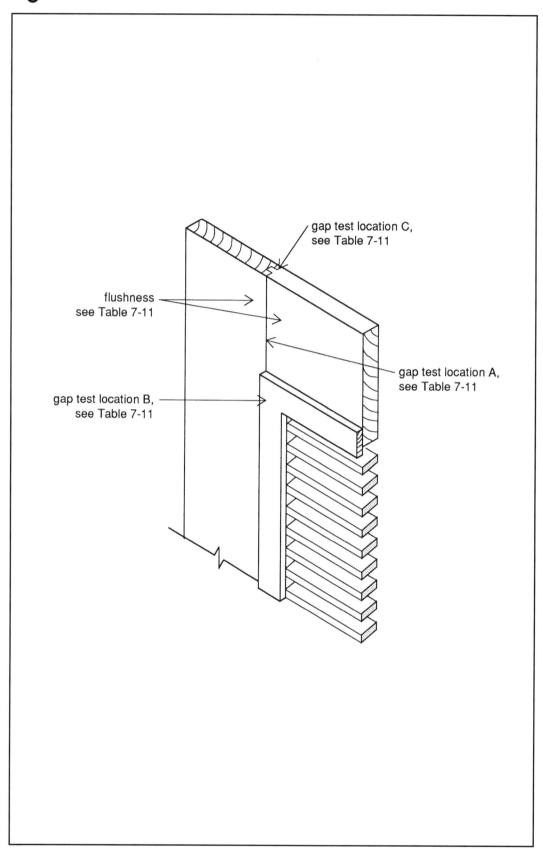

gap test location C,
see Table 7-11

flushness
see Table 7-11

gap test location A,
see Table 7-11

gap test location B,
see Table 7-11

7-13. Blinds and Shutters

Description

This section includes custom-made interior and exterior blinds and shutters built within stile and rail construction.

Industry Standard

Architectural Woodwork Quality Standards, 6th ed., Architectural Woodwork Institute, Centreville, VA, 1993.

Allowable Tolerances

Tolerances for blinds and shutters are shown in Fig. 7-13 and listed in Table 7-11.

In considering the tightness and flushness of plant assembled joints a reasonable assessment should be made between the finished product and absolute compliance with the Architectural Woodwork Institute (AWI) standard. Styles of blinds and shutters are shown in Fig. 7-13.1.

Related Section

7-11. Frames, Jambs, and Windows

Table 7-11
Joint Tolerances for Blinds and Shutters

AWI grade tolerances, in (mm)

	Premium		Custom		Economy	
	Interior	Exterior	Interior	Exterior	Interior	Exterior
Maximum gap: test location A	0.015 (0.38) wide by 20% of joint length	0.025 (0.6) wide by 30% of joint length	0.025 (0.6) wide by 20% of joint length	0.050 (1.3) wide by 30% of joint length	0.050 (1.3) wide by 20% of joint length	0.075 (1.9) wide by 30% of joint length
Maximum gap: test location B	0.015 (0.38) × 3 (75), and no gap may occur within 48 (1200) of a similar gap	0.025 (0.6) × 6 (150), and no gap may occur within 24 (600) of a similar gap	0.025 (0.6) × 6 (150), and no gap may occur within 60 (1500) of a similar gap	0.050 (1.3) × 8 (200), and no gap may occur within 30 (760) of a similar gap	0.050 (1.3) × 8 (200), and no gap may occur within 72 (1830) of a similar gap	0.075 (1.9) × 10 (250), and no gap may occur within 36 (900) of a similar gap
Maximum gap: test location C	0.015 (0.38)	0.025 (0.6)	0.025 (0.6)	0.050 (1.3)	0.050 (1.3)	0.075 (1.9)
Flushness	None	0.015 (0.38)	0.005 (0.13)	0.025 (0.6)	0.025 (0.6)	0.050 (1.3)

SOURCE: Reprinted with permission from *Architectural Woodwork Quality Standards*, 6th ed., Architectural Woodwork Institute.

Figure 7-13.1

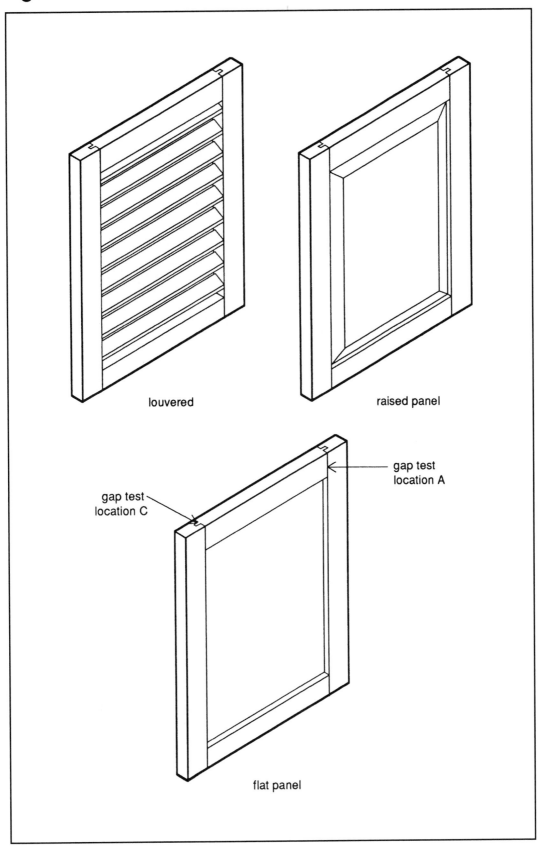

louvered

raised panel

gap test
location A

gap test
location C

flat panel

Figure 7-14

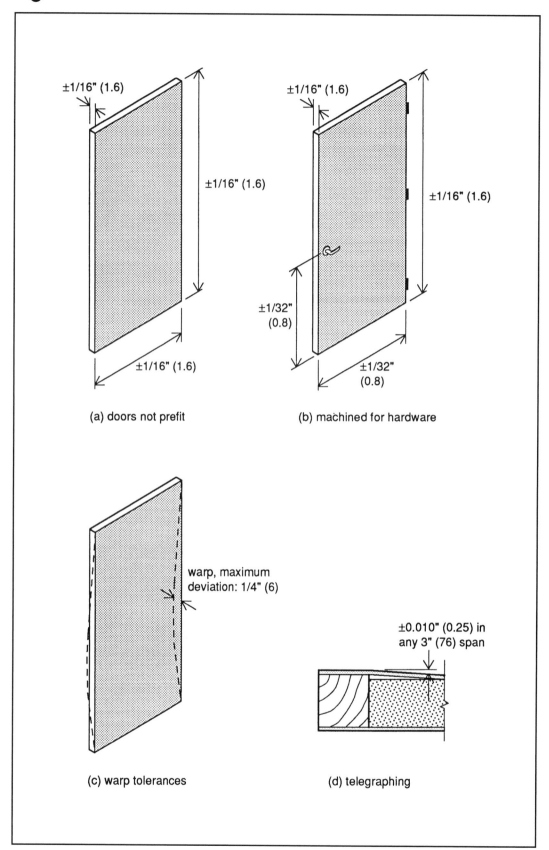

±1/16" (1.6)

±1/16" (1.6)

±1/16" (1.6)

(a) doors not prefit

±1/16" (1.6)

±1/16" (1.6)

±1/32"
(0.8)

±1/32"
(0.8)

(b) machined for hardware

warp, maximum
deviation: 1/4" (6)

(c) warp tolerances

±0.010" (0.25) in
any 3" (76) span

(d) telegraphing

7-14. Architectural Flush Doors

Description

This section includes flush wood doors manufactured according to Architectural Woodwork Institute (AWI) quality standards primarily for commercial construction. Doors conforming to premium, custom, and economy grade are available. Refer to Sec. 11-4 for tolerances for standard flush wood doors manufactured according to National Wood Window and Door Association (NWWDA) standards. However, the tolerances are very similar for both standards.

Industry Standard

Architectural Woodwork Quality Standards, 6th ed., Architectural Woodwork Institute, Centreville, VA, 1993.

Allowable Tolerances

Figure 7-14 illustrates the tolerances of size, warp, and show-through or telegraphing.

The tolerances for hardware location for machined doors include tolerances for locks, hinges, and other hardware.

Warp tolerances apply only to the door and not to its relation to the frame. The maximum deviation of $\frac{1}{4}$ in (6 mm) applies to a maximum door size of 3 ft, 0 in by 7 ft, 0 in (900 mm by 2100 mm) for $1\frac{3}{8}$-in-thick (35-mm-thick) doors and to a maximum door size of 3 ft, 6 in by 7 ft, 0 in (1067 mm by 2100 mm) for $1\frac{3}{4}$-in-thick (44-mm-thick) doors. For larger $1\frac{3}{4}$-in-thick doors, the tolerance is measured in any 3-ft, 6-in by 7-ft, 0-in section.

Telegraphing is the distortion of the face veneer of a door caused by variation in thickness between the core material and the vertical or horizontal edge bands.

Related Sections

11-4. Standard Flush Wood Doors

11-7. Installation of Wood Doors

Figure 7-15

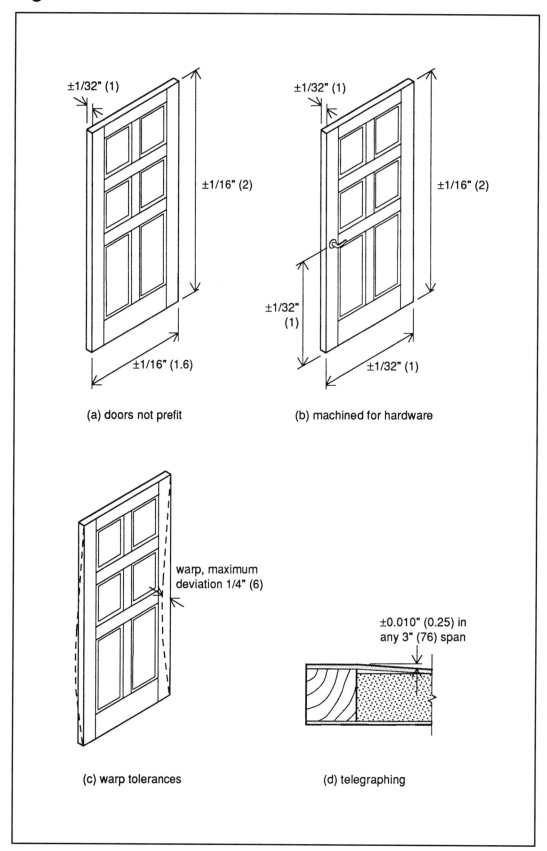

±1/32" (1)

±1/16" (2)

±1/16" (1.6)

(a) doors not prefit

±1/32" (1)

±1/16" (2)

±1/32" (1)

±1/32" (1)

(b) machined for hardware

warp, maximum deviation 1/4" (6)

(c) warp tolerances

±0.010" (0.25) in any 3" (76) span

(d) telegraphing

7-15. Stile and Rail Doors—Size and Flatness

Description

This section includes size and flatness tolerances for stile and rail doors manufactured primarily for commercial construction according to Architectural Woodwork Institute (AWI) standards. Doors conforming to premium, custom, and economy grade are available. Refer to Sec. 11-5 for tolerances for standard stile and rail doors manufactured according to National Wood Window and Door Association (NWWDA) standards.

Industry Standard

Architectural Woodwork Quality Standards, 6th ed., Architectural Woodwork Institute, Centreville, VA, 1993.

Allowable Tolerances

Figure 7-15 illustrates the tolerances of size, warp, and show-through or telegraphing. Joint tightness and flushness tolerances are given in Sec. 7-16.

The tolerances for hardware location for machined doors include tolerances for locks, hinges, and other hardware.

Warp tolerances apply only to the door and not to its relation to the frame. The maximum deviation of $\frac{1}{4}$ in (6 mm) applies to a maximum door size of 3 ft, 0 in by 7 ft, 0 in (900 mm by 2100 mm) for $1\frac{3}{8}$-in-thick (35-mm-thick) doors and to a maximum door size of 3 ft, 6 in by 7 ft, 0 in (1067 mm by 2100 mm) for $1\frac{3}{4}$-in-thick (44-mm-thick) doors. For larger $1\frac{3}{4}$-in-thick doors, the tolerance is measured in any 3 ft, 6 in by 7 ft, 0 in section.

Related Sections

7-16. Stile and Rail Doors—Joint Tightness and Flushness

11-5. Standard Stile and Rail Doors

11-7. Installation of Wood Doors

Figure 7-16

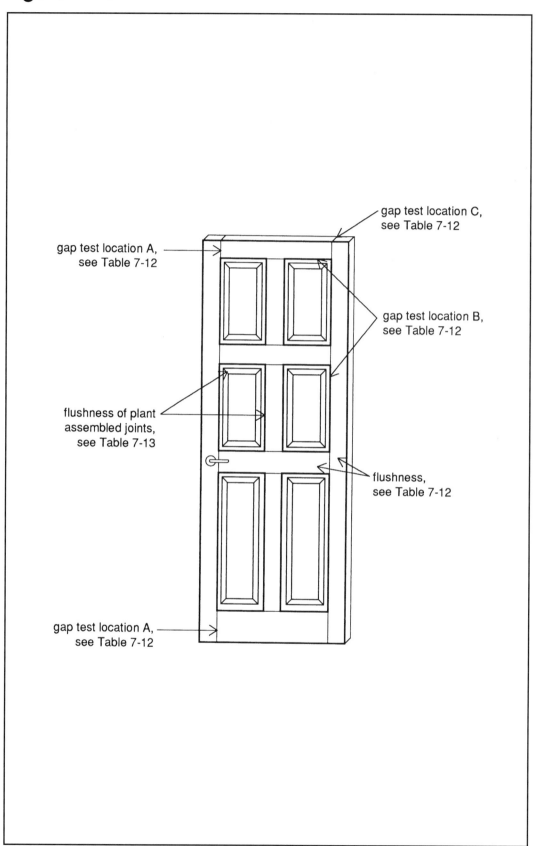

gap test location C,
see Table 7-12

gap test location A,
see Table 7-12

gap test location B,
see Table 7-12

flushness of plant
assembled joints,
see Table 7-13

flushness,
see Table 7-12

gap test location A,
see Table 7-12

7-16. Stile and Rail Doors—Joint Tightness and Flushness

Description

This section includes joint tightness and flushness tolerances for stile and rail doors manufactured primarily for commercial construction according to Architectural Woodwork Institute (AWI) standards. Refer to Sec. 11-5 for tolerances for standard stile and rail doors manufactured according to National Wood Window and Door Association (NWWDA) standards.

Industry Standard

Architectural Woodwork Quality Standards, 6th ed., Architectural Woodwork Institute, Centreville, VA, 1993.

Allowable Tolerances

Joint tightness and flushness for stile and rail intersections are measured at certain standard points on a stile and rail door. These test locations are shown in Fig. 7-16 and the maximum deviations permitted are listed in Table 7-12. Flushness tolerances of other joints are listed in Table 7-13.

Related Sections

7-15. Stile and Rail Doors—Size and Flatness

11-5. Manufacturing Tolerances for Standard Stile and Rail Doors

11-6. Installation of Wood Doors

Table 7-12
Tightness of Plant Assembled Joints

	AWI grade tolerances, in (mm)					
	Premium		Custom		Economy	
	Interior	Exterior	Interior	Exterior	Interior	Exterior
Maximum gap: test location A	0.015 (0.38) wide by 20% of joint length	0.025 (0.6) wide by 30% of joint length	0.025 (0.6) wide by 20% of joint length	0.050 (1.3) wide by 30% of joint length	0.050 (1.3) wide by 20% of joint length	0.075 (1.9) wide by 30% of joint length
Maximum gap: test location B	0.015 (0.38) × 3 (75), and no gap may occur within 48 (1200) of a similar gap	0.025 (0.6) × 6 (150), and no gap may occur within 24 (600) of a similar gap	0.025 (0.6) × 6 (150), and no gap may occur within 60 (1500) of a similar gap	0.050 (1.3) × 8 (200), and no gap may occur within 30 (760) of a similar gap	0.050 (1.3) × 8 (200), and no gap may occur within 72 (1830) of a similar gap	0.075 (1.9) × 10 (250), and no gap may occur within 36 (900) of a similar gap
Maximum gap: test location C	0.015 (0.38)	0.025 (0.6)	0.025 (0.6)	0.050 (1.3)	0.050 (1.3)	0.075 (1.9)
Flushness	None	0.015 (0.38)	0.005 (0.13)	0.025 (0.6)	0.025 (0.6)	0.050 (1.3)

SOURCE: Reprinted with permission from *Architectural Woodwork Quality Standards*, 6th ed., Architectural Woodwork Institute.

Table 7-13
Flushness of Plant Assembled Joints

	AWI grade tolerances, in (mm)					
	Premium		Custom		Economy	
	Interior	Exterior	Interior	Exterior	Interior	Exterior
Stile and rails	None	0.015 (0.38)	0.005 (0.1)	0.025 (0.6)	0.010 (0.2)	0.035 (0.9)
Moldings, beads, rims, etc.	0.007 (0.18)	0.007 (0.18)	0.015 (0.38)	0.015 (0.38)	0.030 (0.76)	0.030 (0.76)

SOURCE: Compiled from information in *Architectural Woodwork Quality Standards,* 6th ed., Architectural Woodwork Institute.

Figure 7-17

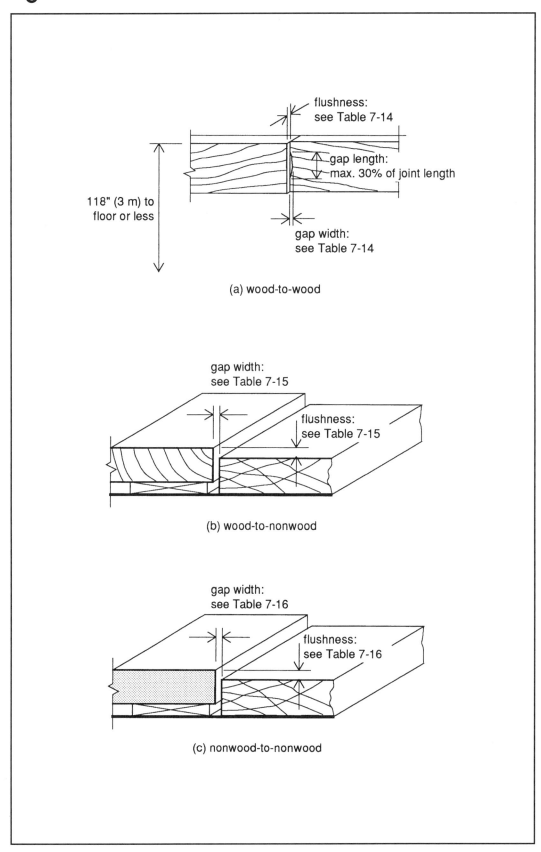

flushness:
see Table 7-14

gap length:
max. 30% of joint length

118" (3 m) to
floor or less

gap width:
see Table 7-14

(a) wood-to-wood

gap width:
see Table 7-15

flushness:
see Table 7-15

(b) wood-to-nonwood

gap width:
see Table 7-16

flushness:
see Table 7-16

(c) nonwood-to-nonwood

7-17. Architectural Woodwork Installation

Description

The *Quality Standards* of the Architectural Woodwork Institute (AWI) provide general installation standards for various types of woodwork based on one of the three grades. Normally, the same woodworking shop that fabricates the material also installs it. This section includes some of the installation standards that relate to dimensional tolerances.

Industry Standard

Architectural Woodwork Quality Standards, 6th ed., Architectural Woodwork Institute, Centreville, VA, 1993.

Allowable Tolerances

Tolerances for field joints of materials vary depending on whether they are wood-to-wood, wood-to-non-wood, or non-wood-to-non-wood. For example, wood trim may be placed next to a stone panel that is part of the woodworker's responsibility. Tolerances also vary depending on the height of the joint above the floor. Tolerances do not apply to joints not open to building occupants or visible to the general public. These tolerances are shown diagrammatically in Fig. 7-17*a,* 7-17*b,* and 7-17*c* and listed in Tables 7-14 through 7-16. In all cases, the maximum allowable length of the gap is 30 percent of the joint length. An example of these conditions is shown in Fig. 7-17.1.

Table 7-14
Wood-to-Wood Field Joints up to 118 in (3 m) above Finished Floor

| | Maximum tolerance, in (mm) | | | | | |
| | Premium | | Custom | | Economy | |
	Flat surface	Shaped surface	Flat surface	Shaped surface	Flat surface	Shaped surface
Gap width	0.012 (0.3)	0.025 (0.65)	0.025 (0.65)	0.050 (1.3)	0.050 (1.3)	0.075 (1.9)
Flushness	0.012 (0.3)	0.025 (0.65)	0.025 (0.65)	0.050 (1.3)	0.050 (1.3)	0.075 (1.9)

SOURCE: Compiled from information in *Architectural Woodwork Quality Standards,* 6th ed., Architectural Woodwork Institute.

Table 7-15
Wood-to-Nonwood Field Joints up to 118 in (3 m) above Finished Floor

| | Maximum tolerance, in (mm) | | | | | |
| | Premium | | Custom | | Economy | |
	Flat surface	Shaped surface	Flat surface	Shaped surface	Flat surface	Shaped surface
Gap width	0.025 (0.65)	0.050 (1.3)	0.050 (1.3)	0.075 (1.9)	0.075 (1.9)	0.100 (2.5)
Flushness	0.025 (0.65)	0.050 (1.3)	0.050 (1.3)	0.075 (1.9)	0.075 (1.9)	0.100 (2.5)

SOURCE: Compiled from information in *Architectural Woodwork Quality Standards,* 6th ed., Architectural Woodwork Institute.

Table 7-16
Nonwood-to-Nonwood Field Joints up to 118 in (3 m) above Finished Floor

| | Maximum tolerance, in (mm) | | | | | |
| | Premium | | Custom | | Economy | |
	Flat surface	Shaped surface	Flat surface	Shaped surface	Flat surface	Shaped surface
Gap width	0.050 (1.3)	0.075 (1.9)	0.075 (1.9)	0.100 (2.5)	0.100 (2.5)	0.125 (3.2)
Flushness	0.050 (1.3)	0.075 (1.9)	0.075 (1.9)	0.100 (2.5)	0.100 (2.5)	0.125 (3.2)

SOURCE: Compiled from information in *Architectural Woodwork Quality Standards,* 6th ed., Architectural Woodwork Institute.

Related Sections

7-2. Site-Built Cabinets and Countertops

7-3. Site-Built Stairs and Trim

7-4. Standing and Running Trim

11-7. Installation of Wood Doors

Figure 7-17.1

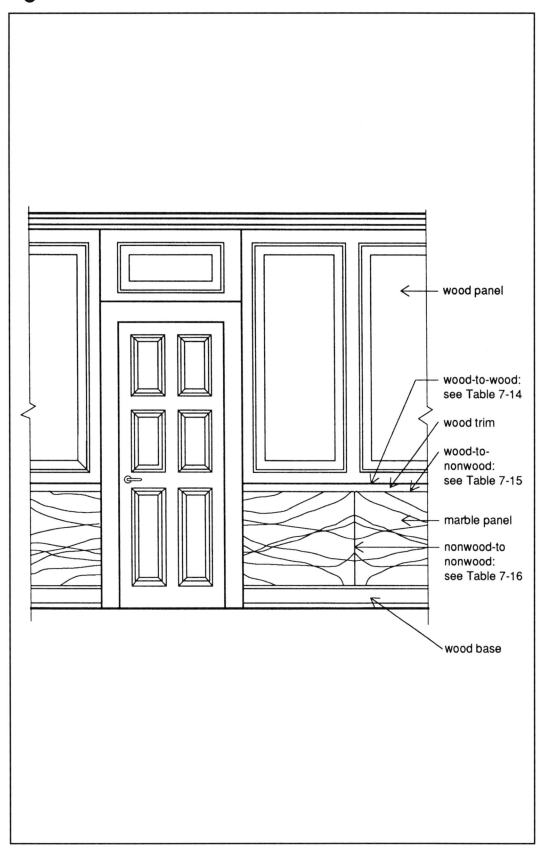

wood panel

wood-to-wood:
see Table 7-14

wood trim

wood-to-
nonwood:
see Table 7-15

marble panel

nonwood-to
nonwood:
see Table 7-16

wood base

Figure 8-1

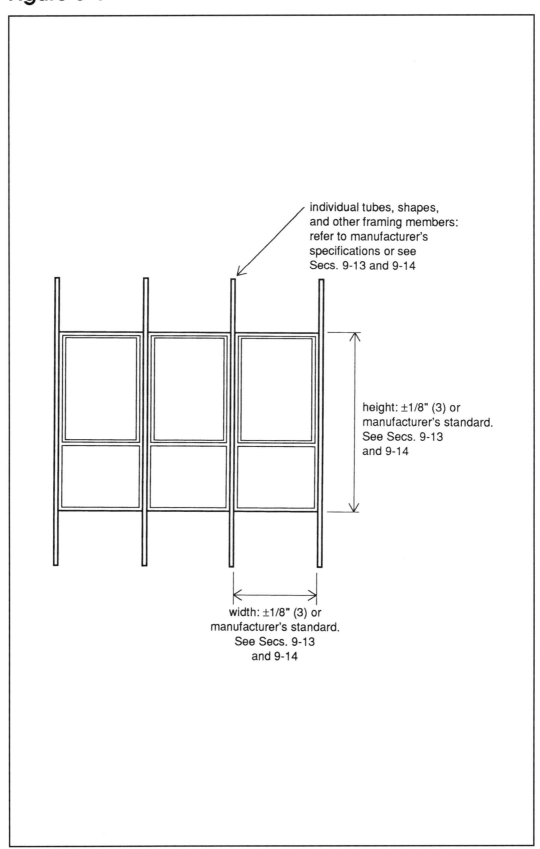

individual tubes, shapes, and other framing members: refer to manufacturer's specifications or see Secs. 9-13 and 9-14

height: ±1/8" (3) or manufacturer's standard. See Secs. 9-13 and 9-14

width: ±1/8" (3) or manufacturer's standard. See Secs. 9-13 and 9-14

Chapter 8

Curtain Walls

8-1. Aluminum Curtain Wall Fabrication

Description

Metal curtain wall construction involves several tolerances in addition to fabrication tolerances. There are basic material tolerances, building frame tolerances, and erection tolerances. In addition, there are required clearances between the curtain wall and other building components that must be provided for. Because metal curtain walls are manufactured from fairly precise components (aluminum tubing and other shapes, for example) and factory fabricated under controlled conditions, the tolerances for the finished product as delivered to the job site are small and normally do not affect installation.

Industry Standards

Metal Curtain Wall Manual, American Architectural Manufacturers Association, Palatine, IL, 1989.

ANSI H35.2-1990, *American National Standard Dimensional Tolerances for Aluminum Mill Products,* The Aluminum Association, Washington, DC., 1990.

Allowable Tolerances

The American Architectural Manufacturers Association does not publish any industrywide standard tolerances for fabrication. Commonly used tolerances are shown in Fig. 8-1. Exact fabricated tolerances should be verified with the manufacturer as they will vary with the size, material, and configuration of each curtain wall system. In nearly all cases, minor manufacturing tolerances are easily accommodated during erection and attachment to the building structure.

Related Sections

8-2. Aluminum Curtain Wall Installation

8-3. Storefront and Entrance Manufacturing

9-13. Extruded Aluminum Tubes

9-14. Aluminum Rods, Bars, and Shapes

Figure 8-2

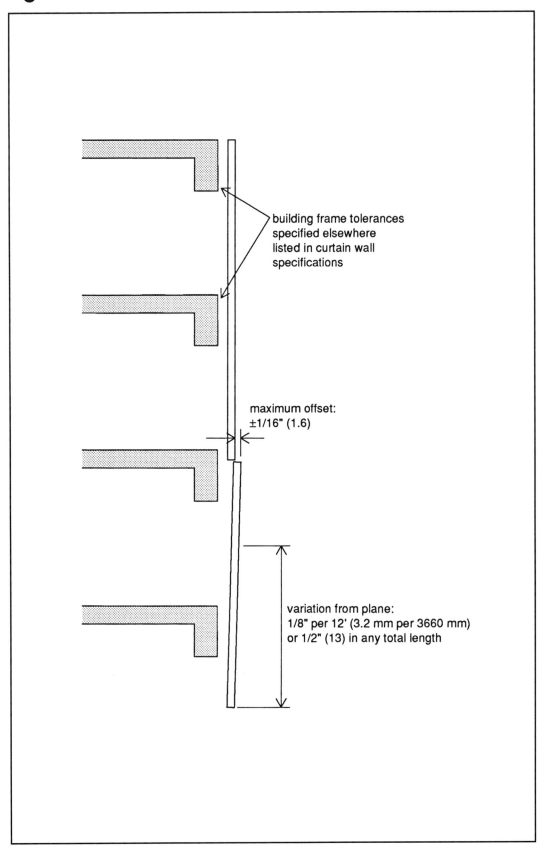

building frame tolerances
specified elsewhere
listed in curtain wall
specifications

maximum offset:
±1/16" (1.6)

variation from plane:
1/8" per 12' (3.2 mm per 3660 mm)
or 1/2" (13) in any total length

8-2. Aluminum Curtain Wall Installation

Description

This section includes installation tolerances for aluminum and other metal curtain walls. In order to meet industry standard tolerances or manufacturers' tolerances it is imperative that the building frame be constructed within acceptable tolerances and that connection details allow for adjustment during erection.

Industry Standards

Metal Curtain Wall Manual, American Architectural Manufacturers Association, Palatine, IL, 1989.

Spectext Section 08920, *Glazed Aluminum Curtain Wall,* Construction Sciences Research Foundation, Baltimore, 1988.

Allowable Tolerances

Tolerances for aluminum and other metal curtain walls should be stated in the specifications. In many cases, a lesser or greater tolerance than is normally used is required. In addition to erection tolerances, the specifications should clearly state what the tolerances for the building frame will be and that the curtain wall manufacturer must accommodate these framing tolerances. In some cases, the manufacturer will give the required curtain wall fabrication and erection tolerances to the architect prior to issuing construction documents so that the required frame tolerances can be stated for other trades.

The tolerances recommended by the Architectural Manufacturers Association for variation from plane and offset of adjacent components are shown in Fig. 8-2.

The Spectext master specifications recommend a maximum plumb misalignment of 0.06 in for every 3 ft (1.5 mm per m) noncumulative or $\frac{1}{2}$ in per 100 ft (12 mm per 30 m), whichever is less, with a maximum misalignment of adjacent members of $\frac{1}{32}$ in (0.8 mm). This is about $\pm\frac{1}{4}$ in in 12 ft (6 mm in 3660 mm), noncumulative.

Related Sections

8-1. Aluminum Curtain Wall Fabrication

8-4. Storefront Installation

12-6. Detailing for Curtain Walls on Concrete Frames

14-7. Detailing for Curtain Walls on Steel Frames

Figure 8-3

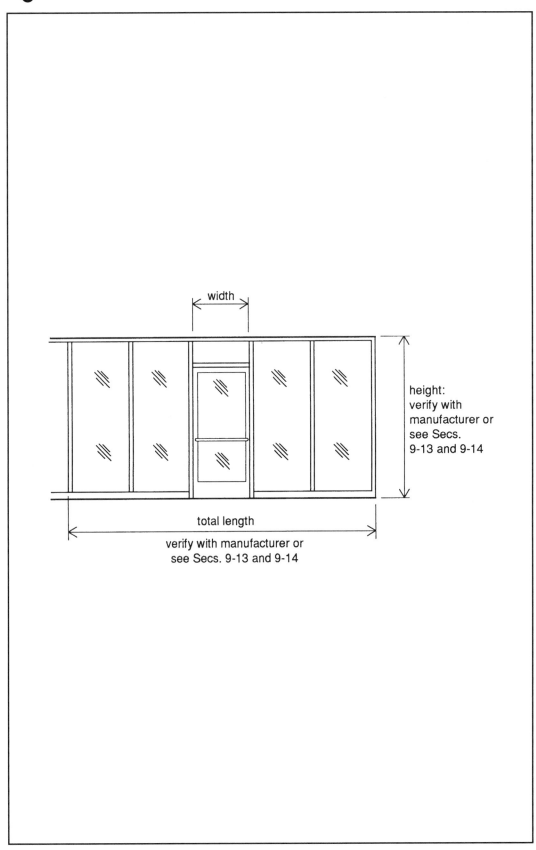

width

height:
verify with
manufacturer or
see Secs.
9-13 and 9-14

total length
verify with manufacturer or
see Secs. 9-13 and 9-14

8-3. Storefront and Entrance Manufacturing

Description

Storefront construction involves several tolerances in addition to manufacturing tolerances. There are basic material tolerances, building substrate tolerances, and installation tolerances. Because storefronts, like curtain walls, are manufactured from fairly precise components (aluminum tubing and other shapes, for example) and factory fabricated under controlled conditions, the tolerances for the finished product as delivered to the job site are small and normally do not affect installation.

Industry Standard

Aluminum Storefront and Entrance Manual, American Architectural Manufacturers Association, Palatine, IL, 1987.

Allowable Tolerances

As shown in Fig. 8-3, the American Architectural Manufacturers Association does not publish any industrywide standard tolerances for storefronts and entrances. Exact fabricated tolerances should be verified with the manufacturer as they will vary with the size, material, and configuration of each system. In nearly all cases, minor manufacturing tolerances are easily accommodated during installation if sufficient clearance is provided between the storefront system and the building substrate. A minimum $\frac{1}{4}$-in (6-mm) clearance is required at each side with a $\frac{1}{2}$-in (13-mm) clearance recommended.

Related Sections

8-1. Aluminum Curtain Wall Fabrication

8-4. Storefront Installation

10-5. All-Glass Entrances

Figure 8-4

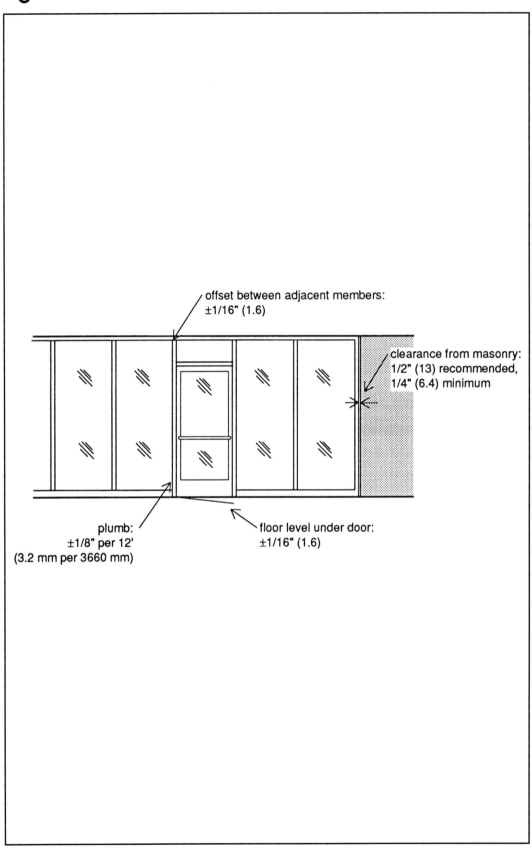

offset between adjacent members:
±1/16" (1.6)

clearance from masonry:
1/2" (13) recommended,
1/4" (6.4) minimum

plumb:
±1/8" per 12'
(3.2 mm per 3660 mm)

floor level under door:
±1/16" (1.6)

8-4. Storefront Installation

Description

Because storefront systems are factory manufactured from precise components, installation tolerances can be quite accurate providing that the substrate tolerances are small enough to allow installation without excessive shimming or caulking.

Industry Standards

Aluminum Storefront and Entrance Manual, American Architectural Manufacturers Association, Palatine, IL, 1987.

Spectext Section 08410, *Aluminum Entrances and Storefronts,* Construction Sciences Research Foundation, Baltimore, 1989.

Allowable Tolerances

Recommended installation tolerances for storefronts are shown in Fig. 8-4. In addition, a clearance of $\frac{1}{4}$ in minimum to $\frac{1}{2}$ in (6 mm to 13 mm) is recommended between the storefront system and masonry and other openings. The floor under a swinging door or revolving door should be level to a tolerance of $\pm\frac{1}{16}$ in (1.6 mm) to prevent the door from binding.

The Spectext master specifications recommend a maximum plumb misalignment of 0.06 in for every 3 ft (1.5 mm per m) noncumulative or $\frac{1}{16}$ in per 10 feet (1.5 mm per 3 m), whichever is less, with a maximum misalignment of adjacent members of $\frac{1}{32}$ in (0.8 mm).

Related Sections

8-2. Aluminum Curtain Wall Installation

8-3. Storefront and Entrance Manufacturing

10-5. All-Glass Entrances

Figure 9-1

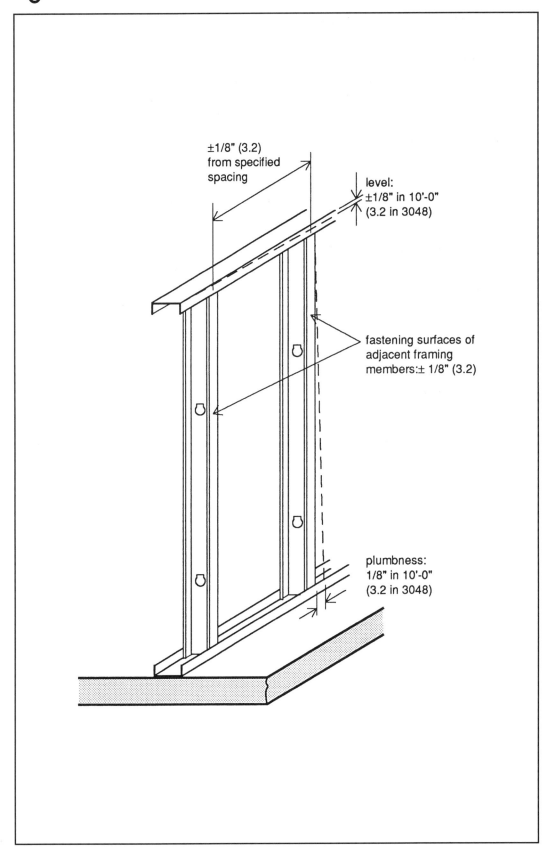

±1/8" (3.2) from specified spacing

level: ±1/8" in 10'-0" (3.2 in 3048)

fastening surfaces of adjacent framing members:± 1/8" (3.2)

plumbness: 1/8" in 10'-0" (3.2 in 3048)

Chapter 9

Finishes

9-1. Lightgage Framing for Gypsum Wallboard

Description

This section includes tolerances for the installation of steel studs for the subsequent application of gypsum wallboard. For gypsum wallboard partitions that are painted or finished with wall covering, the tolerances shown here may not be required. However, if finish materials such as ceramic tile are used or finished clear opening dimensions are required, the smaller tolerances should be specified.

Industry Standards

GA-216, *Recommended Specifications for the Application and Finishing of Gypsum Board,* Gypsum Association, Washington, DC, 1993.

"Specification Guide for Cold-Formed Lightweight Steel Framing," in *Lightweight Steel Framing Systems Manual,* 3d ed., Metal Lath/Steel Framing Association, Chicago, 1987.

ASTM C754, *Standard Specification for Installation of Steel Framing Members to Receive Screw-Attached Gypsum Board,* American Society for Testing and Materials, Philadelphia, 1988.

ASTM C1007, *Standard Specification for Installation of Load Bearing (Transverse and Axial) Steel Studs and Related Accessories,* American Society for Testing and Materials, Philadelphia, 1990.

Allowable Tolerances

The recommended tolerances from several sources are shown in Fig. 9-1. Both the Metal Lath/Steel Framing Association (ML/SFA) and ASTM C1007 recommend that the plumbness and level of studs be within $\frac{1}{960}$ of the span, or $\frac{1}{8}$ in in 10 ft (3.2 mm in 3048 mm). However, ASTM C1007 is for load-bearing studs only while the ML/SFA specifications are for all metal studs. The $\frac{1}{8}$ in per 10 ft tolerance is consistent with the substrate requirements for other finish materials, such as some types of ceramic tile systems.

The Gypsum Association states that adjacent fastening surfaces of framing or furring should not vary by more than $\frac{1}{8}$ in (3.2 mm).

ASTM C754 requires that the spacing of studs and other framing members not vary by more than $\frac{1}{8}$ in (3.2 mm) from the required spacing and that the cumulative error not exceed the requirements of the gypsum wallboard. This is to ensure that the edge of a piece of gypsum board has sufficient bearing on half of a stud for fastening.

If the tolerances shown here are not required and specified, it is more likely that a $\pm\frac{1}{4}$-in (6-mm) tolerance will be observed in actual construction.

Related Sections

6-6. Rough Lumber Framing

9-2. Wallboard Partitions, Ceilings, and Trim

9-4. Installation of Lath and Plaster

9-5. Floor and Wall Tile

Figure 9-2

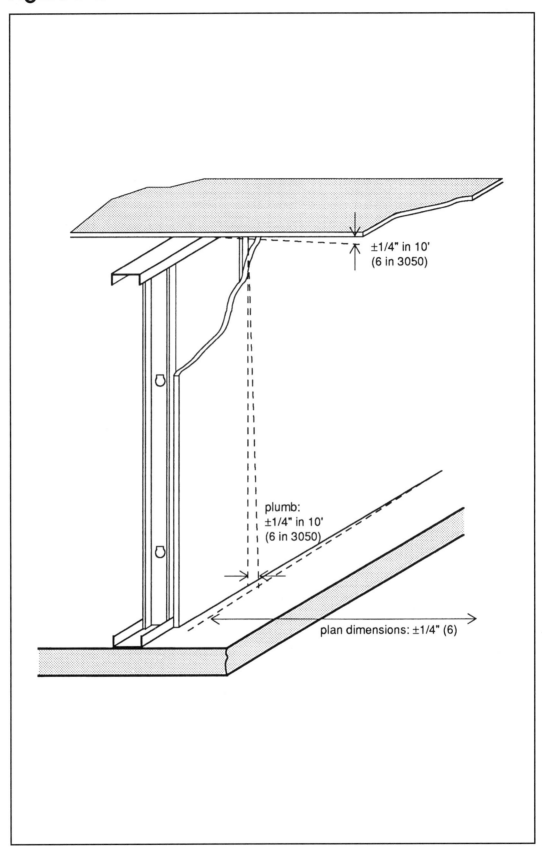

±1/4" in 10'
(6 in 3050)

plumb:
±1/4" in 10'
(6 in 3050)

plan dimensions: ±1/4" (6)

9-2. Wallboard Partitions, Ceilings, and Trim

Description

Although framing tolerances play an important part in the accuracy of gypsum wallboard construction, in most cases the tolerance of the final finished surface is more important than the tolerance of the framing. Several things can affect the final tolerance. For example, the use of trim pieces usually extends the edges of finished wallboard out by about $\frac{1}{8}$ in (3.2 mm) or more because of the small ridge on the trim piece. Shimming the drywall can improve or exaggerate the final surface position. Poor fastening or slightly bent or warped framing can also affect installation.

Industry Standards

ANSI A108.11, *American National Standard for Interior Installation of Cementitious Backer Units,* American National Standards Institute, New York, 1992.

GA-216, *Recommended Specifications for the Application and Finishing of Gypsum Board,* Gypsum Association, Washington, DC, 1993.

Insurance/Warranty Documents, Home Owners Warranty Corporation, Arlington, VA, 1987.

Allowable Tolerances

For noncritical applications finished gypsum wallboard tolerances for metal stud framing should be taken at $\pm\frac{1}{4}$ in (6 mm), as shown in Fig. 9-2. This includes positioning of partitions based on the dimensions shown on the plans as well as plumbness of walls. This takes into account the tolerances of framing ($\frac{1}{8}$ in per 10 ft or 3.2 mm in 3050 mm, at best) and the inaccuracies of fastening and using trim and shim pieces in the application of the wallboard itself. ANSI A108.11 requires framing members of floor joists, wall studs, and ceiling joists for backer board for ceramic tile have a maximum variation from plane of $\pm\frac{1}{8}$ in in 8 ft (3 mm in 2400 mm).

For wood framing, plumbness and positioning tolerances may be slightly greater due to the relatively rough nature of wood studs compared with the accurate manufacture of steel studs. This is reflected in the tolerance of $\pm\frac{1}{4}$ in (6 mm) in any 32-in (813-mm) vertical measurement called for in the *Insurance/Warranty Documents* of the Home Owners Warranty Corporation. This translates to a tolerance of $\pm\frac{3}{4}$ in in an 8-ft (19 mm in a 2400-mm) wall height, although this should be the extreme case.

For ceilings, the Gypsum Association requires that deflection not exceed $L/240$ of the span at full design load, where L is the length of the span. However, this would result in a $\frac{1}{2}$-in (13-mm) drop in the middle of a 10-ft (3050 mm) span. In most cases a level tolerance of $\frac{1}{4}$ in in 10 ft (6 mm in 3050 mm) should be expected for ceilings.

If smaller tolerances are required for additional finish, such as ceramic tile, the required smaller tolerance must be specifically stated in the contract documents.

Related Sections

6-6. Rough Lumber Framing

6-7. Wood Floor Framing and Subflooring

9-1. Lightgage Framing for Gypsum Wallboard

9-4. Installation of Lath and Plaster

9-5. Floor and Wall Tile

Figure 9-3

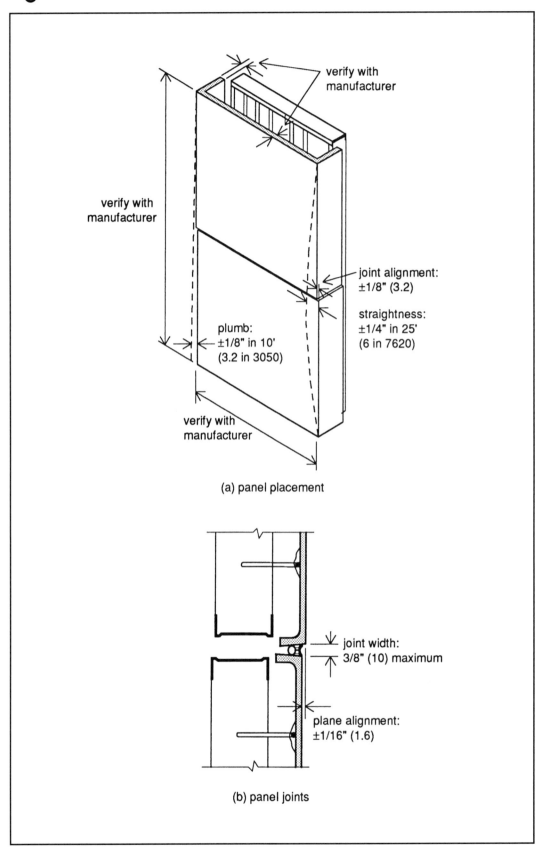

verify with
manufacturer

verify with
manufacturer

joint alignment:
±1/8" (3.2)

straightness:
±1/4" in 25'
(6 in 7620)

plumb:
±1/8" in 10'
(3.2 in 3050)

verify with
manufacturer

(a) panel placement

joint width:
3/8" (10) maximum

plane alignment:
±1/16" (1.6)

(b) panel joints

9-3. Glass Reinforced Gypsum Products

Description

Glass reinforced gypsum products are factory fabricated components made by a molding process using high-strength, high-density gypsum reinforced with continuous filament glass fibers or chopped glass fiber strands. The prefabricated units are attached to steel framing or wood framing, suspended from structure, or otherwise fastened to a suitable substrate.

Industry Standard

Glass Reinforced Gypsum: A Guide, Ceiling and Interior Systems Construction Association, Elmhurst, IL, 1990.

Allowable Tolerances

Tolerances for the fabrication of glass reinforced gypsum products vary with the shape of the component, the final finish, the installed position of the component, and the type of lighting. Tolerances for straightness, length, width, individual dimensions within the overall length, radii, and squareness should be coordinated with the manufacturer and clearly shown on the drawings. All corners should have a radius between $\frac{1}{16}$ in (1.6 mm) and $\frac{1}{8}$ in (3.2 mm) unless otherwise required by the design.

Erection tolerances recommended by the Ceilings and Interior Systems Construction Association are shown in Fig. 9-3.

Related Sections

9-1. Lightgage Framing for Gypsum Wallboard

9-9. Acoustical Ceiling Installation

Figure 9-4

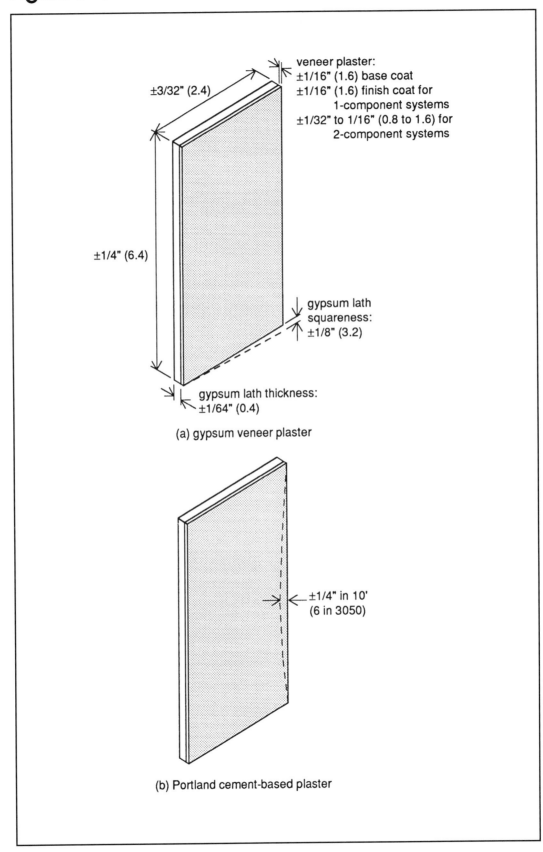

±3/32" (2.4)

veneer plaster:
±1/16" (1.6) base coat
±1/16" (1.6) finish coat for
   1-component systems
±1/32" to 1/16" (0.8 to 1.6) for
   2-component systems

±1/4" (6.4)

gypsum lath
squareness:
±1/8" (3.2)

gypsum lath thickness:
±1/64" (0.4)

(a) gypsum veneer plaster

±1/4" in 10'
(6 in 3050)

(b) Portland cement-based plaster

9-4. Installation of Lath and Plaster

Description

Lath and plaster includes both veneer plaster installations using gypsum lath and standard three-coat plaster work. Because plaster work is site applied and subject to the skills of the plasterer, wide variations in tolerances are possible.

Industry Standards

ASTM C588, *Standard Specification for Gypsum Veneer Base for Veneer Plasters,* American Society for Testing and Materials, Philadelphia, 1992.

ASTM C843, *Standard Specification for Application of Gypsum Veneer Plaster,* American Society for Testing and Materials, Philadelphia, 1992.

ASTM C926, *Standard Specification for Application of Interior Portland Cement-Based Plaster,* American Society for Testing and Materials, Philadelphia, 1990.

Allowable Tolerances

Published tolerances for lath and plaster are shown in Fig. 9-4. Tolerances for gypsum lath are given in ASTM C588 (shown in Fig. 9-4*a*), but these generally do not affect the finished surface. Although there are no tolerances for the plan dimension position of the finished surface of plaster partitions, ASTM C843 does give tolerances for the thickness for the veneer coats of gypsum plaster. ASTM C843 further requires that all protrusions and ridges greater than $\frac{1}{8}$ in (3 mm) be removed and that all depressions greater than $\frac{1}{4}$ in (6 mm) be filled level with the surface.

For standard, full-coat Portland cement plaster work, a plane tolerance of $\pm\frac{1}{4}$ in (6 mm) in 10 ft (3050 mm) is standard as given in ASTM C926, although good plasterers can level a surface to a smaller tolerance than this.

In general, because of possible variations with framing installation, application of lath and trim, and the thickness of plaster, it seems reasonable to expect a tolerance of $\pm\frac{1}{4}$ in in 10 ft (6 mm in 3050 mm) or slightly more for most plaster work.

As with gypsum wallboard, if tighter tolerances are required because of subsequent finish materials, such as ceramic tile, or critical opening dimensions, the tolerances should be clearly stated in the contract documents.

Related Sections

6-6. Rough Lumber Framing

6-7. Wood Floor Framing and Subflooring

9-1. Lightgage Framing for Gypsum Wallboard

9-5. Floor and Wall Tile

Figure 9-5

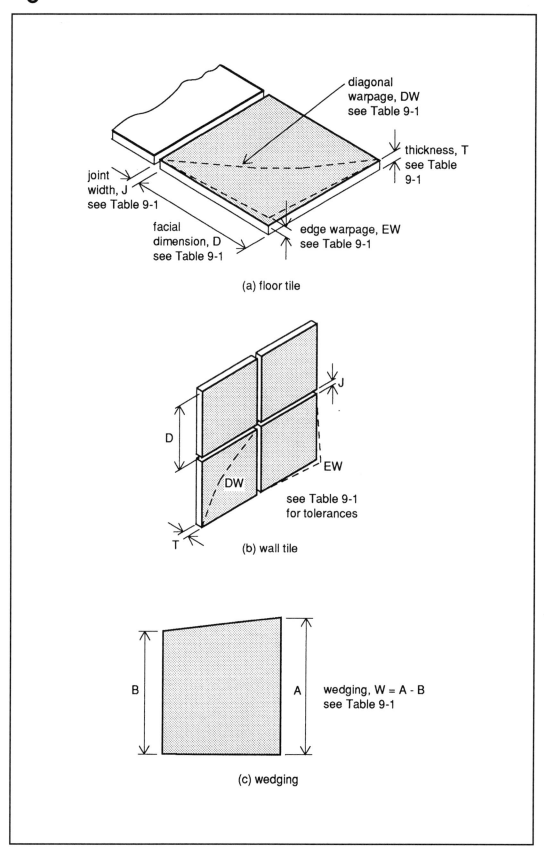

diagonal warpage, DW see Table 9-1

thickness, T see Table 9-1

joint width, J see Table 9-1

facial dimension, D see Table 9-1

edge warpage, EW see Table 9-1

(a) floor tile

D

J

DW

EW

see Table 9-1 for tolerances

T

(b) wall tile

B

A

wedging, W = A - B see Table 9-1

(c) wedging

9-5. Floor and Wall Tile

Description

This section gives tolerances for glazed and unglazed ceramic tile (mosaic and wall tile), quarry tile, and paver tile. *Ceramic mosaic tile* is tile having a facial area less than 6 in². *Wall tile* is a glazed interior tile larger in area than 6 in². There are tolerances for the manufacture of tile but none for the level of the plane of the tile after installation. This depends on the level of the substrate, the warpage, thickness, size and wedging, tolerances of the tile itself, and the skill of the tile setter.

Industry Standards

ANSI A108.1, *American National Standard Specifications for Installation of Ceramic Tile on a Portland Cement Setting Bed,* Tile Council of America, Inc., Princeton, NJ, 1992.

ANSI A108.4, *American National Standard Specifications for Installation of Ceramic Tile with Organic Adhesives or Water Cleanable Epoxy Adhesive,* Tile Council of America, Inc., Princeton, NJ, 1992.

ANSI A108.5, *American National Standard Specifications for Installation of Ceramic Tile with Dry-Set Portland Cement Mortar or Latex-Portland Cement Mortar,* Tile Council of America, Inc., Princeton, NJ, 1992.

ANSI A137.1, *American National Standard Specifications for Ceramic Tile,* Tile Council of America, Inc., Princeton, NJ, 1989.

Ceramic Tile: The Installation Handbook, Tile Council of America, Inc., Princeton, NJ, 1992.

Allowable Tolerances

Tolerances for the manufacture of tile are stated in ANSI A137.1 and summarized in Table 9-1. The locations of these tolerances are shown in Fig. 9-5*a* and 9-5*b*.

Table 9-1
Tile Manufacturing Tolerances

Tile type	T, thickness, in (mm)	D, facial dimension, percent of length	EW, warpage along edges, percent of length	DW, warpage on diagonal, percent	W, wedging, percent
Unglazed ceramic mosaic	±0.030 (0.76)	±10	1.0	0.75	2.0
Glazed ceramic mosaic	±0.030 (0.76)	±10	1.0	0.75	2.0
Glazed wall tile	±0.031 (0.79)	±4.0	0.4 convex 0.3 concave	0.5	0.6
Unglazed quarry tile	±0.050 (1.3)	±4.0	1.5	1.0	1.0
Glazed quarry tile	±0.050 (1.3)	±4.0	1.5	1.0	1.0
Unglazed paver tile	±0.040 (1.0)	±3.0	1.0	0.75	1.0
Glazed paver tile	±0.040 (1.0)	±3.0	1.0	0.75	1.0

SOURCE: Based on information from ANSI A137.1. This material is reproduced with permission from American National Standard A137.1, copyright 1989 by the Tile Council of America, Inc. Copies of this standard may be purchased from the American National Standards Institute at 11 West 42nd Street, New York, NY 10036.

The required tolerances for the plane of the surface over which tile is placed are summarized in Table 9-2 and Fig. 9-5.1 and based on ANSI 108.1 and the Tile Council of America installation handbook.

Table 9-2
Required Tolerance for Plane of Substrate for Tile Installation

Tile installation	Floor substrate tolerances	Wall substrate tolerances
Portland cement mortar bed	$\frac{1}{4}$ in in 10 ft (6 mm in 3000 mm)	$\frac{1}{4}$ in in 8 ft (6 mm in 2400 mm)
Dry-set or latex-Portland cement mortar (thin set)*	$\frac{1}{8}$ in in 10 ft (3 mm in 3000 mm), nor more than $\frac{1}{16}$ in in 12 in (2 mm in 305 mm)	$\frac{1}{8}$ in in 8 ft (3 mm in 2400 mm)
Organic adhesive or epoxy adhesive	$\frac{1}{16}$ in in 3 ft (2 mm in 1000 mm); no abrupt irregularities more than $\frac{1}{32}$ in (1 mm)	$\frac{1}{8}$ in in 8 ft (3 mm in 2400 mm)

*Also includes chemical resistant water cleanable tile-setting and grouting epoxy, furan, and modified epoxy emulsion mortar installations.

SOURCE: Based on information from ANSI A108.1, A108.4, and A108.5. This material is reproduced with permission from American National Standard A108.1, A108.4, A108.5, copyright 1992 by the Tile Council of America, Inc. Copies of these standards may be purchased from the American National Standards Institute at 11 West 42nd Street, New York, NY 10036.

Related Sections

6-6. Rough Lumber Framing

6-7. Wood Floor Framing and Subflooring

9-1. Lightgage Framing for Gypsum Wallboard

9-4. Installation of Lath and Plaster

Figure 9-5.1

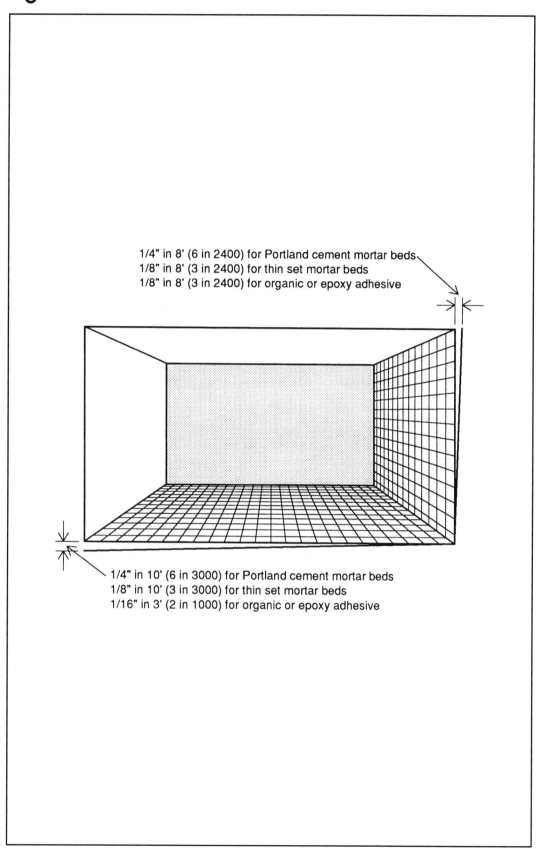

1/4" in 8' (6 in 2400) for Portland cement mortar beds
1/8" in 8' (3 in 2400) for thin set mortar beds
1/8" in 8' (3 in 2400) for organic or epoxy adhesive

1/4" in 10' (6 in 3000) for Portland cement mortar beds
1/8" in 10' (3 in 3000) for thin set mortar beds
1/16" in 3' (2 in 1000) for organic or epoxy adhesive

Figure 9-6

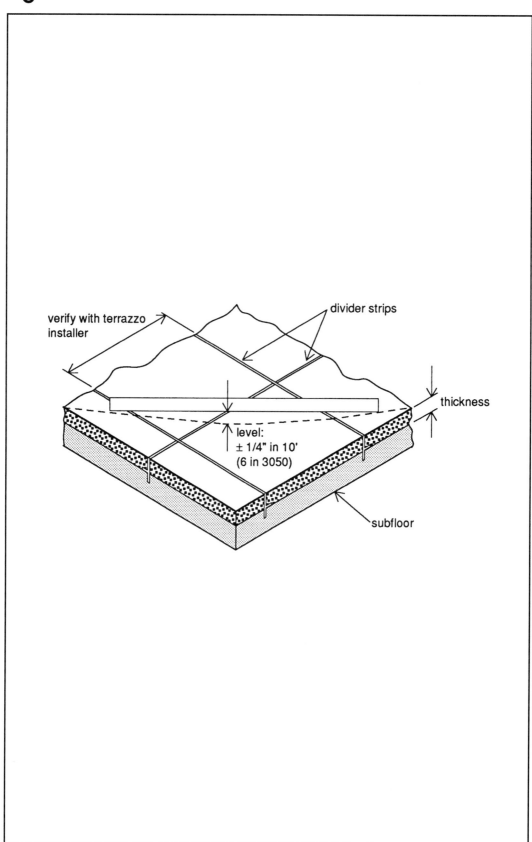

verify with terrazzo installer

divider strips

thickness

level:
± 1/4" in 10'
(6 in 3050)

subfloor

9-6. Terrazzo Flooring

Description

Terrazzo is a composite material consisting of stone chips in a matrix that is cementitious, modified cementitious, or resinous. Terrazzo is poured in place and is normally installed over concrete subfloors, but can be installed over wood floors if deflection is controlled and a sand cushion system is used.

Industry Standard

Terrazzo Information Guide, The National Terrazzo and Mosaic Association, Inc., Des Plaines, IL, 1993.

Allowable Tolerances

Standard tolerances are shown in Fig. 9-6. Because terrazzo is ground smooth after it sets, the level can usually be brought to within $\pm\frac{1}{4}$ in in 10 ft (6 mm in 3050 mm). When the pattern and design of the divider strips are critical for appearance, their location tolerance should be verified with the terrazzo contractor.

For terrazzo floors the subfloor must be within certain tolerances for a satisfactory installation. Concrete subfloors must be level to within $\frac{1}{4}$ in in 10 ft (6 mm in 3050 mm) for monolithic and thin-set terrazzo systems. Concrete subfloors must be level to within $\frac{1}{8}$ in in 10 ft (3 mm in 3050 mm) for monolithic terrazzo, polyacrylate modified terrazzo, epoxy and epoxy modified terrazzo, fine aggregate epoxy, fine aggregate polyester terrazzo, and polyester terrazzo.

Related Sections

2-4. Concrete Slabs-on-Grade

2-8. Cast-in-Place Sectional Tolerances

Figure 9-7

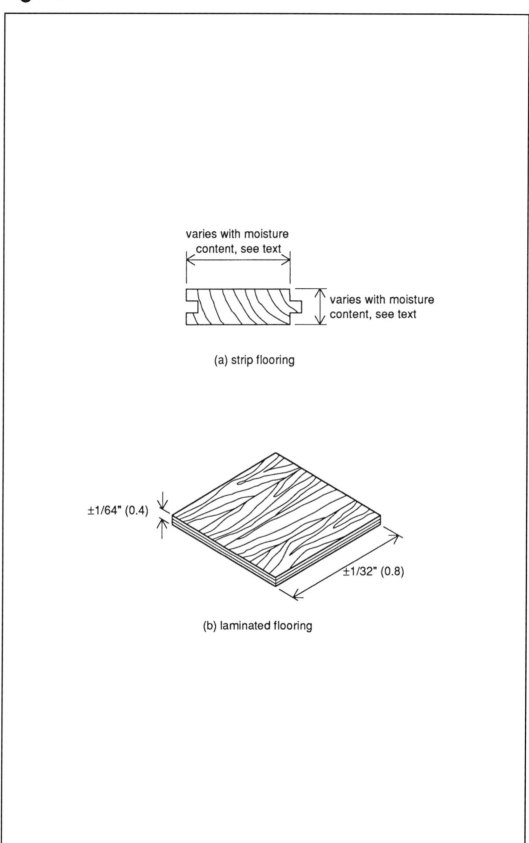

varies with moisture content, see text

varies with moisture content, see text

(a) strip flooring

±1/64" (0.4)

±1/32" (0.8)

(b) laminated flooring

9-7. Wood Flooring

Description

Wood flooring includes standard strip, parquet, and laminated flooring as well as the various types of cushioned wood flooring systems. Because wood flooring is manufactured to exacting tolerances, a successful installation usually depends more on the level and smoothness of the subfloor than on the tolerances of the wood floor itself.

Industry Standards

ANSI/HPMA LHF 1982, *American National Standard for Laminated Hardwood Flooring,* Hardwood Plywood Manufacturers Association, Reston, VA, 1982.

Insurance/Warranty Documents, Home Owners Warranty Corporation, Arlington, VA, 1987.

Quality Standards for the Professional Remodeler, 2d ed., National Association of Home Builders Remodelors™ Council, 1991.

SpecGUIDE, 09550, *Wood Flooring,* The Construction Specifications Institute, Alexandria, VA, May 1988 (out of print).

Allowable Tolerances

There are no industry standards for manufacturing dimensional tolerances for strip flooring, as shown in Fig. 9-7a. Strip flooring is manufactured to fit a metal size gage at the time of manufacturing for the moisture content at the time. As the environmental moisture content changes the strip flooring will change size at the rate of about $\frac{1}{32}$ in (0.8 mm) for each 4 percent change in moisture content according to the Forest Products Laboratory.

Tolerances for laminated flooring are shown in Fig. 9-7b.

There are few standards for tolerances for the final finish surface of wood floors. The *Quality Standards* of the National Association of Home Builders Remodelors™ Council states a total out of level of $\pm\frac{1}{2}$ in in 20 ft (13 mm in 6200 mm) for residential remodeling, but this should be the extreme case. A more reasonable tolerance should be the subfloor tolerance as indicated below.

For strip flooring and parquet flooring, the subfloor should be level to within $\frac{1}{4}$ in in 10 ft (6 mm in 3050 mm) with no abrupt projections or depressions.

The tolerances shown in Table 9-3 for concrete slab substrates for various types of installations were previously recommended by the Construction Specifications Institute.

Table 9-3
Recommended Concrete Slab Tolerances for Wood Flooring

Installation type	Slab tolerance
Cushioned	$\frac{3}{16}$ in in 10 ft (5 mm in 3050 mm)
Laminated	$\frac{3}{16}$ in in 10 ft (5 mm in 3050 mm)
Mastic cushioned	$\frac{1}{4}$ in in 10 ft (6 mm in 3050 mm)
Rubber cushioned	$\frac{3}{16}$ in in 10 ft (5 mm in 3050 mm)
Steel channel	$\frac{1}{8}$ in in 10 ft (3 mm in 3050 mm)

SOURCE: SpecGUIDE, 09550, *Wood Flooring,* The Construction Specifications Institute, May 1988 (out of print).

Related Sections

2-4. Concrete Slabs-on-Grade

2-8. Cast-in-Place Sectional Tolerances

6-7. Wood Floor Framing and Subflooring

Figure 9-8

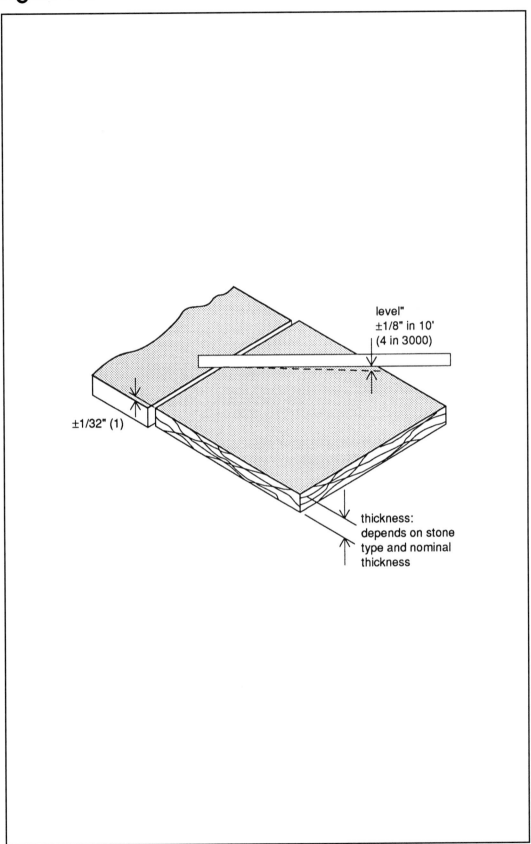

level"
±1/8" in 10'
(4 in 3000)

±1/32" (1)

thickness:
depends on stone
type and nominal
thickness

9-8. Stone Flooring

Description

Stone flooring includes standard thick-set stone (minimum $\frac{3}{4}$ in or 13 mm thick) placed on a thick mortar setting bed and thin stone tiles which are thin-set directly on concrete or wood subfloors.

Industry Standard

Dimension Stone Design Manual IV, Marble Institute of America, Inc., Farmington, MI, 1991.

Allowable Tolerances

For commercial stone floors using $\frac{3}{4}$-in-thick (13-mm-thick) stone on a thick mortar setting bed the maximum variation of the finished surface is $\frac{1}{8}$ in in 10 ft (3 mm in 3050 mm) with no more than $\frac{1}{32}$ in (1 mm) lippage between individual tiles, as shown in Fig. 9-8. *Lippage* is the variation between one edge of a stone tile and the adjacent stone tile edge. It is more pronounced in thin-set stone tile than with thick-set stone floors because there is no thick mortar bed to compensate for minor variations in subfloor level. Natural cleft flooring slate cannot be set to these tolerances because of the unevenness of its thickness.

As with ceramic tile and wood flooring, thin stone tile is manufactured to exacting tolerances and its successful installation depends as much on the level and smoothness of the subfloor as on the skill of the tile setter. The Marble Institute of America recommends that wood subfloors for stone tile have a maximum deflection of no more than $\frac{1}{720}$ of the span and that they be level to within $\frac{1}{16}$ in in 3 ft (1.6 mm in 900 mm). Concrete subfloors for tile should be level to within $\frac{1}{8}$ in (3 mm) of the required plane. When possible the maximum variation of finished surface for stone tile is the same as for thick-set stone floors.

Related Sections

2-4. Concrete Slabs-on-Grade

2-8. Cast-in-Place Sectional Tolerances

5-1. Granite Fabrication

5-2. Marble Fabrication

5-6. Fabrication and Erection Tolerances for Slate

6-7. Wood Floor Framing and Subflooring

Figure 9-9

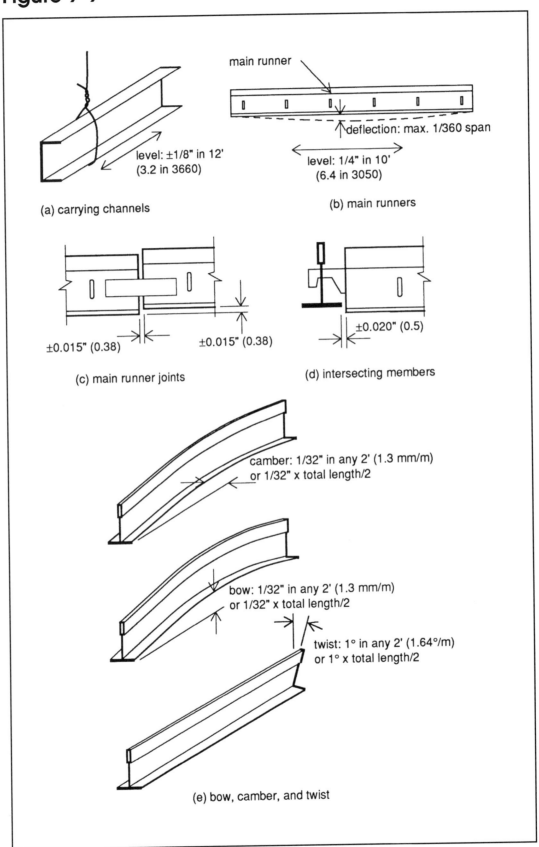

(a) carrying channels

level: ±1/8" in 12'
(3.2 in 3660)

main runner

deflection: max. 1/360 span

level: 1/4" in 10'
(6.4 in 3050)

(b) main runners

±0.015" (0.38)   ±0.015" (0.38)

(c) main runner joints

±0.020" (0.5)

(d) intersecting members

camber: 1/32" in any 2' (1.3 mm/m)
or 1/32" x total length/2

bow: 1/32" in any 2' (1.3 mm/m)
or 1/32" x total length/2

twist: 1° in any 2' (1.64°/m)
or 1° x total length/2

(e) bow, camber, and twist

9-9. Acoustical Ceiling Installation

Description

This section includes tolerances for both steel and aluminum ceiling suspension systems installation for exposed and concealed spline acoustical ceiling systems. However, the ASTM standards only give tolerances for steel systems. For aluminum systems they refer to any tolerances published by the suspension system manufacturer. There are also several manufacturing tolerances for suspension systems given in ASTM C635, but these tolerances are so small that they do not affect the appearance or installation of a ceiling as long as the selected system conforms to the standard.

Industry Standards

ASTM C635, *Standard Specification for the Manufacture, Performance, and Testing of Metal Suspension Systems for Acoustical Tile and Lay-in Panel Ceilings,* American Society for Testing and Materials, Philadelphia, 1991.

ASTM C636, *Standard Practice for Installation of Metal Ceiling Suspension Systems for Acoustical Tile and Lay-in Panels,* American Society for Testing and Materials, Philadelphia, 1991.

Spectext Section 09511, *Suspended Acoustical Ceilings,* Construction Sciences Research Foundation, Baltimore, April 1990.

Allowable Tolerances

Tolerances for connection and level of the various components of a typical ceiling suspension system are shown in Fig. 9-9a, 9-9b, 9-9c, and 9-9d. Although ASTM C636 requires a level of $\frac{1}{4}$ in per 10 ft (6.4 mm in 3050 mm), most ceilings are installed with laser leveling devices and can be leveled to within $\frac{1}{8}$ in in 10 ft (3.2 mm in 3050 mm) and often to within $\frac{1}{8}$ in over the entire room area. Master specifications, such as the Spectext, recommend a tolerance of $\frac{1}{8}$ in in 10 ft.

Bow, camber, and twist tolerances are shown in Fig. 9-9e. Unlike normal construction nomenclature, *bow* here refers to deformation in the *vertical* direction while *camber* refers to deformation in the *horizontal* direction.

Related Section

9-10. Linear Metal Ceiling Installation

Figure 9-10

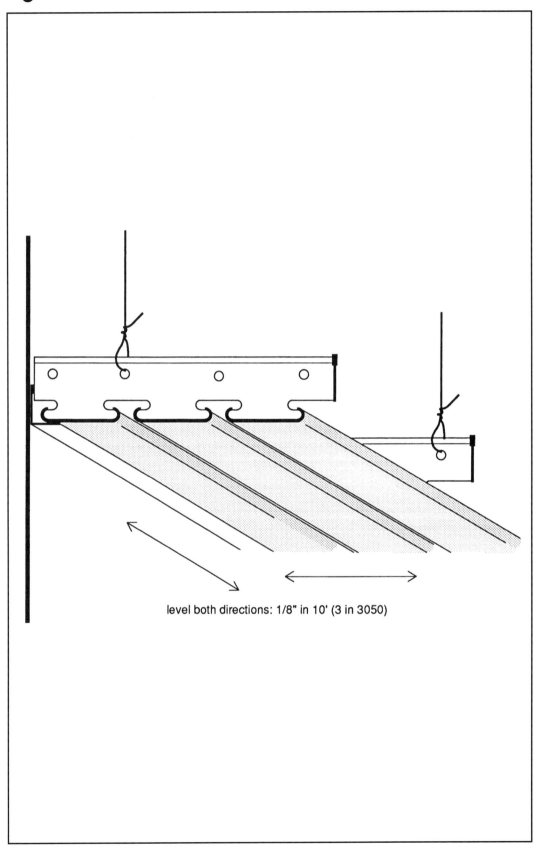

level both directions: 1/8" in 10' (3 in 3050)

9-10. Linear Metal Ceiling Installation

Description

Linear metal ceilings are suspended systems using lengths of prefinished aluminum sections which are clipped to carrier sections suspended with wires attached to the structure above. There is usually a gap between pieces to provide for some sound absorption and for return air movement.

Industry Standard

Spectext Section 09546, *Metal Linear Ceiling System,* Construction Sciences Research Foundation, Baltimore, July 1991.

Allowable Tolerances

There are no industry standards for installation tolerances for linear metal ceilings although the Spectext master specifications recommend a maximum variation from flat plane of $\frac{1}{8}$ in in 10 ft (3 mm in 3050 mm) and a maximum variation from dimensioned position of $\pm\frac{1}{4}$ in (6 mm). They also recommend a maximum variation from plumb of grid members caused by eccentric loads of 2°. As with acoustical ceilings, the suspension system is installed with laser leveling devices in most cases, so a tolerance of $\frac{1}{8}$ in (3 mm) is a reasonable expectation for the precisely manufactured components of these systems.

Manufacturing tolerances are determined by each manufacturer as shown in Fig. 9-10.

Related Section

9-9. Acoustical Ceiling Installation

Figure 9-11

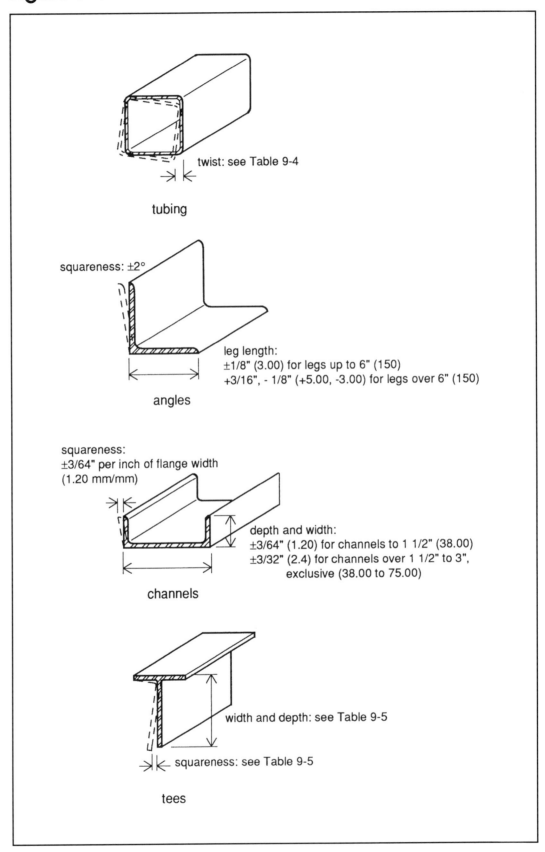

twist: see Table 9-4

tubing

squareness: ±2°

leg length:
±1/8" (3.00) for legs up to 6" (150)
+3/16", - 1/8" (+5.00, -3.00) for legs over 6" (150)

angles

squareness:
±3/64" per inch of flange width
(1.20 mm/mm)

depth and width:
±3/64" (1.20) for channels to 1 1/2" (38.00)
±3/32" (2.4) for channels over 1 1/2" to 3",
exclusive (38.00 to 75.00)

channels

width and depth: see Table 9-5

squareness: see Table 9-5

tees

9-11. Stainless Steel Ornamental Metal Products

Description

This section includes tolerances for some of the shapes and stainless steel alloys commonly used for ornamental construction purposes. There are many ASTM standards for all the alloys and shapes of stainless steel, and for each product type (bars, sheets, tubes, etc.) there are many individual tolerances such as wall thickness, length, squareness, and so on. However, most of these tolerances are so small (on the order of thousandths of an inch) as to be insignificant for most ornamental design and detailing work.

However, when standard stainless steel sections are used for a custom-designed ornamental fabrication, certain tolerances can be important. These are listed in this section.

Industry Standards

ASTM A484, *Standard Specification for General Requirements for Stainless and Heat-Resisting Steel Bars, Billets, and Forgings,* American Society for Testing and Materials, Philadelphia, 1992.

ASTM A554, *Standard Specification for Welded Stainless Steel Mechanical Tubing,* American Society for Testing and Materials, Philadelphia, 1990.

Allowable Tolerances

Tolerances for stainless steel sections that are likely to be important for detailing are shown in Fig. 9-11 and given in Tables 9-4 and 9-5.

Table 9-4
Twist Tolerances for Stainless Steel Tube Sections

Largest size, in (mm)	Twist, max. in/3 ft (mm/m)
½ to 1½ (12.7 to 38.1), inclusive	±0.075 (2.1)
Over 1½ to 2½ (38.1 to 63.5), inclusive	±0.095 (2.6)
Over 2½ (63.5)	±0.125 (3.5)

SOURCE: ASTM A554; copyright ASTM; reprinted with permission.

Table 9-5
Size and Squareness Tolerances for Stainless Steel Tee Sections

Specified size of tee, in (mm)*	Width and depth, in (mm)	Out of square, in (mm)
To 1½ (38.00), inclusive	±⁵⁄₆₄ (2.00)	±³⁄₆₄ (1.20)
Over 1½ to 2 (38.00 to 50.00), inclusive	±³⁄₃₂ (2.40)	±³⁄₃₂ (2.40)
Over 2 to 3 (50.00 to 75.00), exclusive	±⁹⁄₆₄ (3.60)	±⁹⁄₆₄ (3.60)

*The longer member of an unequal tee determines the size for tolerances.
SOURCE: ASTM A484/A484M; copyright ASTM; reprinted with permission.

Related Sections

9-12. Copper Alloy Ornamental Metal Products

9-13. Extruded Aluminum Tubes

Figure 9-12

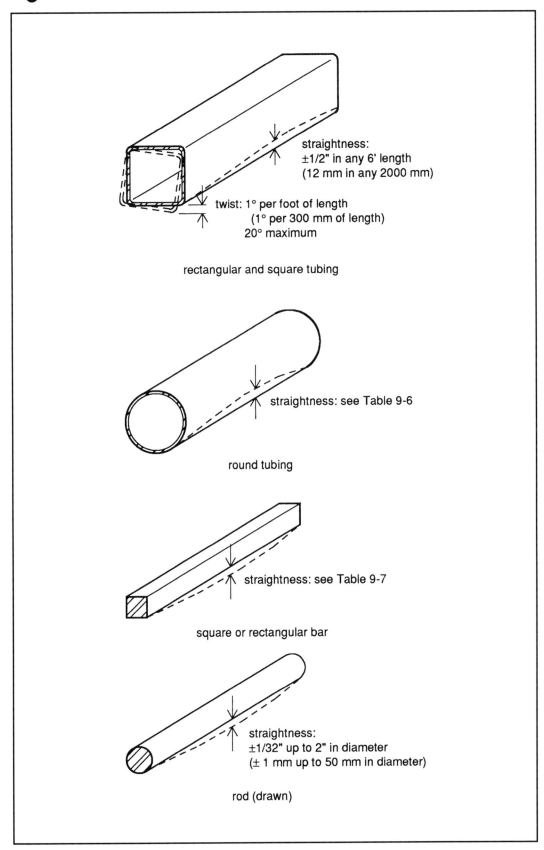

straightness:
±1/2" in any 6' length
(12 mm in any 2000 mm)

twist: 1° per foot of length
(1° per 300 mm of length)
20° maximum

rectangular and square tubing

straightness: see Table 9-6

round tubing

straightness: see Table 9-7

square or rectangular bar

straightness:
±1/32" up to 2" in diameter
(± 1 mm up to 50 mm in diameter)

rod (drawn)

9-12. Copper Alloy Ornamental Metal Products

Description

This section includes tolerances for some of the shapes and alloys of copper commonly used for ornamental construction purposes. There are many ASTM standards for all the alloys and shapes, and for each product type (e.g., bars, sheets, tubes) there are many individual tolerances such as wall thickness, length, squareness, and so on. However, most of these tolerances are so small (on the order of thousandths of an inch) as to be insignificant for most ornamental design and detailing work.

However, when standard copper alloy sections are used for a custom-designed ornamental fabrication, certain tolerances can be important. These are listed in this section for some of the commonly used architectural alloys.

Industry Standards

ASTM B248, *Standard Specification for General Requirements for Wrought Copper and Copper-Alloy Plate, Sheet, Strip, and Rolled Bar*, American Society for Testing and Materials, Philadelphia, 1992.

ASTM B249, *Standard Specification for General Requirements for Wrought Copper and Copper-Alloy Rod, Bar, and Shapes*, American Society for Testing and Materials, Philadelphia, 1991.

ASTM B251/B251M, *Standard Specification for General Requirements for Wrought Seamless Copper and Copper-Alloy Tube*, American Society for Testing and Materials, Philadelphia, 1993.

Allowable Tolerances

Tolerances for copper alloy sections that are likely to be important for detailing are shown in Fig. 9-12 and given in Tables 9-6 and 9-7. The tolerances for rectangular and round tubing include the copper alloys C22000 (commercial bronze), C23000 (red brass), C26000 (cartridge brass), and C28000 (muntz metal). The tolerances shown for drawn rod include the alloy C65500.

Table 9-6
Straightness Tolerances for Round Tubing*

Length of section, ft (mm)†	Maximum curvature, in (mm)
Over 3 to 6 (1000 to 2000), inclusive	±3/16 (5.0)
Over 6 to 8 (2000 to 2500), inclusive	±5/16 (8.0)
Over 8 to 10 (2500 to 3000), inclusive	±1/2 (12)

*Not applicable to pipe, redrawn tube, extruded tube, or any annealed tube.

†For lengths greater than 10 ft (3000 mm) the maximum curvature shall not exceed 1/2 in (12 mm) in any 10-ft (3000-mm) portion of the total length.

SOURCE: ASTM B251/B251M; copyright ASTM; reprinted with permission.

Table 9-7
Straightness Tolerances for Bars Made from Square-Sheared Metal*

Thickness, in (mm)	Tolerance for bars up to 10 in (250 mm) wide†
1/8 and under (3.2)	±1/16 (1.6)
Over 1/8 to 3/16 (3.2 to 5.0), inclusive	±1/8 (3.2)
Over 3/16 (5.0)	±1/8 (3.2)

*Includes alloys C22000 (commercial bronze), C23000 (red brass), and C26000 (cartridge brass).

†Maximum edgewise curvature (depth of arc) in any 72-in (1800-mm) portion of the total length.

SOURCE: ASTM B248/B248M; copyright ASTM; reprinted with permission.

Related Sections

9-11. Stainless Steel Ornamental Metal Products

9-13. Extruded Aluminum Tubes

Figure 9-13

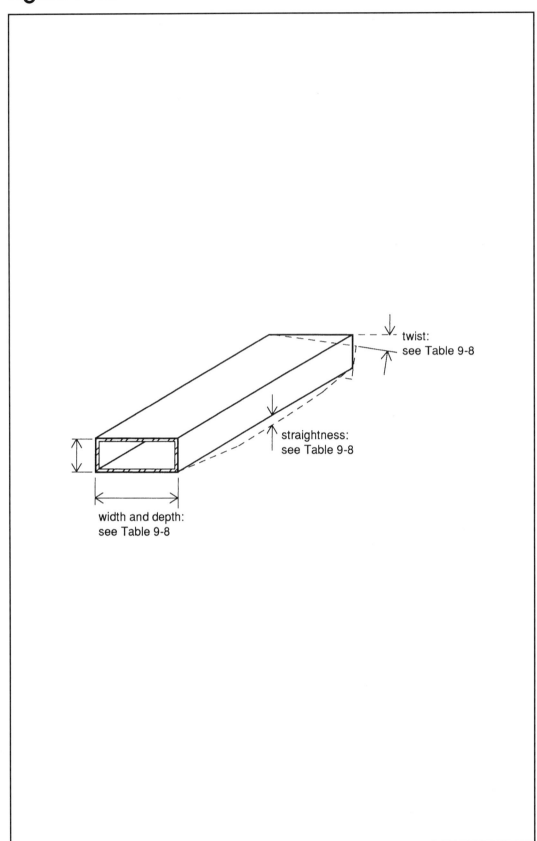

twist:
see Table 9-8

straightness:
see Table 9-8

width and depth:
see Table 9-8

9-13. Extruded Aluminum Tubes

Description

This section includes the aluminum products and tolerances that are most likely to be of concern to a designer detailing a custom-fabricated component using aluminum tubing. Many of the other tolerances for aluminum tubing are not included.

Industry Standard

ANSI-H35.2, *American National Standard Dimensional Tolerances for Aluminum Mill Products, The Aluminum Association, Washington, DC, 1990.*

Allowable Tolerances

ANSI-H35.2 contains many tolerances for individual elements of aluminum tubing. However, most of these tolerances are so small as to be insignificant for most ornamental design and detailing work. Mill tolerances for construction usually affect only the fabrication of components made from aluminum, such as curtain walls and windows. When standard aluminum tubing sections are used for a custom-designed ornamental fabrication certain tolerances can be important, such as width, straightness, and twist. These are listed in Table 9-8 and shown in Fig. 9-13.

Table 9-8
Selected Tolerances for Extruded Aluminum Tube Sections*

Inches		Millimeters	
Specified width, in	Deviation, in or degrees†	Specified width	Deviation, mm or degrees†
Width and Depth			
1.000–1.999	±0.018	25.00–50.00	±0.46
2.000–3.999	±0.025	50.00–100.00	±0.64
4.000–4.999	±0.035	100.00–130.00	±0.88
5.000–5.999	±0.045	130.00–150.00	±1.15
6.000–6.999	±0.055	150.00–180.00	±1.40
7.000–7.999	±0.065	180.00–200.00	±1.65
Straightness			
0.500–5.999	0.010 × measured length, ft‡	12.5–150.00	1 mm/m§
6.000 and over	0.020 × measured length, ft	150.00 and over	2 mm/m
Twist			
0.500–1.499	1° × measured length, ft; max. of 7°	12.50–40.00	3°/m but not greater than 7°
1.500–2.999	0.5° × measured length, ft; max. of 5°	40.00–80.00	1.5°/m but not greater than 5°
3.000 and over	0.25° × measured length, ft; max. of 3°	80.00 and over	1°/m but not greater than 3°

*This table includes tolerances for alloys and sizes normally used in construction. See ANSI-H35.2 for a complete listing of all alloys, sizes, and tolerances.

†Deviation at corners of section. See ANSI-H35.2 for allowable deviation in width between corners.

‡Deviation from straight in total length or in any segment of 1 ft or more of total length.

§Deviation from straight in total length or in any 300-mm or longer chord segment of total length.

SOURCE: Based on information from ANSI-H35.2-1990, The Aluminum Association; reproduced with permission.

Related Sections

8-1. Aluminum Curtain Wall Fabrication

8-4. Storefront and Entrance Manufacturing

11-9. Aluminum Window Manufacturing

Figure 9-14

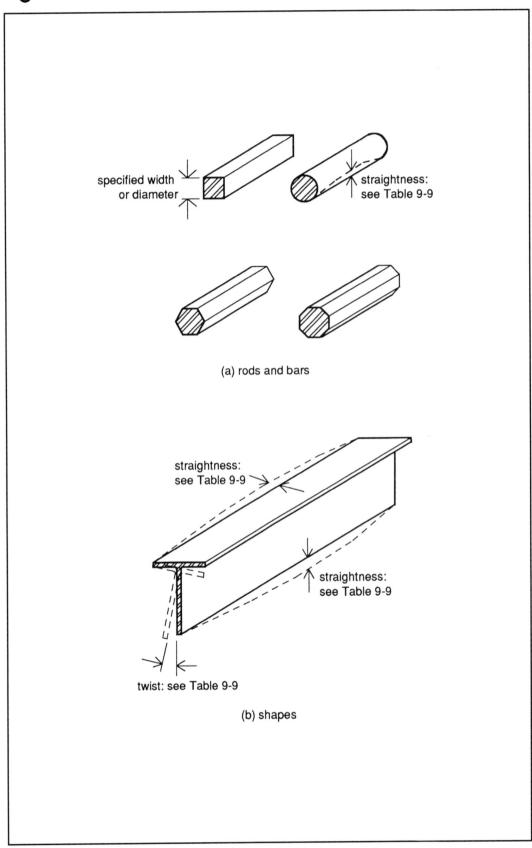

specified width
or diameter

straightness:
see Table 9-9

(a) rods and bars

straightness:
see Table 9-9

straightness:
see Table 9-9

twist: see Table 9-9

(b) shapes

Finishes

9-14. Aluminum Rods, Bars, and Shapes

Description

This section includes the aluminum products and tolerances that are most likely to be of concern to a designer detailing a custom-fabricated component using rods, bars, and various aluminum extruded shapes.

Industry Standard

ANSI-H35.2, *American National Standard Dimensional Tolerances for Aluminum Mill Products,* The Aluminum Association, Washington, DC, 1990.

Allowable Tolerances

ANSI-H35.2 contains many tolerances for individual elements of aluminum rods, bars, and shapes. However, most of these tolerances are so small as to be insignificant for most ornamental design and detailing work. Mill tolerances for construction usually only affect the fabrication of components made from aluminum, such as curtain walls, windows, and railings.

When standard aluminum shapes are used for a custom-designed ornamental fabrication certain tolerances can be important, such as straightness and twist. These are listed in Table 9-9 and shown in Fig. 9-14.

Table 9-9
Selected Tolerances for Aluminum Rods, Bars, and Shapes*

Product type	Inches		Millimeters	
	Specified width or diameter (and thickness)†	Deviation, in or degrees, times the measured length in feet	Specified width or diameter (and thickness)	Deviation, mm or degrees
Straightness				
Shapes	Width up through 1.4999 with thickness up through 0.094	0.050	Width up through 40.00 with thickness up through 2.50	4 mm/m
	Width up through 1.4999 with thickness 0.095 and over	0.0125	Width up through 40.00 with thickness over 2.50	1 mm/m
	Width 1.500 and over of all thicknesses	0.0125	Width over 40.00 of all thicknesses	1 mm/m
Rectangular bar	Width up through 1.499 and thickness up through 0.094	0.050	Width up through 40.00 and thickness up through 2.50	4 mm/m
	Width up through 1.499 with thickness 0.095 and over		Width up through 40.00 and thickness 2.50 and over	1 mm/m
Rod, square, hexagonal, octagonal bar	All	0.0125	All	1 mm/m
Twist				
Shapes/bars	Width up through 1.499	1°, with max. of 7°	Width through 40.00	3°/m; max. of 7°
	1.500–2.999	0.5°, with max. of 5°	40.00–80.00	1.5°/m; max. of 5°
	3.000 and over	0.25°, with max. of 3°	80.00 and over	1°/m; max. of 3°

*This table includes tolerances for alloys and sizes normally used in construction. See ANSI-H35.2 for a complete listing of all alloys, sizes, and tolerances.

†Diameter includes circumscribing circle around shapes like hexagonal bars.

source: Based on information from ANSI-H35.2-1990, The Aluminum Association; reproduced with permission.

Related Sections

8-1. Aluminum Curtain Wall Fabrication

9-13. Extruded Aluminum Tubes

Figure 10-1

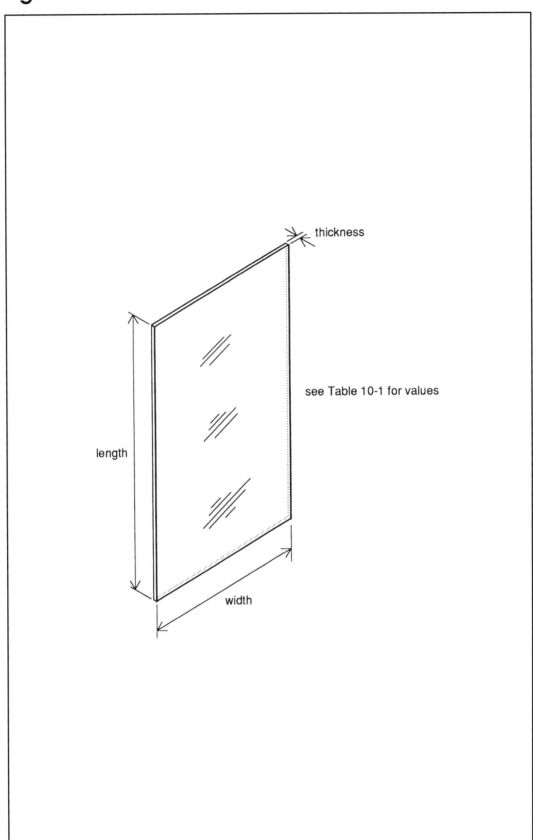

thickness

see Table 10-1 for values

length

width

Chapter 10

Glazing

10-1. Manufacturing Tolerances for Flat Glass

Description

This section includes tolerances for the manufacture of flat glass. It does not include glass as part of a window assembly. Refer to Chap. 11 for window assembly tolerances.

Industry Standards

Glazing Manual, Flat Glass Marketing Association, Topeka, KS, 1986.

ASTM C1036, *Standard Specification for Flat Glass,* American Society for Testing and Materials, Philadelphia, 1991.

Allowable Tolerances

Tolerances for the most common thicknesses of flat glass are shown diagrammatically in Fig. 10-1 and given in Table 10-1. For a complete listing refer to ASTM C1036.

Table 10-1   Allowable Tolerances for Clear, Flat Glass

Ordering thicknesses			Thickness range				Length and width,in (mm)
			in		mm		
Traditional designation, in	Nominal decimal, in	Designation, mm	Min.	Max.	Min.	Max.	
Single	0.09	2.5	0.085	0.101	2.16	2.57	$\pm\frac{1}{16}$ (1.6)
Double, $\frac{1}{8}$	0.12	3.0	0.115	0.134	2.92	3.40	$\pm\frac{1}{16}$ (1.6)
$\frac{5}{32}$	0.16	4.0	0.149	0.165	3.78	4.19	$\pm\frac{1}{16}$ (1.6)
$\frac{3}{16}$	0.19	5.0	0.180	0.199	4.57	5.05	$\pm\frac{1}{16}$ (1.6)
$\frac{7}{32}$	0.21	5.5	0.200	0.218	5.08	5.54	$\pm\frac{1}{16}$ (1.6)
$\frac{1}{4}$	0.23	6.0	0.219	0.244	5.56	6.2	$\pm\frac{1}{16}$ (1.6)
$\frac{5}{16}$	0.32	8.0	0.292	0.332	7.42	8.43	$\pm\frac{5}{64}$ (2.0)
$\frac{3}{8}$	0.39	10.0	0.355	0.406	9.02	10.31	$\pm\frac{3}{32}$ (2.4)
$\frac{1}{2}$	0.49	12.0	0.469	0.531	11.91	13.49	$\pm\frac{1}{8}$ (3.2)
$\frac{5}{8}$	0.63	16.0	0.595	0.656	15.09	16.66	$\pm\frac{5}{32}$ (4.0)
$\frac{3}{4}$	0.75	19.0	0.719	0.781	18.26	19.84	$\pm\frac{3}{16}$ (4.8)
$\frac{7}{8}$	0.87	22.0	0.844	0.906	21.44	23.01	$\pm\frac{7}{32}$ (5.6)
1	1.00	25.0	0.969	1.031	24.61	26.19	$\pm\frac{1}{4}$ (6.4)

SOURCE: ASTM C1036; copyright ASTM; reprinted with permission.

Related Sections

10-2. Manufacturing Tolerances for Patterned and Wired Glass

10-3. Tempered, Heat-Strengthened, and Spandrel Glass

10-4. Sealed Insulated Glass Units

11-11. Lockstrip Gasket Glazing

Figure 10-2

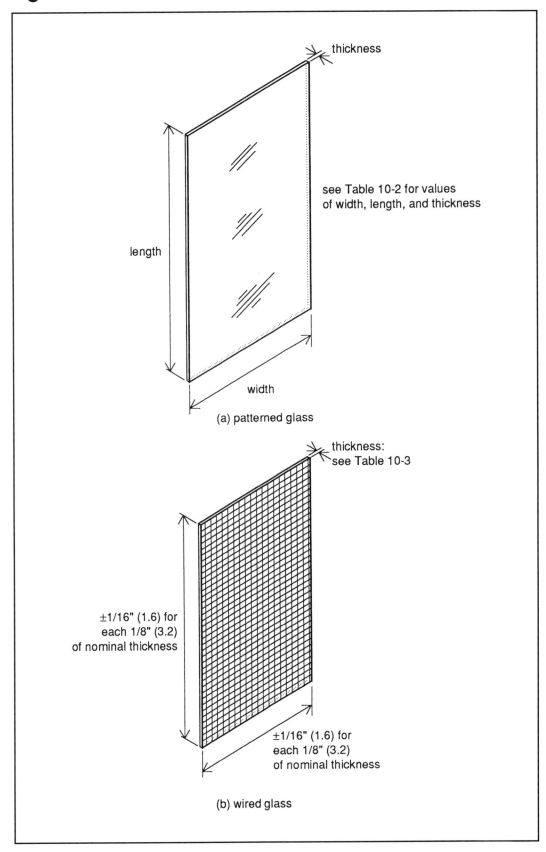

thickness

see Table 10-2 for values
of width, length, and thickness

length

width

(a) patterned glass

thickness:
see Table 10-3

±1/16" (1.6) for
each 1/8" (3.2)
of nominal thickness

±1/16" (1.6) for
each 1/8" (3.2)
of nominal thickness

(b) wired glass

10-2. Manufacturing Tolerances for Patterned and Wired Glass

Description

This section includes tolerances for the manufacture of patterned and wired glass. It does not include glass as part of a window assembly. Refer to Chap. 11 for window tolerances.

Industry Standards

Glazing Manual, Flat Glass Marketing Association, Topeka, KS, 1986.

ASTM C1036, *Standard Specification for Flat Glass,* American Society for Testing and Materials, Philadelphia, 1991.

Allowable Tolerances

Tolerances are shown in Fig. 10-2 and listed in Tables 10-2 and 10-3. Note that Underwriters Laboratories has never approved $\frac{7}{32}$-in wired glass for fire resistance.

Table 10-2
Tolerances for Patterned Glass

Thickness designation,in (mm)	Thickness tolerances, in (mm)		
	Minimum	Maximum	Length and width
SS (2.5)	0.085 (2.2)	0.110 (2.8)	$\pm\frac{1}{16}$ (1.6)
DS (3.0)	0.111 (2.8)	0.134 (3.4)	$\pm\frac{1}{16}$ (1.6)
$\frac{1}{8}$ (3.2)	0.111 (2.8)	0.172 (4.4)	$\pm\frac{1}{16}$ (1.6)
$\frac{5}{32}$ (4.0)	0.142 (3.6)	0.172 (4.4)	$\pm\frac{1}{16}$ (1.6)
$\frac{3}{16}$ (4.8)	0.172 (4.4)	0.219 (5.6)	$\pm\frac{1}{16}$ (1.6)
$\frac{7}{32}$ (5.6)	0.203 (5.2)	0.266 (6.8)	$\pm\frac{3}{32}$ (2.4)
$\frac{1}{4}$* (6.4)	0.234 (6.0)	0.297 (7.6)	$\pm\frac{1}{8}$ (3.2)

*Available only from foreign sources.
SOURCE: ASTM C1036; copyright ASTM; reprinted with permission.

Table 10-3
Tolerances for Wired Glass

Thickness designation, in (mm)	Thickness tolerances, in (mm)	
	Minimum	Maximum
$\frac{7}{32}$ (5.6)	0.203 (5.1)	0.250 (6.4)
$\frac{1}{4}$ (6.4)	0.250 (6.4)	0.297 (7.6)
$\frac{3}{8}$* (9.5)	0.328 (8.3)	0.391 (9.9)

*$\frac{3}{8}$-in thickness is available only from foreign sources.
SOURCE: ASTM C1036; copyright ASTM; reprinted with permission.

Related Sections

10-1. Manufacturing Tolerances for Flat Glass

10-3. Tempered, Heat-Strengthened, and Spandrel Glass

10-4. Sealed Insulated Glass Units

11-11. Lockstrip Gasket Glazing

Figure 10-3

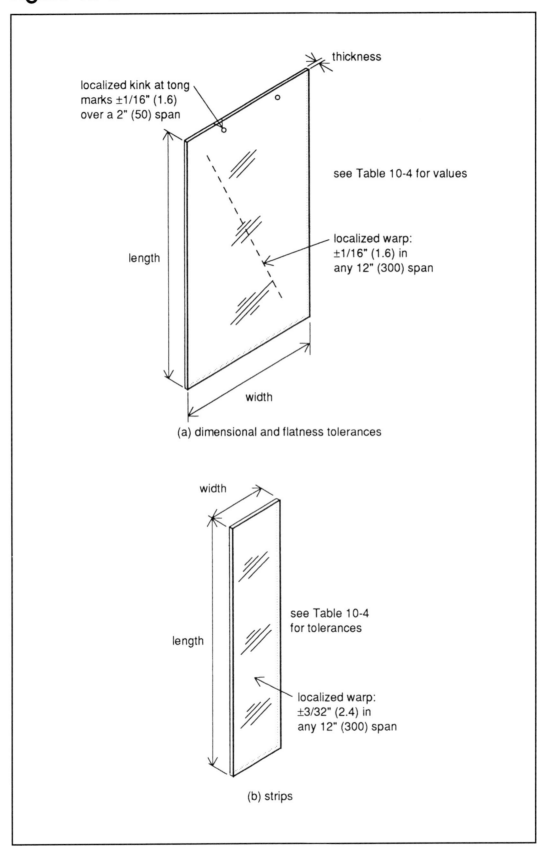

thickness

localized kink at tong marks ±1/16" (1.6) over a 2" (50) span

see Table 10-4 for values

length

localized warp: ±1/16" (1.6) in any 12" (300) span

width

(a) dimensional and flatness tolerances

width

see Table 10-4 for tolerances

length

localized warp: ±3/32" (2.4) in any 12" (300) span

(b) strips

10-3. Tempered, Heat-Strengthened, and Spandrel Glass

Description

This section includes tolerances for the manufacture of the various types of heat-treated flat glass.

Industry Standard

ASTM C1048, *Standard Specification for Heat Treated Flat Glass,* American Society for Testing and Materials, Philadelphia, 1992.

Allowable Tolerances

Tolerances are shown in Figs. 10-3 and 10-3.1 and listed in Tables 10-4 and 10-5. In Table 10-4 three conditions are noted. *Strips* are defined when one of the following three conditions are met: (1) for glass up to 72 in (1829 mm) long when the width is equal to or less than the length divided by 8; (2) for glass over 72 to 96 in (1829 to 2438 mm) when the width is equal to or less than the length divided by 7; (3) for glass over 96 to 132 in (2438 to 3353 mm) when the width is equal to or less than the length divided by 5. The ratios of length to width can be increased by substituting thicknesses greater than $\frac{1}{4}$ in (6 mm). Glass for all types of heat treating must conform to ASTM C1036 for flat glass.

Table 10-4
Dimensional Tolerances for Tempered, Heat-Strengthened, and Spandrel Glass

Dimensions	Plus, in (mm)	Minus, in (mm)
Transparent glass and coated glass (conditions 1 and 3)		
Neither dimension over 76 in (1930 mm)	$\frac{1}{16}$ (1.6)	$\frac{1}{8}$ (3.2)
One or more dimensions from 76 to 96 in and not over 40 ft^2 in area (1930 to 2438 and not more than 3.7 m^2)	$\frac{1}{16}$ (1.6)	$\frac{1}{8}$ (3.2)
Either dimension over 96 in (2438) or over 40 ft^2 in area (3.7 m^2)	$\frac{1}{16}$ (1.6)	$\frac{3}{16}$ (4.8)
Strips: dimensions not over 96 in (2438)	$\frac{1}{8}$ (3.2)	$\frac{1}{8}$ (3.2)
Strips: dimensions over 96 in (2438)	$\frac{3}{16}$ (4.8)	$\frac{3}{16}$ (4.8)
Spandrel glass, one surface ceramic coated (condition 2)		
Dimensions not over 96 in (2438)	0	$\frac{3}{16}$ (4.8)
Dimensions over 96 in (2438)	0	$\frac{1}{4}$ (6.4)
Strips: dimensions not over 96 in (2438)	0	$\frac{1}{4}$ (6.4)
Strips: dimensions over 96 in (2438)	0	$\frac{5}{16}$ (8.0)

SOURCE: Based on information from ASTM C1048; copyright ASTM; reprinted with permission.

Related Section

10-1. Manufacturing Tolerances for Flat Glass

Table 10-5
Bow Tolerances for Tempered, Heat-Strengthened, and Spandrel Glass

Edge length, in (mm)	Nominal glass thickness, in (mm)				
	$\frac{1}{8}$, $\frac{5}{32}$, $\frac{3}{16}$ (3.0, 4.0, 5.0)	$\frac{1}{4}$ (6.0)	$\frac{5}{16}$ (8.0)	$\frac{3}{8}$ (10.0)	$\frac{1}{2}$–$\frac{7}{8}$ (12.0–22.0)
0–18 (0–460)	$\frac{1}{8}$ (3.2)	$\frac{1}{16}$ (1.6)	$\frac{1}{16}$ (1.6)	$\frac{1}{16}$ (1.6)	$\frac{1}{16}$ (1.6)
18–36 (460–910)	$\frac{3}{16}$ (4.8)	$\frac{1}{8}$ (3.2)	$\frac{3}{32}$ (2.4)	$\frac{3}{32}$ (2.4)	$\frac{1}{16}$ (1.6)
36–48 (910–1220)	$\frac{9}{32}$ (7.1)	$\frac{3}{16}$ (4.8)	$\frac{5}{32}$ (4.0)	$\frac{1}{8}$ (3.2)	$\frac{3}{32}$ (2.4)
48–60 (1220–1520)	$\frac{3}{8}$ (9.5)	$\frac{9}{32}$ (7.1)	$\frac{7}{32}$ (5.6)	$\frac{3}{16}$ (4.8)	$\frac{1}{8}$ (3.2)
60–72 (1520–1830)	$\frac{1}{2}$ (12.7)	$\frac{3}{8}$ (9.5)	$\frac{9}{32}$ (7.1)	$\frac{1}{4}$ (6.4)	$\frac{3}{16}$ (4.8)
72–84 (1830–2130)	$\frac{5}{8}$ (15.9)	$\frac{1}{2}$ (12.7)	$\frac{11}{32}$ (8.7)	$\frac{5}{16}$ (7.9)	$\frac{1}{4}$ (6.4)
84–96 (2130–2440)	$\frac{3}{4}$ (19.0)	$\frac{5}{8}$ (15.9)	$\frac{7}{16}$ (11.1)	$\frac{3}{8}$ (9.5)	$\frac{9}{32}$ (7.1)
96–108 (2440–2740)	$\frac{7}{8}$ (22.2)	$\frac{3}{4}$ (19.0)	$\frac{9}{16}$ (14.3)	$\frac{1}{2}$ (12.7)	$\frac{3}{8}$ (9.5)
108–120 (2740–3050)	1 (25.4)	$\frac{7}{8}$ (22.2)	$\frac{11}{16}$ (17.5)	$\frac{5}{8}$ (15.9)	$\frac{1}{2}$ (12.7)
120–132 (3050–3350)	—	1 (25.4)	$\frac{13}{16}$ (20.6)	$\frac{3}{4}$ (19.0)	$\frac{5}{8}$ (15.9)
132–144 (3350–3660)	—	$1\frac{1}{8}$ (28.6)	$\frac{15}{16}$ (23.8)	$\frac{7}{8}$ (22.2)	$\frac{3}{4}$ (19.0)
144–156 (3660–3960)	—	$1\frac{1}{4}$ (31.8)	$1\frac{1}{16}$ (27.0)	1 (25.4)	$\frac{7}{8}$ (22.2)

SOURCE: Compiled from ASTM C1048; copyright ASTM; reprinted with permission.

Figure 10-3.1

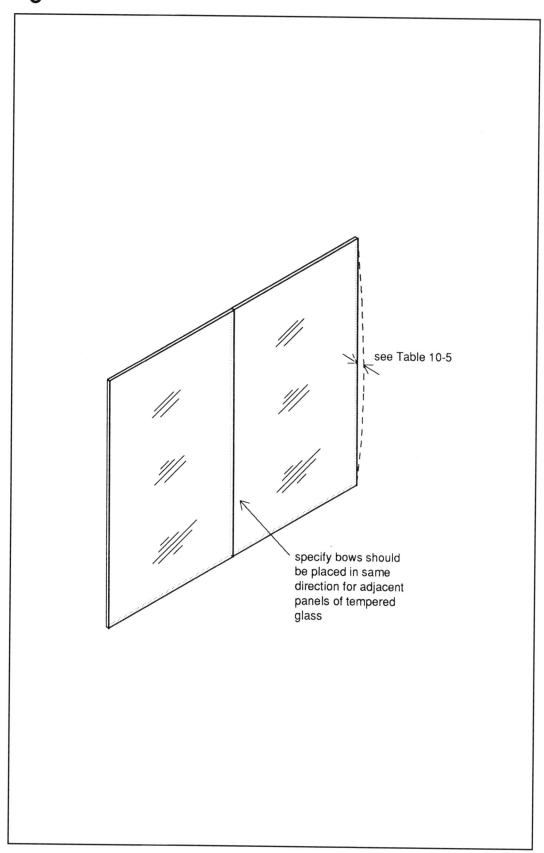

see Table 10-5

specify bows should
be placed in same
direction for adjacent
panels of tempered
glass

Figure 10-4

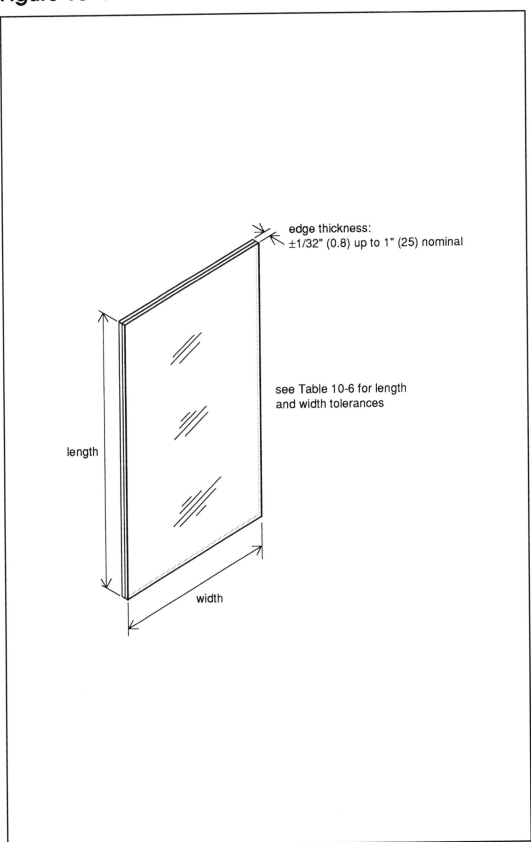

edge thickness:
±1/32" (0.8) up to 1" (25) nominal

see Table 10-6 for length
and width tolerances

length

width

10-4. Sealed Insulated Glass Units

Description

Insulated glass units consist of two panes of glass that enclose a hermetically sealed air space. The panes are held apart by a spacer around the perimeter.

Industry Standard

Voluntary Guidelines for Commercial Insulating Glass—Dimensional Tolerances, Sealed Insulated Glass Manufacturers Association, Chicago, 1983.

Allowable Tolerances

Recommended tolerances are shown in Fig. 10-4 and listed in Table 10-6. For insulating units fabricated from flat glass these tolerances can usually be maintained. When tempered glass is used the bow tolerance is often the controlling factor. In many cases the tempered glass manufacturer must reduce the range of bow tolerances to allow the insulating unit to be fabricated to within or close to the tolerances recommended by the Sealed Insulated Glass Manufacturers Association.

Table 10-6
Dimensional Tolerances for Insulating Glass Units

Width or length, in (mm)	Plus, in (mm)	Minus, in (mm)
Up to 30 (760)	$\frac{1}{8}$ (3.2)	$\frac{1}{16}$ (1.6)
Over 30 to 60 (760 to 1525)	$\frac{5}{32}$ (4.0)	$\frac{1}{16}$ (1.6)
Over 60 to 84 (1525 to 2134)	$\frac{3}{16}$ (4.8)	$\frac{1}{16}$ (1.6)
Over 84 (2134)	Consult manufacturer	

SOURCE: Sealed Insulated Glass Manufacturers Association.

Related Sections

10-1. Manufacturing Tolerances for Flat Glass

10-3. Tempered, Heat-Strengthened, and Spandrel Glass

Figure 10-5

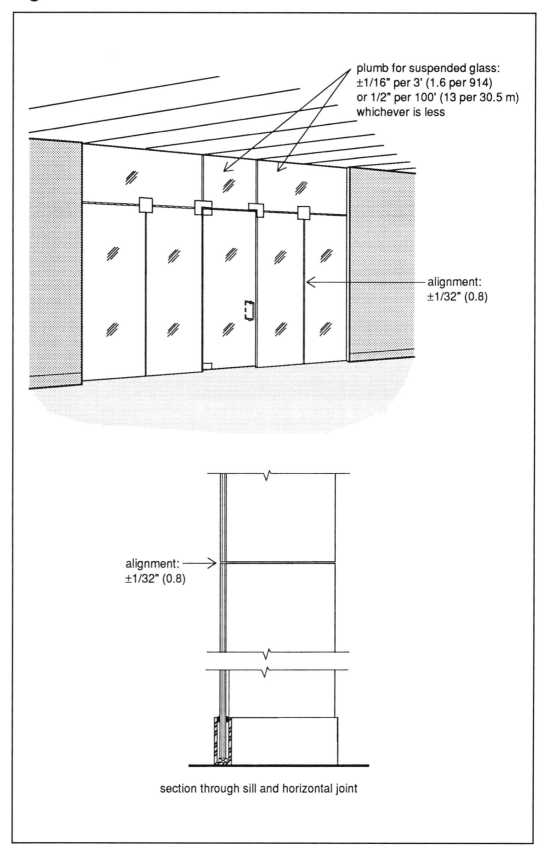

plumb for suspended glass:
±1/16" per 3' (1.6 per 914)
or 1/2" per 100' (13 per 30.5 m)
whichever is less

alignment:
±1/32" (0.8)

alignment:
±1/32" (0.8)

section through sill and horizontal joint

10-5. All-Glass Entrances

Description

All-glass entrances consist of a glazing system using a minimum of visible framing members, relying instead on silicon sealant, suspended glazing, glass mullions, clamps, and other special fittings to support fixed glass and glass doors.

Industry Standards

ASTM C1048, *Standard Specification for Heat Treated Flat Glass,* American Society for Testing and Materials, Philadelphia, 1992.

Spectext Section 08971, *Suspended Glass,* Construction Sciences Research Foundation, Baltimore, July 1988.

Allowable Tolerances

Because all-glass systems do not rely on rigid framing members of aluminum, steel, wood, or other materials, the accuracy of the installation depends primarily on the tolerances of the glass. Most all-glass entrances are in hazardous locations so tempered or laminated glass is used. For tempered glass installations, the bow tolerances listed in Table 10-5 often govern. These affect both the plumbness of the glass and the relative alignment of two butt jointed pieces. To minimize misalignment, adjacent tempered glass units should be installed with the bow in the same direction. When tempered glass is installed in concealed framing at the floor and ceiling, the dimensional tolerances listed in Table 10-4 must also be accommodated.

For suspended glazing, the Spectext master specifications recommend a noncumulative plumb tolerance of $\frac{1}{16}$ in (1.6 mm) in every 3 ft (900 mm) or $\frac{1}{2}$ in (13 mm) per 100 ft (30.5 m), whichever is less. See Fig. 10-5. Spectext also recommends a maximum misalignment of adjoining glass units of $\frac{1}{32}$ in (0.8 mm).

Related Sections

10-1. Manufacturing Tolerances for Flat Glass

10-3. Tempered, Heat-Strengthened, and Spandrel Glass

10-4. Sealed Insulated Glass Units

Figure 11-1

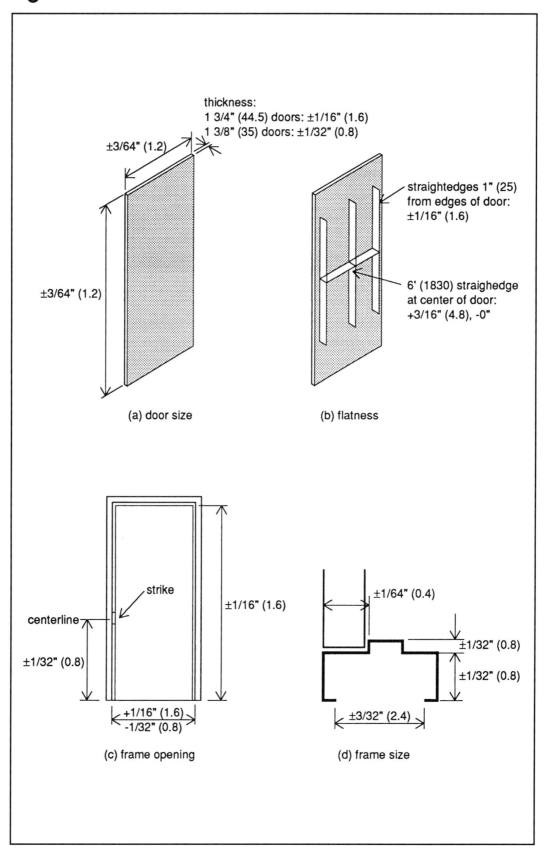

thickness:
1 3/4" (44.5) doors: ±1/16" (1.6)
1 3/8" (35) doors: ±1/32" (0.8)

±3/64" (1.2)

±3/64" (1.2)

(a) door size

straightedges 1" (25)
from edges of door:
±1/16" (1.6)

6' (1830) straighedge
at center of door:
+3/16" (4.8), -0"

(b) flatness

strike

centerline

±1/32" (0.8)

±1/16" (1.6)

+1/16" (1.6)
-1/32" (0.8)

(c) frame opening

±1/64" (0.4)

±1/32" (0.8)

±1/32" (0.8)

±3/32" (2.4)

(d) frame size

Chapter 11

Doors and Windows

11-1. Standard Steel Doors and Frames

Description

Standard steel doors and frames include products manufactured according to SDI-100, *Recommended Specifications—Standard Steel Doors and Frames,* and include both single- and double-rabbeted frames. This section does not include special or unusual doors or frame conditions.

Industry Standard

SDI 117, *Manufacturing Tolerances, Standard Steel Doors and Frames,* Steel Door Institute, Cleveland, OH, 1988.

Allowable Tolerances

Tolerances for door and frame size, flatness, and frame preparation are shown in Fig. 11-1. In addition to the door size tolerances shown, the squareness of a door is determined by measuring the diagonals. The two diagonals should not vary by more than $\frac{1}{16}$ in (1.6 mm). To determine flatness three measurements are taken: once with a 6-ft (1830-mm) straight-edge across the center of the door in a vertical direction, once across the center of the door in a horizontal direction, and once at positions 1 in (25 mm) from the lock and hinge edges of the door.

For additional tolerances on hinge cutout and placement refer to SDI 117.

Related Sections

11-2. Insulated Steel Door Systems

11-3. Detention Security Hollow Metal Doors and Frames

Figure 11-2

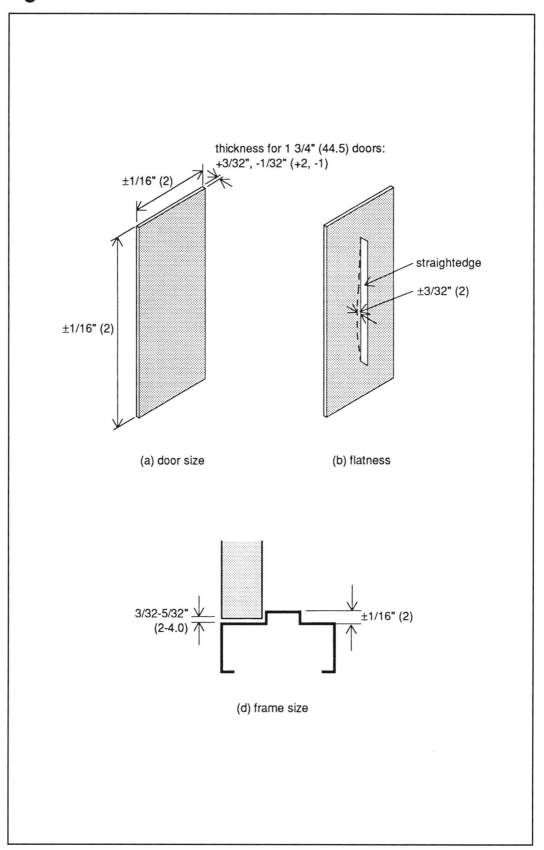

thickness for 1 3/4" (44.5) doors:
+3/32", -1/32" (+2, -1)

±1/16" (2)

±1/16" (2)

straightedge

±3/32" (2)

(a) door size

(b) flatness

3/32-5/32"
(2-4.0)

±1/16" (2)

(d) frame size

11-2. Insulated Steel Door Systems

Description

The tolerances in this section cover doors and frames. Doors are manufactured to fit the standard frame opening sizes listed in Table 11-1 with a $\frac{3}{32}$-in to $\frac{5}{32}$-in (2-mm to 4-mm) clearance between the door and the frame. The width is measured from inside of jamb to inside of jamb and the height is measured from the top of the threshold to the inside of the header rabbet.

Table 11-1
Standard Insulated Steel Door Opening Sizes

Standard width, ft-in (mm)*
2 ft-6 in (762)
2 ft-8 in (813)
2 ft-10 in (864)
3 ft-0 in (914)
3 ft-6 in (1067)
3 ft-8 in (1118)
5 ft-0 in (1524)
5 ft-4 in (1626)
6 ft-0 in (1829)
6 ft-8 in (2032)

*All heights 6 ft-8 in (2032 mm). Midline indicates double door opening sizes.

SOURCE: ISDI 100-79, Insulated Steel Door Institute.

Industry Standard

ISDI-100, *Door Size Dimensional Standard and Assembly Tolerances for Insulated Steel Door Systems,* Insulated Steel Door Institute, Cleveland, 1990.

Allowable Tolerances

Tolerances for door and frame size and flatness are shown in Fig. 11-2. The flatness tolerances shown apply to warpage of the door as well as other surface irregularities.

Related Sections

11-1. Standard Steel Doors and Frames

11-3. Detention Security Hollow Metal Doors and Frames

Figure 11-3

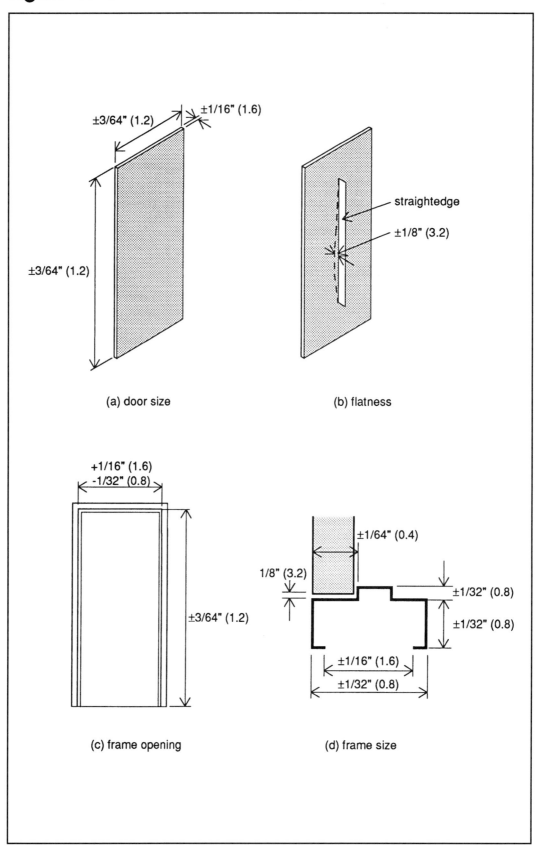

(a) door size

(b) flatness

(c) frame opening

(d) frame size

11-3. Detention Security Hollow Metal Doors and Frames

Description

This section includes tolerances for heavy duty doors and frames used for detention facilities. Standard steel doors and frames include products manufactured according to SDI-100, *Recommended Specifications—Standard Steel Doors and Frames,* and include both single- and double-rabbeted frames.

Industry Standard

ANSI/NAAMM HMMA 863, *Guide Specifications for Detention Security Hollow Metal Doors and Frames,* Hollow Metal Manufacturers Association, Division of National Association of Architectural Metal Manufacturers, Chicago, 1990.

Allowable Tolerances

Tolerances for door and frame size and flatness are shown in Fig. 11-3. The flatness tolerances shown apply to warpage and bow of the door.

For swinging and sliding doors the hardware cutout dimension tolerance is the template dimension plus 0.015 in and minus 0 in (plus 0.38 mm and minus 0 mm). Hardware location tolerance is $\pm\frac{1}{32}$ in (±0.8 mm). Refer to ANSI/HMMA 863 for standardized hardware locations and standard clearances.

Related Sections

11-1. Standard Steel Doors and Frames

11-2. Insulated Steel Door Systems

Figure 11-4

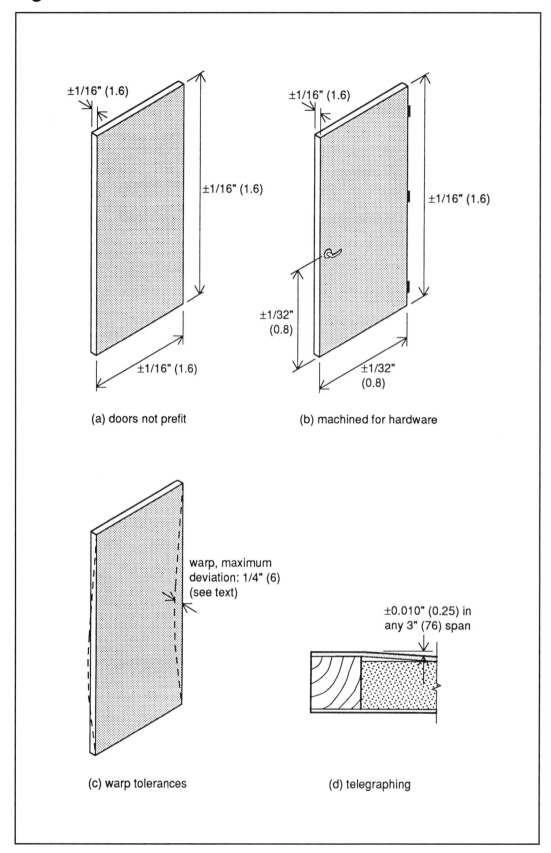

(a) doors not prefit

(b) machined for hardware

(c) warp tolerances

(d) telegraphing

11-4. Standard Flush Wood Doors

Description

This section includes tolerances for flush wood doors manufactured according to the National Wood Window and Door Association standards. Refer to Sec. 7-14 for tolerances for standard flush wood doors manufactured according to Architectural Woodwork Institute standards. However, the tolerances are very similar for both standards.

Industry Standards

NWWDA I.S. 1-A, *Architectural Wood Flush Doors,* National Wood Window and Door Association, Des Plaines, IL, 1991.

Quality Standards for the Professional Remodeler, 2d ed., National Association of Home Builders Remodelors™ Council, Washington, DC, 1991.

Insurance/Warranty Documents, Home Owners Warranty Corporation, Arlington, VA, 1987.

Allowable Tolerances

Figure 11-4 illustrates the tolerances of size, warp, and show-through or telegraphing. The tolerances for hardware location for machined doors pertain to locks, hinges, and other hardware.

Warp tolerances apply only to the door and not to its relation to the frame. The maximum deviation of $\frac{1}{4}$ in (6 mm) applies to a maximum door size of 3 ft, 0 in by 7 ft, 0 in (900 mm by 2100 mm) for $1\frac{3}{8}$-in-thick (35-mm-thick) doors and to a maximum door size of 3 ft, 6 in by 7 ft, 0 in (1067 mm by 2100 mm) for $1\frac{3}{4}$-in-thick (44-mm-thick) doors. For doors larger than 3 ft, 0 in by 7 ft, 0 in (900 mm by 2100 mm) the tolerance is measured in any 3 ft, 6 in by 7 ft, 0 in section.

Telegraphing is the distortion of the face veneer of a door caused by variation in thickness between the core material and the vertical or horizontal edge bands.

The *Insurance/Warranty Documents* of the Home Owners Warranty Corporation and the *Quality Standards for the Professional Remodeler* of the National Association of Home Builders Remodelors™ Council both use the $\frac{1}{4}$-in (6-mm) maximum tolerance for warping of interior doors.

Related Sections

7-14. Architectural Flush Doors

11-5. Standard Stile and Rail Doors

11-7. Installation of Wood Doors

Figure 11-5

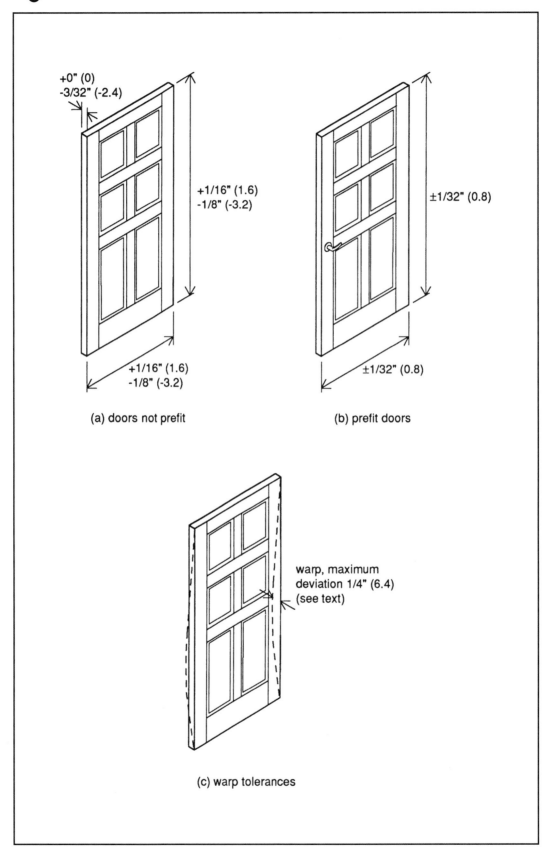

+0" (0)
-3/32" (-2.4)

+1/16" (1.6)
-1/8" (-3.2)

+1/16" (1.6)
-1/8" (-3.2)

(a) doors not prefit

±1/32" (0.8)

±1/32" (0.8)

(b) prefit doors

warp, maximum
deviation 1/4" (6.4)
(see text)

(c) warp tolerances

11-5. Standard Stile and Rail Doors

Description

This section includes size and flatness tolerances for stile and rail doors manufactured according to the National Wood Window and Door Association standards. Refer to Sec. 7-15 for tolerances for standard stile and rail doors manufactured according to Architectural Woodwork Institute standards.

Industry Standard

NWWDA I.S. 6-91, *Wood Stile and Rail Doors,* National Wood Window and Door Association, Des Plaines, IL, 1991.

Allowable Tolerances

Figure 11-5 illustrates the size tolerances for both prefit and non-prefit doors as well as tolerances for warp. Warp is measured by placing a straightedge or taut string on the concave face of the door at any angle and measuring the distance between the bottom of the straightedge and the face of the door. Warp tolerance is based on a $1\frac{3}{4}$-in-thick door that is 3 ft, 6 in wide and 7 ft, 0 in high (44 mm by 1070 mm by 2130 mm). The $\frac{1}{4}$-in (6-mm) maximum warp dimension does not apply to larger doors.

The height and width tolerances for doors not prefit do not apply to bifold doors. These are considered prefit at the time of manufacture and must conform to tolerances for prefit doors shown in Fig. 11-5*b.*

Related Sections

7-15. Stile and Rail Doors—Size and Flatness

7-16. Stile and Rail Doors—Joint Tightness and Flushness

11-4. Standard Flush Wood Doors

11-7. Installation of Wood Doors

Figure 11-7

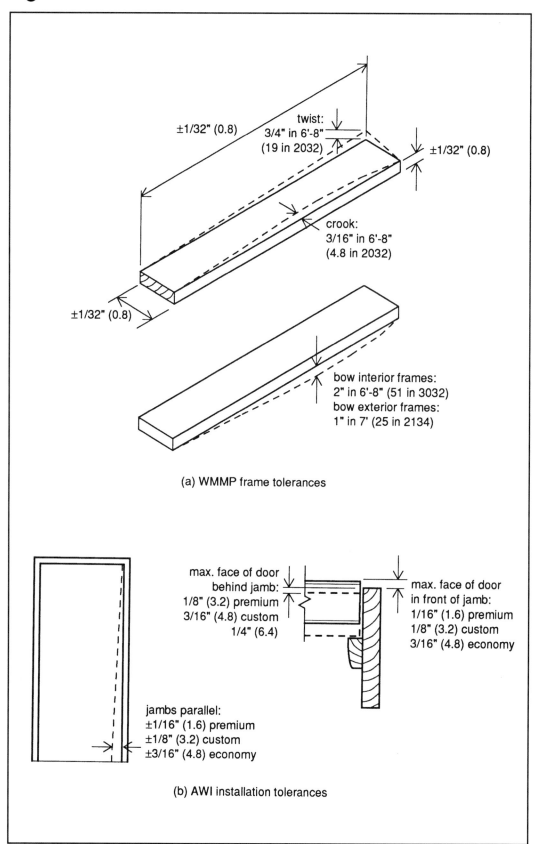

±1/32" (0.8)

twist:
3/4" in 6'-8"
(19 in 2032)

±1/32" (0.8)

crook:
3/16" in 6'-8"
(4.8 in 2032)

±1/32" (0.8)

bow interior frames:
2" in 6'-8" (51 in 3032)
bow exterior frames:
1" in 7' (25 in 2134)

(a) WMMP frame tolerances

max. face of door
behind jamb:
1/8" (3.2) premium
3/16" (4.8) custom
1/4" (6.4)

max. face of door
in front of jamb:
1/16" (1.6) premium
1/8" (3.2) custom
3/16" (4.8) economy

jambs parallel:
±1/16" (1.6) premium
±1/8" (3.2) custom
±3/16" (4.8) economy

(b) AWI installation tolerances

11-7. Installation of Wood Doors

Description

Installation of wood doors includes the manufacture and installation of the frame pieces as well as the hanging of the door. The Wood Moulding and Millwork Producers (WMMP) publishes quality standards for the fabrication of one-piece and two-piece interior wood jambs and for exterior wood frames. However, they do not state any tolerances for hanging doors within the frames. Prefit clearances of $\frac{1}{8}$ in (3 mm) between the door and the frame are given in *Architectural Wood Flush Doors* (NWWDA I.S. 1-A) published by the National Wood Window and Door Association (NWWDA).

The Architectural Woodwork Institute (AWI) lists tolerances for frames fabricated according to one of their grades (see Sec. 7-11) and also publishes installation standards which are summarized in this section. For AWI installation standards to apply they must be specifically called out in the specifications and the doors manufactured according to AWI standards.

Industry Standards

WM 1-89, *Quality Standards, Hinged Interior Wood Door Jambs,* Wood Moulding and Millwork Producers, Portland, OR, 1989.

WM 3-89, *Quality Standards, Exterior Wood Door Frames,* Wood Moulding and Millwork Producers, Portland, OR, 1989.

Architectural Woodwork Quality Standards, 6th ed., Architectural Woodwork Institute, Centreville, VA, 1993.

Allowable Tolerances

WMMP standards for jamb fabrication are summarized in Fig. 11-7a. The tolerance for *cupping,* which is a deviation in the face of a piece from a straight line drawn from edge to edge, is limited to $\frac{1}{32}$ in (0.8 mm) in widths less than 4 in (100 mm) and to $\frac{1}{16}$ in (1.6 mm) in widths 4 in and over.

AWI tolerances for installation are shown in Fig. 11-7b.

Related Sections

7-11. Frames, Jambs, and Windows

11-4. Standard Flush Wood Doors

11-5. Standard Stile and Rail Doors

11-6. Wood Swinging Patio Doors

Figure 11-8

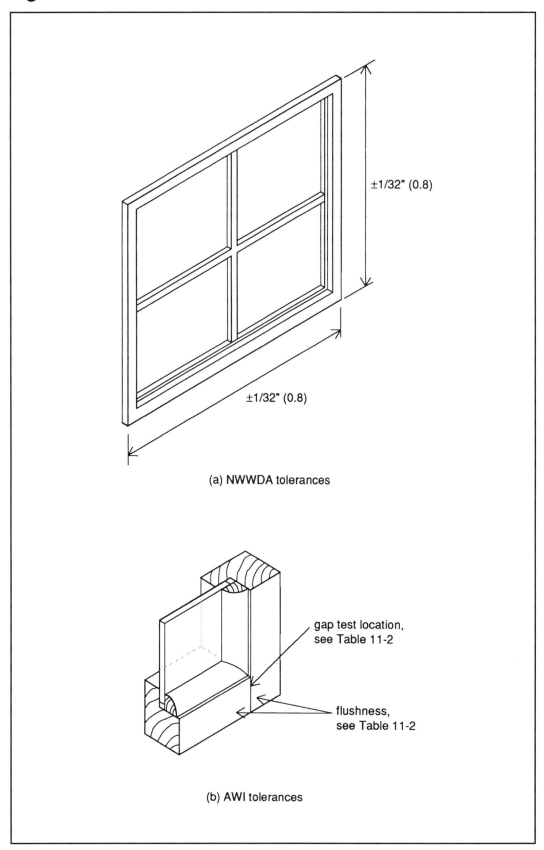

±1/32" (0.8)

±1/32" (0.8)

(a) NWWDA tolerances

gap test location,
see Table 11-2

flushness,
see Table 11-2

(b) AWI tolerances

11-8. Wood Windows

Description

This section includes windows manufactured according to National Wood Window and Door Association (NWWDA) standards or custom-built windows made according to Architectural Woodwork Institute (AWI) standards. Most wood windows for residential or commercial construction are factory-built units fabricated to very close tolerances. Therefore, in most cases, the tolerances shown in Fig. 11-8a apply.

Industry Standards

NWWDA I.S. 2-93, *Wood Windows,* National Wood Window and Door Association, Des Plaines, IL, 1993.

Architectural Woodwork Quality Standards, 6th ed., Architectural Woodwork Institute, Centreville, VA, 1993.

Allowable Tolerances

NWWDA tolerances are shown in Fig. 11-8a and AWI tolerances are indicated in Fig. 11-8b, with specific tolerances listed in Table 11-2.

Table 11-2
AWI Joint Tolerances for Factory Assembled Windows

	AWI grade tolerances, in (mm)					
	Premium		Custom		Economy	
	Interior	Exterior	Interior	Exterior	Interior	Exterior
Maximum gap at test location	0.015 (0.38)	0.025 (0.6)	0.025 0.6	0.050 (1.3)	0.050 (1.3)	0.075 (1.9)
Flushness	None	0.015 (0.38)	0.005 (0.13)	0.025 (0.6)	0.025 (0.6)	0.050 (1.3)

SOURCE: Reprinted with permission from *American Woodwork Quality Standards,* 6th ed., Architectural Woodwork Institute.

Related Section

7-11. Frames, Jambs, and Windows

Figure 11-9

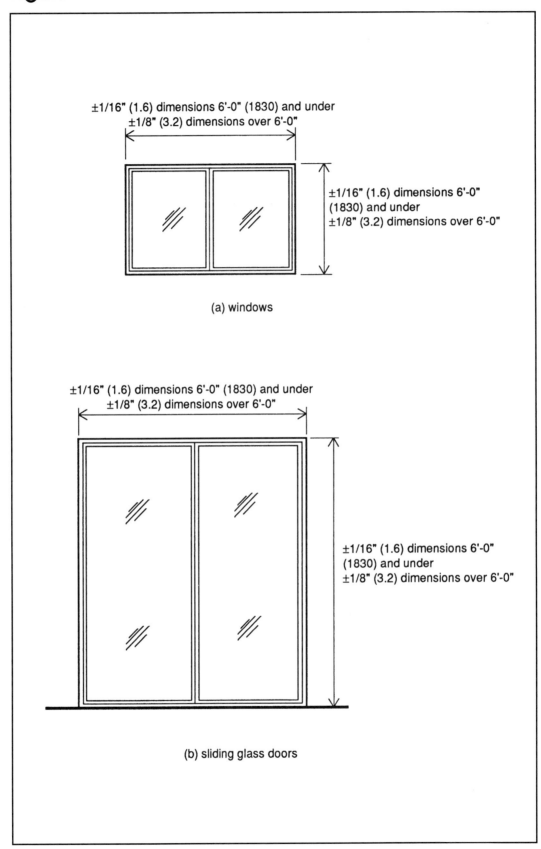

±1/16" (1.6) dimensions 6'-0" (1830) and under
±1/8" (3.2) dimensions over 6'-0"

±1/16" (1.6) dimensions 6'-0"
(1830) and under
±1/8" (3.2) dimensions over 6'-0"

(a) windows

±1/16" (1.6) dimensions 6'-0" (1830) and under
±1/8" (3.2) dimensions over 6'-0"

±1/16" (1.6) dimensions 6'-0"
(1830) and under
±1/8" (3.2) dimensions over 6'-0"

(b) sliding glass doors

11-9. Aluminum Windows and Sliding Doors

Description

This section includes tolerances for aluminum prime windows and sliding glass doors that are manufactured according to ANSI/AAMA 101-88. As with other premanufactured window and door units, aluminum windows and doors seldom present problems with installation or operation due to dimensional tolerance problems.

Industry Standard

ANSI/AAMA 101-88, *Voluntary Specifications for Aluminum Prime Windows and Sliding Glass Doors,* American Architectural Manufacturers Association, Des Plaines, IL, 1988.

Allowable Tolerances

Tolerances are shown in Fig. 11-9. In addition to these size tolerances, the tolerances of wall thicknesses and other cross-sectional dimensions of aluminum extrusions given in ANSI H35.2 apply. (Refer to Sec. 9-14.) Note that the tolerances shown in Fig. 11-9 do not apply to diagonal measurements.

Related section

9-14. Aluminum Rods, Bars, and Shapes

Figure 11-10

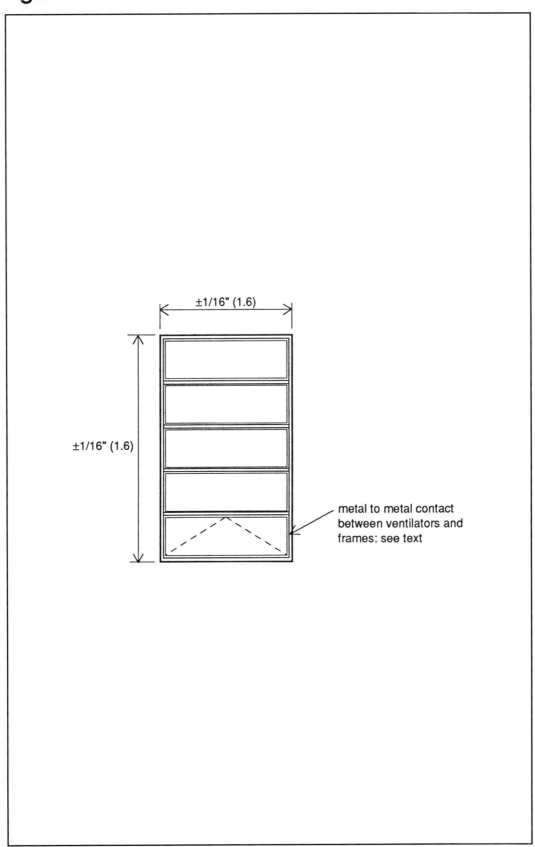

±1/16" (1.6)

±1/16" (1.6)

metal to metal contact
between ventilators and
frames: see text

11-10. Steel Windows

Description

This section includes tolerances for standard and detention steel window units that are manufactured according to the specifications of the Steel Window Institute (SWI). As with other premanufactured windows, steel windows seldom present problems with installation or operation due to tolerance problems.

Industry Standard

Steel Windows, Specifications, Steel Window Institute, Cleveland, 1983.

Allowable Tolerances

Dimensional tolerances are shown in Fig. 11-10. In addition, SWI specifications require limits on gaps between metal when ventilator units are locked and tested before leaving the factory. For commercial side hung ventilators, is should not be possible to freely insert, without forcing, a steel feeler gage 2 in (50 mm) wide by 0.020 in (0.51 mm) thick between the inside contacts of more than 40 percent of the contacts. For projected ventilators it should not be possible to insert a feeler gage 0.031 in (0.79 mm) thick between the inside contacts or to freely insert a 0.020-in (0.51-mm) feeler gage between more than 40 percent of the contacts.

For residential window units it should not be possible to insert a feeler gage 0.031 in (0.79 mm) thick between the inside contacts or to freely insert a 0.020-in (0.51-mm) feeler gage between more than 40 percent of the contacts.

Framing members must be designed so that the deflection at the required wind load will not exceed $\frac{1}{175}$ of the span of the member. A 3 percent mill tolerance in the minimum weights of sections is allowed. Outside frame members must be designed to lap masonry by at least $\frac{1}{2}$ in (13 mm).

Figure 11-11

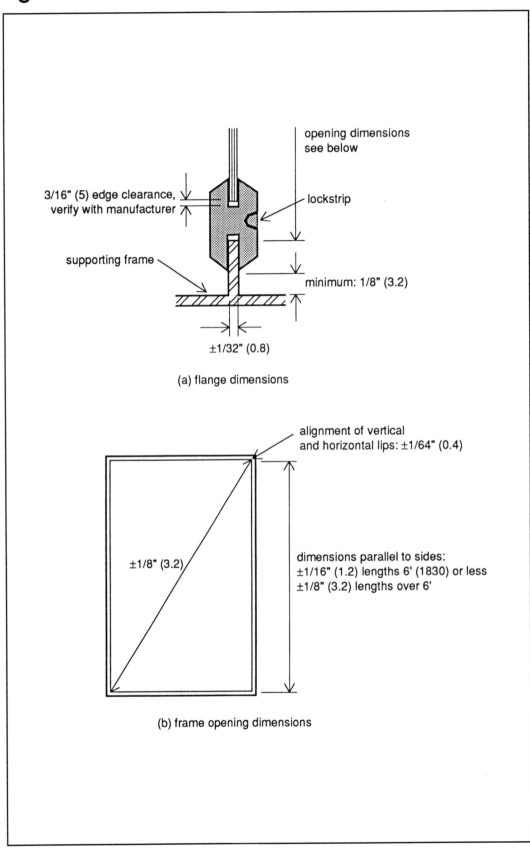

3/16" (5) edge clearance, verify with manufacturer

opening dimensions see below

lockstrip

supporting frame

minimum: 1/8" (3.2)

±1/32" (0.8)

(a) flange dimensions

alignment of vertical and horizontal lips: ±1/64" (0.4)

±1/8" (3.2)

dimensions parallel to sides:
±1/16" (1.2) lengths 6' (1830) or less
±1/8" (3.2) lengths over 6'

(b) frame opening dimensions

11-11. Lockstrip Gasket Glazing

Description

Lockstrip glazing consists of an elastomeric member that holds and seals glass to a supporting framework without standard metal frames. The gasket is made in two parts: (1) the main body, which has a grooved recess in one side, and (2) a separate wedge-shaped lockstrip which is inserted in the recess after the glass is installed. The pressure the lockstrip exerts on the gasket holds both the glass and gasket firmly in place against the framing. There are two basic types of lockstrip gaskets. One is an H-shaped piece as shown in Fig. 11-11*a* and the other is a gasket which is designed to fit into a reglet cast into a concrete wall.

Industry Standard

Aluminum Curtain Wall Design Guide Manual, American Architectural Manufacturers Association, Palatine, IL, 1979.

Allowable Tolerances

Because the gasket is the only thing holding the glass in place, the tolerances for the frame and the gasket must be small. Tolerances for the supporting frame are shown in Fig. 11-11*b* while the required clearances and tolerances for H-shaped gaskets are shown in Fig. 11-11*a*. Refer to the individual manufacturer's catalogue for specific tolerance recommendations for particular gasket designs.

Related Sections

8-2. Aluminum Curtain Wall Installation

10-3. Tempered, Heat-Strengthened, and Spandrel Glass

10-4. Sealed Insulated Glass Units

Part 2

Accommodating Construction Tolerances

Accommodating Construction Tolerances

The tolerances shown in Part 1 describe generally accepted industry standard variations in the manufacture, fabrication, and installation of individual materials and construction components. However, nearly all finished building construction is composed of two or more materials, either in contact with each other or in close proximity. These materials usually have different manufacturing and installation tolerances, come from different sources, and have different capacities to be field-adjusted. To make matters more difficult, some materials are field-fabricated, which can create problems by requiring relatively large tolerances or which can alleviate problems because they allow custom fitting. Therefore, it is critical for the designer to consider the cumulative effect of different material and erection tolerances when developing details.

In addition to providing for tolerances, the designer must also account for building movement and for required clearances. *Clearance* is the space between two components and is normally provided to accommodate tolerances and building movement, but clearance can also be required for attached materials, such as fireproofing on steel, or for working space as the building is constructed, such as space for a worker to tighten a bolt.

Tolerances can be accommodated in several ways. The first is by specifying and enforcing tolerances as small as practical for field-fabricated components. (Prefabricated component tolerances usually don't pose as much of a problem because industry standard tolerances are smaller and can be controlled in the shop.) While this method can minimize assembly problems and improve the appearance of visible portions of the building, tight tolerances generally increase construction costs and place an additional burden on the architect or construction supervisor to make sure that all tolerances are being met. Even strict supervision is not always practical. For example, under a strict interpretation of the specifications a contractor could be required to demolish an entire section of concrete construction because it exceeded the specified tolerances by $\frac{1}{4}$ in, but this could seriously delay construction, lead to litigation, make for an adversarial work environment for the remainder of the project, and increase cost unnecessarily.

Figure P2-1

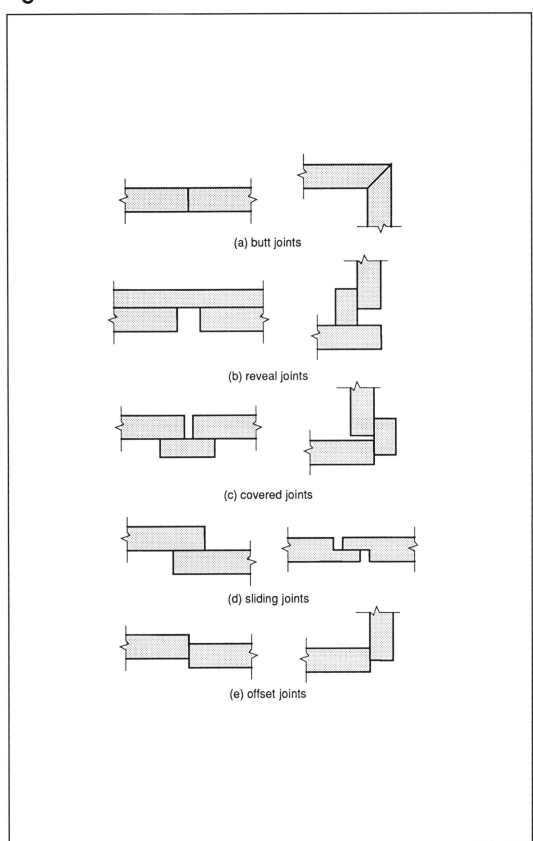

(a) butt joints

(b) reveal joints

(c) covered joints

(d) sliding joints

(e) offset joints

Accommodating Construction Tolerances

The more practical method is to understand the reality of construction methods and plan for them in the design and detailing of the building. This usually comes down to designing joints and connections with sufficient clearance and adjustability to accommodate the majority of expected problems, including the fact that many times actual erection tolerances exceed recommended industry standard tolerances. If visual appearance is critical, the design of the joint or connection to make irregularities less noticeable is also a possibility. For example, a wide reveal between two surfaces can conceal a slight misalignment of surfaces or an overlapping joint easily hides variations in material length and installation tolerance.

Joint Design

A *joint* is a place where two or more materials come together, either rigidly fastened or with provision for movement. There are several basic methods of creating a joint; some are better than others for accommodating construction tolerances and building movement. These are shown in Fig. P2-1.

A butt joint, Fig. P2-1*a*, is normally used where two identical materials meet and no movement is expected. However, even two normally rigid pieces of material, such as interior wood trim, can shrink or move just enough to be noticeable. When movement is expected and tolerances must be allowed, the two materials may be separated slightly and the joint filled with sealant. When sealant is not required, a reveal joint, shown in Fig. P2-1*b*, can be used; the reveal both concealing minor misalignments of the material faces as well as allowing for some sideways movement.

Covered joints, Fig. P2-1*c*, can accommodate either small or large clearances and movement, but impose a particular appearance on the joint. Sliding joints, Fig. P2-1*d*, also allow for a wide range of clearance and movement without requiring a third piece of material. Offset joints, shown in Fig. P2-1*e*, also articulate a joint and conceal minor movement. However, if size or installation tolerances must be accommodated, a reveal or space is required when the two materials are in the same plane or when sealant is required.

For nearly all exterior materials and many interior materials a joint must be filled with sealant. The size of the joint is critical for proper performance. For example, if a joint that is too narrow expands beyond the capability of the sealant, the sealant will fail. This is shown in Fig. P2-2.

The size of a joint depends on the movement expected, construction tolerances, and the movement capability of the sealant. Joint movement may be caused by factors such as thermal expansion and contraction, moisture absorption, and the various forms of structural movement. Construction tolerances include both manufacturing and erection tolerances. The movement capability of the sealant is measured in terms of the percentage from original size the sealant can expand or contract without failing. Common sealant performances are $7\frac{1}{2}$, 10, $12\frac{1}{2}$, and 25 percent. Some high-performance sealants are capable of 50 percent movement.

Joint width can be calculated using the following formula:

$$J = \frac{100(e\Delta tL + S)}{M} + T$$

where J = joint width, in (mm);
$\quad e$ = coefficient of thermal expansion, in/in/°F (mm/mm/°C);
$\quad \Delta t$ = expected temperature change, °F (°C);
$\quad L$ = length of the material being joined, in (mm);
$\quad M$ = movement capability of sealant, in percent expressed as whole numbers;
$\quad T$ = construction tolerance of the material, in (mm);
$\quad S$ = other expected movement caused by seismic forces or other nonthermal causes

For example, what would be the minimum joint width between two granite panels, each 5 ft wide and exposed to a temperature change of 120°F if a 25 percent performance sealant

Figure P2-2

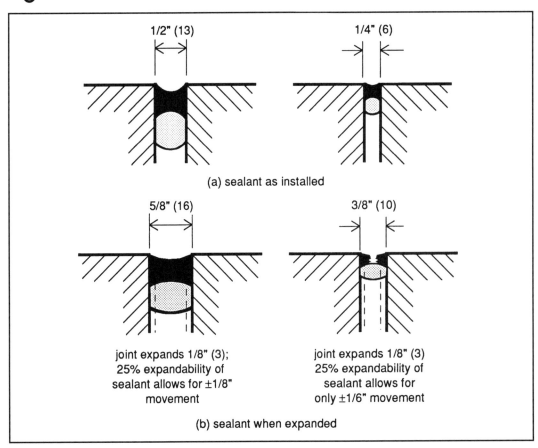

1/2" (13)

1/4" (6)

(a) sealant as installed

5/8" (16)

3/8" (10)

joint expands 1/8" (3);
25% expandability of
sealant allows for ±1/8"
movement

joint expands 1/8" (3)
25% expandability of
sealant allows for
only ±1/6" movement

(b) sealant when expanded

Figure P2-3

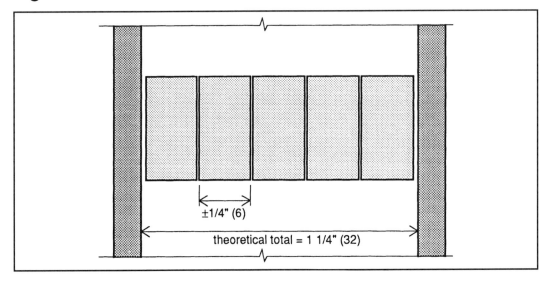

±1/4" (6)

theoretical total = 1 1/4" (32)

was used? Assume that the coefficient of thermal expansion for granite is 4.7×10^{-6} and that no other movement is expected. From Secs. 5-1 and 5-4 the dimensional tolerance for granite is $\pm\frac{1}{4}$ in (6 mm) and the relative alignment tolerance is $\pm\frac{1}{8}$ in (3 mm). Joint width would be calculated as follows:

$$J = \frac{100[(4.7 \times 10^{-6})120(60)]}{25} + 0.25 + 0.125$$

$$= 0.1354 + 0.25 + 0.125$$

$$= 0.5104, \text{ or about } \frac{1}{2} \text{ in}$$

Using the tolerance figures of $\frac{1}{4}$ in (6 mm) and $\frac{1}{8}$ in (3 mm) and adding them gives the worst case. This assumes that two adjacent panels will be oversized by the full $\frac{1}{4}$-in (6-mm) dimension tolerance and one of the panels will be misaligned by $\frac{1}{8}$ in (3 mm). However, if this occurred, then there would only be about a $\frac{1}{8}$-in joint at the time of construction. Besides being less than the recommended minimum joint of $\frac{1}{4}$ in, any bead of sealant would be crushed when the panels expanded the remaining $\frac{1}{8}$ in or the joint would break if the panels contracted and stressed the sealant beyond its 25 percent capability. In the case of only two panels, the joint size might have to be enlarged to accommodate this worst case. However, as discussed in the next section, it is statistically improbable that all three conditions would occur simultaneously or that there would be only one joint. Chances are greater that several panels would be in line and create a number of joints, each of which could accommodate a portion of the total required tolerance clearance.

Accumulated Tolerances

When several construction components are combined it is entirely possible that the tolerance for each component will vary to the allowable maximum in the same direction. For instance, if the allowable tolerance on a stone panel is $\pm\frac{1}{4}$ in (6 mm) and five of them are installed in a row, the total length could be as much as $1\frac{1}{4}$ in (32 mm) shorter or longer than designed (not accounting for joints). See Fig. P2-3.

However, statistically it is unlikely that this would occur; some panels will be a little longer, some a little shorter than the specified size. This statistically probable total tolerance resulting from several combined tolerances can be calculated according to the following formula:

$$T = \sqrt{t_1^2 + t_2^2 + t_3^2 + \ t_n^2}$$

where T is the total tolerance and t_1^2, t_2^2, to t_n^2 are the tolerances of the number n of the individual components. When the tolerances of the individual components are different in the plus and minus direction, two calculations are required to determine the probable plus and minus tolerances. This formula is applicable where all components have the same individual tolerances, or where various materials and components are combined.

Using this formula and the above example of five stone panels, the total tolerance would be

$$T = \sqrt{0.25^2 + 0.25^2 + 0.25^2 + 0.25^2 + 0.25^2}$$

$$= \sqrt{0.313}$$

$$= 0.559 \text{ in (about } \frac{9}{16} \text{ in), in this case, slightly less than one half of the tolerance based on simple addition.}$$

The following sections in Part 2 illustrate some common construction and detailing situations and show how accumulated and multiple tolerances can be accommodated.

Figure 12-1

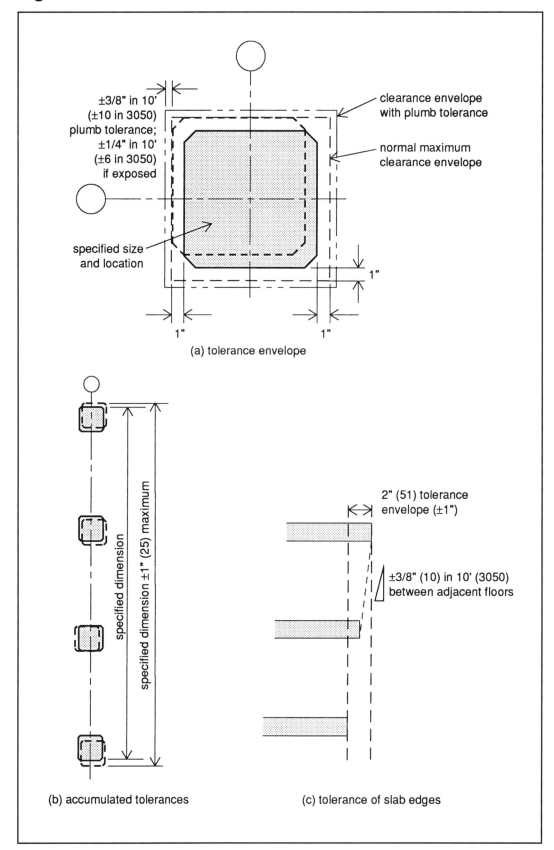

±3/8" in 10'
(±10 in 3050)
plumb tolerance;
±1/4" in 10'
(±6 in 3050)
if exposed

clearance envelope
with plumb tolerance

normal maximum
clearance envelope

specified size
and location

1"

1"   1"

(a) tolerance envelope

specified dimension

specified dimension ±1" (25) maximum

(b) accumulated tolerances

2" (51) tolerance
envelope (±1")

±3/8" (10) in 10' (3050)
between adjacent floors

(c) tolerance of slab edges

Chapter 12

Cast-in-Place Concrete Systems

12-1. Accumulated Concrete Frame Tolerances

There are several tolerances for the lateral alignment of the structural frame of a cast-in-place building as stated in ACI 117, *Standard Tolerances for Concrete Construction and Materials.* In general, columns, walls, and edges of slabs can vary as much as 1 in (25 mm) and the edges of horizontal openings can vary as much as $\frac{1}{2}$ in (13 mm). Any material adjacent or connected to a concrete frame must take these tolerances into account. Although ACI 117 specifically states that tolerances are not cumulative and that the most restrictive tolerance controls, it is possible that, in any 10 ft (3.0 m), the plumb line of a column or wall could vary another $\frac{3}{8}$ in (9.5 mm). In the worst case, a total clearance envelope of $1\frac{3}{8}$ in (35 mm) beyond the expected size and location of a column or wall should be accommodated. See Fig. 12-1*a*.

However, the lateral position tolerance is not cumulative along several columns or walls. As shown in Fig. 12-1*b,* the total length of a frame should vary no more than 1 in (25 mm) one way or the other. When exposed, the outside corners of exterior columns have a tighter tolerance. They can vary from plumb no more than $\frac{1}{2}$ in (13 mm) for building heights 100 ft (30.48 m) or less and no more than $\frac{1}{2000}$ of the height, or a maximum of 3 in (76 mm), for buildings over 100 ft (30.5 mm). (See Sec. 2-7.)

A common problem in attaching a facing material, such as brick veneer or curtain wall, to a concrete frame is the misalignment of the faces of the concrete spandrel beams or slab edges. As shown in Fig. 12-1*c,* in a multistory building the faces of the concrete can vary 1 in (25 mm) on either side of the theoretical edge line for buildings under 100 ft and $\frac{1}{1000}$ of the building height (up to a maximum of 6 in or 152 mm) for higher structures. This creates a total required clearance envelope of 2 in (51 mm) for buildings under 100 ft (30.48 m) and much more for higher buildings. However, between any two adjacent floors, the misalignment cannot exceed $\frac{3}{8}$ in (10 mm) as stated in the ACI requirements for relative alignment. Refer to the following sections in this chapter for common methods of accommodating concrete frame misalignments.

For level alignment, or the position of the tops and bottoms of slabs and beams, the tolerance is $\pm\frac{3}{4}$ in (19 mm) from the specified elevation. Even though the thickness of slabs or the depth of beams can vary (see Sec. 2-8), the final position of the member must fall within this $\frac{3}{4}$-in tolerance. The tolerance is not cumulative from floor to floor.

Although all concrete tolerances have been set by the American Concrete Institute, experience has shown that many times actual construction exceeds recommended tolerances, even when specifically written into the specifications. When conditions warrant, tighter tolerances may need to be specified and carefully controlled as construction progresses, even though this may increase costs beyond what normal tolerances would.

Related Sections

2-7. Cast-in-Place Plumb Tolerances

2-8. Cast-in-Place Sectional Tolerances

2-9. Cast-in-Place Concrete Elements in Plan

Figure 12-2

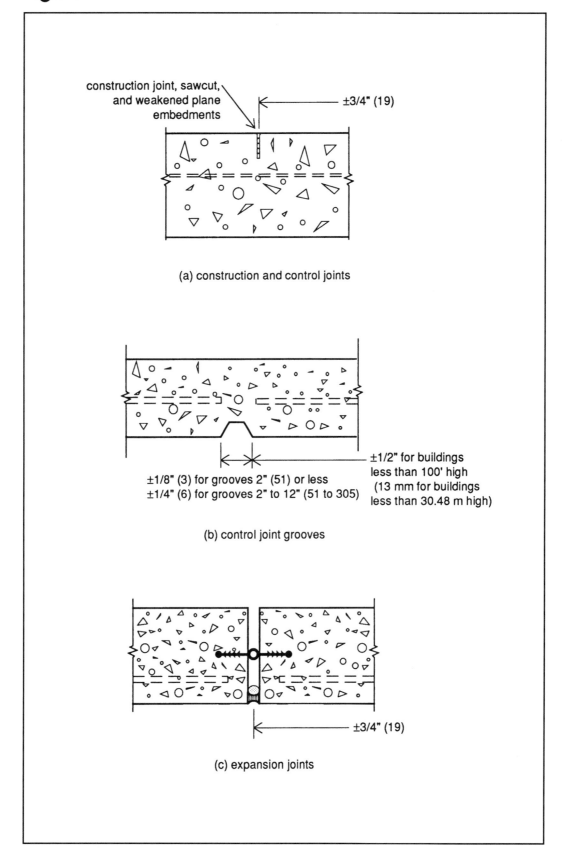

construction joint, sawcut, and weakened plane embedments

±3/4" (19)

(a) construction and control joints

±1/8" (3) for grooves 2" (51) or less
±1/4" (6) for grooves 2" to 12" (51 to 305)

±1/2" for buildings less than 100' high (13 mm for buildings less than 30.48 m high)

(b) control joint grooves

±3/4" (19)

(c) expansion joints

12-2. Joint Tolerances

Cast-in-place concrete joints include construction, control, isolation, expansion, and building joints. The location tolerance of these joints, either in the horizontal or vertical plane, varies depending on the type of joint and whether or not it is exposed to view.

As shown in Fig. 12-2a construction joints, sawcuts, control joints, and weakened plane embedments can vary $\frac{3}{4}$ in (19 mm) from their location on the plans. The vertical alignment for grooves for control joints (see Fig. 12-2b) may vary $\frac{1}{2}$ in (13 mm) for buildings less than 100 ft (30.48 m) high and $\frac{1}{2000}$ of the height of the building for taller structures, with a maximum misalignment of 3 in (76 mm). The relative alignment of control joint grooves in concrete exposed to view should vary no more than $\frac{1}{4}$ in in 10 ft (6 mm in 3050 mm). The width of grooves must be within $\frac{1}{8}$ in (3 mm) for grooves 2 in (51 mm) or less in width and within $\frac{1}{4}$ in (6 mm) for grooves from 2 to 12 in wide (51 to 305 mm).

The relative alignment of the faces of the two separate sections of concrete can vary depending on which class of surface is specified. These are summarized in Table 12-1. *Class A surfaces* are those prominently exposed to public view where appearance is of special importance. *Class B surfaces* are for coarse-textured concrete intended for plaster, stucco, or similar coverings. The *Class C surface* is the general standard for exposed surfaces where other finishes are not specified. *Class D surfaces* are for concealed concrete elements where roughness is not objectionable. For walls poured in two separate operations, such as the expansion joint shown in Fig. 12-2c, alignment is usually not a problem because the cured portion of the wall is used to align the formwork for the second pour.

Table 12-1
Offset Between Adjacent Pieces of Formwork Facing

Class of surface	Offset tolerance,in (mm)
Class A	$\pm\frac{1}{8}$ (3)
Class B	$\pm\frac{1}{4}$ (6)
Class C	$\pm\frac{1}{2}$ (13)
Class D	±1 (25)

SOURCE: ACI 117-90; reproduced with permission, American Concrete Institute.

Related Sections

2-7. Cast-in-Place Plumb Tolerances

2-9. Cast-in-Place Concrete Elements in Plan

Figure 12-3

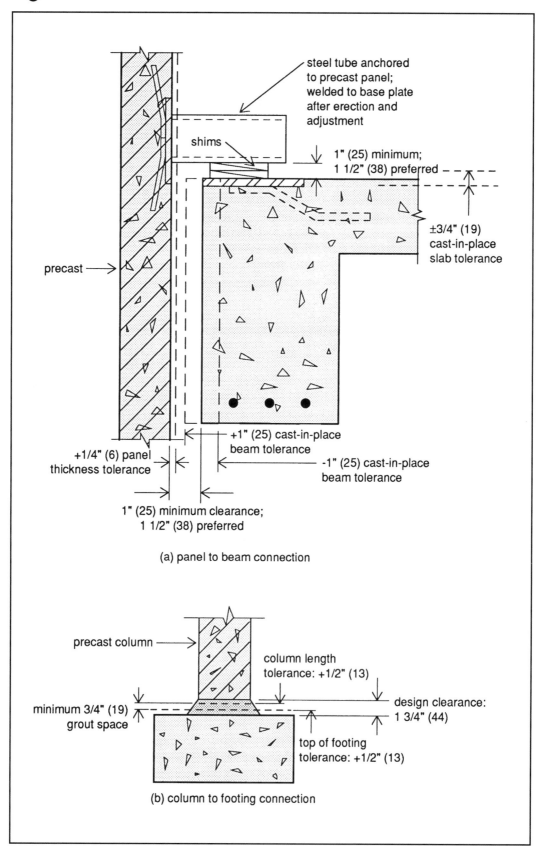

steel tube anchored to precast panel; welded to base plate after erection and adjustment

shims

1" (25) minimum; 1 1/2" (38) preferred

±3/4" (19) cast-in-place slab tolerance

precast →

+1/4" (6) panel thickness tolerance

+1" (25) cast-in-place beam tolerance

-1" (25) cast-in-place beam tolerance

1" (25) minimum clearance; 1 1/2" (38) preferred

(a) panel to beam connection

precast column →

column length tolerance: +1/2" (13)

minimum 3/4" (19) grout space

design clearance: 1 3/4" (44)

top of footing tolerance: +1/2" (13)

(b) column to footing connection

12-3. Detailing for Cast-in-Place and Precast Systems

Cast-in-place and precast concrete are normally used together when precast architectural panels are supported with a cast-in-place structural frame or when columns are supported by cast-in-place foundations. Because both systems have relatively large tolerances, connection detailing must accommodate the worst expected combination of tolerances while still providing for erection clearances and minimizing erection time.

A common condition is shown in Fig. 12-3a, where a precast cladding panel is attached to a cast-in-place beam. This detail shows only one of many possible ways to accommodate tolerances. In addition to clip angles anchored to the precast panel and set on shims, angles, channels, and other support members can be cast into the cladding panel. Vertical adjustment can also be accomplished with leveling bolts instead of shims. The recommended design clearance is $1\frac{1}{2}$ in (38 mm). This allows for the beam to be out by the maximum of 1 in (25 mm) and for the panel thickness to be over by the allowable $\frac{1}{4}$ in (6 mm).

In order to minimize cost, the connections should be designed to minimize the time the panel must be held in place with a crane while adjustments are made and fastening is done. Connections should also be designed for the top of the concrete frame so access is not required between the back of the panel and the face of the beam.

For horizontal alignment of several panels within a cast-in-place structural bay, the vertical joints are typically used to accommodate tolerance problems, with each joint accommodating a portion of the total expected tolerance. Because it is highly unlikely that *all* panels will be either oversized or undersized by the maximum allowable tolerance, the formula described in the introduction to Part 2 can be used to estimate the total tolerance likely from several individual panels. Procedures for determining joint width are also given in the introduction to Part 2.

Another condition is shown in Fig. 12-3b, where a precast column is supported on a cast-in-place footing. The footing length must be designed to accommodate possible variations in length of the column and placement tolerances of the footing while providing for sufficient clearance for grouting under the base plate cast onto the bottom of the column. The column length may vary by $\frac{1}{2}$ in (13 mm) and the top of the footing may vary by up to $\frac{1}{2}$ in (13 mm) higher than specified or as much as 2 in (51 mm) lower. Assuming the haunch is set at its intended elevation, the worst case when allowing for grouting would be when the column is $\frac{1}{2}$ in too long and the footing is $\frac{1}{2}$ in too high. If a $\frac{3}{4}$-in (19-mm) grout space is required, the total required clearance should be $1\frac{3}{4}$ in (44 mm). In case the column is $\frac{1}{2}$ in short and the footing is 2 in below the specified elevation, there will be a potential grout space of $3\frac{1}{4}$ in (83 mm). If this is too much, it could be decreased by setting the haunch at an acceptable $\frac{1}{2}$ in (13 mm) below its intended elevation (see Sec. 2-23) and shimming at the haunch.

In both of these examples, the relevant tolerances for each system must be determined along with any required clearances for erection, insulation, mechanical and electrical interface, or other construction components. Then, the extreme conditions must be determined based on the worst case tolerances. Finally, the connection or joint must be designed to accommodate all the required tolerances and clearances. If the worst case situation results in a connection that is too large for economical construction, a judgment must be made concerning whether to increase the tolerances, possibly increasing construction costs, or recognize that some compromises in the position, plumb, or level of some elements may need to be made.

Related Sections

2-5. Footings

2-7. Cast-in-Place Plumb Tolerances

2-8. Cast-in-Place Sectional Tolerances

2-21. Precast Columns

2-23. Precast Column Erection

Figure 12-4

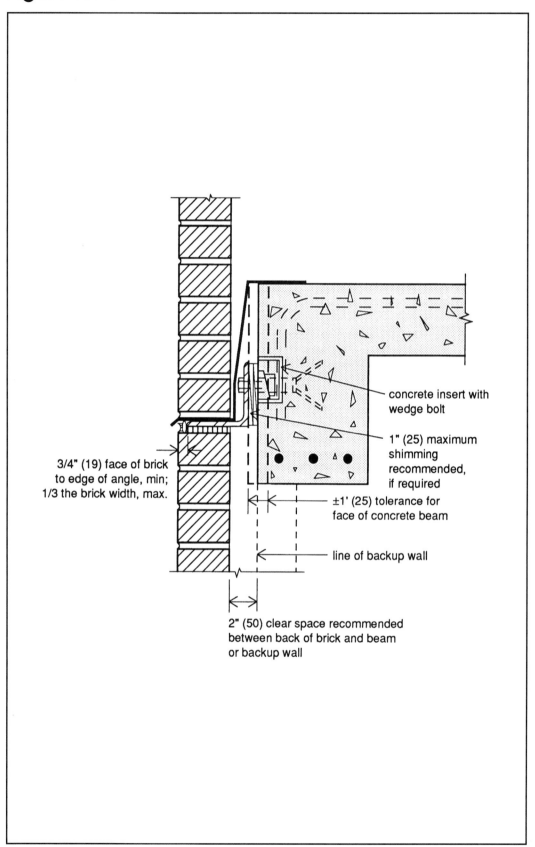

concrete insert with
wedge bolt

1" (25) maximum
shimming
recommended,
if required

3/4" (19) face of brick
to edge of angle, min;
1/3 the brick width, max.

±1' (25) tolerance for
face of concrete beam

line of backup wall

2" (50) clear space recommended
between back of brick and beam
or backup wall

12-4. Detailing Brick on Cast-in-Place Concrete

When brick and cast-in-place concrete are used together, the construction tolerance of the concrete frame usually dictates the method of detailing. Dimensional and distortion tolerances of brick are relatively minor, as described in Sec. 4-5. At most, a surface of an individual, standard-size brick may be out of specified plane by about $\frac{5}{32}$ in (4 mm) due to a worst case combination of size and warp tolerance.

When brick is laid as an exterior veneer to a backup wall of other masonry or metal studs in a one-story building, the recommended 2-in (50-mm) cavity between the walls is adequate to accommodate any minor tolerance of brick manufacturing or construction. When brick is used with multistory cast-in-place concrete buildings the exterior faces of the columns, beams, and slabs may vary as much as 1 in (25 mm) in either direction.

Because brick is normally supported at each floor line in multistory buildings, the connection and support systems must be designed to accommodate the concrete frame tolerance as well as provide the required clearance between the back of the brick wall and the structural frame and whatever backup wall is used. The Brick Institute of American recommends that brick veneer should vary no more than $\frac{1}{2}$ in (13 mm) out of plumb, and most masons lay up walls to an even closer plumb tolerance.

Figure 12-4 shows a common brick veneer support system using a shelf angle bolted to the concrete frame. The shelf angle is installed over a compressible filler so that minor deflection of the wall above can occur without bearing on the brick below and cracking or collapsing it. Because the actual elevation of the top of the last brick below the shelf angle may vary slightly, the shelf angle must be adjustable in the vertical direction. This is usually accomplished with a concrete insert with a wedge bolt or with slotted holes in the vertical leg of the angle.

Horizontal adjustment is made by shimming behind the angle if necessary. The maximum recommended shimming distance is 1 in (25 mm), which can accommodate the maximum concrete frame tolerance toward the inside. However, horseshoe-shaped shims (not washers) should be used with a length about equal to the length of the vertical leg of the angle so there is full bearing against the concrete. If the concrete frame is constructed at the theoretical location, then no shimming will be necessary. If the concrete beam extends too far outward, some of the horizontal leg of the angle can be slid farther outward, but the minimum $\frac{3}{4}$-in (19-mm) recess should not be decreased so there is adequate room for applying the sealant. In extreme cases, an angle with a shorter horizontal leg may be used, subject to engineering review.

Note that potential problems can arise if the clearance becomes so small that there is not adequate space for the bolt head, flashing, and any material which is used to prevent the bolt head from puncturing the flashing. Depending on the thickness of the angle, the size of the fastener, and the method of flashing, the 2-in clearance may need to be increased, especially in tall buildings. This also provides extra space to allow for oversize manufacturing tolerances of the brick.

Related Sections

2-7. Cast-in-Place Plumb Tolerances

2-8. Cast-in-Place Sectional Tolerances

2-9. Cast-in-Place Concrete Elements in Plan

4-5. Brick Manufacturing

4-6. Brick Wall Construction

15-2. Detailing Brick and Masonry Systems

Figure 12-5

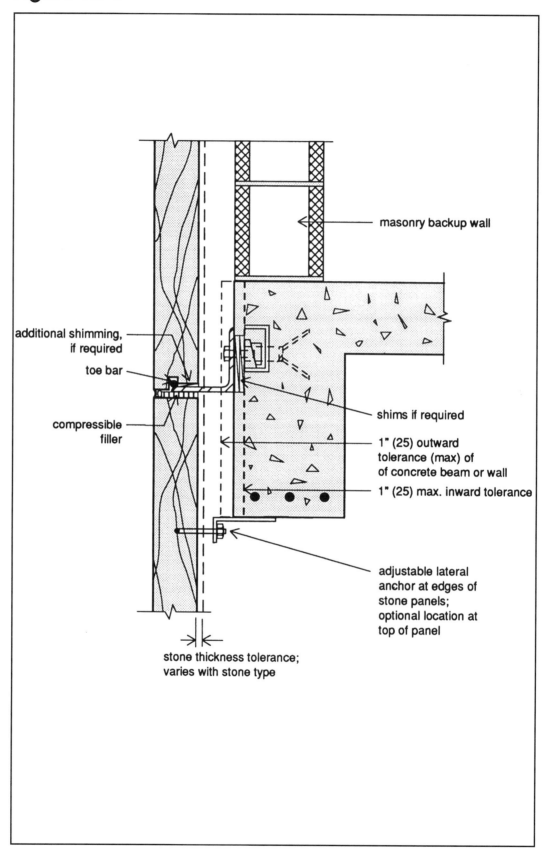

masonry backup wall

additional shimming, if required

toe bar

compressible filler

shims if required

1" (25) outward tolerance (max) of of concrete beam or wall

1" (25) max. inward tolerance

adjustable lateral anchor at edges of stone panels; optional location at top of panel

stone thickness tolerance; varies with stone type

12-5. Detailing for Stone on Concrete

In order to maintain the installation tolerances for granite, marble, and limestone shown in Secs. 5-4 and 5-5, adequate clearances and adjustable connections must be detailed when stone is attached to concrete. Detailing for stone is similar to that for brick, but there are some important differences. Among them are the wider variety of anchoring systems available, larger thickness tolerances, and the ability for stone panels to be installed slightly out of plumb (within the standards described in Secs. 5-4 and 5-5) along the height of a building to partially accommodate minor irregularities of the frame, if absolutely necessary.

Figure 12-5 shows a typical gravity support and anchor at a spandrel beam. This is the most critical connection to accommodate the structural frame tolerances and the stone tolerances. A variety of lateral anchors is available for various types of backup walls which provides for sufficient adjustment to maintain the erection tolerances shown in Secs. 5-4 and 5-5. As with brick, vertical deviations of the concrete frame are accommodated with adjustable concrete inserts or slotted angles. Deviations perpendicular to the building face are taken up by shimming the support angles. Additional vertical adjustment can be made by shimming between the angle and the bottom edge of the stone.

When determining the minimum design clearance, the following tolerances and construction elements must be combined: the ± 1 in (25 mm) tolerance of the face of the concrete beam or wall; the thickness of the stone, which will vary depending on the type of stone and thickness (see Secs. 5-1, 5-2, and 5-3); the thickness of the angle; the size of the bolt head; working space required for erection and fastening; and any flashing, weep tubes, or other accessories behind the stone.

As with precast panels, horizontal joints and stone movement are normally accommodated by designing the vertical joints between stone sections large enough to absorb both movement and dimensional tolerances of the stone and concrete frame. Refer to the introduction to Part 2 for procedures for estimating total expected tolerance of several panels and the method for calculating joint width.

Because Fig. 12-5 shows a pressure relieving joint, there is a separate lateral anchor for the bottom panel. If the joint does not have to accommodate deflection of the panel above or building movement, both gravity anchorage of the upper panel and lateral anchorage of the lower panel can be made with the same connection.

Because the exact method of anchorage varies with the type of structural frame, the type of stone, loading, and other factors, along with the preferences of individual fabricators and installers, final details should be verified with the stone fabricator and contractor.

Related Sections

2-7. Cast-in-Place Plumb Tolerances

2-8. Cast-in-Place Sectional Tolerances

2-9. Cast-in-Place Concrete Elements in Plan

5-1. Granite Fabrication

5-2. Marble Fabrication

5-3. Limestone Fabrication

5-4. Granite and Marble Installation

5-5. Limestone Installation

Figure 12-6

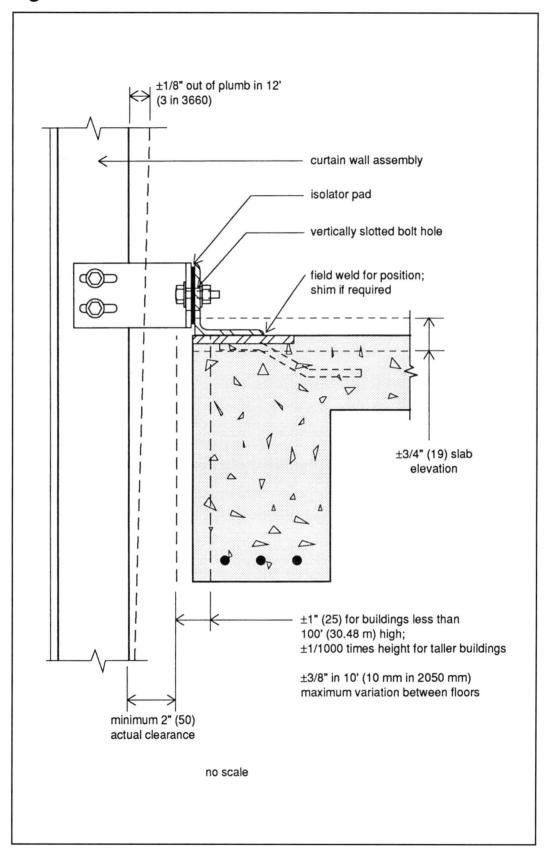

±1/8" out of plumb in 12'
(3 in 3660)

curtain wall assembly

isolator pad

vertically slotted bolt hole

field weld for position;
shim if required

±3/4" (19) slab
elevation

±1" (25) for buildings less than
100' (30.48 m) high;
±1/1000 times height for taller buildings

±3/8" in 10' (10 mm in 2050 mm)
maximum variation between floors

minimum 2" (50)
actual clearance

no scale

12-6. Detailing for Curtain Walls on Concrete Frames

If adequate allowance is made for concrete frame tolerances and these tolerances are controlled during construction, most curtain walls can be installed to the tolerances indicated in Sec. 8-2. Adjustment needs to be provided in three directions: vertical, horizontal, and lateral. In addition, a minimum clearance of 2 in (50 mm) between the curtain wall and the frame is recommended for curtain wall construction. If adjustment and clearances are provided, then the minor manufacturing and fabrication tolerances of the curtain wall can be accommodated, as well as any movement of the building frame and expansion and contraction of the curtain wall. In extreme cases, where the frame exceeds tolerances, the curtain wall can be installed slightly out of plumb, following the line of the frame along the height of the building.

Figure 12-6 shows one typical method of accommodating tolerances. The exact detail varies with the type of curtain wall used, the interior finishes, and other construction details. The curtain wall manufacturer and structural engineer should be consulted for recommended details and for the tolerances that the manufacturer's system requires. Generally, the connection should be made at the top of the slab to make erection easier. Serrated angles and bolts, T-shaped clips, slotted holes, embedded anchors, and shims can all be used to provide the necessary adjustments. When shims are used, the height of the shim stack should not exceed the diameter of the fastener securing the anchor. If the anchor must be higher, special shims and connection details may be required.

Lateral tolerances of the frame can be accommodated by proper design of the vertical joints of the curtain wall. The lateral frame tolerance can be up to 1 in (25 mm) between columns or in the total length of the building. At individual connectors, lateral alignment can be made by field-welding clip angles, with slotted bolt holes, or by other means. Refer to the introduction to Part 2 for joint design procedures.

Related Sections

2-7. Cast-in-Place Plumb Tolerances

2-8. Cast-in-Place Sectional Tolerances

2-9. Cast-in-Place Concrete Elements in Plan

8-1. Aluminum Curtain Wall Fabrication

8-2. Aluminum Curtain Wall Installation

9-13. Extruded Aluminum Tubes

Figure 12-7

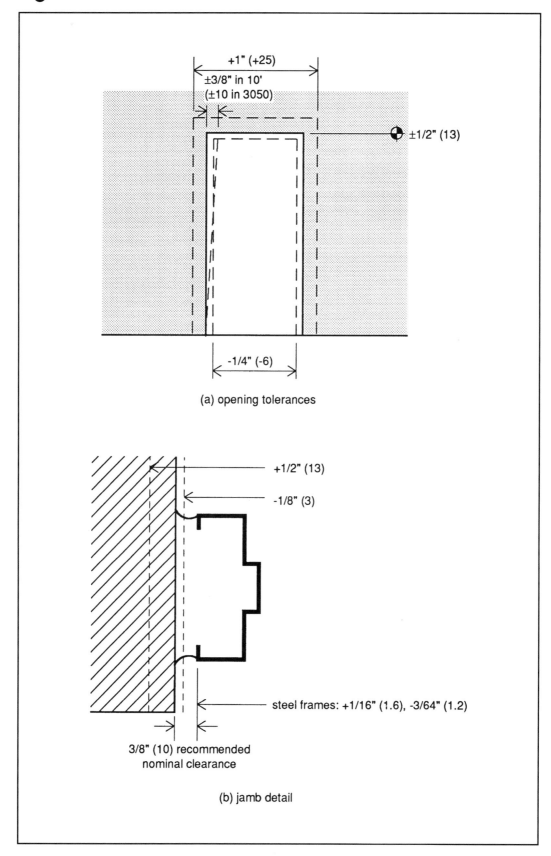

+1" (+25)

±3/8" in 10'
(±10 in 3050)

±1/2" (13)

-1/4" (-6)

(a) opening tolerances

+1/2" (13)

-1/8" (3)

steel frames: +1/16" (1.6), -3/64" (1.2)

3/8" (10) recommended
nominal clearance

(b) jamb detail

12-7. Detailing Doors in Cast-in-Place Concrete

In most construction, only steel or aluminum door frames are used with cast-in-place concrete. If wood frames are used, there is usually a rough wood buck placed between the two materials which can be trimmed or shimmed to accommodate the concrete tolerances. Steel frames are fixed in size so the frame detail and clearance are critical to sizing the opening to allow for tolerances and to provide a good sealant joint.

Figure 12-7 shows the possible tolerances of both the concrete opening and a steel frame. Detailing a nominal $\frac{1}{4}$-in (6-mm) clearance between the concrete and door frame just barely accommodates a maximum inward concrete tolerance of $\frac{1}{8}$ in (3 mm) and a maximum possible oversize tolerance of the frame of $\frac{1}{16}$ in (1.6 mm). (See Sec. 11-1.) However, this only leaves a $\frac{1}{16}$-in space for sealant and it does not allow for any variation in plumb of one or both sides of the opening. Although American Concrete Institute (ACI) requirements state that tolerances are not cumulative, an additional variation is possible. A minimum $\frac{3}{8}$-in (10-mm) nominal clearance is a better choice. If both the concrete opening and the door frame vary in the opposite direction, there can be as much as a $\frac{15}{16}$-in (23-mm) gap that must be shimmed and filled with sealant. (This includes the $\frac{3}{8}$-in nominal sealant space.) Although it is unlikely that all tolerances would combine in this fashion, it is a possibility.

The horizontal portion of the opening can vary as much as $\frac{1}{2}$ in (13 mm). The clearance of the head joint needs either to be increased by an additional $\frac{3}{8}$ in (10 mm) to $\frac{3}{4}$ in (19 mm) total or the extra tolerance accommodated in the sill detail.

Related Sections

2-7. Cast-in-Place Plumb Tolerances

2-8. Cast-in-Place Sectional Tolerances

2-9. Cast-in-Place Concrete Elements in Plan

11-1. Standard Steel Doors and Frames

Figure 12-8

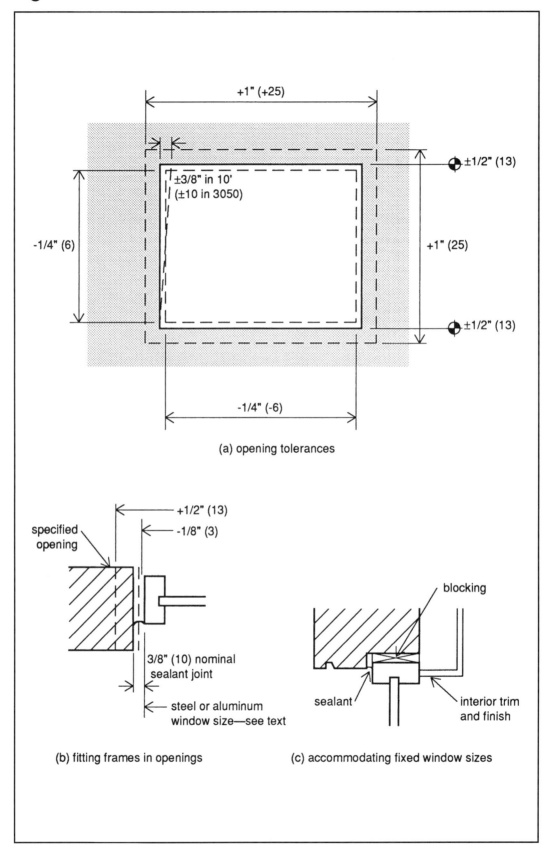

±3/8" in 10'
(±10 in 3050)

+1" (+25)

±1/2" (13)

-1/4" (6)

+1" (25)

±1/2" (13)

-1/4" (-6)

(a) opening tolerances

specified
opening

+1/2" (13)

-1/8" (3)

3/8" (10) nominal
sealant joint

steel or aluminum
window size—see text

(b) fitting frames in openings

blocking

sealant

interior trim
and finish

(c) accommodating fixed window sizes

12-8. Detailing Windows in Cast-in-Place Concrete

Several types of windows can be used in cast-in-place concrete. These include steel, aluminum, wood, and lockstrip gasket glazing. Standard details for steel and aluminum windows are usually the most sensitive to construction tolerances because these window types are commonly placed directly in the opening. When wood windows are used they are usually framed into a rough wood buck and the exterior and interior joints are covered with some type of trim which conceals any accommodation for construction tolerances. Lockstrip gasket glazing is a special condition which requires a much tighter tolerance of the concrete in both size and squareness. Only steel and aluminum windows are considered here.

For a window opening the finished size can be as much as $\frac{1}{4}$ in (6 mm) too small or 1 in (25 mm) too large. This means a possible variation of $\frac{1}{8}$ in (3 mm) inward and $\frac{1}{2}$ in (13 mm) outward for any jamb, head, or sill section (see Fig. 12-8a). This does not include any variation in plumb or level for any of the four sides. Although American Concrete Institute (ACI) requirements state that tolerances are not cumulative, some additional variation is possible.

If an aluminum window is used, one jamb may be as much as $\frac{1}{16}$ in (1.6 mm) large (see Sec. 11-9) and the concrete opening may be as much as $\frac{1}{8}$ in (3 mm) too small. If a nominal $\frac{1}{4}$-in (6-mm) clearance is provided, this would provide only a $\frac{1}{16}$-in (1.6-mm) space for sealant. As with doors, a minimum $\frac{3}{8}$-in (10-mm) nominal clearance is a better choice (see Fig. 12-8b). For storefronts, a $\frac{1}{2}$-in (13-mm) clearance between framing and the concrete is recommended.

Although misformed openings are not a problem if each is field measured for a custom window, this is generally not the case. One method of accommodating fixed window sizes is shown in Fig. 12-8c. By casting a notch in the concrete opening both in and out tolerances can be concealed and the joint can be properly sealed without oversizing the sealant joint. Although this increases formwork costs slightly, in some cases it is a preferable option.

Related Sections

2-7. Cast-in-Place Plumb Tolerances

2-8. Cast-in-Place Sectional Tolerances

2-9. Cast-in-Place Concrete Elements in Plan

11-9. Aluminum Windows and Sliding Doors

11-10. Steel Windows

11-11. Lockstrip Gasket Glazing

Figure 13-1

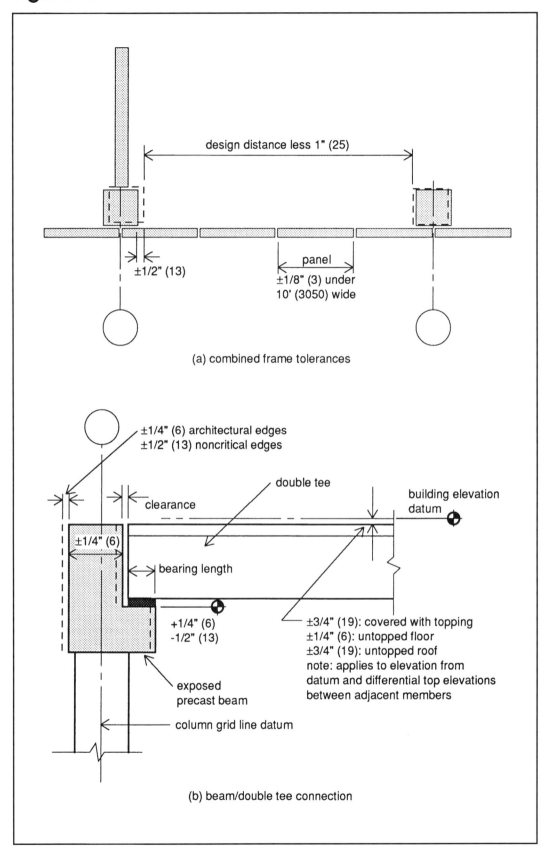

(a) combined frame tolerances

(b) beam/double tee connection

Chapter 13

Precast Concrete Systems

13-1. Combined Precast Concrete Frame Tolerances

There are three types of tolerances in precast work that, when combined, can affect the performance and appearance of a structure. These are product tolerances, erection tolerances, and interfacing tolerances. Product and erection tolerances are given in Chap. 2. *Interfacing tolerances* are the clearances required for joining different materials in contact with or in close proximity to the precast work. Interface tolerances also allow for building movement. Because precast work has larger tolerances than many other materials connected to it, such as masonry, doors, and windows, designing connections, joints, and details is critical to a successful project. This chapter describes some of the more common types of interfaces.

When precast is joined to other precast work the product tolerances may or may not be additive to the erection tolerances depending on what part of the precast governs erection. When erection tolerances govern the setting of a primary control surface of a member, that erection tolerance is *not* additive to the product tolerances. A *primary control surface* is a surface on a precast element that is dimensionally set and controlled during the erection process. Two examples are the exposed face of an architectural panel and the elevation of a bearing haunch on a column.

However, erection tolerances of secondary control surfaces and product tolerances *are* additive. A *secondary control surface* is one that is dependent on the location tolerance of the primary control surface. For example, if the top of an exposed L-shaped beam is designated as the primary control surface for purposes of appearance, then the tolerance for the secondary control surface of the bearing ledge is added to the dimensional tolerance from the top of the beam to the bearing ledge.

Figure 13-1a shows one typical example of combined frame tolerances. Two nonexposed columns may be erected to within $\frac{1}{2}$ in (13 mm) of their designed locations, creating a possible total variance of 1 in (25 mm). See Sec. 2-23 for column erection tolerances. The panels enclosing the frame would have to be adjusted at the joints in order to accommodate the frame tolerances as well as the width of the panels. In an extreme case the panels could be shifted toward the corners of the building to accommodate a large difference. Refer to the introduction to Part 2 for information on calculating combined tolerances.

Figure 13-1b illustrates a case where the primary control surface would have to be designated. In this case the floor elevation might be the controlling factor for the erection of the double tee, while the primary control surface for the exposed beam might be the bottom of the beam so it aligns with adjacent construction. Sufficient clearance for the bearing pad would then have to be determined to accommodate both of these tolerances: the product size tolerance of both beam and double tee as well as the combined erection tolerances of the bottom of the double tee and the bearing elevation of the beam. The clearance between the inside of the beam and the end of the double tee also depends on erection tolerances and the product tolerances of both beam and double tee.

Figure 13-2

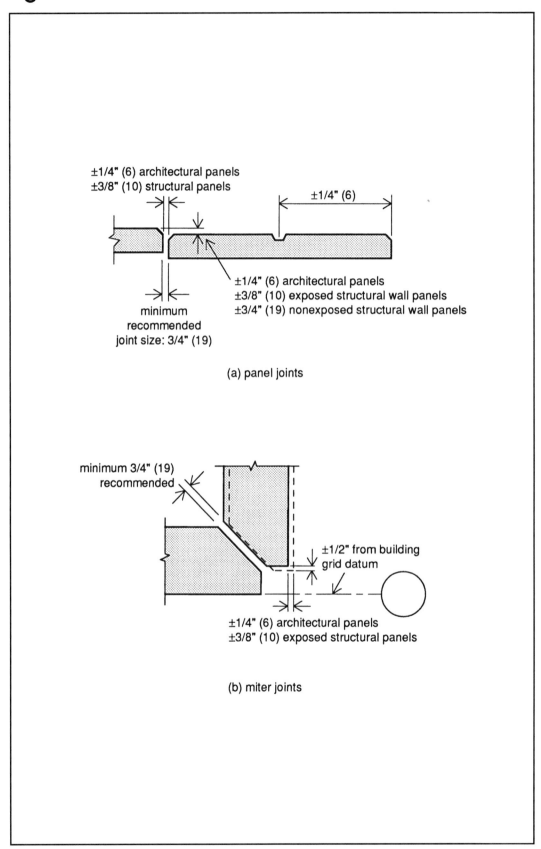

±1/4" (6) architectural panels
±3/8" (10) structural panels

±1/4" (6)

±1/4" (6) architectural panels
±3/8" (10) exposed structural wall panels
±3/4" (19) nonexposed structural wall panels

minimum
recommended
joint size: 3/4" (19)

(a) panel joints

minimum 3/4" (19)
recommended

±1/2" from building
grid datum

±1/4" (6) architectural panels
±3/8" (10) exposed structural panels

(b) miter joints

13-2. Joint Tolerances

Joints are sized to allow for building movement as well as to accommodate product and erection tolerances. In addition, joints between precast elements have their own tolerance. These apply primarily to exposed wall panels. The tolerances of a joint depend on whether it is part of an architectural panel, an exposed structural wall panel, or a nonexposed structural panel.

As shown in Fig. 13-2a tolerances for joints between panels can vary from $\pm\frac{1}{4}$ in (6 mm) for architectural panels to $\pm\frac{3}{8}$ in (9.5 mm) for structural panels. False joints may be expected to fall within $\pm\frac{1}{4}$ in (6 mm) from the designated location as measured from the edge of a panel.

The alignment between two panels varies from $\pm\frac{1}{4}$ in (6 mm) for architectural panels to a maximum of $\pm\frac{3}{4}$ in (19 mm) for nonexposed structural wall panels. If the outside surface is designated as a primary control surface, then this possible lateral variation must be taken into account when calculating the clearance between the back of the panel and the structural frame, but it would not be additive to the product thickness tolerance. Chamfered or reveal joints should be used to conceal misalignment.

Usually, joints are sized so that product and erection tolerances can be apportioned among the joints. Refer to the introduction to Part 2 for the method of doing this. Generally, a $\frac{3}{4}$-in (19-mm) joint between panels is considered as a minimum to account for tolerances and building movement while still providing a large enough joint for sealant.

Figure 13-2b illustrates the possible tolerances in a miter joint. Some accumulated panel tolerances can be accommodated with a miter joint, but if large deviations along a series of panels are expected and if the variation is designed to be taken up at the corners of the building then a quirk miter should not be used. Some type of an overlapping joint is a better alternative. See Sec. 13-3.

Related Sections

2-25. Precast Floor and Roof Member Erection

2-26. Precast Structural Wall Panel Erection

2-27. Precast Architectural Wall Panel Erection

Figure 13-3

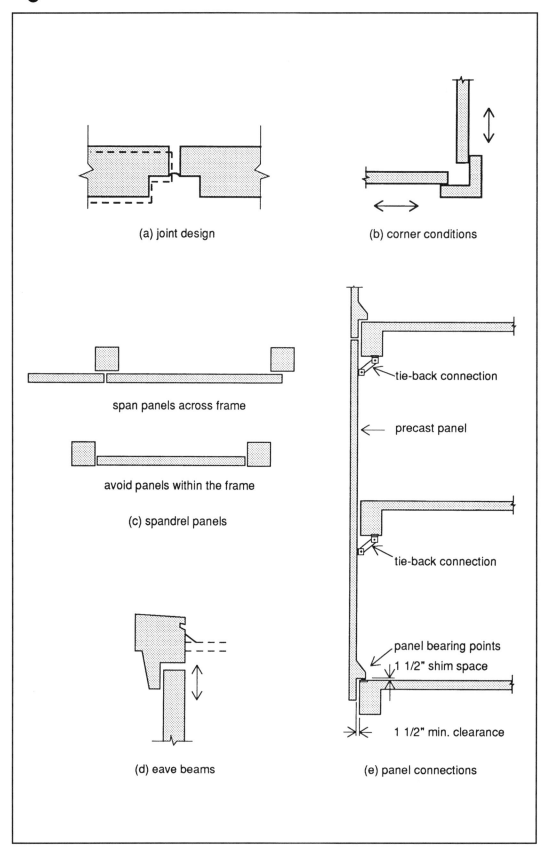

(a) joint design

(b) corner conditions

span panels across frame

avoid panels within the frame

(c) spandrel panels

(d) eave beams

tie-back connection

precast panel

tie-back connection

panel bearing points

1 1/2" shim space

1 1/2" min. clearance

(e) panel connections

13-3. Detailing for Precast Systems

Most precast-to-precast tolerances can be easily accommodated by using some basic design concepts as shown in Fig. 13-3. Either reveal joints or chamfered joints should be used and butt joints avoided. These minimize any minor misalignments by creating a strong shadow line at each joint. See Fig. 13-3a.

If possible, create overlapping joints at the corners to accommodate accumulated panel tolerances along the length of the building as diagrammatically illustrated in Fig. 13-3b. Avoid miter joints, because these have very little room for adjustment.

Spanning across beams and exposed structural columns with spandrel panels and infill panels is preferable to placing panels within the frame. See Fig. 13-3c. The accumulated tolerances of the columns and panels may result in uneven or oversized joints. If articulated columns or beam lines are desired, they can be covered with separate precast architectural panels.

As shown in Fig. 13-3d, eave beams can be used to accommodate inaccuracies in panel length and erection tolerances at the roof line in much the same way as corner panels are used. Because eave beams span across several panels, they can also accommodate reglets for flashing more accurately than trying to align reglets at each panel joint.

When non-load-bearing panels are attached to a structural frame, only two points of bearing should be designed into the panel support system as illustrated in Fig. 13-3e. These are the points where erection tolerances are accommodated, usually with shims or leveling bolts. Various types of tieback connections are used at other points to provide lateral support while accommodating product and erection tolerances and allowing for panel movement.

Related Sections

Chapter 2, Secs. 2-16 through 2-27. Precast Product and Erection Tolerances Sections

13-1. Combined Precast Concrete Frame Tolerances

13-2. Joint Tolerances

Figure 13-4

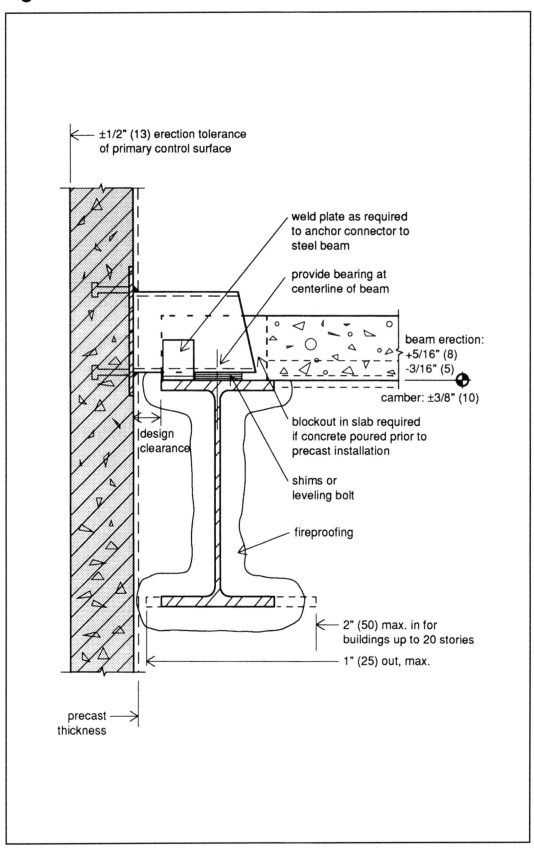

±1/2" (13) erection tolerance
of primary control surface

weld plate as required
to anchor connector to
steel beam

provide bearing at
centerline of beam

beam erection:
+5/16" (8)
-3/16" (5)

camber: ±3/8" (10)

design
clearance

blockout in slab required
if concrete poured prior to
precast installation

shims or
leveling bolt

fireproofing

2" (50) max. in for
buildings up to 20 stories

1" (25) out, max.

precast
thickness

13-4. Detailing for Precast and Steel Systems

Detailing combined precast and steel systems can be difficult because the accumulated tolerances can be substantial and tolerances for both systems vary depending on the size and type of member. For example, wide-flange tolerances vary with length and size of flange, and variation of vertical alignment of the frame varies with building height. Each detail has to be evaluated individually based on product tolerances, erection tolerances, and clearance for fireproofing and other building systems.

Figure 13-4 illustrates a common condition where an architectural precast panel is attached to a steel frame in a perfectly plumb condition for the entire height of the building. In order to determine the horizontal design clearance required between the back of the precast panel and the outside edge of the beam and also the possible minimum and maximum variation in bearing length of the precast anchor, several tolerances must be accounted for.

First, fabrication and erection tolerances of the steel are the most critical. In a building up to 20 stories high the steel may vary as much as 1 in (25 mm) out and 2 in (50 mm) in. (See Sec. 3-6 for exact values.) In addition, the width of the flange can vary $\pm\frac{1}{4}$ in (6 mm) or $\frac{1}{8}$ in (3 mm) on one side. Beam sweep varies with the length of the beam but can account for another $\frac{3}{8}$ in (10 mm) for a 30-ft (9140-mm) length. In the worst case, these might place the outside edge of the beam $1\frac{1}{2}$ in (38 mm) toward the precast. The precast thickness can vary by $\frac{1}{4}$ in (6 mm) and precast bowing could add about $\frac{1}{8}$ in (3 mm) for a 5-ft (1525-mm) panel. If the outside face was the primary control surface, this additional $\frac{3}{8}$ in (10 mm) would need to be accommodated in the clearance space. These tolerances add up to a total minimum clearance of $1\frac{7}{8}$ in (48 mm), not accounting for fireproofing.

If the maximum possible clearance is calculated using this $1\frac{7}{8}$-in design clearance, in the worst case the edge of the steel will be almost 5 in (125 mm) from the back of the column (2-in design clearance plus $\frac{3}{8}$-in outward tolerance of the panel plus $2\frac{1}{2}$-in total inward tolerance of the steel). If the length of the precast anchor from the edge of the beam to the center of the beam is added, this gives a large and uneconomical structural connection for the precast.

A design judgment has to be made concerning the likelihood of all tolerances acting together, and whether it would be better to have the line of the precast follow the line of the steel framing so the precast is slightly out of plumb, but the eccentricity of the anchor bearing is reduced.

The design clearance between the floor slab and the precast anchor can be estimated in a similar way. For example, the top of the beam can be set $\frac{5}{16}$ in (8 mm) high and camber can add another $\frac{3}{8}$ in (10 mm).

Related Sections

2-12. Architectural Precast Concrete Panels

2-27. Precast Architectural Wall Panel Erection

3-1. Mill Tolerances for W and HP Shapes

3-6. Steel Column Erection Tolerances

3-7. Location of Exterior Steel Columns in Plan

3-8. Beam/Column Connections

14-4. Detailing for Precast on Steel

Figure 13-5

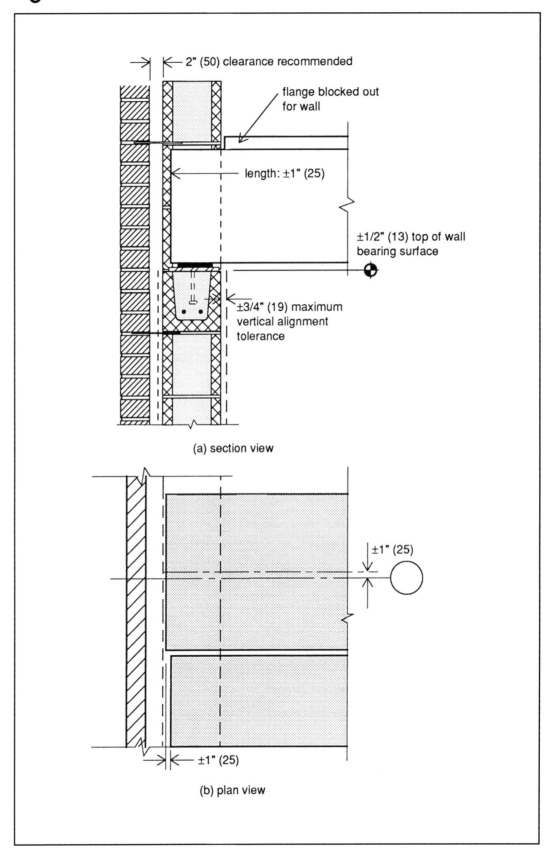

2" (50) clearance recommended

flange blocked out
for wall

length: ±1" (25)

±1/2" (13) top of wall
bearing surface

±3/4" (19) maximum
vertical alignment
tolerance

(a) section view

±1" (25)

±1" (25)

(b) plan view

13-5. Detailing Masonry and Precast Systems

When masonry and precast concrete are used together, the construction tolerance of the precast frame usually dictates the method of detailing. Dimensional and distortion tolerances of concrete block and brick are relatively minor, as described in Secs. 4-1 and 4-5. At most, an individual concrete block may be $\frac{1}{8}$ in (3 mm) larger or smaller than specified. American Concrete Institute (ACI) tolerance standards require masonry walls to be laid up to within a $\pm\frac{3}{4}$-in (19-mm) vertical alignment along the total height of the wall with a maximum vertical misalignment of $\frac{1}{4}$ in in any 10-ft section (6.4 mm in 3 m). The top of bearing walls must be within $\frac{1}{2}$ in (13 mm) of the specified elevation.

Figure 13-5 shows one of many possible combinations of masonry and precast: a double tee supported by a reinforced concrete block wall with a self-supporting brick veneer. The end of the double tee (or any other floor or roof member used) should not extend into the recommended 2-in (50-mm) cavity, so the minimum clearance between the end of the tee and the outside face of the block wall should be determined.

In the worst case, the block wall could slope inward up to $\frac{3}{4}$ in (19 mm) and the tee could be 1 in (25 mm) too long so a total clearance of $1\frac{3}{4}$ in (44 mm) could be specified. (Other types of members, such as hollow-core slabs, have other length tolerances.) The wall and tee might also vary in opposite directions at some point along the wall so the $1\frac{3}{4}$-in design clearance added to a $\frac{3}{4}$-in outward slope of wall and a tee that is 1 in short could result in as much as a $3\frac{1}{2}$-in (89-mm) clearance leaving only a $4\frac{1}{8}$-in (105-mm) bearing surface on a standard 8-in block. This is too small and results in eccentric bearing on the wall creating structural problems or requiring an expensive connection and additional wall reinforcing. To alleviate this problem the minimum design clearance could be reduced to 1 in and the recommended 2-in cavity increased slightly to account for any tees that might extend slightly into the cavity. Required clearances for other types of masonry/precast details can be estimated in a similar manner.

Related Sections

2-20. Prestressed Double Tees

2-25. Precast Floor and Roof Member Erection

 4-3. Concrete Unit Masonry Construction

Figure 13-6

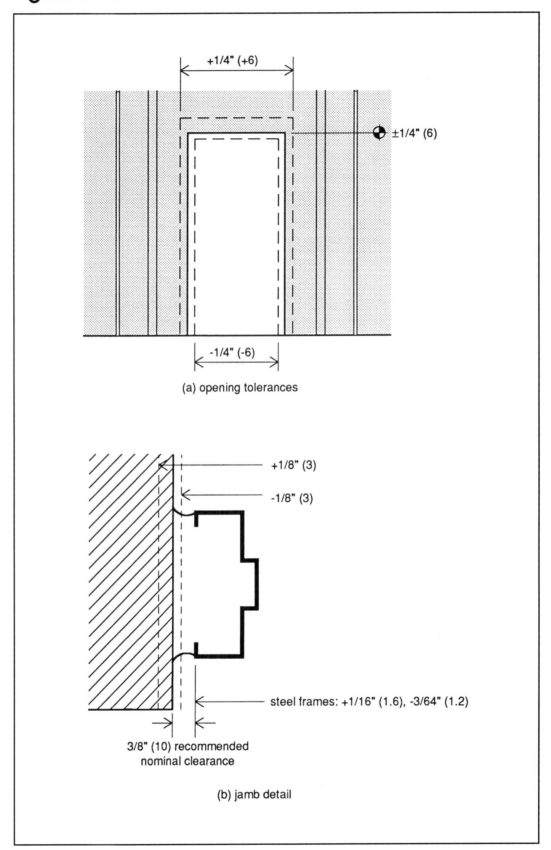

(a) opening tolerances

(b) jamb detail

13-6. Detailing Doors in Precast Concrete

As with cast-in-place concrete, doors in precast concrete are typically framed with steel and in some cases aluminum. If wood frames are used, there is usually a rough wood buck placed between the two materials which can be trimmed or shimmed to accommodate tolerances of the concrete.

Figure 13-6 shows the possible tolerances of both the precast opening and a steel frame. Tolerances for precast are tighter than they are for cast-in-place so accommodating a door is usually not a problem. Because the total opening size has a $\pm\frac{1}{4}$-in (6-mm) tolerance [or $\frac{1}{8}$ in (3 mm) on each side], a nominal $\frac{3}{8}$-in (10-mm) clearance is sufficient. Even if the opening is $\frac{1}{8}$ in smaller and the steel door is $\frac{1}{16}$ in (1.6 mm) larger, there is still a $\frac{3}{16}$-in (5-mm) sealant joint. Aluminum frames have about the same tolerance. Height tolerances can be adjusted either at the door head or by modifying the clearance at the floor line.

For large garage doors that span across two or more panels framing is more difficult. The edges of each precast panel at the head of the opening can be over $\frac{1}{2}$ in (13 mm) off (depending on the type of panel) unless the top of the opening is designated as a primary control surface. If the edges of adjacent panels are offset, the irregular head section can be framed with steel angles or channels to provide a straight, true rough opening.

Related Sections

2-12. Architectural Precast Concrete Panels

2-13. Precast Ribbed Wall Panels

2-14. Precast Insulated Wall Panels

 8-4. Storefront Installation

11-1. Standard Steel Doors and Frames

Figure 13-7

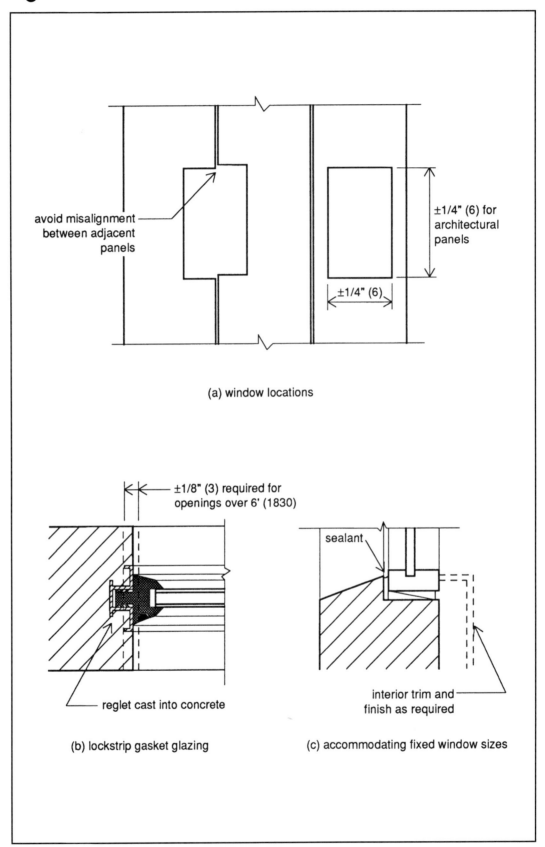

avoid misalignment
between adjacent
panels

±1/4" (6) for
architectural
panels

±1/4" (6)

(a) window locations

±1/8" (3) required for
openings over 6' (1830)

sealant

reglet cast into concrete

interior trim and
finish as required

(b) lockstrip gasket glazing

(c) accommodating fixed window sizes

13-7. Detailing Windows in Precast Concrete

Several types of windows can be used in precast concrete. These include steel, aluminum, wood, and lockstrip gasket glazing. Standard details for steel and aluminum windows are usually the most sensitive to construction tolerances because these window types are commonly placed directly in the opening. When wood windows are used they are usually framed into a rough wood buck and the exterior and interior joints are covered with trim which conceals any accommodation for construction tolerances. Lockstrip gasket glazing is a special condition which requires a much tighter tolerance of the concrete in both size and squareness. Only steel and aluminum windows are considered here.

For a window opening the finished size can be as much as $\frac{1}{4}$ in (6 mm) too small or too large in architectural panels and $\pm\frac{1}{2}$ in (13 mm) in ribbed and insulated wall panels. This means a possible variation of $\frac{1}{8}$ in (or $\frac{1}{4}$ in) in and out for any jamb, head, or sill section. See Fig. 13-7a. This does not include any variation in plumb or level for any of the four sides.

If an aluminum window is used, one jamb may be as much as $\frac{1}{16}$ in (1.6 mm) large (see Sec. 11-9) and the concrete opening may be as much as $\frac{1}{8}$ in (3 mm) too small. If a nominal $\frac{1}{4}$-in (6-mm) clearance is provided, this provides only a $\frac{1}{16}$-in (1.6-mm) space for sealant. A minimum $\frac{3}{8}$-in nominal clearance is a better choice. For storefronts, a $\frac{1}{2}$-in (13-mm) clearance between framing and the concrete is recommended.

Openings for glazing reglets must be cast to a tighter tolerance as described in Sec. 11-11. A separate reglet should be cast into the concrete to provide a smooth, true surface for the gasket. See Fig. 13-7b.

One method of accommodating fixed window sizes is shown in Fig. 13-7c. By casting a notch in the concrete opening, both in and out tolerances can be concealed and the joint can be properly sealed without oversizing the sealant joint. Although this increases formwork costs slightly, in some cases it is a preferable option. With steel windows part of the steel sash can be cast directly into the concrete.

Related Sections

2-12. Architectural Precast Concrete Panels

2-13. Precast Ribbed Wall Panels

2-14. Precast Insulated Wall Panels

8-4. Storefront Installation

11-9. Aluminum Windows and Sliding Doors

11-10. Steel Windows

11-11. Lockstrip Gasket Glazing

Figure 14-1

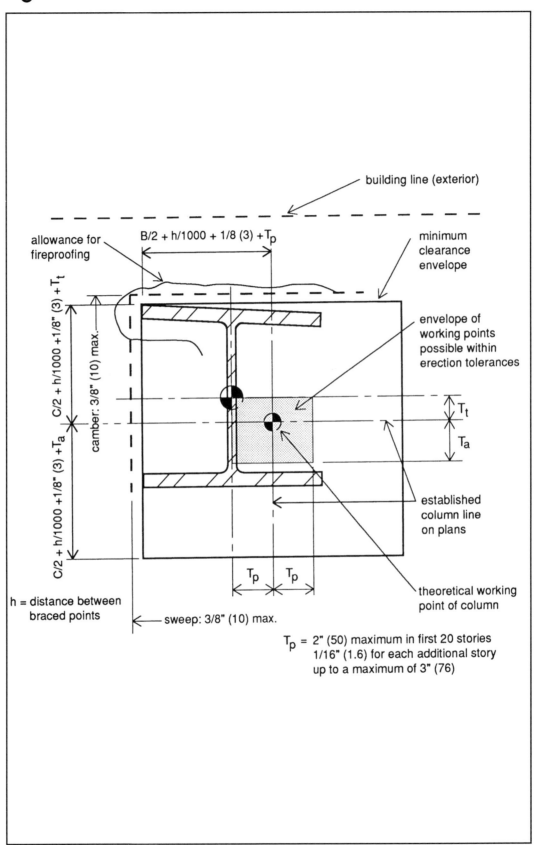

building line (exterior)

allowance for fireproofing

$B/2 + h/1000 + 1/8 (3) + T_p$

minimum clearance envelope

$C/2 + h/1000 + 1/8" (3) + T_t$

$C/2 + h/1000 + 1/8" (3) + T_a$

$C/2 + h/1000 + 1/8" (3) + T_a$

camber: 3/8" (10) max.

envelope of working points possible within erection tolerances

T_t

T_a

established column line on plans

T_p T_p

theoretical working point of column

h = distance between braced points

sweep: 3/8" (10) max.

T_p = 2" (50) maximum in first 20 stories
1/16" (1.6) for each additional story
up to a maximum of 3" (76)

Chapter 14

Steel Frame Systems

14-1. Accumulated Column Tolerances

Total in-place tolerances for exterior steel columns result from a combination of mill, fabrication, and erection tolerances. This section shows how these tolerances can accumulate. Refer to Secs. 3-1 and 3-6 for mill tolerances and individual column erection tolerances.

Figure 14-1 shows the minimum clearance envelope based on the actual column size, erection tolerances, dimensional mill tolerance, and out-of-straightness between braced points as allowed by the American Institute of Steel Construction (AISC) standards. An additional allowance for sweep or camber should be added in critical situations. The clearance envelope is measured from the theoretical working point of the column which is the actual center of the steel column at the end of the shipping piece.

Because the various tolerances vary with beam size and height of the building, a tolerance envelope can be calculated for each story, but in most cases the worst condition is determined for detailing purposes. For example, in a 20-story building the column can vary up to 1 in (25 mm) toward the building line or 2 in (50 mm) away from the building line due to erection tolerances. If the column is $\frac{1}{8}$ in (3 mm) oversize and straightness varies by $h/1000$, the envelope could be as much as $1\frac{1}{4}$ in (32 mm) out or as much as $2\frac{1}{4}$ in (57 mm) in (assuming a 12-ft, or 3660-mm, distance between braced points). At the midpoint of the column between splice points, camber or sweep could add as much as $\frac{3}{8}$ in (10 mm) to the basic erection tolerance envelope. See Fig. 3-1 and Table 3-1 for sweep and camber tolerances.

Even though the envelope of working point tolerance for an individual column can be up to 3 in (76 mm) for a 20-story building, AISC standards require that all exterior columns along one side of a building at each splice line be limited to a $1\frac{1}{2}$-in-wide (38-mm-wide) band as shown in Sec. 3-7. The adjacent envelope above or below each band must be within the 1:500 slope restriction illustrated in Sec. 3-6.

In general, if connections between the steel frame and exterior cladding provide for a total adjustment of 3 in (76 mm) in a 20-story building, the exterior building line can be maintained in a true vertical plane. Above this, the facade can be erected to within $\frac{1}{16}$ in (1.6 mm) of plumb per story. If dimensional or erection tolerances of the cladding material are substantial, these should be added to the steel tolerances as illustrated in the following sections of this chapter.

Related Sections

3-1. Mill Tolerances for W and HP Shapes

3-6. Steel Column Erection Tolerances

3-7. Location of Exterior Steel Columns in Plan

3-8. Beam/Column Connections

Figure 14-2

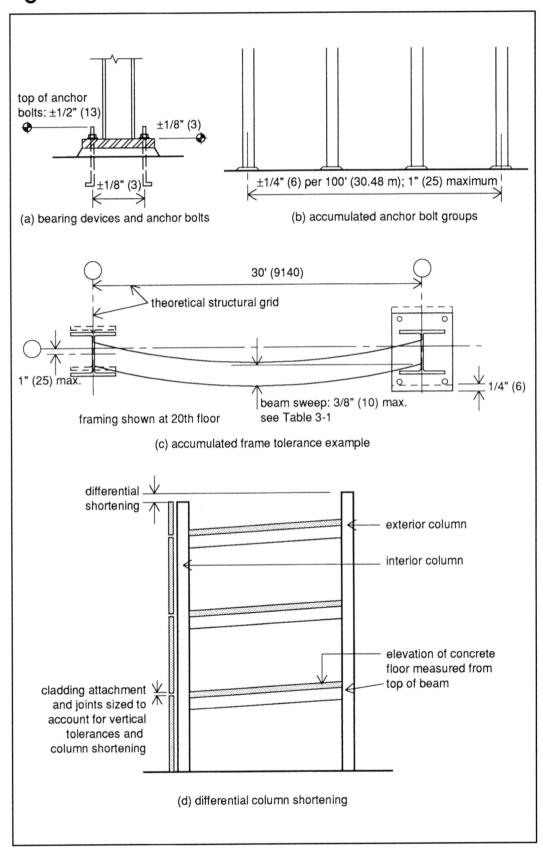

top of anchor
bolts: ±1/2" (13)

±1/8" (3)

±1/8" (3)

(a) bearing devices and anchor bolts

±1/4" (6) per 100' (30.48 m); 1" (25) maximum

(b) accumulated anchor bolt groups

30' (9140)

theoretical structural grid

1" (25) max.

1/4" (6)

beam sweep: 3/8" (10) max.
see Table 3-1

framing shown at 20th floor

(c) accumulated frame tolerance example

differential
shortening

exterior column

interior column

elevation of concrete
floor measured from
top of beam

cladding attachment
and joints sized to
account for vertical
tolerances and
column shortening

(d) differential column shortening

14-2. Accumulated Steel Frame Tolerances

Accumulated tolerances of an entire building frame are a combination of mill, fabrication, and erection tolerances. How these combine depends on the particular configuration of each building frame. The tolerances given in Chap. 3 can be used to determine specific overall tolerances. Some of the common conditions are illustrated in this section.

Steel framing begins with the connection of the frame to the foundation with anchor bolts. Figure 14-2a shows acceptable tolerances of bearing devices and anchor bolt groups. Although these are normally set by a contractor other than the steel erector, individual bolts within a group must be set within $\frac{1}{8}$ in (3 mm) of each other and the group must be set to within $\frac{1}{4}$ in (6 mm) of the established column line. There cannot be more than a $\frac{1}{4}$-in (6-mm) variation between adjacent anchor bolt groups. As shown in Fig. 14-2b the accumulated variance per 100 ft (30.48 m) is also limited to $\frac{1}{4}$ in (6 mm) with a maximum overall variance of 1 in (25 mm) along the entire length of the building.

The location of beam edges relative to other parts of the building can vary due to a combination of tolerances on base plate location, column erection, column out-of-straightness, member size, and beam sweep. Figure 14-2c shows an example of a possible condition at the twentieth floor of a building with 30-ft (9140-mm) spacing between columns. In the worst case, the base plate could be out by $\frac{1}{4}$ in (6 mm), the column out by the maximum of 1 in (25 mm), the column oversize by $\frac{1}{8}$ in (3 mm), and the column out of straightness by about $\frac{1}{8}$ in (3 mm) assuming a 12 ft (3.66 m) distance between braced points ($h/1000$). The beam connecting two columns could be oversized by $\frac{1}{8}$ in ($\frac{1}{4}$ in total but only half of this on one side), and have a sweep up to $\frac{3}{8}$ in (10 mm). Direct addition of all these tolerances gives a maximum possible outside variance at the midpoint of the beam of $1\frac{7}{8}$ in (47 mm). It is unlikely that all of these would occur simultaneously so the total probable tolerance can be calculated by taking the square root of the sum of the squares of the individual tolerances according to the method described in the introduction to Part 2. Using this calculation the total tolerance in this example would be about $1\frac{1}{8}$ in (29 mm).

Steel frame tolerances also vary in the vertical direction as diagrammed in Fig. 14-2d. The elevation of any beam as measured from the splice point can vary by $+\frac{5}{16}$ in (7.9 mm) or $-\frac{3}{16}$ in (4.8 mm) as shown in Fig. 3-8. In addition, allowable variations in length of columns can accumulate in a tall building. As the building is constructed, the interior columns may carry a greater percentage of load depending on the sequence of construction, resulting in a differential shortening between interior and exterior columns. Because of this, construction elements on each floor should be installed based on the elevation of the beams or splice points rather than on a fixed benchmark on the ground. There should be enough vertical adjustment in the connections between the steel frame and the exterior cladding to account for these accumulated tolerances and shortening of the building frame. Joints should allow for a $\pm\frac{5}{8}$-in (16-mm) vertical adjustment.

Related Sections

3-8. Beam/Column Connections

Introduction to Part 2

Figure 14-3

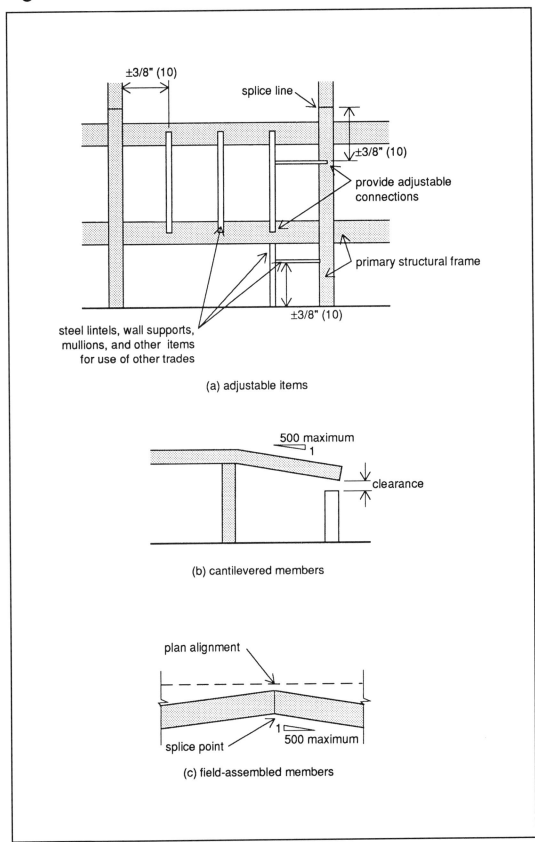

±3/8" (10)

splice line

±3/8" (10)

provide adjustable connections

primary structural frame

±3/8" (10)

steel lintels, wall supports, mullions, and other items for use of other trades

(a) adjustable items

500 maximum

1

clearance

(b) cantilevered members

plan alignment

splice point

1

500 maximum

(c) field-assembled members

14-3. Detailing for Steel Structural System Tolerances

In addition to the mill, fabrication, and erection tolerances described in the preceding sections and in Chap. 3, there are some additional tolerances that must be considered in some circumstances.

Secondary steel members attached to the primary structural frame for the purpose of supporting work of other trades have their own tolerances. These members are known as "adjustable items" and are shown diagrammatically in Fig. 14-3a. The tolerance for both horizontal and vertical positioning is $\pm\frac{3}{8}$ in (10 mm). This tolerance is valid only if sufficient clearance and adjustment are shown on the drawings so the steel erector can meet the tolerances. Vertical position is measured to the upper milled splice line of the nearest column and horizontal position is measured relative to the established finish line at any floor. Architectural exposed structural steel must meet tolerances which are one-half those for structural steel.

For cantilevered steel the member is considered plumb, level, and aligned if the angular variation from a working line of the installed piece to a straight line extending in the plan direction does not exceed 1:500. See Fig. 14-3b.

When steel members are field assembled the same angular variation applies. The member is considered plumb, level, or aligned if the actual installed alignment does not vary from the planned alignment by more than this amount. For example, in a 10-ft (3050-mm) length this means that the member could be as much as $\frac{1}{4}$ in (6 mm) off. See Fig. 14-3c. For irregular shapes, if the fabricated member is within tolerance and the supporting members are erected with standard tolerances, then the irregular shape is considered to be within acceptable tolerance.

Related Sections

3-7. Location of Exterior Steel Columns in Plan

3-9. Architecturally Exposed Structural Steel

Figure 14-4

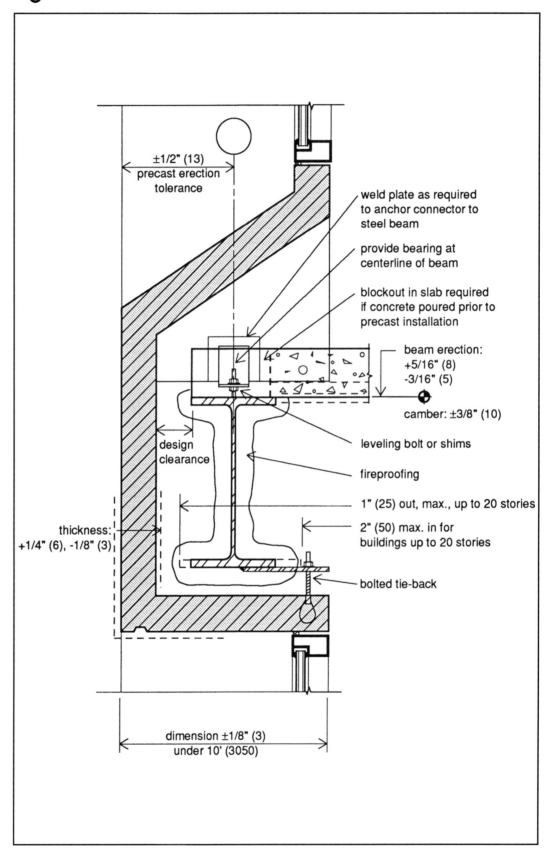

±1/2" (13)
precast erection
tolerance

weld plate as required
to anchor connector to
steel beam

provide bearing at
centerline of beam

blockout in slab required
if concrete poured prior to
precast installation

beam erection:
+5/16" (8)
-3/16" (5)

camber: ±3/8" (10)

design
clearance

leveling bolt or shims

fireproofing

1" (25) out, max., up to 20 stories

thickness:
+1/4" (6), -1/8" (3)

2" (50) max. in for
buildings up to 20 stories

bolted tie-back

dimension ±1/8" (3)
under 10' (3050)

14-4. Detailing for Precast on Steel

Detailing for precast concrete on steel framing requires that the mill, fabrication, and erection tolerances for the steel be calculated and added to the possible fabrication and erection tolerances of the precast. Because tolerances for both materials vary depending on the type and size of member as well as the height of the building, separate calculations need to be made for various conditions and locations in the building.

Figure 14-4 shows an example of a precast/steel detail. The location of the steel beam can vary as much as 1 in (25 mm) out and 2 in (50 mm) in on a building up to 20 stories. For shorter structures the rate of slope from plumb is 1:500 as described in Sec. 3-6. In addition, the width of the flange can vary $\pm\frac{1}{4}$ in (6 mm) or $\frac{1}{8}$ in (3 mm) on one side. Beam sweep varies with the length of the beam but can account for another $\frac{3}{8}$ in (10 mm) for a 30-ft (9140-mm) length. In the worst case, these might place the outside edge of the beam $1\frac{1}{2}$ in (38 mm) toward the precast.

The precast thickness can vary up to $\frac{1}{4}$ in (6 mm) oversize, but the precast erector is allowed to have the primary control surface within $\frac{1}{2}$ in (13 mm) from the centerline of the structural grid. If fireproofing is required around the steel, this must also be added to the tolerances to determine the total design clearance between the back of the precast and the edge of the beam.

Related Sections

2-12. Architectural Precast Concrete Panels

2-15. Hollow-Core Slabs

2-27. Precast Architectural Wall Panel Erection

 3-6. Steel Column Erection Tolerances

 3-8. Beam/Column Connections

13-4. Detailing for Precast and Steel Systems

Figure 14-5

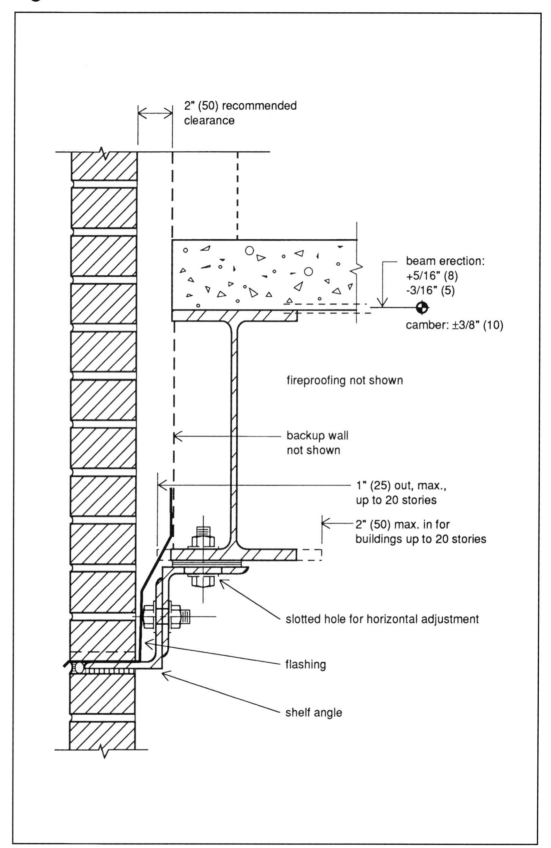

2" (50) recommended clearance

beam erection:
+5/16" (8)
-3/16" (5)

camber: ±3/8" (10)

fireproofing not shown

backup wall not shown

1" (25) out, max., up to 20 stories

2" (50) max. in for buildings up to 20 stories

slotted hole for horizontal adjustment

flashing

shelf angle

14-5. Detailing for Brick on Steel

When brick and steel framing are used together, the construction tolerance of the steel frame usually dictates the method of detailing. Dimensional and distortion tolerances of brick are relatively minor as described in Sec. 4-5. At most, a surface of an individual, standard-size brick may be out of specified plane by about $\frac{5}{32}$ in (4 mm) due to a worst case combination of size and warp tolerance.

In buildings taller than one or two stories the brick is usually supported on shelf angles at every story. A compressible filler below the angle allows for deflection of the angle as well as building movement and expansion of the brick panel below. The connection and support systems must be designed to accommodate the steel frame tolerance as well as provide the recommended 2-in (50-mm) clearance between the back of the brick wall and the structural frame and whatever backup wall is used. Vertical adjustment must also be provided so the shelf angle can match the joint location as the brick is laid. In designing the adjustable connection both the erection and fabrication tolerances of the steel beam should be considered.

Figure 14-5 shows only one possible way of attaching the shelf angle to the beam. With this detail vertical adjustment can be provided by shimming or with vertically slotted holes. Horizontal adjustment can be provided with slotted holes. Generally, shimming should not exceed 1 in (25 mm) and should be done with horseshoe-shaped shims with a length equal to the length of the angle. Where the steel frame varies at its maximum, the size of the shelf angle can be decreased or increased subject to engineering review.

Note that potential problems can arise if the clearance becomes so small that there is not adequate space for the bolt head, flashing, and any material which is used to prevent the bolt head from puncturing the flashing. Depending on the thickness of the angle, the size of the fastener, and the method of flashing, the 2-in (50-mm) clearance may need to be increased, especially in tall buildings.

Related Sections

3-6. Steel Column Erection Tolerances

3-7. Location of Exterior Steel Columns in Plan

3-8. Beam/Column Connections

4-5. Brick Manufacturing

4-6. Brick Wall Construction

12-4. Detailing Brick on Cast-in-Place Concrete

15-2. Detailing Brick and Masonry Systems

Figure 14-6

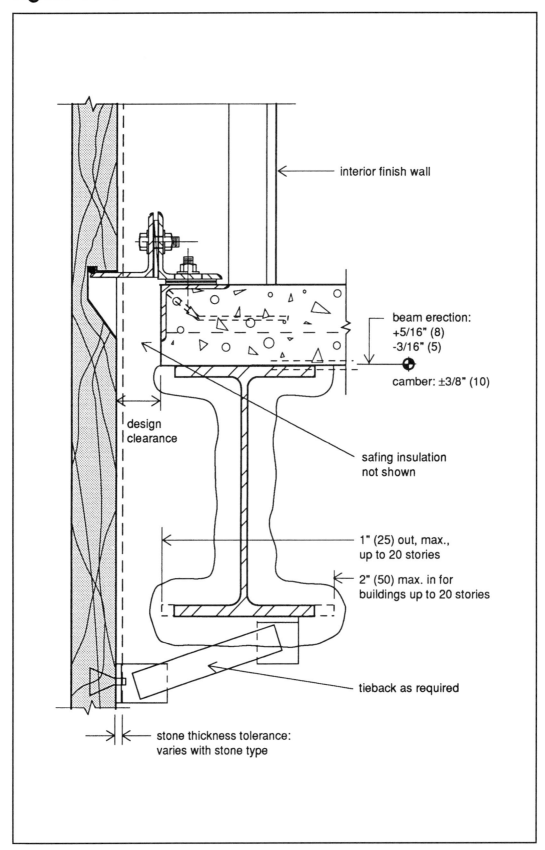

interior finish wall

beam erection:
+5/16" (8)
-3/16" (5)

camber: ±3/8" (10)

design
clearance

safing insulation
not shown

1" (25) out, max.,
up to 20 stories

2" (50) max. in for
buildings up to 20 stories

tieback as required

stone thickness tolerance:
varies with stone type

14-6. Detailing for Stone on Steel Systems

Detailing for stone facades attached to steel framing is similar to that for stone on concrete except that the tolerances for steel framing can be larger for tall buildings. However, in most cases stone can be installed slightly out of plumb (within the standards described in Secs. 5-4 and 5-5) along the height of a building to partially accommodate minor irregularities of the frame, if absolutely necessary.

Figure 14-6 shows a typical gravity support and anchor at a spandrel beam. This is the most critical connection to accommodate both the steel and stone tolerances. A variety of lateral anchors is available for various types of backup walls which provides for sufficient adjustment to maintain the erection tolerances shown in Secs. 5-4 and 5-5. Vertical deviations of the steel frame are accommodated with shims or vertically slotted holes in the angles. Deviations perpendicular to the building face are taken up by shimming the support angles or with slotted holes where the angle is attached to the anchor plate in the slab.

When determining the minimum design clearance the following tolerances and construction elements must be combined: the erection tolerance of the steel beam, which varies with height (see Sec. 3-6); the thickness of the stone, which will vary depending on the type of stone and thickness (see Secs. 5-1, 5-2, and 5-3); working space required for erection and fastening; and allowance for fireproofing of the steel, if required.

As with precast panels, horizontal joints and stone movement are normally accommodated by designing the vertical joints between stone sections large enough to absorb both movement and dimensional tolerances of the stone and steel frame. Refer to the introduction to Part 2 for procedures for estimating total expected tolerance of several panels and the method for calculating joint width.

Because the exact method of anchorage varies with the type of structural frame, the type of stone, loading, and other factors, along with the preferences of individual fabricators and installers, final details should be verified with the stone fabricator and contractor.

Related Sections

3-6. Steel Column Erection Tolerances

3-7. Location of Exterior Steel Columns in Plan

3-8. Beam/Column Connections

5-1. Granite Fabrication

5-2. Marble Fabrication

5-3. Limestone Fabrication

5-4. Granite and Marble Installation

5-5. Limestone Installation

14-1. Accumulated Column Tolerances

14-3. Detailing for Steel Structural System Tolerances

Figure 14-7

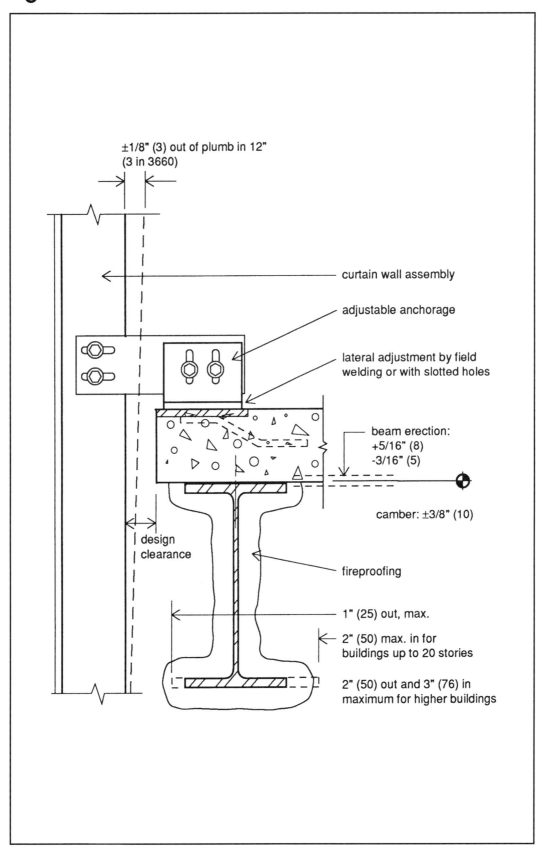

±1/8" (3) out of plumb in 12"
(3 in 3660)

curtain wall assembly

adjustable anchorage

lateral adjustment by field
welding or with slotted holes

beam erection:
+5/16" (8)
-3/16" (5)

camber: ±3/8" (10)

design
clearance

fireproofing

1" (25) out, max.

2" (50) max. in for
buildings up to 20 stories

2" (50) out and 3" (76) in
maximum for higher buildings

14-7. Detailing for Curtain Walls on Steel Frames

Steel framing is one of the most common structural systems used to support curtain walls. Even though steel frames have large tolerances, especially for high-rise buildings, the curtain wall can be installed to the tolerances indicated in Sec. 8-2 if adequate adjustable connections are detailed and sufficient design clearance is provided. Figure 14-7 shows some of the tolerance requirements for a typical curtain wall/spandrel beam connection. Because individual conditions will vary, exact details should be verified with the curtain wall fabricator and the structural engineer.

Adjustment needs to be provided in three directions: vertical, horizontal, and lateral. In addition, a minimum clearance of 2 in (50 mm) between the curtain wall and the frame is recommended. If adjustment and clearances are provided, then the minor manufacturing and fabrication tolerances of the curtain wall can be accommodated as well as any movement of the building frame and expansion and contraction of the curtain wall. In extreme cases, where the frame exceeds tolerances, the curtain wall can be installed slightly out of plumb, following the line of the frame along the height of the building.

Generally, the connection should be made at the top of the slab to make erection easier. Serrated angles and bolts, T-shaped clips, slotted holes, embedded anchors, and shims can all be used to provided the necessary adjustments. When shims are used the height of the shim stack should not exceed the diameter of the fastener securing the anchor. If the anchor must be higher, special shims and connection details may be required.

Lateral tolerances of the frame can be accommodated by proper design of the vertical joints of the curtain wall, or in extreme cases, at the building corners. The lateral deviation from plumb of exterior column as indicated in Sec. 3-6 can vary at a slope of 1:500 up to a maximum of 1 in (25 mm) up to the twentieth story and up to 2 in (50 mm) beyond that. At individual connectors, lateral alignment can be made by field welding clip angles, with slotted bolt holes, or other means. Refer to the introduction to Part 2 for joint design procedures.

Related Sections

3-6. Steel Column Erection Tolerances

3-7. Location of Exterior Steel Columns in Plan

3-8. Beam/Column Connections

8-1. Aluminum Curtain Wall Fabrication

8-2. Aluminum Curtain Wall Installation

9-13. Extruded Aluminum Tubes

14-1. Accumulated Column Tolerances

14-3. Detailing for Steel Structural System Tolerances

Figure 15-1

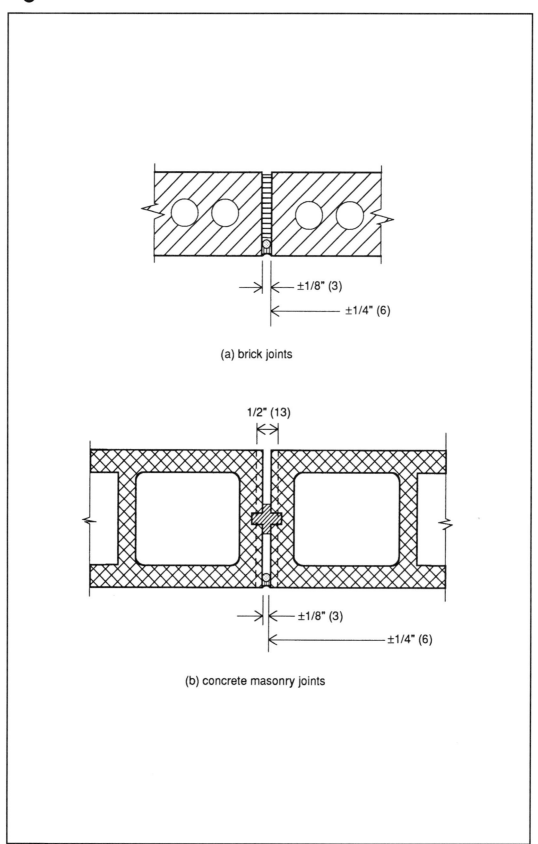

(a) brick joints

(b) concrete masonry joints

Chapter 15

Masonry Systems

15-1. Masonry Joint Tolerances

The thickness of masonry joints can usually be held to a $\pm\frac{1}{8}$-in (3-mm) tolerance with the edges of all vertically aligned joints within a $\frac{1}{2}$-in (13-mm) envelope. See Fig. 15-1. These tolerances allow for both minor size variations of the masonry and inaccuracies in laying up the wall. The end of a wall can usually be held to within $\frac{1}{4}$ in (6 mm) of the location shown on the plans.

When expansion joints are required they should be sized to account for both expansion and contraction caused by temperature changes and for expansion caused by moisture absorption as well as for size and construction tolerances. The expansion joint size for a brick wall depends on the distance between the expansion joints as well as the maximum expected temperature differential. In most cases, a $\frac{1}{2}$-in (13-mm) expansion joint will accommodate joint spacing of 20 ft (6100 mm) and a 140°F (60°C) temperature differential. A $\frac{5}{8}$-in (16-mm) joint will allow expansion joints spaced 25 ft (7620 mm) apart at the same temperature differential. If allowances for size tolerances are added and a sealant with a 25 percent movement capacity is used, most masonry expansion joints will be in the range of $\frac{3}{4}$ in to 1 in (38 mm to 50 mm).

Related Sections

4-1. Concrete Unit Masonry Manufacturing

4-3. Concrete Unit Masonry Construction

4-5. Brick Manufacturing

4-6. Brick Wall Construction

Figure 15-2

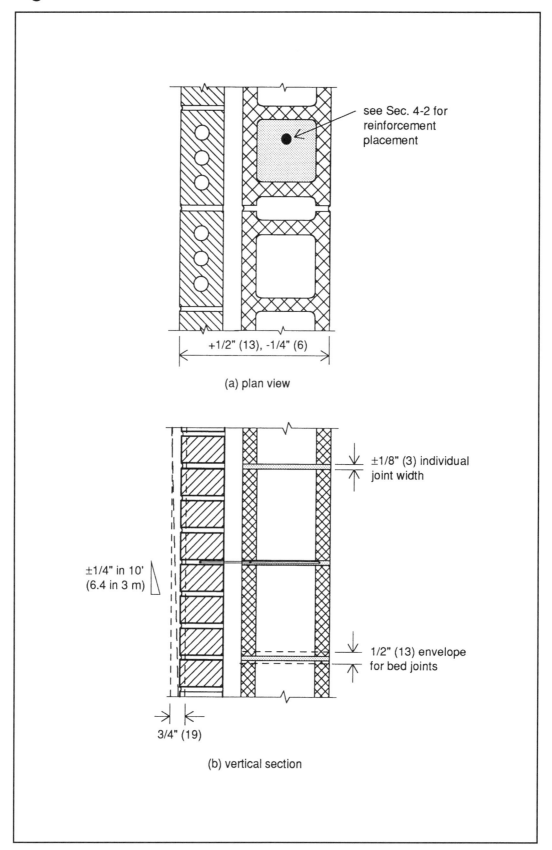

see Sec. 4-2 for reinforcement placement

+1/2" (13), -1/4" (6)

(a) plan view

±1/8" (3) individual joint width

±1/4" in 10' (6.4 in 3 m)

1/2" (13) envelope for bed joints

3/4" (19)

(b) vertical section

15-2. Detailing Brick and Masonry Systems

Brick and masonry systems usually consist of a backup wall of concrete unit masonry with a brick facing as shown in Fig. 15-2. If the multiwythe construction is a bearing wall, the concrete block is reinforced and grouted. As shown in Fig. 15-2a the tolerances for the total width of multiwythe construction are $+\frac{1}{2}$ in (13 mm) and $-\frac{1}{4}$ in (6 mm). This is based on American Concrete Institute (ACI) standards. Any furring or interior dimensions that are critical should take this into account. The face of both wythes must fall within a $\frac{3}{4}$-in (19-mm) envelope along the total height of the wall with no more than a $\frac{1}{4}$ in per 10 ft (6.4 mm in 3 m) variation in vertical slope. See Fig. 15-2b.

Because the cavity between the brick and concrete block is so large (recommended width is 2 in or 50 mm), any variation in the size of either masonry unit is easily accommodated in the cavity.

Related Sections

4-2. Concrete Masonry Reinforcement Placement

4-3. Concrete Unit Masonry Construction

4-6. Brick Wall Construction

Figure 15-3

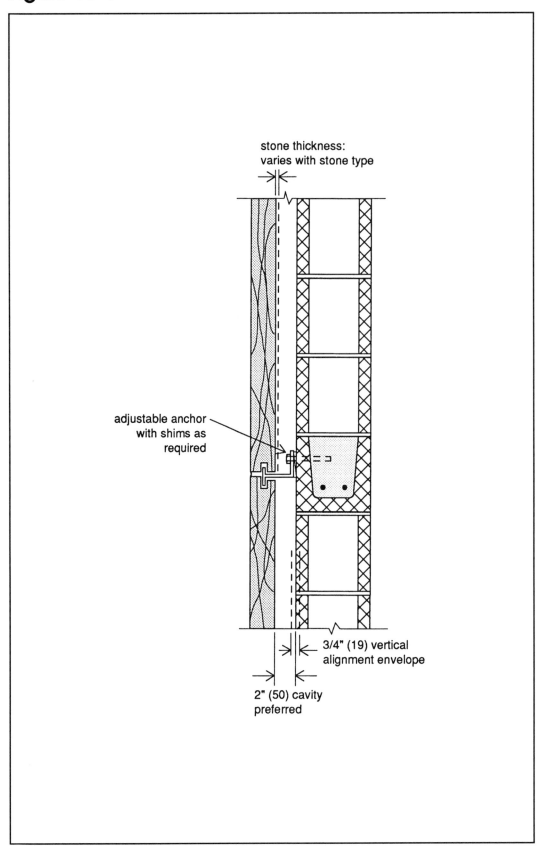

stone thickness:
varies with stone type

adjustable anchor
with shims as
required

3/4" (19) vertical
alignment envelope

2" (50) cavity
preferred

15-3. Detailing for Stone on Masonry Backup

In order to maintain the installation tolerances for granite, marble, and limestone shown in Secs. 5-4 and 5-5, adequate clearances and adjustable connections must be detailed when stone is attached to masonry. Detailing for stone on masonry is similar to detailing for stone on concrete, but there are some differences. Among them is the need for the stone gravity anchor locations to be coordinated with the coursing of the masonry. Generally, these anchors must be made in bond beams as shown in Fig. 15-3. As with concrete backup, the stone panels can be installed slightly out of plumb (within the standards described in Secs. 5-4 and 5-5) along the height of a building to partially accommodate minor irregularities of the frame if absolutely necessary. However, if sufficient clearance and adjustable anchors are provided, this is usually not necessary.

Figure 15-3 shows a typical gravity support and anchor at a bond beam. This is the most critical connection to accommodate the tolerances of the masonry and the stone. A variety of lateral anchors are available which provide for sufficient adjustment to maintain the erection tolerances shown in Secs. 5-4 and 5-5. Vertical deviations of the masonry are accommodated with adjustable anchors or slotted angles. Additional vertical adjustment can be made by shimming between the angle and the bottom edge of the stone. In some cases, a separate steel grid system is attached to the masonry wall and the stone is adjusted as it is anchored to the grid. Deviations perpendicular to the building face are taken up by shimming the support angles.

When determining the minimum design clearance the following tolerances and construction elements must be combined: the $\frac{3}{4}$-in (19-mm) tolerance envelope of the face of the wall; the thickness of the stone, which will vary depending on the type of stone and thickness (see Secs. 5-1, 5-2, and 5-3); the thickness of the angle; the size of the bolt head; working space required for erection and fastening; and any flashing, weep tubes, or other accessories behind the stone. Generally, a 2-in (50-mm) clearance is considered minimum. For adhered veneer the mortar between the masonry and stone should be between $\frac{1}{2}$ and $1\frac{1}{4}$ in (13 to 32 mm) thick.

Horizontal size tolerances and stone movement are normally accommodated by designing the vertical joints between stone sections large enough to absorb both movement and dimensional tolerances of the stone. Refer to the introduction to Part 2 for procedures for estimating total expected tolerance of several panels and the method for calculating joint width.

Because the exact method of anchorage varies with the type of masonry structure, the type of stone, loading, and other factors, along with the preferences of individual fabricators and installers, final details should be verified with the stone fabricator and contractor.

Related Sections

4-3. Concrete Unit Masonry Construction

5-1. Granite Fabrication

5-2. Marble Fabrication

5-3. Limestone Fabrication

5-4. Granite and Marble Installation

5-5. Limestone Installation

Figure 15-4

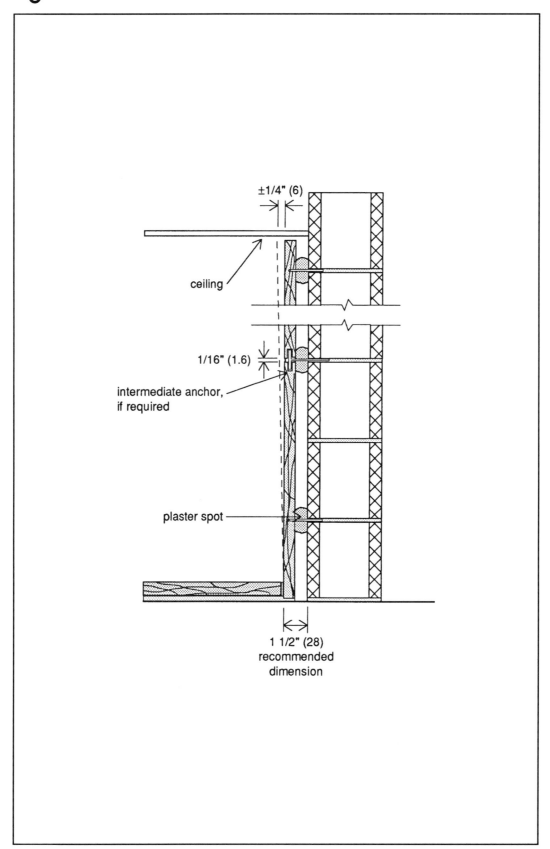

±1/4" (6)

ceiling

1/16" (1.6)

intermediate anchor,
if required

plaster spot

1 1/2" (28)
recommended
dimension

15-4. Detailing Interior Stone on Masonry

Stone can be applied to interior walls by directly applying the stone to the masonry with mortar or by using the standard-set method as shown in Fig. 15-4. Direct application is normally used only with thin stone tiles placed in a mortar setting bed, so any variation in the masonry must be concealed within the thickness of the mortar or the stone must follow the irregularities of the masonry.

The standard-set method uses anchors set into the masonry coursing and plaster spots at each anchor to hold the assembly tightly together. Because of the gap between the stone and the masonry and the adjustability of the anchors and plaster spots, the finished surface of the stone can be installed almost perfectly plumb in installations with standard ceiling heights.

For high spaces where several stone panels are used vertically, intermediate gravity supports may be required. This can be accomplished by using a steel angle anchored to the backup wall similar to the detail shown in Fig. 15-3. Adjustable anchors can be used in much the same way they are in exterior applications so the final wall finish is within $\frac{1}{4}$ in (6 mm) of plumb.

Related Sections

4-3. Concrete Unit Masonry Construction

5-1. Granite Fabrication

5-2. Marble Fabrication

9-8. Stone Flooring

Figure 15-5

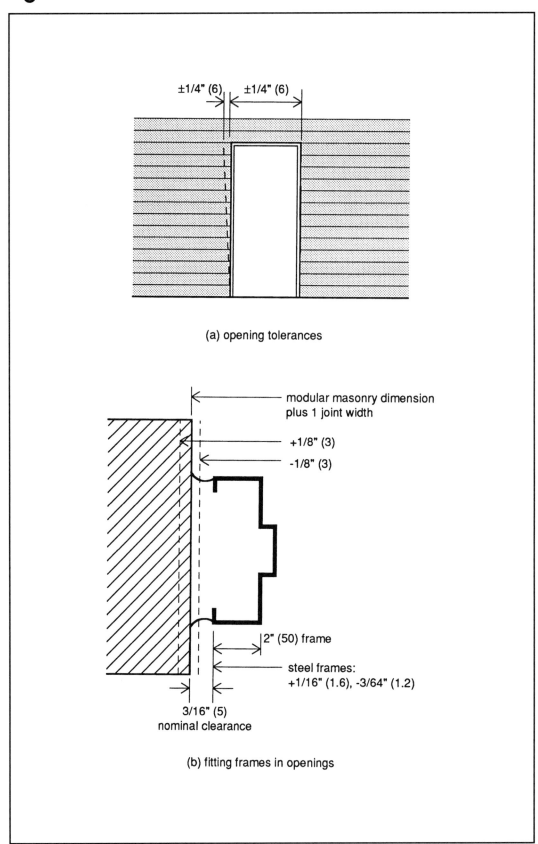

±1/4" (6)   ±1/4" (6)

(a) opening tolerances

modular masonry dimension
plus 1 joint width

+1/8" (3)

-1/8" (3)

2" (50) frame

steel frames:
+1/16" (1.6), -3/64" (1.2)

3/16" (5)
nominal clearance

(b) fitting frames in openings

15-5. Detailing Doors in Masonry

In most masonry construction, only steel door frames are used. If wood frames are used, a rough wood buck is usually placed between the two materials which can be trimmed or shimmed to accommodate the concrete tolerances. Steel frames are fixed in size so the frame detail and clearance are critical to sizing the opening to allow for tolerances and to provide a good sealant joint. When possible, the masonry opening size should conform to standard modular masonry sizes (8 in, or 200 mm) to avoid the expense of cutting the masonry. This way either full or half-size blocks can be used.

Figure 15-5 shows the possible tolerances of both the masonry opening and a steel frame. For example, using a 36-in (914-mm) door with 2-in (51-mm) frames gives a total frame width of 40 in (1016 mm). The total width of the masonry opening is 40 in plus the width of one joint [about $\frac{3}{8}$ in (10 mm)]. This leaves just $\frac{3}{16}$ in (5 mm) on each side to accommodate the door and any tolerances that may exist. If the steel frame is oversized by its tolerance of $\frac{1}{16}$ in (1.6 mm) and the masonry is inward by $\frac{1}{8}$ in (3 mm) and slightly out of plumb, there may be inadequate space for the frame. Normally, this problem is prevented by placing the frames in position and building the wall around them. If this is not possible, it is better to use $1\frac{1}{2}$-in (38-mm) frames to provide more clearance. Other door sizes may require cutting the blocks.

Related Sections

4-3. Concrete Unit Masonry Construction

4-6. Brick Wall Construction

11-1. Standard Steel Doors and Frames

11-3. Detention Security Hollow Metal Doors and Frames

Figure 15-6

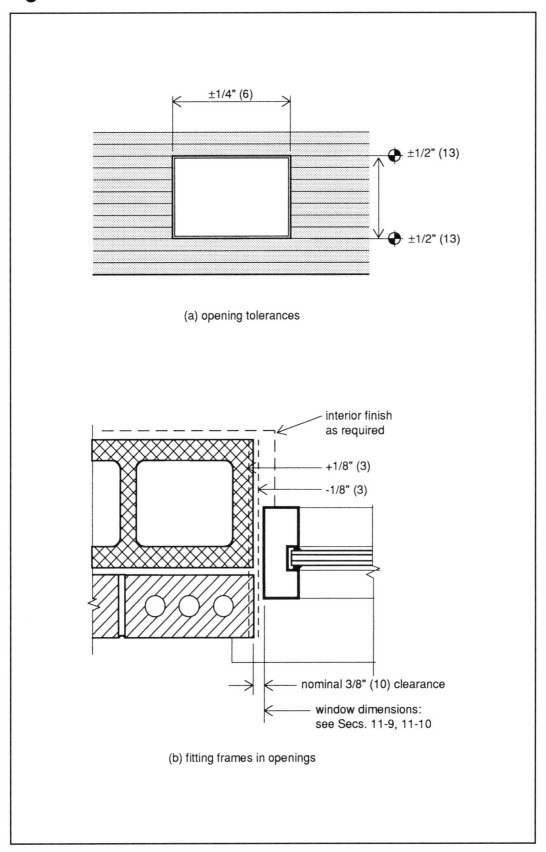

±1/4" (6)

±1/2" (13)

±1/2" (13)

(a) opening tolerances

interior finish
as required

+1/8" (3)

-1/8" (3)

nominal 3/8" (10) clearance

window dimensions:
see Secs. 11-9, 11-10

(b) fitting frames in openings

15-6. Detailing Windows in Masonry

Several types of windows can be used in masonry openings. These include steel, aluminum, and wood. Standard details for steel and aluminum windows are usually the most sensitive to construction tolerances because these window types are commonly placed directly in the opening. When wood windows are used they are usually framed into a rough wood buck and the exterior and interior joints are covered with some type of trim which conceals any accommodation for construction tolerances. Only steel and aluminum windows are considered here.

As with doors, the masonry opening size should conform to standard modular masonry sizes to avoid cutting the masonry. For a window opening the finished size can be as much as $\frac{1}{4}$ in (6 mm) too small or too large, or a possible variation of $\frac{1}{8}$ in at each jamb. See Fig. 15-6a. Although American Concrete Institute (ACI) standards allow bed joints to fall within a $\frac{1}{2}$-in (13 mm) tolerance envelope, the vertical dimension of a masonry opening usually varies no more than $\frac{1}{4}$ in in 10 ft (6 mm in 3050 mm).

The flange of steel windows is usually placed between the wythes of masonry so tolerances are easily accommodated. If aluminum windows are used, one jamb may be as much as $\frac{1}{16}$ in (1.6 mm) large (see Sec. 11-9), and the masonry opening may be as much as $\frac{1}{8}$ in (3 mm) too small. If a nominal $\frac{1}{4}$-in (6-mm) clearance is provided, this would provide only a $\frac{1}{16}$-in (1.6-mm) space for sealant and for expansion of the window and masonry and any movement that may occur. A minimum $\frac{3}{8}$-in (10-mm) nominal clearance is a better choice. For storefronts, a $\frac{1}{2}$-in (13-mm) clearance between framing and the masonry is recommended.

Related Sections

4-3. Concrete Unit Masonry Construction

4-6. Brick Wall Construction

11-9. Aluminum Windows and Sliding Doors

11-10. Steel Windows

Figure 16-1

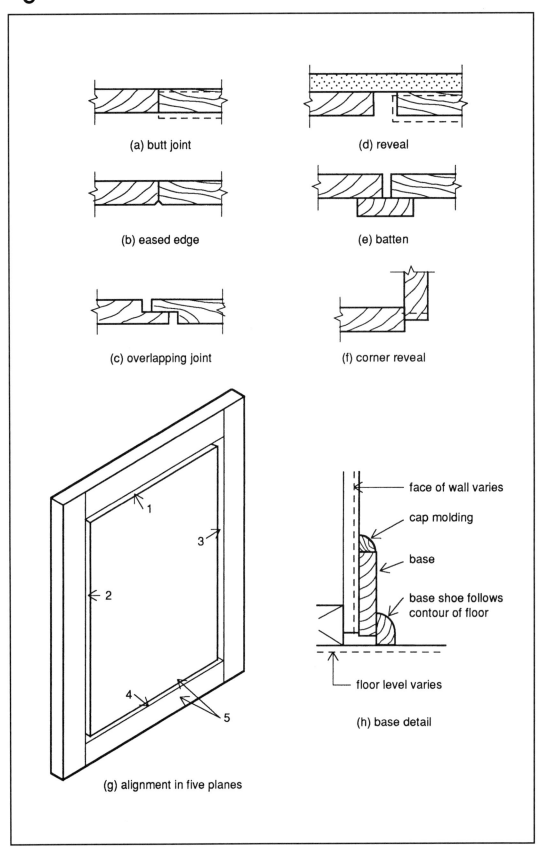

(a) butt joint

(d) reveal

(b) eased edge

(e) batten

(c) overlapping joint

(f) corner reveal

1

3

2

4

5

(g) alignment in five planes

face of wall varies

cap molding

base

base shoe follows
contour of floor

floor level varies

(h) base detail

Chapter 16

Timber and Carpentry Construction

16-1. Detailing Wood Joints

Tolerances of rough carpentry, finish carpentry, and architectural woodwork are normally accommodated by designing joints which conceal or allow for size and movement deviations. Even when wood is precisely cut to fit a particular construction detail, either on the job site or in the millshop, the tendency for wood to shrink and expand with changes in moisture content requires joints that conceal movement.

A typical butt joint, as shown in Fig. 16-1*a,* may be perfectly fit in the shop but any slight movement or change in moisture will cause it to open. Using an eased edge as shown in Fig. 16-1*b* conceals any slight movement or cracking at the joint line. However, even this type of joint cannot accommodate larger movement or size tolerances of the wood or the substrate to which it is applied. An overlapping joint with a reveal can easily accommodate fabrication and installation tolerances and any movement that may occur. One type of overlapping joint is shown in Fig. 16-1*c.*

Other types of joints that accommodate tolerances and movement by emphasizing the joint are shown in Fig. 16-1*d,* 16-1*e,* and 16-1*f.* These concepts work with finish carpentry as well as architectural woodwork. For example, any misalignment of the two planes of wood shown in Fig. 16-1*d* is not noticeable because of the space separating them. In addition, if one piece is slightly undersize or oversize, the reveal space can take up the extra dimension.

Whenever possible, joints or details that require alignment in three, four, or five planes should be avoided because it is very difficult to get everything aligned and all joints equal. Figure 16-1*g* shows one example: a cabinet door for which maintaining alignment and allowance for tolerances throughout the life of the cabinet is nearly impossible.

Figure 16-1*h* shows one common example of how wood trim is used to accommodate and conceal tolerances of adjacent construction. The wood base covers the crack between the wall and floor while the relatively flexible base shoe follows any contour variations of an uneven floor. The cap molding is flexible enough to follow any contour variations of the wall.

Related Sections

7-1. Manufacturing Tolerances for Board Lumber

7-2. Site-Built Cabinets and Countertops

7-3. Site-Built Stairs and Trim

7-4. Standing and Running Trim

7-17. Architectural Woodwork Installation

Figure 16-2

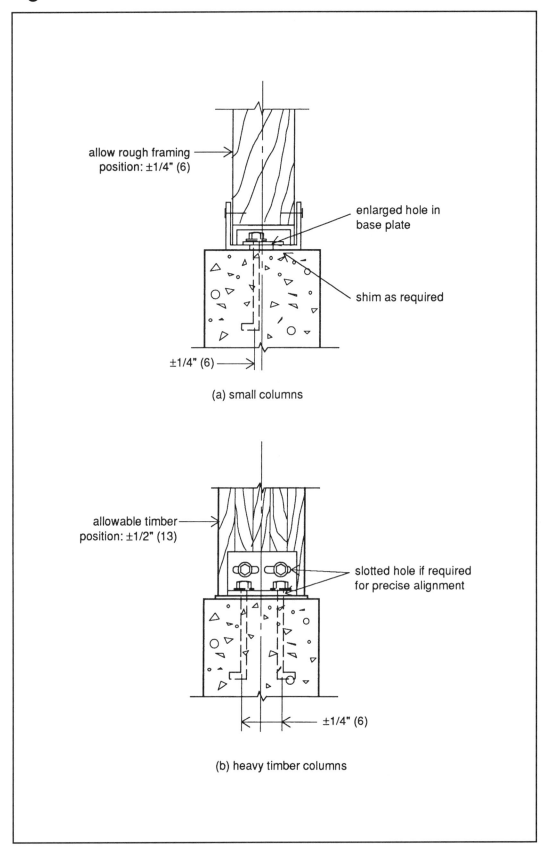

allow rough framing
position: ±1/4" (6)

enlarged hole in
base plate

shim as required

±1/4" (6)

(a) small columns

allowable timber
position: ±1/2" (13)

slotted hole if required
for precise alignment

±1/4" (6)

(b) heavy timber columns

16-2. Detailing for Timber Columns

Timber columns can be either dimensional lumber [up to $4\frac{1}{2}$ in (114 mm) in thickness], heavy timber [5 in (127 mm) or over], or glued laminated timber. In each case the construction tolerances involved include the size and installation tolerances of the timber, and the tolerances of any attached construction such as concrete foundations and anchoring devices.

Figure 16-2 illustrates how timber columns can be positioned accurately when attached with anchor bolts to concrete foundations. As shown in Fig. 16-2a column base plates are available with enlarged holes allowing the plate to be positioned even when the anchor bolt is out of location by $\frac{1}{4}$ in (6 mm) or more. If such an adjustable anchor is *not* used, the position of the column should still be within its allowable $\frac{1}{4}$-in (6-mm) position tolerance as described in Sec. 6-6.

For heavy timber and laminated columns anchors with slotted holes can be used if precise alignment is required and the columns are predrilled. However, in most cases the position of the timber is not critical and can be off by the allowable $\frac{1}{4}$ in (6 mm) of the anchor bolts and still be within allowable tolerances for heavy timber position. To accommodate size and squareness tolerances and expansion there should be a $\frac{1}{8}$-in (3-mm) clearance between the timber and any steel anchorage device.

Related Sections

6-1. Glued Laminated Timber Fabrication

6-2. Manufacturing Tolerances for Structural Lumber

6-6. Rough Lumber Framing

16-3. Detailing for Timber Beams

Figure 16-3

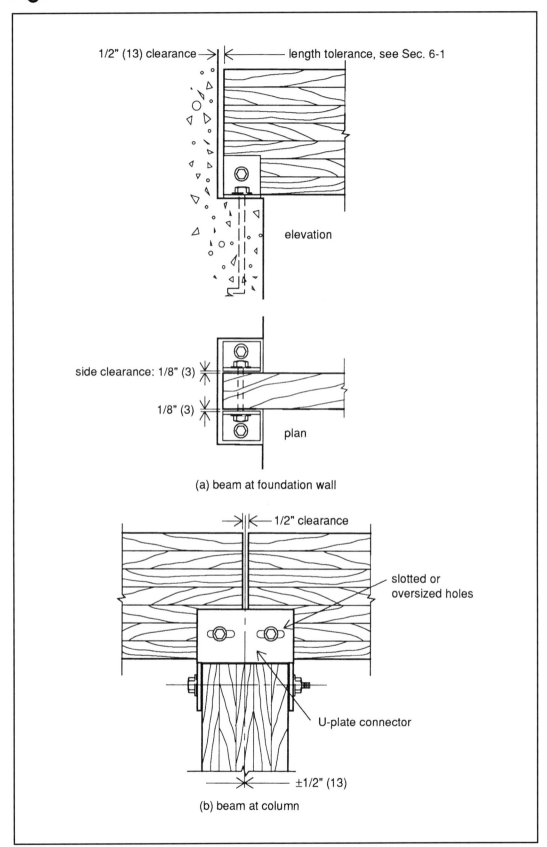

1/2" (13) clearance → length tolerance, see Sec. 6-1

elevation

side clearance: 1/8" (3)

1/8" (3)

plan

(a) beam at foundation wall

1/2" clearance

slotted or oversized holes

U-plate connector

±1/2" (13)

(b) beam at column

16-3. Detailing for Timber Beams

As with columns, timber beams can be either dimensional lumber [thickness up to $4\frac{1}{2}$ in (114 mm)], heavy timber [5 in (127 mm) or over], or glued laminated timber. There are generally few problems with dimensional lumber because it can be cut, trimmed, and shimmed on the job site to meet positioning tolerances of $\pm\frac{1}{4}$ in (6 mm) shown in Sec. 6-6. Any misalignments are normally concealed with finish materials.

Heavy timber and glued laminated timber construction require more thought in detailing because these are often exposed and are part of the design aesthetic of the building. Figure 16-3 shows two common framing situations where clearances for construction tolerances are critical. At least a $\frac{1}{2}$-in (13-mm) clearance should be detailed between the end of a beam and any other structure, such as a concrete beam pocket. See Fig. 16-3a. The clearance allows for any length tolerance of the beam and minor misalignments of the anchor device and bolt hole position. As with any heavy timber framing, there should be a $\frac{1}{8}$-in (3-mm) clearance between the timber and any steel anchorage device.

As shown in Fig. 16-3b, oversized or slotted holes can be used in steel connectors to accommodate size and position tolerances if positioning is critical and if allowed by the structural requirements of the bolted connection. If steel columns are used, their erection tolerance must also be considered.

Related Sections

6-1. Glued Laminated Timber Fabrication

6-2. Manufacturing Tolerances for Structural Lumber

6-6. Rough Lumber Framing

16-2. Detailing for Timber Columns

Figure 16-4

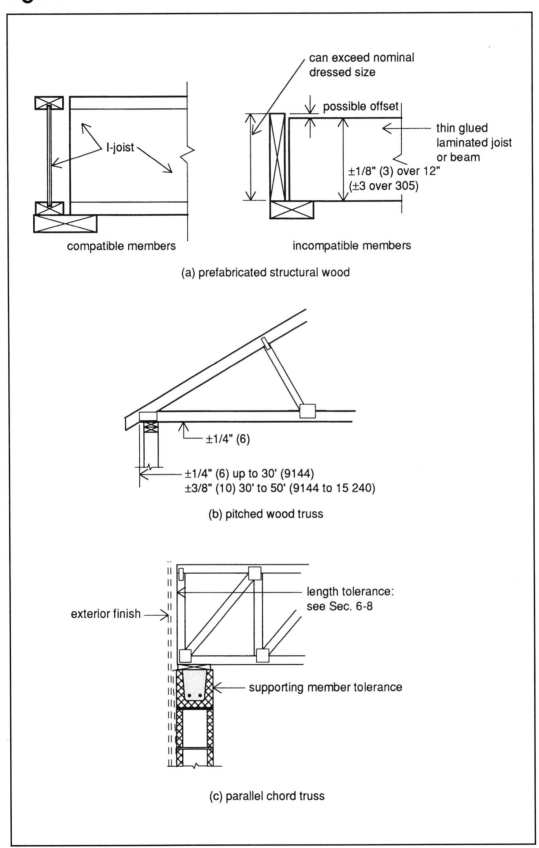

can exceed nominal dressed size

possible offset

thin glued laminated joist or beam

±1/8" (3) over 12" (±3 over 305)

I-joist

compatible members

incompatible members

(a) prefabricated structural wood

±1/4" (6)

±1/4" (6) up to 30' (9144)
±3/8" (10) 30' to 50' (9144 to 15 240)

(b) pitched wood truss

exterior finish

length tolerance: see Sec. 6-8

supporting member tolerance

(c) parallel chord truss

16-4. Detailing for Prefabricated Structural Wood

Prefabricated structural wood members—such as trusses, I-joists, and thin, glued laminated framing—are made to exacting standards and their manufacturing tolerances are clearly defined. However, when used with other structural components such as dimensional lumber, masonry, and steel, the combined effects of all tolerances must be considered to prevent misfits during erection, field cutting or trimming, or overly tight fits that do not allow for wood expansion or building movement.

Whenever possible, prefabricated structural wood should be used with compatible framing. Even using prefabricated structural wood members with standard dimensional lumber can result in undesirable offsets because the manufacturing tolerances of the two materials are different. For example, as shown in Fig. 16-4a, a thin, glued laminated joist over 12 in (305 mm) deep could be $\frac{1}{8}$ in (3 mm) shorter than its nominal depth dimension. An adjacent piece of dimensional lumber could be oversized by the same amount resulting in a misalignment of $\frac{1}{4}$ in (6 mm) or more.

Supporting framework for either pitched or parallel chord trusses should be dimensioned to accommodate the length tolerances of the trusses as well as possible out-of-alignment plan tolerances of the supporting members. This is especially critical where sheathing or other exterior finish materials must be applied over both construction assemblies. See Fig. 16-4b and 16-4c. In most cases elevation tolerances for trusses are not critical.

Related Sections

6-8. Metal Plate Connected Wood Truss Fabrication

6-9. Metal Plate Connected Wood Truss Erection

6-10. Prefabricated Structural Wood

Figure 16-5

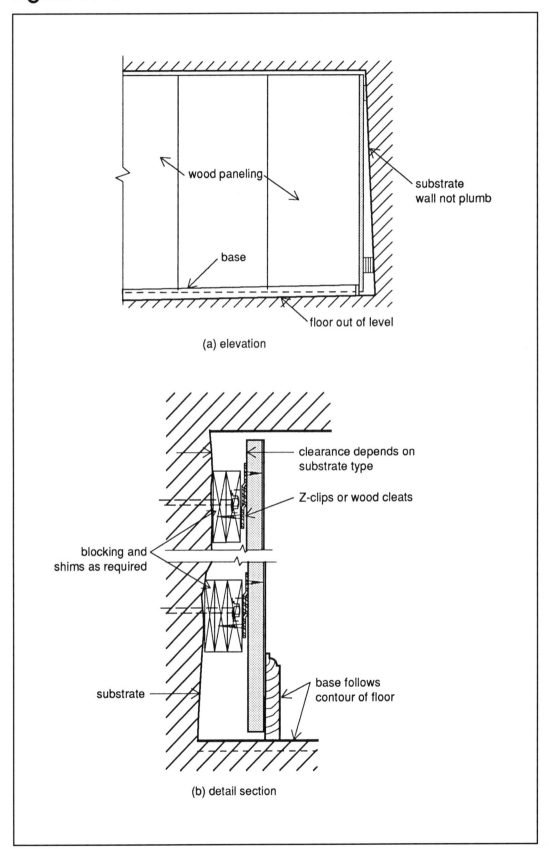

wood paneling

substrate
wall not plumb

base

floor out of level

(a) elevation

clearance depends on
substrate type

Z-clips or wood cleats

blocking and
shims as required

substrate

base follows
contour of floor

(b) detail section

16-5. Detailing for Paneling and Site-Built Substrates

Wood paneling is fabricated in the millshop to exact sizes and squareness but must be installed on substrates that are usually not level, plumb, or square. See Fig. 16-5*a*. If sufficient clearance is provided, blocking can be installed against the wall substrate so a line connecting the faces of the blocking is plumb. When the paneling is suspended or fastened on the blocking it will also be plumb. In some cases, such as with accurately constructed gypsum wallboard partitions, only minor shimming of the Z-clips or wood cleats used to suspend the paneling is required. In other situations, such as on rough concrete walls or in older buildings, extensive blocking and shimming may be required to build out to a plumb and level plane. See Fig. 16-5*b*.

If floors or ceilings are extremely out of level, base trim or cornice molding can be used to conceal the variation in gap size between the bottom or top edge of the paneling and the ceiling or floor, respectively.

Corner details must also be developed which allow the paneling to be installed in rooms that are out of square.

Related Sections

7-4. Standing and Running Trim

7-8. Flush Paneling

7-9. Stile and Rail Paneling

7-17. Architectural Woodwork Installation

Figure 16-6

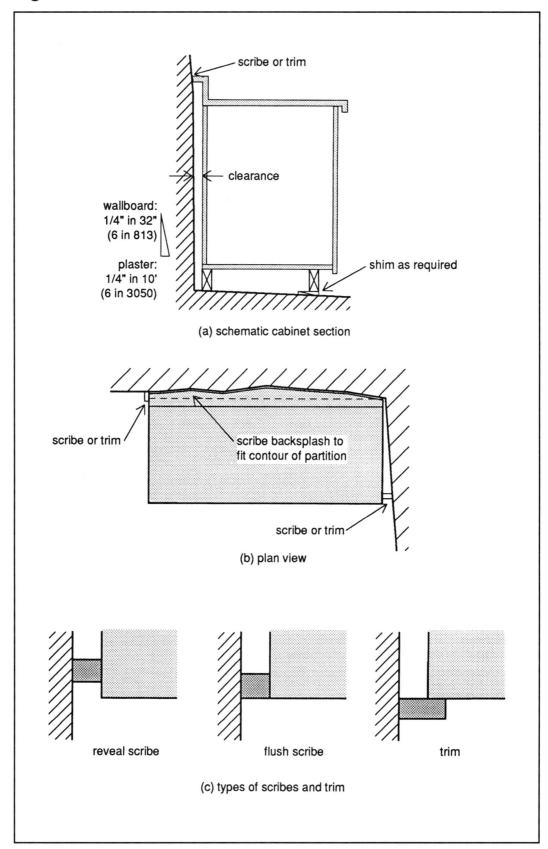

scribe or trim

clearance

wallboard:
1/4" in 32"
(6 in 813)

plaster:
1/4" in 10'
(6 in 3050)

shim as required

(a) schematic cabinet section

scribe or trim

scribe backsplash to
fit contour of partition

scribe or trim

(b) plan view

reveal scribe

flush scribe

trim

(c) types of scribes and trim

16-6. Detailing for Cabinetry and Site-Built Substrates

Most cabinets are manufactured in a shop or factory to exact sizes and squareness and must be fit into less exacting construction where walls are not plumb, floors level, or corners square. Even site-built cabinets must be fit into less than perfect existing construction. Cabinet detailing should provide ways to tightly mate the cabinets to adjacent construction while maintaining the overall design style of the installation.

Figure 16-6a and Fig. 16-6b schematically illustrate the places where typical cabinets must be matched to the surrounding construction. For upper cabinets and shelving, similar fits must also be made at the ceiling. Because most partitions are not exactly plumb or perfectly smooth, there should be a clearance behind the cabinet back so that the cabinet only touches the partition at the countertop. The dimension of the clearance depends on the condition of the partition, but is normally $\frac{1}{4}$ in to $\frac{1}{2}$ in (6 mm to 13 mm). In most cases, the top of the backsplash is built wider than necessary so it can be scribed to fit the outline of the partition when the countertop is installed. Any shimming required to level the cabinet must be concealed with a finish base.

Where a vertical edge of a cabinet or other woodwork touches the partition the joint can be finished with one of the methods diagrammed in Fig. 16-6c.

Related Sections

7-2. Site-Built Cabinets and Countertops

7-5. Architectural Cabinets

7-6. Modular Cabinets

7-7. Countertops

7-17. Architectural Woodwork Installation

List of Sources

Chapter 1. Sitework

ACI 117-90, *Standard Tolerances for Concrete Construction and Materials* and *Commentary*, ACI 117R-90, American Concrete Institute, Detroit, 1990.

J. K. Latta, "Inaccuracies in Construction," Canadian Building Digest 171, April 1975, in *Canadian Building Digests*, 151-200, Institute for Research in Construction, National Research Council of Canada, Ottawa, March 1989.

Landscape Specification Guidelines, 3d ed., Associated Landscape Contractors of America, Falls Church, VA, 1986.

SITESPEC Section 02200, "Earthwork," p. 1, *SITESPEC Handbook, Version II*, James Burkart, Upper Arlington, OH, 1991.

SITESPEC Section 02510, "Asphalt Concrete Paving," p. 1, *SITESPEC Handbook, Version II*, James Burkart, Upper Arlington, OH, 1991.

Spectext Section 02211, *Rough Grading*, Construction Sciences Research Foundation, Baltimore, MD, July 1989, p. 6.

Spectext Section 02510, *Asphaltic Concrete Paving*, Construction Sciences Research Foundation, Baltimore, MD, July 1989, p. 8.

Spectext Section 02923, *Landscape Grading*, Construction Sciences Research Foundation, Baltimore, MD, July 1989, p. 3.

SS-1, *Model Construction Specifications for Asphalt Concrete and Other Plant-Mix Types*, Asphalt Institute, Lexington, KY, November 1984.

Chapter 2. Concrete

ACI 117-90, *Standard Tolerances for Concrete Construction and Materials*, American Concrete Institute, Detroit, 1990.

ACI Compilation No. 9, *Concrete Floor Flatness and Levelness*, American Concrete Institute, Detroit, undated.

ASTM E1155-87, *Standard Test Method for Determining Floor Flatness and Levelness Using the F-Number System*, American Society for Testing and Materials, Philadelphia, 1987.

MSP-1-86, *Manual of Standard Practice*, 24th ed., Concrete Reinforcing Steel Institute, Schaumburg, IL, 1986.

Recommended Practice for Glass Fiber Reinforced Concrete Panels, Precast/Prestressed Concrete Institute, Chicago, 1993.

Tolerances for Precast and Prestressed Concrete, Precast/Prestressed Concrete Institute, reprinted from *Journal of the Prestressed Concrete Institute*, vol. 30, no. 1, January–February 1985.

Chapter 3. Steel

ASTM A500, *Standard Specification for Cold-Formed Welded and Seamless Carbon Steel Structural Tubing in Rounds and Shapes,* American Society for Testing and Materials, Philadelphia, 1990.

ASTM A6/A6M, *General Requirements for Rolled Steel Plates, Shapes, Sheet Piling, and Bars for Structural Use,* American Society for Testing and Materials, Philadelphia, 1991.

ASTM A618, *Standard Specification for Hot-Formed Welded and Seamless High-Strength Low-Alloy Structural Tubing,* American Society for Testing and Materials, Philadelphia, 1990.

Code of Standard Practice for Steel Buildings and Bridges, American Institute of Steel Construction, Chicago, 1990.

Vertical Transportation Standards, National Elevator Industry, Inc., Fort Lee, NJ, 1990.

Chapter 4. Masonry

ACI 117-90, *Standard Specifications for Tolerances for Concrete Construction and Materials,* and *Commentary,* ACI 117R-90, American Concrete Institute, Detroit, 1990.

ACI 531.1-76, *Specification for Concrete Masonry Construction,* American Concrete Institute, Detroit, 1976, revised 1983.

AIA File No. 9, *Public Works Specifications, Ceramic Veneer,* Architectural Terra Cotta Institute, October 1961. (Out of print; available from Gladding, McBean, Lincoln, CA.)

ASTM C34, *Standard Specification for Structural Clay Load-Bearing Wall Tile,* American Society for Testing and Materials, Philadelphia, 1991.

ASTM C55, *Standard Specification for Concrete Building Brick,* American Society for Testing and Materials, Philadelphia, 1985.

ASTM C56, *Standard Specification for Structural Clay Non-Load Bearing Tile,* American Society for Testing and Materials, Philadelphia, 1991.

ASTM C62-91, *Standard Specification for Building Brick,* American Society for Testing and Materials, Philadelphia, 1991.

ASTM C90, *Standard Specification for Hollow Load-Bearing Concrete Masonry Units,* American Society for Testing and Materials, Philadelphia, 1992.

ASTM C126, *Standard Specification for Ceramic Glazed Structural Clay Facing Tile, Facing Brick, and Solid Masonry Units,* American Society for Testing and Materials, Philadelphia, 1991.

ASTM C129, *Standard Specification for Non-Load Bearing Concrete Masonry Units,* American Society for Testing and Materials, Philadelphia, 1992.

ASTM C212, *Standard Specification for Structural Clay Facing Tile,* American Society for Testing and Materials, Philadelphia, 1991.

ASTM C216-91, *Standard Specification for Facing Brick,* American Society for Testing and Materials, Philadelphia, 1991.

ASTM C652-91, *Standard Specification for Hollow Brick,* American Society for Testing and Materials, Philadelphia, 1991.

ASTM C744, *Standard Specification for Prefaced Concrete and Calcium Silicate Masonry Units,* American Society for Testing and Materials, Philadelphia, 1985.

ASTM C901-90, *Standard Specification for Prefabricated Masonry Panels,* American Society for Testing and Materials, Philadelphia, 1990.

ASTM C1088-91, *Standard Specification for Thin Veneer Brick Units Made from Clay or Shale,* American Society for Testing and Materials, Philadelphia, 1991.

BIA 9, *Manufacturing, Classification and Selection of Brick,* BIA Tech. Note 9, Brick Institute of America, Reston, VA, revised March 1986.

BIA llC, *Guide Specification for Brick Masonry,* BIA Tech. Note 11C, Brick Institute of America, Reston, VA, revised December 1984.

NCMA-TEK 36A, *ASTM Specifications for Concrete Masonry Units,* NCMA-TEK 36A, National Concrete Masonry Association, Herndon, VA, 1986.

Uniform Building Code, Section 2407(j)2, "Mortar Joints in Glass Block Construction," International Conference of Building Officials, Whittier, CA, 1991.

Uniform Building Code, Sections 2404(d)1 and 2404(e), "Placement of Reinforcing Steel in Concrete Masonry Units," International Conference of Building Officials, Whittier, CA, 1991.

Chapter 5. Stone

CSI Standard Specification 04435-90, Cast Stone Institute, Winter Park, FL, 1990.

Dimension Stone Design Manual IV, Marble Institute of America, Farmington, MI, 1991.

Indiana Limestone Handbook, 19th ed., Indiana Limestone Institute of America, Inc., Bedford, IN, 1992.

Marble and Stone Slab Veneer, Masonry Institute of America, Farmington, MI, 1986, pp. 20–22.

Specifications for Indiana Limestone (Exterior Applications), 2d ed., Indiana Limestone Institute of America, Inc., Bedford, IN, undated.

Chapter 6. Lumber

AITC 113-86, *Standard for Dimensions of Structural Glued Laminated Timber,* American Institute of Timber Construction, Englewood, CO, 1986.

ANSI/AITC A190.1, *American National Standard for Wood Products—Structural Glued Laminated Timber,* American Institute of Timber Construction, Englewood, CO, 1992.

ANSI A208.1-1993, *American National Standard, Particleboard,* American National Standards Institute, New York, 1993.

ANSI A208.2-1994, *Medium Density Fiberboard for Interior Use,* American National Standards Institute, New York, 1994.

HIB-91, *Handling, Installing & Bracing Metal Plate Connected Wood Trusses,* Truss Plate Institute, Madison, WI, 1991.

Insurance/Warranty Documents, Home Owners Warranty Corporation, Arlington, VA, 1987.

PS 1-83, *U.S. Product Standard PS 1-83 for Construction and Industrial Plywood,* National Institute for Standards and Technology, Office of Product Standards Policy, Gaithersburg, MD, 1983.

PS 20-70, *Voluntary Product Standard, PS 20-70, American Softwood Lumber Standard,* National Institute for Standards and Technology, Gaithersburg, MD, 1970.

Quality Standards for the Professional Remodeler, 2d ed., National Association of Home Builders Remodelors™ Council, Washington, DC, 1991.

Spectext Section 06112, *Framing and Sheathing,* Construction Sciences Research Foundation, Baltimore, MD, October 1989, p. 12.

Spectext Section 06151, *Wood Chord Metal Joists,* Construction Sciences Research Foundation, Baltimore, MD, January 1990, p. 7.

Spectext Section 06181, *Glued Laminated Structural Units,* Construction Sciences Research Foundation, Baltimore, MD, July 1989, p. 7.

Spectext Section 06193, *Plate Connected Wood Trusses,* Construction Sciences Research Foundation, Baltimore, MD, January 1990, p. 8.

Standard Grading Rules for Southern Pine Lumber, Southern Pine Inspection Bureau, Pensacola, FL, 1991.

TPI-85, *TPI-85 Addendum, Appendix P, Quality Standard for Metal Plate Connected Wood Trusses,* Truss Plate Institute, Madison, WI, 1985.

Chapter 7. Finish Carpentry and Architectural Woodwork

ANSI/KCMA A161.1-1990, *Recommended Performance and Construction Standards for Kitchen and Vanity Cabinets,* Kitchen Cabinet Manufacturers Association, Reston, VA, 1990.

Architectural Woodwork Quality Standards, 6th ed., Architectural Woodwork Institute, Centreville, VA, 1993.

Insurance/Warranty Documents, Home Owners Warranty Corporation, Arlington, VA, 1987.

PS 20-70, *Voluntary Product Standard PS 20-70, American Softwood Lumber Standard,* National Institute for Standards and Technology, Gaithersburg, MD, 1970.

Quality Standards for the Professional Remodeler, 2d ed., National Association of Home Builders Remodelors™ Council, Washington, DC, 1991.

Spectext Section 06200, *Finish Carpentry,* Construction Sciences Research Foundation, Baltimore, MD, October 1990.

Spectext Section 06410, *Custom Casework,* Construction Sciences Research Foundation, Baltimore, MD, April 1989.

Standard Grading Rules for Southern Pine Lumber, Southern Pine Inspection Bureau, 1991.

WM 4-85, *General Requirements for Wood Moulding,* Wood Moulding and Millwork Producers, Inc., Portland, OR, 1985.

Chapter 8. Curtain Walls

Aluminum Curtain Wall Design Manual, American Architectural Manufacturers Association, Palatine, IL, 1989.

Aluminum Storefront and Entrance Manual, American Architectural Manufacturers Association, Palatine, IL, 1987.

CWG-I-89, *Installation of Aluminum Curtain Walls,* American Architectural Manufacturers Association, Palatine, IL, 1989.

Spectext Section 08410, *Aluminum Entrances and Storefronts,* Construction Sciences Research Foundation, Baltimore, MD, October 1989.

Spectext Section 08920, *Glazed Aluminum Curtain Wall,* Construction Sciences Research Foundation, Baltimore, MD, July 1988.

Chapter 9. Finishes

ANSI A108.1, *American National Standard Specifications for Installation of Ceramic Tile on a Portland Cement Setting Bed,* American National Standards Institute, New York, 1992.

ANSI A108.11, *American National Standard for Interior Installation of Cementitious Backer Units,* American National Standards Institute, New York, 1992.

ANSI A108.4, *American National Standard Specifications for Installation of Ceramic Tile with Organic Adhesives or Water Cleanable Epoxy Adhesive,* American National Standards Institute, New York, 1992.

ANSI A108.5, *American National Standard Specifications for Installation of Ceramic Tile with Dry-Set Portland Cement Mortar or Latex-Portland Cement Mortar,* American National Standards Institute, New York, 1992.

ANSI A137.1, *American National Standard Specifications for Ceramic Tile,* American National Standards Institute, New York, 1980.

ANSI-H35.2, *American National Standard Dimensional Tolerances for Aluminum Mill Products,* The Aluminum Association, Washington, DC, 1990.

ANSI/HPMA LHF, *American National Standard for Laminated Hardwood Flooring,* Hardwood Plywood Manufacturers Association, Reston, VA, 1982.

ASTM A484, *Standard Specification for General Requirements for Stainless and Heat-Resisting Steel Bars, Billets, and Forgings,* American Society for Testing and Materials, Philadelphia, 1992.

ASTM A554, *Standard Specification for Welded Stainless Steel Mechanical Tubing,* American Society for Testing and Materials, Philadelphia, 1990.

ASTM B248, *Standard Specification for General Requirements for Wrought Copper and Copper-Alloy Plate, Sheet, Strip, and Rolled Bar,* American Society for Testing and Materials, Philadelphia, 1992.

ASTM B249, *Standard Specification for General Requirements for Wrought Copper and Copper-Alloy Rod, Bar, and Shapes,* American Society for Testing and Materials, Philadelphia, 1991.

ASTM B251/B251M, *Standard Specification for General Requirements for Wrought Seamless Copper and Copper-Alloy Tube,* American Society for Testing and Materials, Philadelphia, 1993.

ASTM C1007, *Standard Specification for Installation of Load-Bearing (Transverse and Axial) Steel Studs and Related Accessories,* American Society for Testing and Materials, Philadelphia, 1990.

ASTM C588, *Standard Specification for Gypsum Veneer Base for Veneer Plasters,* American Society for Testing and Materials, Philadelphia, 1992.

ASTM C635, *Standard Specification for the Manufacture, Performance, and Testing of Metal Suspension Systems for Acoustical Tile and Lay-in Panel Ceilings,* American Society for Testing and Materials, Philadelphia, 1991.

ASTM C636, *Standard Practice for Installation of Metal Ceiling Suspension Systems for Acoustical Tile and Lay-in Panels,* American Society for Testing and Materials, Philadelphia, 1991.

ASTM C754, *Standard Specification for Installation of Steel Framing Members to Receive Screw-Attached Gypsum Board,* American Society for Testing and Materials, Philadelphia, 1988.

ASTM C843, *Standard Specification for Application of Gypsum Veneer Plaster,* American Society for Testing and Materials, Philadelphia, 1992.

ASTM C926, *Standard Specification for Application of Interior Portland Cement-Based Plaster,* American Society for Testing and Materials, Philadelphia, 1990.

Ceramic Tile: The Installation Handbook, Tile Council of America, Inc., Princeton, NJ, 1992.

Dimension Stone Design Manual IV, Marble Institute of America, Inc., Farmington, MI, 1991.

GA-216, *Recommended Specifications for the Application and Finishing of Gypsum Board,* Gypsum Association, Washington, DC, 1993.

Glass Reinforced Gypsum: A Guide, Ceilings and Interior Systems Construction Association, Elmhurst, IL, 1990.

Insurance/Warranty Documents, Home Owners Warranty Corporation, Arlington, VA, 1987.

SpecGUIDE, 09550, *Wood Flooring,* The Construction Specifications Institute, Alexandria, VA, May 1988 (out of print).

"Specification Guide for Cold-Formed Lightweight Steel Framing," in *Lightweight Steel Framing Systems Manual,* 3d ed., Metal Lath/Steel Framing Association, Chicago, 1987.

Spectext Section 09511, *Suspended Acoustical Ceilings,* Construction Sciences Research Foundation, Baltimore, MD, April 1990.

Spectext Section 09546, *Metal Linear Ceilings,* Construction Sciences Research Foundation, Baltimore, July 1991.

Terrazzo Information Guide, The National Terrazzo and Mosaic Association, Inc., Des Plaines, IL, undated.

Chapter 10. Glazing

ASTM C1036-91, *Standard Specification for Flat Glass,* American Society for Testing and Materials, Philadelphia, 1991.

ASTM C1048-92, *Standard Specification for Heat Treated Flat Glass,* American Society for Testing and Materials, Philadelphia, 1992.

Engineering Standards Manual, Glass Tempering Association, Topeka, 1991.

Glazing Manual, Flat Glass Marketing Association, Topeka, 1986.

Spectext Section 08971, *Suspended Glass,* Construction Sciences Research Foundation, Baltimore, July 1988.

Voluntary Guidelines for Commercial Insulating Glass, Dimensional Tolerances, Sealed Insulated Glass Manufacturers Association, Chicago, 1983.

Chapter 11. Doors and Windows

Aluminum Curtain Wall Design Guide Manual, American Architectural Manufacturers Association, Palatine, IL, 1979.

ANSI/AAMA 101-88, *Voluntary Specifications for Aluminum Prime Windows and Sliding Glass Doors,* American Architectural Manufacturers Association, Palatine, IL, 1988.

ANSI/NAAMM 863, *Guide Specifications for Detention Security Hollow Metal Doors and Frames,* Hollow Metal Manufacturers Association, division of National Association of Architectural Metal Manufacturers, Chicago, 1990.

Architectural Woodwork Quality Standards, 6th ed., Architectural Woodwork Institute, Centreville, VA, 1993.

ISDI-100, *Door Size Dimensional Standard and Assembly Tolerances for Insulated Steel Door Systems,* Insulated Steel Door Systems Institute, Cleveland, 1990.

NWWDA I.S. 1-A, *Architectural Wood Flush Doors,* National Wood Window and Door Association, Des Plaines, IL, 1991.

NWWDA I.S. 2-93, *Wood Windows,* National Wood Window and Door Association, Des Plaines, IL, 1993.

NWWDA I.S. 6-91, *Wood Stile and Rail Doors,* National Wood Window and Door Association, Des Plaines, IL, 1991.

NWWDA I.S. 8-88, *Wood Swinging Patio Doors,* National Wood Window and Door Association, Des Plaines, IL, 1988.

SDI 117, *Manufacturing Tolerances, Standard Steel Doors and Frames,* Steel Door Institute, Cleveland, OH, 1988.

Steel Windows, Specifications, Steel Window Institute, Cleveland, OH, 1983.

WM 1-89, *Quality Standards, Hinged Interior Wood Door Jambs,* Wood Moulding and Millwork Producers, Portland, OR, 1989.

WM 3-89, *Quality Standards, Exterior Wood Door Frames,* Wood Moulding and Millwork Producers, Portland, OR, 1989.

Index

Index

Accommodating tolerances, 269–273
Accumulated tolerances, 273
Acoustical ceilings, 223
All-glass entrances, 245
Aluminum doors, 263
Aluminum rods, bars, and shapes, 233
Aluminum tubing, 231
Aluminum windows, 263, 329
Anchor bolt placement, 83
Anchor bolts, 307, 333
Angles, steel (*see* Steel, mill tolerances)
Architectural precast concrete panels, 37
Architectural woodwork, 331
Architectural woodwork installation, 193
Architecturally exposed structural steel (AESS), 89
Asphalt paving, 9
Asphalt walks, (illus.) 10

Beams:
    concrete, 279
    concrete reinforcement, 15
    concrete thickness, 29
    erection of precast, 61
    erection of steel, 83, 85, 87, 307, 309
    prestressed, 49
    timber, 335
Bifold doors, 255
Blinds, 181
Board lumber, 151
Brass, 229
Brick, 321
    building, 101
    on cast-in-place concrete, 281
    facing, 101, 107
    hollow, 101
    manufacturing, 101
    with precast systems, 299
    prefabricated panels, 99
    with steel framing, 313
    thin veneer, 101
    veneer, 281
    veneer on masonry, 321
    wall construction, 105, 281
Bronze, 229
Building brick, 101
Building joints, 277
Building movement, 271
Butcher block, 165
Butt joints, 271

Cabinets, 153, 161, 163, 341
Cast-in-place concrete (*see* Concrete, cast-in-place)
Cast stone, 129

Ceiling suspension systems, 223
Ceilings, 143, 207, 223, 225
Ceramic mosaic tile, 213
Ceramic tile, 213
Ceramic veneer, 113
Clay facing tile, 111
Clay tile, 107
Clearances, 269, 279, 283, 297
    between glass fiber reinforced concrete and structure, 69
    between masonry and precast, 299
    between steel frames and brick, 313
    between steel frames and precast, 297
    between steel frames and stone, 315
    between stone and masonry, 323
    in stone installation, 123
Columns:
    concrete, 275, 279
    concrete reinforcement, 17
    concrete thickness, 29
    erection of precast, 59
    erection of steel, 83, 85, 87, 305
    precast, 55
    timber, 333
Concrete:
    cast-in-place, 27, 29, 31, 275, 279, 281, 283, 285, 287
    cast-in-place joints, 277
    cast-in-place stairs, 33
    elevator shafts, 91
    frames, 275, 285
    glass fiber reinforced, 35, 69
    openings in, (illus.) 30, (illus.) 36
    paving, 7
    piers, 25
    precast:
        beams, 49, 291
        columns, 55, 291
        double tees, 53, 291
        hollow core slabs, 43
        insulated wall panels, 41
        joists, 57
        panels, 37
        pilings, 47
        ribbed wall panels, 39
        single tees, 51
        slabs, 43
        stairs, 45
        systems, 279
        (*See also* Precast concrete, erection)
    prestressed, 19
    reinforcement, 15, 17
    slabs-on-grade, 21
    slip-formed, 27
    steps, 11
    surface classes, 277

Concrete block, 93, 321
Concrete block reinforcement, 95
Concrete block walls, 97
Concrete brick, 93
Construction joints, 277
Control joints, 277
Copper alloys, 229
Cored slabs, 43
Countertops, 153, 165, 341
Covered joints, 271
Cubic stone, 119
Curtain walls, 197, 199, 275, 285, 317

Detention doors and frames, 251
Detention steel windows, 265
Dimensional lumber, 133, 333
Dimensional stone, 117
Door frames, 177
Doors:
    aluminum sliding, 263
    bifold, 255
    in concrete walls, 287
    detention, 251
    flush wood, 253
    installation of wood, 259
    insulated steel, 249
    in precast concrete, 301
    steel, 247
    stile and rail, 187, 189, 255
    wood frames for, 259
    wood patio, 257
Double tees, 53
Drilled piers, 25
Driveways:
    asphalt, 9
    concrete, 7

Elevator shafts, 91
Embedments, 277
Erection tolerances, 269, 271, 297
Expansion joints, 277, 319

F-number system, 21
Facing brick, 101, 107
Facing clay tile, 111
Fiberboard, 139
Finish carpentry, 151, 153, 331
Flat glass, 235
Flatness of concrete slabs, 21
Floors:
    ceramic tile, 213
    erection of precast, 63
    hollow-core slab, 43
    stone, 221
    terrazzo, 217
    wood, 143, 219
Flush wood doors, 185, 253
Footings, 23, (illus.) 28, 279
Foundations, 3, 23

Frames:
    door, 247, 253, 259, 287, 301, 327
    window, 289, 303
Framing, rough lumber, 141, 143, 207

Gaskets, 267
GFRC (see Glass fiber reinforced concrete)
Glass:
    entrances, 245
    flat, 235
    heat-strengthened, 239
    patterned, 237
    sealed insulated, 243
    spandrel, 239
    tempered, 239, 243
    wired, 237
Glass block, 115
Glass fiber reinforced concrete (GFRC), 35, 69
Glass reinforced gypsum products, 209
Glazing (see Glass)
Glued laminated timber, 131, 141, 333, 335
Grading, 13
Granite, 117, 123
Gypsum lath, 211
Gypsum wallboard, 141, 143, 207
Gypsum wallboard framing, 205

Heat-strengthened glass, 239
Heat-treated flat glass, 239
Heavy timber, 131, 133, 141, 333, 335
High-pressure decorative laminate (HPDL), 161,
    163, 165, 167
Hollow brick, 101
Hollow-core slabs, 43
Hollow metal doors (see Steel doors)

I-joists, 337
Instruments, 3, 5
Insulated steel doors, 249
Insulated wall panels, concrete, 41
Interfacing tolerances, 291
Isolation joints, 277

Joint design, 271–273
Joint width, 271
Joints:
    in brick walls, (illus.) 104
    in cabinets, (illus.) 160, (illus.) 162
    in concrete, 277
    in concrete block walls, (illus.) 96
    in countertops, 165
    in curtain walls, 285
    designing, 271–273
    glass block, (illus.) 114
    between glass fiber reinforced concrete pan-
        els, (illus.) 68
    between glass reinforced gypsum products,
        (illus.) 208

Joints: (*Continued*)
   masonry, 319
   in paneling, (illus.) 166
   between precast beams, (illus.) 60
   in precast construction, 279, 295
   between precast floor members, (illus.) 62
   between precast wall panels, (illus.) 36, (illus.)
      64, (illus.) 66, 279, 293
   sizing, 271–273
   in steel beams, 89
   in stile and rail wood doors, 189
   stone, 283
   types, (illus.) 270
   wood, 331
   in wood trim, (illus.) 158
   in woodwork, 193
Joists, 143

Laminated lumber, 131, 141, 149
Lath and plaster, 211
Level:
   of building layout, 5
   of cast-in-place concrete, 29
   of concrete block walls, (illus.) 96
   of concrete slabs, 21, 275
   of lightgage framing, (illus.) 204
   of limestone installation, 125
   of wood floors, 143
Lightgage framing, (illus.) 204, 205
Limestone, 121, 125
Linear metal ceilings, 225
Lockstrip gasket glazing, 267, 289, 303
Lumber, 133, 141, 151

Marble, 119, 123
Marble tile, 119
Masonry:
   openings for doors, 327
   openings for windows, 329
   with precast concrete, 299
Masonry backup, 323, 325
Masonry joints, 319
Medium density fiberboard, 139
Micropter transits, (illus.) 2
Mill tolerances:
   of S and M shapes, 77
   of structural angles and tees, 79
   of structural pipe and tubing, 81
   of W and HP shapes, 71, 75
Modular cabinets, 163
Moulding, 157

Offset joints, 271
Optical levels, (illus.) 4
Optical plumbing devices, (illus.) 4
Optical squares, (illus.) 2
Ornamental metal, 227, 229, 231, 233

Paneling, 167, 339
Particleboard, 137

Partitions, 205, 207
Patio doors, 257
Patterned glass, 237
Piers, 25
Pilings, 47
Pipe, structural steel, 81
Plaster, 211
Plumb bobs, (illus.) 4, 5
Plumbness:
   of brick veneer, 281
   of building layout, 5
   of cast-in-place concrete, 27, 29
   of concrete block walls, (illus.) 96
   of concrete frames, 275
   of limestone installation, 125
   of steel columns, 83, 85
   of steel studs, (illus.) 204
   of wood framing, 141
Plywood, 135
Plywood web joists, 149
Preassembled stone units, 121
Precast concrete:
   architectural panels, 37, 279, 293
   beams, 49, 291
   columns, 55, 291
   doors in, 301
   double tees, 53, 291
   erection of, 59, 61, 63, 65, 67, 69, 291
   hollow-core slabs, 43
   insulated wall panels, 41
   joints in, 293
   keystone joists, 57
   with masonry, 299
   pilings, 47
   ribbed wall panels, 39
   single tees, 51
   stairs, 45
   with steel frames, 311
   system design, 293, 295, 297
   tee joists, 57
   windows in, 303
Precise levels, (illus.) 4
Prefabricated masonry panels, 99
Prefabricated structural wood, 149, 337
Prefaced concrete block, 93
Prestressed concrete:
   beams, 49
   double tees, 53
   reinforcement, 19
   single tees, 51
Prestressing steel, 19
Primary control surface, 291

Quarry tile, 213

Rebar (*see* Reinforcement)
Reinforcement in unit masonry, 95
Reinforcement of concrete, 15, 17
Reveal joints, 271
Ribbed wall panels, concrete, 39
Roofs, precast concrete erection, 63
Rotation of slip-formed concrete, 27

Rough carpentry, 337
Running trim, 157

Screens, 179
Sealant, 271, 319
Sealed insulated glass, 243
Secondary control surface, 291
Shelf angles, 281, 313
Shutters, 181
Sidewalks, 7, 11
Single tees, 51
Site-cast concrete (*see* Precast concrete)
Site paving, 7
Slabs, concrete, 275
Slabs-on-grade, 21
Slate, 127
Sliding aluminum doors, 263
Sliding joints, 271
Solid laminated tops, 165
Spandrel beams, 83
Spandrel glass, 239
Spirit levels, (illus.) 4, 5
Stainless steel, 227
Stairs:
    concrete, 11, 33
    millwork, 175
    precast, 45
    site-build wood, 155
Standing and running trim, 157
Steel:
    architecturally exposed structural steel, 89
    with brick veneer, 313
    connections, 87
    with curtain walls, 317
    elevator shafts, 91
    erection, 83, 85, 87, 89, 297, 305, 307, 309
    frames, 307
    mill tolerances, 71, 75, 77, 79, 81
    with precast, 311
    with precast concrete, 297
    secondary members, 309
    with stone panels, 315
    system design, 297, 305, 307, 309
    weathering steel, 89
Steel door frames, 327
Steel doors, 247
Steel frames, 247
Steel studs, 205
Steel tapes, (illus.) 2, 3
Steel tubing, 81
Steel windows, 265
Steel windows in masonry, 329
Stile and rail doors, 187, 189, 255
Stile and rail paneling, 171
Stone:
    on cast-in-place concrete, 283
    granite, 117
    installation, 123, 125
    limestone, 121
    marble, 119
    on masonry, 323, 325

Stone (*Continued*):
    slate, 127
    on steel frames, 315
Stone flooring, 221
Storefronts, 201, 203, 329
Structural clay facing tile, 107, 111
Structural lumber, 133
Structural steel pipe, 81
Studs:
    plumbness, 141
    steel, 205, 207
    wood, 207
Subflooring, 143
Survey instruments, 3, 5

Telegraphing, 253
Tempered glass, 239, 243
Terra cotta, 113
Terrazzo, 217
Theodolites, 3
Thin brick veneer, 101
Thin glued laminated framing, 149, 337
Thin stone panels, 117, 119
Timber beams, 335
Timber columns, 333
Transits, 3, (illus.) 4
Translation of slip-formed concrete, 27
Trusses, 145, 147, 337
Tubing, steel, 81

Vernier transits, (illus.) 2

Wall tile, 213
Walls:
    brick, 105
    ceramic tile, 213
    concrete, 275
    concrete block, 97
    erection of precast concrete, 65, 67
    precast, 37, 39, 41
    prefabricated masonry, 99
    reinforcement in concrete, 17
    thickness of concrete, 29
Water levels, (illus.) 4
Weakened plane joints, 277
Weathering steel, 89
Window frames, 177
Windows:
    aluminum, 263
    detention, 265
    frames, 289
    lockstrip glazed, 267, 289
    in masonry walls, 329
    in precast concrete, 303
    steel, 265
    wood, 261
Wired glass, 237
Wood:
    blinds and shutters, 181

Wood (*Continued*):
  cabinets, 153, 161, 163
  doors, 185, 187, 189
  flooring, 219
  flush paneling, 167
  installation of millwork, 193
  screen framing, 179
  stairs, 155, 175
  stile and rail paneling, 171

Wood (*Continued*):
  trim, 157, 177
Wood chord metal joists, 149
Wood door framing, 259, 143
Wood framing plumbness, 141,
    207
Wood paneling installation, 339
Wood trusses, 145, 147
Wood windows, 261

About the Author

David Kent Ballast, AIA, CSI, is the head of Architectural Research Consulting, a Denver-based consulting firm offering a variety of research and management services to architects, interior designers, and the construction industry. He is also an instructor in interior construction and computer-aided design at Arapahoe Community College. Mr. Ballast is a contributing editor to *Architectural Record* magazine, and the author of numerous books, including *The Architect's Handbook, Practical Guide to Computer Applications for Architecture and Design, The Architect's Handbook of Construction Detailing,* and *Interior Construction and Detailing for Designers and Architects.*